Building and Managing
Virtual Private Networks

Building and Managing Virtual Private Networks

DAVE KOSIUR

WILEY COMPUTER PUBLISHING

John Wiley & Sons, Inc.
New York • Chichester • Weinheim • Brisbane • Singapore • Toronto

Publisher: Robert Ipsen
Editor: Carol A. Long
Managing Editor: Micheline Frederick
Text Design & Composition: North Market Street Graphics

This book is printed on acid-free paper. ∞

Published by John Wiley & Sons, Inc.

Published simultaneously in Canada.

Library of Congress Cataloging-in-Publication Data:
Kosiur, David R.
　　Building and managing virtual private networks / Dave Kosiur.
　　　　p.　　　cm.
　　"Wiley Computer Publishing."
　　Includes index.
　　ISBN 0-471-29526-4 (pbk. : alk. paper)
　　1. Extranets (Computer networks)　2. Business enterprises—Computer networks).　I. Title.
HD30.382.K67　　　1998
650'.0285'46—dc21　　　　　　　　　　　　　　　　　　　　　98-26717
　　　　　　　　　　　　　　　　　　　　　　　　　　　　　　　　CIP

Printed in the United States of America.

10 9 8 7 6 5 4 3

C O N T E N T S

PREFACE   **xiii**

PART I: THE INTERNET AND BUSINESS   **1**

CHAPTER 1   Business on the Internet   **3**

The Changing Business Environment   **4**

The Internet   **6**

     The Internet's Infrastructure   8

     What the Internet Delivers   9

Using Internet Technology   **11**

Summary   **14**

CHAPTER 2   Virtual Private Networks   **17**

The Evolution of Private Networks   **18**

What Is an Internet VPN?   **23**

Why Use an Internet VPN?   **24**

     Cost Savings   25

     Some Detailed Cost Comparisons   26

       Scenario 1   26
       Scenario 2   28
       Scenario 3   29
   Flexibility   31
   Scalability   31
   Reduced Tech Support   32
   Reduced Equipment Requirements   33

Meeting Business Expectations   **33**
Summary   **37**

CHAPTER 3   A Closer Look at Internet VPNs   **39**
The Architecture of a VPN   **39**
   Tunnels: The "Virtual" in VPN   40
   Security Services: The "Private" in VPN   41
The Protocols behind Internet VPNs   **44**
   Tunneling and Security Protocols   44
   Management Protocols   47
VPN Building Blocks   **48**
   The Internet   48
   Security Gateways   51
   Other Security Components   54
Summary   **54**

PART II: SECURING AN INTERNET VPN   **55**

CHAPTER 4   Security: Threats and Solutions   **57**
Security Threats on Networks   **59**
   Spoofing   59
   Session Hijacking   60
   Electronic Eavesdropping or Sniffing   61
   The Man-in-the-Middle Attack   62
Authentication Systems   **63**
   Traditional Passwords   63
   One-Time Passwords   64
   Other Systems   65
      Password Authentication Protocol (PAP)   65
      Challenge Handshake Authentication Protocol (CHAP)   66
      Terminal Access Controller Access-Control System (TACACS)   67
      Remote Authentication Dial-In User Service   68
   Hardware-Based Systems   69
      Smart Cards and PC Cards   69
      Token Devices   70
   Biometric Systems   71

An Introduction to Cryptography   **72**

   What Is Encryption?   72

   What Is Public-Key Cryptography?   74

   Two Important Public-Key Methods   76

      The Diffie-Hellman Technique   77

      RSA Public-Key Cryptography   79

   Selecting Encryption Methods   79

   Public-Key Infrastructures   82

      Public-Key Certificates   82

      Generating Public Keys   84

      Certificate and Key Distribution   84

      Certificate Authorities   85

Summary   **89**

CHAPTER 5   Using IPSec to Build a VPN   **91**

What Is IPSec?   **92**

The Building Blocks of IPSec   **95**

   Security Associations   95

   The Authentication Header   96

   ESP: The Encapsulating Security Payload   98

   A Question of Mode   101

Key Management   **103**

   ISAKMP's Phases and Oakley's Modes   106

      Main Mode   107

      Aggressive Mode   108

      Quick Mode   109

   Negotiating the SA   110

Using IPSec   **111**

   Security Gateways   112

   Wild Card SAs   113

   Remote Hosts   113

   Tying It All Together   116

   Sample Deployment   116

Remaining Problems with IPSec   **118**

Summary   **119**

CHAPTER 6   Using PPTP to Build a VPN   **121**

What Is PPTP?   **122**

The Building Blocks of PPTP   **124**

   PPP and PPTP   124

   Tunnels   127

   RADIUS   130

   Authentication and Encryption   133

   LAN-to-LAN Tunneling   134

Using PPTP   **135**
　　PPTP Servers   137
　　PPTP Client Software   137
　　Network Access Servers   138
　　Sample Deployment   139
Applicability of PPTP   **142**
Summary   **143**

CHAPTER 7   Using L2TP to Build a VPN   **145**
What Is L2TP?   **146**
The Building Blocks of L2TP   **147**
　　PPP and L2TP   148
　　Tunnels   150
　　Authentication and Encryption   152
　　LAN-to-LAN Tunneling   156
　　Key Management   157
Using L2TP   **159**
　　L2TP Network Servers   160
　　L2TP Client Software   161
　　Network Access Concentrators   161
　　Sample Deployment   162
Applicability of L2TP   **164**
Summary   **164**

CHAPTER 8   Designing Your VPN   **167**
Determining the Requirements for Your VPN   **168**
Some Design Considerations   **174**
　　Network Issues   174
　　Security Issues   178
　　ISP Issues   182
Planning for Deployment   **184**
Summary   **186**

PART III: BUILDING BLOCKS OF A VPN   **187**

CHAPTER 9   The ISP Connection   **189**
ISP Capabilities   **190**
　　Types of ISPs   190
　　What to Expect from an ISP   195
　　Learning an ISP's Capabilities   196
　　　ISP Infrastructure   196

Network Performance and Management   *197*
Connectivity Options   *198*
Security and VPNs   *198*

Service Level Agreements   **201**
Preparing for an SLA   203
Monitoring ISP Performance   203

In-House or Outsourced VPNs?   **205**
Commercial VPN Providers   **208**
ANS VPDN Services   208
AT&T WorldNet VPN   209
CompuServe IP Link   210
GTE Internetworking   211
InternetMCI VPN   211
UUNET ExtraLink   212
Other VPN Providers   213

Future Trends in ISPs   **213**
Summary   **214**

CHAPTER 10   Firewalls and Routers   **215**
A Brief Primer on Firewalls   **216**
Types of Firewalls   217
Packet Filters   *217*
Application and Circuit Proxies   *219*
Stateful Inspection   *222*
General Points   223
Firewalls and VPNs   **224**
Firewalls and Remote Access   225
Product Requirements   227
Common Requirements   *227*
IPSec   *228*
PPTP and L2TP   *230*
An Overview of the Products   *230*
Routers   **234**
Product Requirements   234
An Overview of the Products   *236*
Summary   **237**

CHAPTER 11   VPN Hardware   **239**
Types of VPN Hardware   **240**
The Price of Integration   **241**
Different Products for Different VPNs   **242**

Product Requirements   **247**
An Overview of the Products   **249**
Summary   **255**

CHAPTER 12   VPN Software   **257**
Different Products for Different VPNs   **258**
Tunneling Software   258
VPNs and NOS-Based Products   259
Host-to-Host VPNs   260
Product Requirements   **261**
An Overview of the Products   **263**
Summary   **266**

PART IV: MANAGING A VPN   **269**

CHAPTER 13   Security Management   **271**
Corporate Security Policies   **272**
Selecting Encryption Methods   **274**
Protocols and Their Algorithms   274
Key Lengths   275
Key Management for Gateways   **276**
Identification of Gateways   276
Handling Session Keys   278
Key Management for Users   **279**
Authentication Services   **280**
Managing an In-House CA   **283**
Controlling Access Rights   **286**
Summary   **288**

CHAPTER 14   IP Address Management   **289**
Address Allocation and Naming Services   **290**
Static and Dynamic Address Allocation   291
Internal versus External DNS   295
Private Addresses and NAT   **297**
Multiple Links to the Internet   **299**
IPv6   **300**
Summary   **302**

CHAPTER 15   Performance Management   **303**
Network Performance   **304**
Requirements of Real-Time Applications   305
Supporting Differentiated Services   **307**

VPN Performance   *312*
Policy-Based Management   *314*
Monitoring ISP Performance and SLAs   *317*
Summary   *319*

PART V: LOOKING AHEAD   **321**

CHAPTER 16   Extending VPNs to Extranets   **323**
Reasons for an Extranet   *325*
Turning a VPN into an Extranet   *328*
Summary   *333*

CHAPTER 17   Future Directions   **335**
VPN Deployment   *335*
ISPs and the Internet   *336*
VPN Standards   *338*
Security and Digital Certificates   *339*
VPN Management   *340*
Product Trends   *341*
Keeping Up   *343*

Appendix A   Resources   **345**
Books   *345*
IETF Documents—RFCS   *345*
IETF Documents—Internet Drafts   *350*
   Access, Searching, and Indexing of Directories   350
   Authenticated Firewall Traversal   350
   Differentiated Services   351
   Domain Name System Security   351
   Dynamic Host Configuration   351
   Electronic Data Interchange-Internet Integration   352
   IP Performance Metrics   352
   IP Security Protocol   352
   Multiprotocol Label Switching   353
   Next Generation (IPv6) Transition   354
   Point-to-Point Protocol Extensions   354
   Public Key Infrastructure (X.509)   355
   Remote Authentication Dial-In User Service   355
   RSVP Admission Policy   356
   Individual Submissions   356
Web Sites   *358*
   Internet and ISP Information   358

Security   358
VPN-Related Information   358

Appendix B   VPN Vendors and Products   **361**
   Commercial VPN Providers   *367*

Appendix C   What's on the Web Site?   **369**

Glossary   **371**

Index   **381**

Preface

The world of *virtual private networks* (VPNs) has exploded in the last year, with more and more vendors offering what they call VPN solutions for business customers. Unfortunately, each vendor has his own definition of what a VPN is; to add to the confusion, each potential customer has his own idea of what comprises a VPN as well. Mix in the usual portion of marketing hype, and you've got quite a confusing situation indeed.

One of the purposes of this book is to dispell as much of the confusion surrounding VPNs as possible. Our approach has been based on three main ideas: relate the current usage of the term VPN to past private networks so that both experienced and new network managers can see how they're related; carefully describe and compare the various protocols so that you, the reader, will see the advantages and disadvantages of each; and always keep in mind that more than one kind of VPN fits into the business environment. With the wide variety of technologies available for VPNs, it should be the customer who decides what kind of VPN—and, therefore, what protocols and products—meets his business needs best.

To that end, this book aims to provide you with the background on VPN technologies and products that you need to make appropriate business decisions about the design of a VPN and expectations for its use.

Who Should Read This Book

This book is aimed at business and IS managers, system administrators, and network managers who are looking to understand what Internet-based VPNs are and how they can be set up for business use. Our goal is to provide the reader with enough background to understand the concepts, protocols, and systems associated with VPNs so that his company can decide whether it wants to deploy a VPN and what might be the best way to do so, in terms of cost, performance, and technology.

How This Book Is Organized

This book has been organized into five parts:

1. The Internet and Business
2. Securing an Internet VPN
3. Building Blocks of a VPN
4. Managing a VPN
5. Looking Ahead

Part I, *The Internet and Business,* covers the relationship between business and Internet, including how VPNs can provide competitive advantages to businesses. The first three chapters of the book make up Part I.

Chapter 1, "Business on the Internet," discusses today's current dynamic business environment, the basics of the Internet, and how Internet technology meshes with business needs using intranets, extranets, and VPNs.

Chapter 2, "Virtual Private Networks," covers the different types of private networks and *virtual private networks* (VPNs) that have been deployed by businesses over the past 30 years and introduces the focus of this book, virtual private networks created using the Internet. Here, you'll find details on cost justifications for Internet-based VPNs, along with other reasons for using VPNs.

Chapter 3, "A Closer Look at Internet VPNs," delves into the nature of Internet-based VPNs, introducing their architecture as well as the components and protocols that can be used to create a VPN over the Internet.

Part II, *Securing an Internet VPN,* focuses on the security threats facing Internet users and how the three main VPN protocols—IPSec, PPTP, and L2TP—deal with these security issues so that you can properly design a VPN to meet your needs. Chapters 4 through 8 are included in Part II.

Chapter 4, "Security: Threats and Solutions," describes the major threats to network security and then moves on to detail the principles of different systems for authenticating users and how cryptography is used to protect your data.

Chapter 5, "Using IPSec to Build a VPN," is the first of three chapters presenting the details of the main protocols used to create VPNs over the Internet. The first of the trio covers the *IP Security Protocol* (IPScc) and the network components you can use with IPSec for a VPN.

Chapter 6, "Using PPTP to Build a VPN," discusses the details of PPTP, the Point-to-Point Tunneling Protocol. Like Chapter 5, it includes a discussion of protocol details and the devices that can be deployed to create a VPN.

Chapter 7, "Using L2TP to Build a VPN," is the last chapter dealing with VPN protocols; it covers L2TP, the Layer2 Tunneling Protocol. It shows how L2TP incorporates some of the features of PPTP and IPSec and how its VPN devices differ from those of the other two protocols.

Chapter 8, "Designing Your VPN," focuses on the issues you should deal with in planning your VPN. The major considerations you'll most likely face in VPN design are classified into three main groups—network issues, security issues, and ISP issues. This chapter aims to serve as a transition from many of the theoretical and protocol-related issues discussed in the first seven chapters of the book to the more pragmatic issues of selecting products and deploying and managing the VPN, which is the focus of the remainder of the book.

Part III, *Building Blocks of a VPN*, moves into the realm of the products that are available for creating VPNs, as well as the role the ISP can play in your VPN.

Chapter 9, "The ISP Connection," focuses on Internet Service Providers, showing how they relate to the Internet's infrastructure and the service you can expect from them. Because your VPN is likely to become mission-critical, the role of the ISP is crucial to the VPN's success. We, therefore, cover how service level agreements are used to state expected ISP performance and how they can be monitored. The last part of this chapter summarizes some of the current ISPs that offer special VPN services, including outsourced VPNs.

Chapter 10, "Firewalls and Routers," is the first of three chapters that deal with VPN products. This chapter discusses how firewalls and routers can be used to create VPNs. For each type of network device, we cover the principal VPN-related requirements and summarize many of the products that are currently available in the VPN market.

Chapter 11, "VPN Hardware," continues the product coverage, focusing on VPN hardware. One main issue covered in the chapter is the network services that should be integrated in the hardware and the resulting effects on network performance and management.

Chapter 12, "VPN Software," deals with VPN software, mainly the products that can be used with existing servers or as adjuncts to Network Operating Systems. As in the previous two chapters, this chapter includes a list of requirements and a summary of the available products.

Part IV, *Managing a VPN*, includes three chapters that cover the three main issues of management—security, IP addresses, and performance.

Chapter 13, "Security Management," describes how VPNs have to mesh with corporate security policies and the new policies that may have to be formulated, particularly for managing cryptographic keys and digital certificates. The chapter includes suggestions on selecting encryption key lengths, deploying authentication services, and how to manage a certificate server for digital certificates.

Chapter 14, "IP Address Management," covers some of the problems network managers face in allocating IP addresses and naming services. It describes the solutions using *Dynamic Host Configuration Protocol* (DHCP) and *Dynamic Domain Name System* (DDNS) and points out some of the problems VPNs can cause with private addressing, *Network Address Translation* (NAT), and DNS.

Chapter 15, "Performance Management," is concerned with the basics of network performance and how the demands of new network applications like interactive multimedia can be met both on networks and VPNs. The chapter describes the five major approaches to providing differentiated services and how network management can be tied to VPN devices, especially through policy-based network management.

Part V, the last part of the book, is called *Looking Ahead* and covers likely ways to expand your VPN and what the future may hold.

Chapter 16, "Extending VPNs to Extranets," deals specifically with the issues of extending your VPN to become an extranet to link business partners together for electronic commerce. It covers some of the main reasons for creating an extranet and points out some of the issues you'll have to deal with while getting all the parts of an extranet to work together.

Chapter 17, "Future Directions," is our attempt to project where the VPN market is going and what's likely to happen in the next few years, in the development of VPN protocols, the products that support them, and the uses businesses will create for VPNs.

The Internet and Business

Virtual Private Networks (VPNs) now can provide cost savings of 50 to 75 percent by replacing more costly leased lines and remote access servers and reducing equipment and training costs; but they also help keep your business network flexible, enabling it to respond faster to changes in business partnerships and the marketplace.

As you evaluate your corporate structure for designing a VPN, keep in mind which sites require full-time connections and what type of data will cross the VPN, as well as how many telecommuters and mobile workers you'll need to support.

1

Business on the Internet

Communication is the heart of business. Not only do companies depend on communication to run their internal affairs, but they also have to communicate with their suppliers, customers, and markets if they expect to stay in business.

In the 90s, the Internet has become the star of communication. It has captured the imaginations of individuals and business owners alike as a new medium for communicating with customers as well as business partners. But, the Internet is a great melting pot of many different technologies. Many of the technologies necessary for reliable, secure business quality communications are still in the process of being rolled out for routine use. The everyday use of the Internet for business communication holds great promise, but we've yet to achieve the plug-and-play stage for many business applications of the Internet.

Today's advances in technology at every level of networking can make it difficult, if not impossible, to find a single integrated solution for your business needs. Thus, we find ourselves in the midst of a time in which not only are new higher-speed media being introduced for residential and business communication, but in which new application environments, such as the Web, not only unify diverse services but offer added opportunities such as the new marketing and sales channels found in electronic commerce.

The terminology surrounding the Internet seems to change every day as vendors seek to define new market niches and offer their versions of "marketectures." One aim of this book is to address the confusion surrounding the technologies that fall under the umbrella term *Virtual Private Networks* (VPNs), providing you with a framework for distinguishing between the different types of VPNs and selecting the ones that will meet your business needs.

This book focuses on running VPNs over the Internet. Using the Internet for a Virtual Private Network enables you to communicate securely among your offices—wherever they may be located—with greater flexibility and at a lower cost than using private networks set up with pre-Internet technologies, such as leased lines and modem banks.

This chapter serves as a brief introduction to the structure and capabilities of today's Internet and how the Internet can be used by businesses to improve their operations. Later chapters will cover the details of many of the concepts we introduce here.

The Changing Business Environment

Business today isn't like it was in the good old days, even if old is only 3–5 years ago. Amidst all the downsizing, automation, and increasing numbers of small businesses as well as mega-mergers, one trend seems self-evident: Flexibility is the order of the day.

A cornerstone of business flexibility is an adaptable communications network. Well-designed networking can help your business deal with many of the changes in current-day business environments—for example, improved customer and partner relations, an increasingly mobile workforce, flattened organizational structures, virtual teams, etc. (see Figure 1.1).

Businesses are faced not only with quickly changing projects and markets but also with short-term associations with suppliers and other business partners as they attempt to compete. Customers demand more—not just more quality and variety in products but also more information about, and support for, the products. As customers demand more, they also can offer more to sellers; smart marketers look to increased interactivity with customers to learn more of their needs, leaning towards more individuality and treating each customer as a market of one rather than a

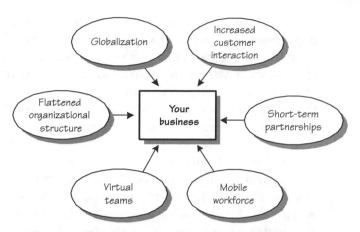

FIGURE 1.1 Changes in today's business environments.

large number of individuals lumped into a single group with average tastes and needs.

Even as businesses struggle with these sources and sinks of information, they find their own employees dispersed across the planet, trying to get their jobs done in markets that have become increasingly global. Businesspersons may well hope that phone calls and videoconferences can make the deal or solve a problem, but we're still stuck in a physical world in which face-to-face contacts are valued, useful, and often a necessity. Thus, we're faced with an increasingly mobile workforce, and I'm not referring to job-switching (although that happens often enough), just to the number of miles the modern-day worker travels to meet business obligations. Yet, amidst all this travel across the planet, each employee needs to stay in touch with the home office, wherever it is.

One of the common business trends in the past decade has been a flattening of the business organization, a move from a hierarchical management structure to one including fewer managers and more interacting teams. Flatter organizations, however, require more coordination and communication in order to function properly, providing yet another reason for the growth of networks.

In these flatter organizations, it's not uncommon to see an increasing number of teams formed. These teams, which are formed quickly to attack a particular problem and then disbanded, consist of members scattered throughout the company, often in more than one country. Much of their work and coordination is conducted electronically, transmitted across networks at any and all times of the day. In a global business, the sun never sets.

As businesses change, so too must the Information Technology (IT) departments helping to maintain the communication infrastructure that's so important to the company's success. Three major shifts in information technology have occurred during the past few years—from personal computing to workgroup computing, from islands of isolated systems to integrated systems, and from intra-enterprise computing to inter-enterprise computing. To deal with all these changes and help synchronize the organization with business, the IT staff have to maintain flexibility so they can respond to the regular order of the day—change.

A primary aim of this book is to illustrate how the Internet and *Internet Protocol* (IP)-based technologies can provide your business with new methods for creating a more flexible and less costly private network that better meets today's business needs. Let's investigate the Internet a bit before we move on to the details of these Internet-based Virtual Private Networks.

The Internet

In spite of all the hype and heightened expectations surrounding it, the Internet has truly become one of the major technological achievements of this century. Starting out as a simple network connecting four computers scattered around the United States, the Internet has become the largest public data network, crisscrossing the globe and connecting peoples of all ages, nationalities, and ways of life. Even as it's become a common mode of communication among individuals using computers at home and at the workplace, the Internet has become more of a commercial network, offering businesses new forms of connectivity, both with other business partners and with their customers.

For all its success, the Internet can be difficult for some to fathom. For instance, the Internet has no central governing body that can compel its users to follow a particular procedure. A number of organizations deal with different aspects of the Internet's governance. For instance, the *Internet Society* (ISOC) helps promote policies and the global connectivity of the Internet, while the *Internet Engineering Task Force* (IETF) is a standards setting body for many of the technical aspects. The *World Wide Web Consortium* (W3C) focuses on standards for the Web and interacts with the IETF in setting standards. Addressing and naming of entities on the Internet is important to the functioning of the Internet, and that task currently is shared by Network Solutions Inc. and the *Internet Assigned*

Numbers Authority (IANA), although the parties involved in this procedure may change before long.

The Internet is a somewhat loose aggregation of networks that work together by virtue of running according to a common set of rules, or protocols, the *Transfer Control Protocol/Internet Protocol* (TCP/IP) protocols. These protocols have proven to be an important cornerstone of the Internet, which has evolved in a very open environment guided by a group of selfless, dedicated engineers under the guidance of the *Internet Architecture Board* (IAB), the overseer of the IETF, and a related task force, the *Internet Research Task Force* (IRTF). Despite the proliferation of numerous other networking protocols, the TCP/IP protocols have become the preferred means for creating open, extensible networks, both within and among businesses as well as for public networking. The seemingly never-ending exponential growth of the Internet that started roughly three decades ago is but one proof of the Internet's popularity and flexibility.

The growth of the Internet has been phenomenal by any measure (see Figure 1.2). The Internet's predecessor, ARPANET, was started in 1969 and connected only four computers at different locations in the United States. During the past few years, the number of computers attached to the Internet has been doubling annually. According to the sur-

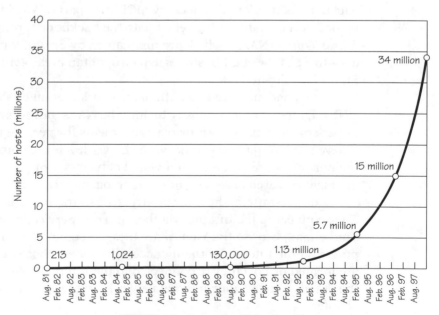

FIGURE 1.2 Growth of the Internet.

vey of Internet domains that's been run periodically since 1987 by Network Wizards, more than 30 million computers were connected to the Internet as of February, 1998. Depending on whom you ask, 50 million users of the Internet may live in the United States alone. With this growth has come a change in the direction of the Internet. Although the Internet may have started out as a network designed primarily for academic research, it's now become a commercialized network frequented largely by individuals outside universities and populated by a large number of business enterprises.

Business usage of the Internet has grown as well. It's difficult to measure business-related traffic in any reliable coherent fashion. But, one sample indicator of phenomenal growth of business use is the increase in the number of computers in what are called *.com domain names* (reserved for businesses only)—the number of these business-related computers rose from 774,735 in July, 1994, to 8,201,511 in August, 1997.

The Internet's Infrastructure

The Internet is global in scope and strongly decentralized with no single governing body. The physical networks comprising the Internet form a hierarchy (see Figure 1.3) whose top level is composed of the high-speed backbone network maintained by MCI (now part of Worldcom); the majority of Internet traffic is funnelled onto the backbone through the *Network Access Points* (NAPs), which are maintained by Sprint, Worldcom, and others—these are located in strategic metropolitan areas across the United States (see Figure 1.4).

Independently-created national networks set up by PSInet and UUNET, among others, mostly tie into the NAPs, but some service providers have made their own arrangements for peering points to help relieve some of the load at the NAPs. Lower levels are composed of regional networks, then the individual networks found on university campuses, at research organizations, and in businesses.

For most users, the internal structure of the Internet is transparent. They connect to the Internet via their *Internet Service Provider* (ISP) and send e-mail, browse the Web, share files, and connect to other host computers on the Internet without concern for where those other computers are located or how they're connected to the Internet. We'll cover some of the details of tying your internal networks to the Internet in the following chapters.

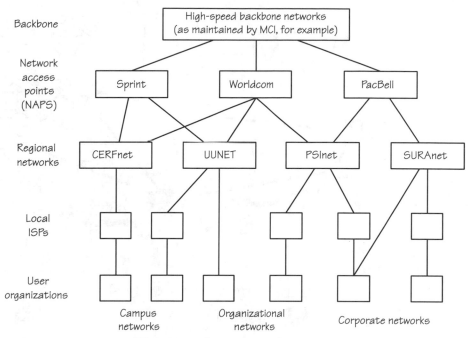

FIGURE 1.3 The Internet hierarchy.

What the Internet Delivers

For a moment, put aside any specific business needs that you may have. Instead, just concentrate on what the Internet can offer its users.

The Internet offers its users a wide range of connectivity options, many at low cost. These options range from a very high-speed (megabits per second) direct link to the Internet backbone to support data exchange or multimedia applications between company sites to the low-end option of using a dial-up connection through regular phone lines at speeds of 9,600 to 28,800 bits per seconds.

The near-ubiquity of the Internet makes setting up connections much easier than with any other data network. These could be either permanent connections for branch offices or on-the-fly links for your mobile workers. While Internet coverage isn't equal throughout the world, the Internet makes it possible to achieve global connectivity at a cost lower than if your business created its own global network.

As mentioned before, the Internet is built on a series of open protocols. This foundation has made it much easier for developers to write networked applications for just about any computing platform, promoting a

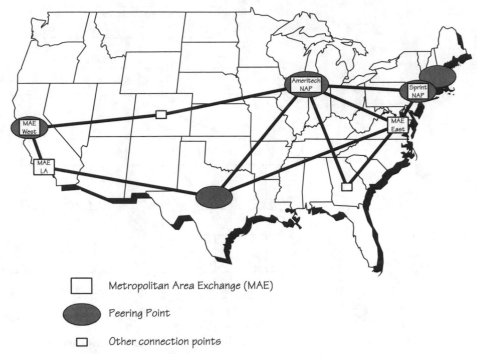

FIGURE 1.4 Map of U.S. Internet.

great deal of interoperability. It's not unusual to find a wide range of Internet applications that run on all major operating systems, making your job of offering common networked services easier. The World Wide Web has gone even farther by offering developers and content designers alike the possibility of working within a single user interface that spans multiple operating systems as well.

The Internet also offers you the opportunity of having a more manageable network. Because you've outsourced much of the national and global connectivity issues to your Internet Service Provider, you can focus more of your attention on other internal network management issues.

The Internet is not without its shortcomings, however. In many ways, it's become a victim of its own success. For example, the bandwidth available on the Internet backbone and offered by many ISPs has barely been able to keep up with the explosive increase in Internet usage that's taken place during the past few years. That, in turn, has raised some concerns about the reliability of Internet traffic. Brownouts and other localized network outages have occurred, but new equipment and policies continue to improve the robustness of Internet links.

A related concern has been the Internet's capability to handle multimedia traffic, especially real-time interactive multimedia. In general, the delays of data transmissions over the Internet make real-time multimedia transmissions difficult, but certain ISP networks have been designed with such applications in mind, and efforts at improving quality-of-service have started to address the problem. Currently, guaranteed performance is restricted by most ISPs to network uptime, but you should expect to see minimum delay guarantees offered in the next year or two.

Lastly, and this is an issue we'll repeatedly address in this book, is the problem of security. Admittedly, the majority of data transmitted on the Internet is transmitted in the clear and can be intercepted by others. But, methods exist for encrypting data against illegal viewing as well as for preventing unauthorized access to private corporate resources, even when they're linked to the Internet. Many of the reported illegal intrusions into networks are due more to poorly-implemented security policies than to any inherent insecurity of the Internet. We'll see later in this book that robust security is available for every aspect of data communications over the Internet.

Using Internet Technology

The Internet offers business opportunities on what we'll call a *private level* as well as a *public level*. The public level is where a great deal of attention has been focused over the past few years, as proponents of electronic commerce have aimed at the buying and selling of goods and services over the public Internet, either to the general public or to other businesses.

But, the private Internet is what this book is all about. Businesses can use the Internet as a means of transmitting corporate information privately among their corporate sites, without fear that either hackers or the general public will see the information. The plumbing and many of the techniques are the same for both the public Internet and private businesses using the Internet, but the goal differs—open data for public access versus protected, private data for businesses. We'll see in this book that the two goals are not contradictory nor are they mutually exclusive.

The fact that these two uses can share many of the same telecommunications resources offers new opportunities for business (see Figure 1.5).

Moving private business data on the Internet can also simplify, or at least ease, the setup of more business-to-business opportunities. The commonality of the Internet—its protocols, plumbing, the popular Web interface, and so on—make it easier to ensure compatibility between two or

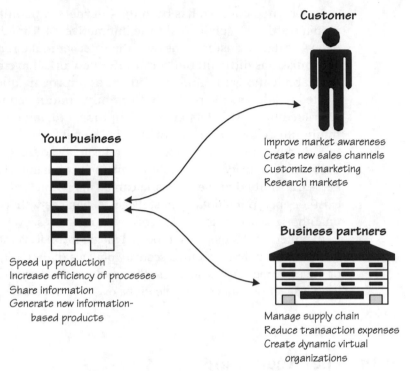

Customer

Your business

Improve market awareness
Create new sales channels
Customize marketing
Research markets

Business partners

Speed up production
Increase efficiency of processes
Share information
Generate new information-
    based products

Manage supply chain
Reduce transaction expenses
Create dynamic virtual
    organizations

FIGURE 1.5 Using the Internet for business.

more business partners (if they've embraced the use of the Internet). If you're already distributing private business data on the Internet to a select group of employees, it's not difficult to expand the membership of that select group to include a new corporate partner. Today's techniques make setting up links between new business partners a matter of days, if not hours—as long as you're on the Internet.

The openness of the TCP/IP protocols and the interoperability that the protocols promote hasn't escaped the attention of the business world. Now we're seeing not only increased usage of that grand-daddy of TCP/IP networks, the Internet (with a capital I), but more and more businesses are using TCP/IP to create their own corporate networks or intranets, tying together disparate technologies and different types of computers into intranets. Now the same applications and expertise that have been used on the Internet can be deployed within corporate networks for their own private uses.

It seems only natural that, if your company's using TCP/IP for its internal networks and if you want to communicate with business partners, suppliers, and the like (who are also using TCP/IP), the Internet can become the link between your business and theirs. This underlying concept of extranets means that you control access to your computing resources and your business partner does likewise for his resources, but you use TCP/IP over the Internet to share common data and increase the efficiency of communications between the two of you (see Figure 1.6).

We'll return to extranets later. The majority of this book is going to focus on another aspect of TCP/IP networks for business, using the Internet to link together a company's sites and mobile workers into one private, secure network. VPNs make secure multisite intranets possible. While intranets primarily focus on a set of applications, notably the Web, within a corporate organization, VPNs provide the lower-layer network services (or plumbing). Extranets also have a focus on applications that's similar to that found in intranets, but they're between business partners. VPNs also make extranets easier to implement, because the security services offered by VPNs enable you to control access to your corporate resources, and that access can include business partners and suppliers.

Internet-based VPNs, the subject of this book, enable you to leverage many of the Internet's inherent advantages—global connectivity, distributed resources, and location-independence, for example—to add value to your business's internal operations (see Figure 1.7). Not only can you

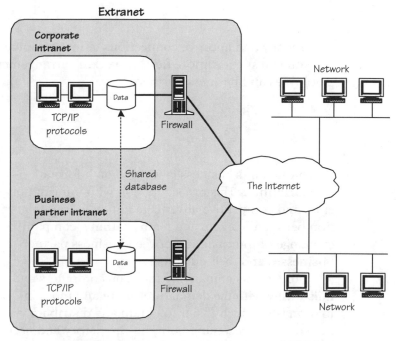

FIGURE 1.6 Intranets, extranets, and VPNs.

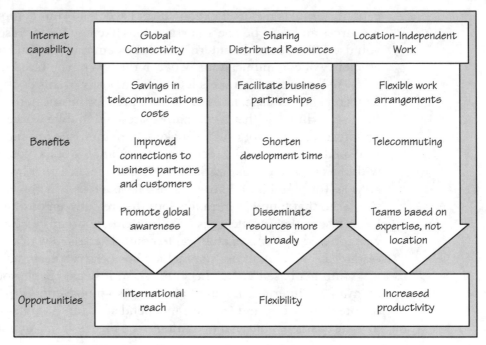

FIGURE 1.7 Using the Internet's capabilities to improve business.

save money and improve connections to international business partners, but you can support more flexible working arrangements, both for your employees and business partners.

Summary

Much of today's business is focused on information—its creation, analysis, or distribution. This preoccupation with information as a source of revenue and competitive advantage not only drives the exchange of information between workers and teams within a company but also drives the exchange of information between business partners as well as between businesses and their customers.

Today's accompanying focus on computers and things digital dovetails nicely with the demand for more and more information. Digital information is so much easier to obtain and distribute via electronic means that networks are becoming both the circulatory and nervous systems of the business world.

While private networks have long proven their usefulness in many corporate environments, the current-day trend to obtain information from a multitude of sources, many of them outside the corporate walls, has business managers and network architects alike looking for ways to tie together their internal private electronic networks with external, more public ones.

The Internet offers businesses the means to improve communications not only with their customers and business partners but also with other parts of the company. Creating secure, private corporate networks using the shared infrastructure of the Internet is what the remainder of this book is about.

2

Virtual Private Networks

Ever since businesses started to use computers in more than one location, there's been the desire and the need to connect them together in a private, secure fashion to facilitate corporate communications. Setting up a private network on a local campus of office buildings can be relatively simple, because the company usually owns the physical plant. But, installing a corporate network involving other offices or plants located miles away in another county or state makes things more difficult. In many cases, businesses have had no choice but to use special phone lines leased from their local exchange or long-distance carriers in order to link together geographically separated locations.

You'll see as we go through the following section that businesses have long had various ways to interconnect their sites, forming private corporate networks. But, until recently, these networks were essentially *hardwired*, offering little flexibility. After network services were offered to connect sites over shared public links, the term *Virtual Public Network* or VPN became part of the vernacular. The word "virtual" was tacked on as a modifier to indicate that although you could treat the circuit between two sites as a private one, it was, in fact, not hard-wired and existed only as a link when traffic was passing over the circuit. *It was a virtual circuit.* As we see later in this chapter, a major concern when setting up virtual circuits for transmitting private data on Internet VPNs is protecting that data from illegal interception and unauthorized viewing.

The Evolution of Private Networks

During the past 30 plus years, the nature and architecture of private corporate networks have evolved as new technologies have become available and business environments have changed. What started out as private networks using phone lines leased from AT&T have now become virtual private networks using the Internet as the primary communications medium.

If you were to trace corporate networking back to the 1960s, you would see that business managers had little choice but to connect their sites using analog phone lines and 2,400-bps modems leased from AT&T. Eventually, as the telephone monopoly and government policies changed, other companies pushed modem technology forward, enabling businesses to link their sites at higher speeds, reaching 9,600 bps in the early '80s.

Although we may be accustomed to the idea of using a laptop and a modem just about anywhere we go these days, many modem-based links 30 years ago were statically-defined links between stationary sites, not the dynamic mobile ones of today. The best quality analog lines were specially-selected ones, called *conditioned lines,* that were permanently wired to a site; there also weren't that many mobile workers running around with portable computers and modems.

For most, the leased lines used for intersite corporate connectivity were dedicated circuits that connected two endpoints on a network (see Figure 2.1). The dedicated circuits were not switched via the *public switched telephone network* (PSTN) like regular phone calls but were configured for full-time use by a single party—the corporate customer. The bandwidth of that circuit was dedicated to the customer's use and was not shared with other customers. The advantage of this architecture is that the customer is guaranteed both bandwidth and privacy on the line. One disadvantage is that the customer must pay for the full bandwidth on the line at all times, even when the line is not being used.

Although these networks were private, in that they consisted of point-to-point connections over lines devoted just to the client's traffic, these networks couldn't be called virtual private networks, because more than one customer of the network provider (i.e., the phone companies) didn't share the transmission media. VPNs were to come later.

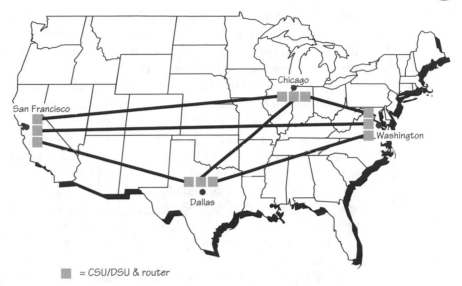

= CSU/DSU & router

FIGURE 2.1 A private network of leased lines.

The next significant advance for connecting sites came with the introduction of *Digital Data Service* (DDS) in the mid 1970s. DDS was the first digital service for private line applications, offering 56-Kbps connections to corporate customers.

As digital services became more readily available, interest in *Wide Area Networks* (WANs) using these services grew. Connections using T1 services running at 1.544 Mbps were particularly useful. A T1 datastream consists of 24 separate channels, each of which can carry up to 64 Kbps of traffic

Defining the VPN

Many different definitions of Virtual Private Network are floating around the marketplace; many of these definitions have been tweaked to meet the product lines and focus of the vendors. We've settled on one rather simple definition for VPNs that we'll use throughout this book—a *Virtual Private Network is a network of virtual circuits for carrying private traffic.*

A virtual circuit is a connection set up on a network between a sender and a receiver in which both the route for the session and bandwidth is allocated dynamically. VPNs can be established between two or more Local Area Networks (LANs), or between remote users and a LAN.

(called a DSO stream or channel), either voice or data. Because these channels could be assigned to different uses, a company could use a single T1 line to service both its voice and data networking needs, assigning different numbers of channels to each use according to its internal requirements.

In the early 1990s, the driving force for private networks was voice communications, not data. Phone companies traditionally sold T1 services to corporate clients as a way to create their own lower cost private telephone systems, pointing out that the cost savings of this approach to voice communications enabled clients to let data traffic between sites piggy-back on the otherwise unused bandwidth of the T1 links.

But, as markets changed and the cost of voice communications through the telcos dropped, the cost savings of private voice networks disappeared, or at least was greatly reduced. At the same time, data traffic had increased, and interest in using either T1s or 56-Kbps lines for mainly data traffic grew.

During the past few years, other networking technologies like frame relay and *Asynchronous Transfer Mode* (ATM) have become available for forming corporate networks. Frame relay has become particularly popular for connecting different sites together. Less equipment is needed at each endpoint, because a router at each endpoint can take care of directing the traffic to more than one destination (see Figure 2.3 on page 22). That's because the service provider maintains a "cloud" of frame relay connections, and the links are assigned only as needed.

Because the frame-relay links are assigned only when needed, frame relay corporate nets probably are the first modern-day virtual private networks. (It's worth noting that X.25 packet-switched networks also used virtual circuits and used *Closed User Groups* [CUGs] to restrict recipients of data. The X.25 networks probably also should be classified as VPNs, but newer technologies like frame-relay appear to be deployed more frequently these days.)

Although this frame-relay net can simplify connections somewhat when compared to the mesh of leased lines because you need to connect only each site to the provider's frame-relay cloud and although it offers less expensive connectivity than leased lines, the frame-relay net does not address the needs of mobile workers or teams that require dynamic off-site links. Using private networks of leased lines or frame-relay links, a company still has to maintain modem banks to provide connectivity to mobile workers, which has become more of a problem as the demand for mobile communications and remote access has increased.

The conventional response to corporate growth—adding another frame-relay link or modem bank—doesn't mesh well with today's dynamic

Designing the Net

Because leased lines are dedicated to handling only traffic between two points, the number of lines in a simple network connecting all branch offices to the corporate headquarters grows linearly as the number of branch offices increases. But, this star network topology requires all traffic to pass through headquarters, which can be a single point-of-failure. If the connection to HQ goes down, communications between branch offices are cut as well.

One answer is to build in redundant links, forming a mesh including additional links between the branch offices, like that shown in Figure 2.1. But, that becomes an expensive solution, especially if the redundant links aren't used much. Another solution is to create what's called a *hub-and-spoke topology* (see Figure 2.2.), which makes it possible to maintain some local connectivity should one of the major connection points (a hub) go down.

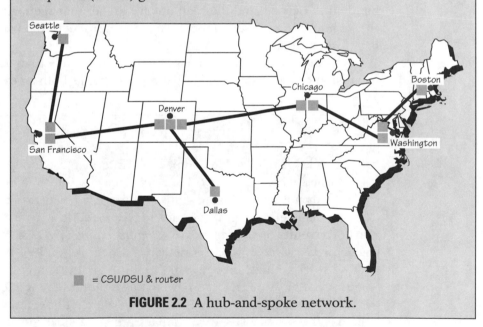

FIGURE 2.2 A hub-and-spoke network.

business environments. The problem with leased lines and frame relay is that setting them up takes too long. And, even if the frame-relay circuits could be set up quickly enough, each WAN interface is expensive and requires attention, not only during setup but for ongoing maintenance. Although modems can be set up fairly quickly, they may not support the

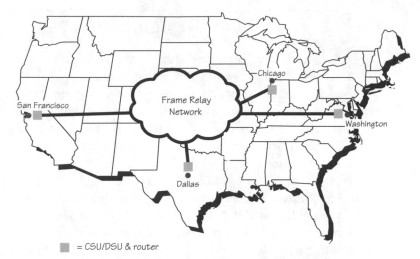

FIGURE 2.3 A private network using a frame-relay net.

bandwidth needed, and they can involve higher management overhead in the form of remote user support. The management of the two systems also is not integrated.

Nowadays, the situation has changed sufficiently to make further expansion of leased lines and larger modem banks both an expensive

Frame Relay Notes

Frame relay is a data-oriented network interface used to send bursts of data over a wide area network. As a packet-based technology, frame relay does not allocate bandwidth until real data is transmitted. Instead, frame relay defines virtual circuits in the network, known as permanent virtual circuits or *permanent virtual connections* (PVC). A PVC typically is defined between two corporate sites. Effectively, a PVC sets up a logical network connection between the sites over the shared frame-relay network. Unfortunately, you have to pay a monthly rental fee for each PVC you need to connect your sites, regardless of how much you use them. When you lease a PVC from a frame-relay provider, part of the agreement is a *Committed Information Rate* (CIR). This CIR sets the minimum bandwidth the provider guarantees will be available for your traffic 24 hours a day, 7 days a week. A CIR is not tied in any way to the speed of your physical connection; you could have a T1 connection, but pay for a 64-Kbps CIR.

proposition and one requiring increased management and support resources. And, if flexible business arrangements are required with partners or temporary offices, or mobile teams of workers are needed, the delays associated with requesting and installing new leased lines or frame-relay links become counter-productive if not downright unacceptable. What's required is a single solution that not only provides for the security of corporate traffic but also provides the flexibility of configuration and connectivity that today's businesses require. That solution is the Internet VPN.

What Is an Internet VPN?

Rather than depend on dedicated leased lines or frame relay's PVCs, an Internet-based VPN uses the open, distributed infrastructure of the Internet to transmit data between corporate sites. In essence, companies using an Internet VPN set up connections to the local connection points, called *Points-of-Presence* (POPs), of their *Internet Service Provider* (ISP) and let the ISP ensure that the data is transmitted to the appropriate destinations via the Internet, leaving the rest of the connectivity details to the ISP's network and the Internet infrastructure (see Figure 2.4).

The link created to support a given communications session between sites is dynamically formed, reducing the load on the network; permanent

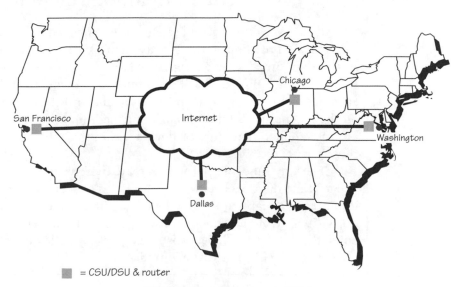

FIGURE 2.4 An Internet VPN.

links aren't part of the Internet VPN's structure. In other words, the bandwidth required for a session isn't allocated until it's required and is freed up for other uses when a session is finished. In many ways, this aspect resembles the properties of a frame-relay network, but it's extended to other types of connections on the Internet.

Because the Internet is a public network with open transmission of most data, Internet VPNs include the provision for encrypting data passed between VPN sites, which protects the data against eavesdropping and tampering by unauthorized parties.

As an added advantage, an Internet VPN also supports secure connectivity for mobile workers by virtue of the numerous dial-in connections that ISPs typically offer clients at their POPs.

Why Use an Internet VPN?

Whether you're building a VPN from scratch or converting your traditional VPN to one using the Internet, a number of benefits arise from the use of Internet-based VPNs. These benefits are direct and indirect cost savings, flexibility, and scalability.

Virtual Circuit or Tunnel?

Technically speaking, virtual circuits are restricted to a single type of transmission medium—frame-relay virtual circuits are one example. But, we are, in effect, creating virtual circuits between sites using the Internet for a VPN, so what's the difference? Because the Internet embraces a number of transmission media, an Internet VPN cannot rely on the mechanisms built into just one medium to form a virtual circuit but must depend on other protocols within the TCP/IP suite to form these virtual circuits.

The way that Internet VPNs create these virtual circuits is to encapsulate data packets within special IP packets for transmission on the Internet, enabling them to be transmitted on any medium that supports IP. To avoid any confusion with the media-dependent virtual circuits, the paths that the encapsulated packets follow in Internet VPNs are called *tunnels,* not virtual circuits.

Cost Savings

First and foremost are the cost savings of Internet VPNs when compared to traditional VPNs. A traditional VPN built using leased T1 (1.5 Mbps) links and T3 (45 Mbps) links has to deal with tariffs structured to include an installation fee, a monthly fixed cost, and a mileage charge. For example, a T3 line has an average fixed charge (without the mileage charge) in the range of $25,000 to $27,000 per month; the mileage pricing is around $60 to $65 per month, per mile. For a T1 line, the average fixed charge is $3,400 to $3,800 per month, with a mileage charge of $4 to $6 per month, per mile. For a leased line between New York and Chicago, a T1 would cost about $8,000 per month.

The costs associated with frame-relay networks differ from those for leased lines; frame-relay networks are usually less expensive than dedicated leased lines, but they also require fees for the Permanent Virtual Circuits that the provider allocates between each of your sites. A typical T1 connection to a frame-relay net would cost around $2,000 per month, with an additional cost of $1,400 per month for each PVC. Frame-relay fees do not include a charge for distance.

Internet Service Providers offer digital connections in a number of bandwidths: 56 Kbps, T1, fractional T1, burstable T1, T3, fractional T3, and burstable T3. Leased line prices from ISPs, which are not the same as an RBOC leased line because it only travels to the ISP's local POP, include a one-time installation fee and a monthly fixed fee, with no mileage charges. A dedicated T1 Internet circuit lists for around $2,400 per month; a full T3 circuit costs about $55,000 per month.

Leased Internet lines offer another cost advantage because many providers offer prices that are tiered according to usage. With Local Exchange Carriers [LECs], you pay the same fee for a fixed-bandwidth leased line, regardless of how much of the bandwidth you use and how often you use it. For businesses that require the use of a full T1 or T3 only during busy times of the day but don't need the full bandwidth the majority of the time, ISP services such as burstable T1 are an excellent option. Burstable T1 provides on-demand bandwidth with flexible pricing. For example, a customer who signs up for a full T1 but whose traffic averages 512 Kbps of usage on the T1 circuit will pay less than a T1 customer whose average monthly traffic is 768 Kbps if burstable T1 rates are used.

Eliminating long-distance charges is another cost savings resulting from Internet VPNs. Rather than require mobile employees or off-site teams to dial-in via long-distance lines to the corporate modem bank, a company's VPN enables them to place local calls to the ISP's POP in order to connect to the corporate network.

It's also conceivable that your costs can be reduced by outsourcing the entire VPN operation (aside from setting security rights for your employees) to the service provider. Some of the providers we discuss in Chapter 9 include full technical support, help-desk services, and security audits, which can reduce your own internal support requirements.

Some Detailed Cost Comparisons

It's often been written that the cost savings alone makes it worthwhile to adopt Internet VPNs in your business. Although it's impossible to offer enough details to cover all possible network configurations, this section includes three different network scenarios to show how costs differ between private networks using leased lines, the Internet, and remote-access-only. One scenario is aimed at a small company of three offices; one focuses on a large company with four regional/main offices and six branch offices; and the last covers a company interested in providing only remote access for its mobile workers.

In all cases, we've simplified the calculations somewhat by not including the charges for a local loop, which each site would need, and we've not included any support personnel costs. Each of these calculations is an approximation of the costs; your mileage may vary . . .

SCENARIO 1

This scenario (see Figure 2.5) is the simplest of the group, consisting of three offices located on the East Coast—Boston, New York City, and Washington D.C.—that want to have a full-time virtual network between them. They're running only a single T1 line between each office in the first part of this scenario.

Capital outlays for equipment and installation at each site include $2,000 per router, $1,000 for a CSU/DSU, and $300 for installation of the T1. The center link in the network (New York City) has to install two CSU/DSUs and two routers. The resulting setup cost is therefore $13,200. The T1 fees were figured as an average of late 1997 fees (i.e., $3,600 per month plus $5/mile/month). (See Table 2.1.)

For a network setup using an Internet VPN, the router and CSU/DSU costs are assumed to be the same as for the T1 case, but the initial installation costs are higher (i.e., $3,000 per site, adding up to a setup cost of $18,000). The Internet access fee for a T1-speed link to the ISP was assumed to be $1,900 per site.

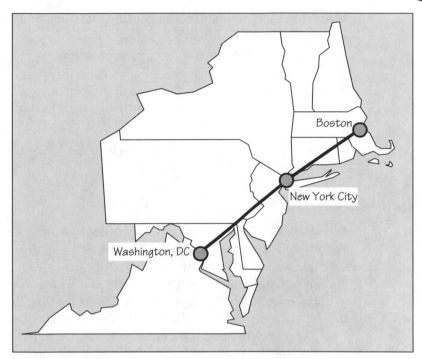

FIGURE 2.5 Map of regional three-office network.

Although the T1 lines are less expensive to install than the Internet VPN, running a simple trunk, or bus, of T1 lines between the three sites costs almost three times as much per month. Given the preceding situation, MegaGlobal Corp. would recoup its expenditures for the Internet VPN in less than one month of operation. Obviously, if the company already had the capital equipment and switched from the leased lines to an Internet VPN, the time for recovering the costs would be even less.

The second part of this scenario has MegaGlobal Corp. create a mesh between all three cities for improved reliability (see Table 2.2). The assumptions are the same as before, but now each site has to install two CSU/DSUs and two routers for the leased lines (see Figure 2.5), which adds

TABLE 2.1 Monthly Costs for Single Leased-Line Networks versus Internet VPN

City	Distance (mi.)	T1 Fees	Internet VPN Fee
Boston–NYC	194	$4,570	$1,900
NYC–Washington DC	235	$4,775	$1,900
Total		$9,345	$3,800

TABLE 2.2 Monthly Costs for Leased-Line Mesh and Internet VPN

City	Distance (mi.)	T1 Fees	Internet VPN Fee
Boston–NYC	194	$4,570	$1,900
NYC–Washington DC	235	$4,775	$1,900
Boston–Washington DC	463	$5,915	$1,900
Total		$15,260	$5,700

up to a capital outlay of $19,800. The Internet VPN setup costs remain the same as before.

SCENARIO 2

The second scenario describes company MegaGlobal Corp. with four major regional offices across the country—in San Francisco, Denver, Chicago, and New York City. MegaGlobal Corp. also has six additional branch offices in the United States, which it wants to connect to the regional offices. These offices are located in Los Angeles, Salt Lake City, Dallas, Minneapolis, Washington DC, and Boston.

For a leased-line network, MegaGlobal Corp. has chosen to use a hub-and-spoke model, with the four regional offices serving as hubs and the branch offices connecting to the closest hub on the spoke (see Figure 2.6). To improve reliability between the regional offices, two T1s are run between each hub; the branch offices have a single T1 each.

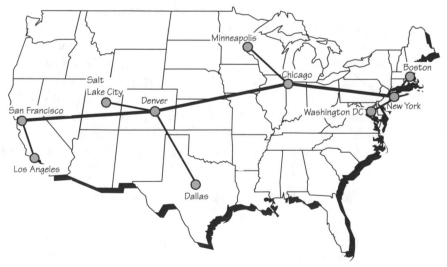

FIGURE 2.6 Map for national corporate network.

Capital outlays for equipment and installation at each site include $2,000 per router, $1,000 for a CSU/DSU, and $300 for installation of the T1. Because of the redundant lines, 24 CSU/DSUs and 24 routers are needed (assuming a separate device for each link). The resulting setup cost is therefore $79,200. The T1 fees were picked as an average of late 1997 fees (i.e., $3,600 per month plus $5/mile/month). (See Table 2.3.)

For a network using an Internet VPN, the router and CSU/DSU costs are assumed to be the same as for the T1 case, but the initial installation costs are higher (i.e., $3,000 per site, adding up to a setup cost of $60,000). The Internet access fee for a T1 speed link to the ISP was assumed to be $1,900 per site.

It's easy to see that the Internet VPN is a money saver after the first month of operation. Using single T1s between the hubs reduces the cost somewhat, to an initial setup cost of $59,400 and monthly fees of $60,655, but that doesn't significantly change the point at which the Internet VPN costs less than the T1 solution.

Even if lower-speed links, say 56 Kbps, were used for connecting the branch offices to the regional offices, the Internet solution would cost less.

SCENARIO 3

Because some products marketed as VPN products seek to replace dial-in remote access products with Internet access, this last scenario focuses on remote access only. In this case, MegaGlobal Corp. wants to support 100 remote users with dial-in access via the Internet. We are assuming that there will be 25 percent local calls and 75 percent long-distance calls into the office. We also assume that each worker using remote access averages

TABLE 2.3 Monthly Costs for Leased-Line Netwotk and Internet VPN

City	Distance (mi.)	T1 Fees	Internet VPN Fee
SF–Denver	1,267	$13,535	$1,900
Denver–Chicago	1,023	$12,315	$1,900
Chicago–NYC	807	$11,235	$1,900
SF–LA	384	$5,520	$1,900
Denver–Salt lake	537	$6,285	$1,900
Denver–Dallas	794	$7,570	$1,900
Chicago–Minneapolis	410	$5,650	$1,900
NYC–DC	235	$4,775	$1,900
NYC–Boston	194	$4,570	$1,900
Total		$71,455	$17,100

one hour of connectivity per working day, for a total of 20 hours per month. Long-distance call charges average $10 per hour, which results in long-distance charges of $15,000 per month (0.75*2,000 hrs./month *$10/hr.). (See Table 2.4.)

Comparative monthly charges for the Internet VPN solution include the $20 per month ISP fees for each user's dial-up account and the T1 access fee of $1,900 per month for the main site.

Required equipment or software that we haven't discussed before would be a terminal server for the remote-access case and security gateway software for the Internet VPN solution. Although MegaGlobal Corp. wants to support 100 remote users, we assume that it will provide only a fraction of that number of lines and a configured 10-port terminal server; at a cost of $550 per port, the terminal server would cost $5,500.

Capital outlays for the Internet VPN are the same as in previous scenarios, but only one router and CSU/DSU are needed because everyone is connecting to the main office. Thus, only one T1 line to the ISP has to be installed.

There's a wide variation in the cost of security software, as we'll see later in this book. At the low end, software bundled with Microsoft's Windows NT server is the most cost-effective. Assume that a suitable NT server and software license would run around $2,600 and do not factor in any additional client costs, assuming that each user already will have installed the appropriate version of Windows for their daily work. At the high end, the security gateway software for a router can cost around $15,000, with added costs for the client software (at $100 per user).

Thus, the capital outlay for the low-end Internet VPN solution would be $8,600, while the high-end solution costs $31,000 (T1 installation + router + CSU/DSU + security gateway software + 100 security clients). With a monthly savings of $11,100, the Internet VPN solution allows MegaGlobal Corp. to recoup its initial investment in one month for the low-end solution and in about three months for the high-end solution.

Are there occasions when the Internet VPN is not a cost-effective solution? A few. First, if a company has to use only a single leased-line between two locations that are relatively close, the fees for a T1 line can be

TABLE 2.4 Monthly Costs for Remote Access Via Direct Dial-in and Internet VPN

Direct Dial-in		Internet VPN	
Long-distance charges	$15,000	ISP dial-in accounts	$2,000
		T1 line	$1,900
Total	$15,000		$3,900

less than the equivalent ISP installation for the Internet VPN. Second, if all of the sites are close to each other and form a small regional network, a set of leased lines can prove to be less costly. Third, if most of the remote users are local telecommuters that do not require long-distance calls, a modem bank will most likely be less expensive than ISP charges.

Using frame relay to form the private network also can bring the costs down, because no mileage fees are charged. But, with either solution, bear in mind that you'll still have to maintain a different infrastructure for dial-in access from mobile workers and telecommuters, which adds to the cost of capital equipment as well as network management and support. Internet VPNs still offer more flexibility and scalability than other alternatives.

Flexibility

With traditional VPNs, the other connections that serve smaller branch offices, telecommuters, and mobile works—xDSL, ISDN, and high-speed modems—have to be maintained with separate equipment (modem banks, for instance) that are not part of the setup for either leased lines or frame relay.

In an Internet-based VPN, not only can T1 and T3 lines be used between your offices and the ISP, but many other connection types can be used to connect smaller offices and mobile workers to the ISP and, therefore, to your VPN. The only restriction is the media that the ISP supports, and the number of supported media is constantly growing.

Because point-to-point links aren't a part of the Internet VPN, your company doesn't have to support the same media and speeds at each site, further reducing equipment and support costs. If your mobile workers are using 56-Kbps modems and telecommuters use ISDN to connect to the ISP and the Internet, the appropriate equipment is required only on their end, the client side. By the time their traffic makes its way to the corporate net, it's been aggregated with other corporate traffic and is being transmitted over the main connection that your corporate net maintains to the Internet, such as a T1 or T3 link (see Figure 2.7). The third scenario presented earlier is a good example of this.

Scalability

Because VPNs use the same media and underlying technologies as the Internet, they're able to offer businesses two dimensions of scalability that are difficult to achieve otherwise.

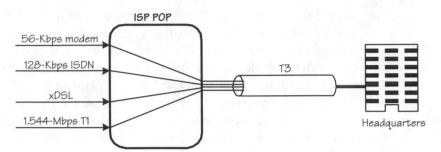

FIGURE 2.7 Consolidation of incoming traffic.

First, there's geographic scalability. With an Internet VPN, offices, teams, telecommuters, and mobile workers can become part of a VPN wherever the ISP offers a *Point-of-Presence* (POP). Most large ISPs have a significant number of POPs scattered throughout the United States and Canada, with many also offering POPs in Europe and Asia. This scalability also can be dynamic; a field office at a customer's site can be linked easily to a local POP within a matter of minutes (using a regular phone line and a modem, for instance) and just as easily removed from the VPN when the office closes up shop. Of course, higher bandwidth links may take longer to set up, but the task is often easier than installing a leased line on someone else's premises.

Second, there's bandwidth scalability. We've already mentioned that ISPs charge by usage, so fees for a little-used T1 are less than those for a highly used T1. But, ISPs can also quickly offer your choice of bandwidths according to the needs of your sites. Your home office may require a T1 or even a T3 connection, for instance, while your branch offices might be able to get by with a dial-up modem line or an ISDN line. And, if a branch office requires more bandwidth, it can upgrade from a plain phone line to a 56-Kbps or ISDN connection or from ISDN to a T1. Your network can grow as needed; since links aren't hard wired between each site, you don't have to upgrade the equipment at every site to support changes at one site.

Reduced Tech Support

VPNs also can reduce the demand for technical support resources. Much of this reduction stems from standardization on one type of connection (IP) from mobile users to an ISP's POP and standardized security requirements. As mentioned earlier, outsourcing the VPN also can reduce your internal technical support requirements, because the service providers take over many of the support tasks for the network.

Reduced Equipment Requirements

Lastly, by offering a single solution for enterprise networking, dial-in access, and Internet access, Internet VPNs require less equipment. Rather than maintaining separate modem banks, terminal adapters, and remote access servers, a business can set up its *customer premises equipment* (CPE) for a single medium, such as a T3 line, with the rest of the connection types handled by the ISP. The IT department can reduce WAN connection setup and maintenance by replacing modem banks and multiple frame-relay circuits with a single wide area link that carries remote user, LAN-to-LAN, and Internet traffic at the same time.

Meeting Business Expectations

When it comes to integrating any new technology into a business network, a number of common concerns always have to be addressed. These concerns are standards, manageability, scalability, legacy integration, reliability, and performance.

Corporate managers and planners like to see that products and services comply with the common standards of the day, partly to ensure longevity of the products, but also, and perhaps more importantly, to ensure that products from different vendors will interoperate. Even though many companies still choose to go with a single vendor for their networking equipment, thus reducing the demand for vendor interoperability, these same companies still like to keep their options open should better- or lower-priced components become available.

As networks become more complicated and as the number of users increases, network managers find themselves between a rock and a hard place. Not only do they have to manage, monitor, and configure more network devices, but they usually have to perform these tasks with either a fixed or a reduced number of staff. It's rare to see the network staff grow as quickly as the network itself. Thus, adding any new components or services to the network has to fit into existing network management systems or, even better, the existing management tasks have to be simplified. And, considering the importance of security in VPNs, it's just as important that VPN security management fit nicely into a corporation's security plans.

Network managers must plan for growth as they review products and services for their networks. They don't want to be faced with replacing one product or technology with another in a few months or a year when the demand for a service increases. Using the same software, but on a faster server, for instance, is a scalability approach managers can deal with; scrapping both the software and the hardware isn't. Similarly, a vendor offering a series of hardware products that offer the same functionality, but support more users or faster bandwidth, often fits better into a network designer's plan than does a company offering only one solution.

These days, few, if any, businesses have the luxury of starting their computing and networking infrastructure from scratch. There's a great deal of older data, systems, and networks that usually have to be supported in order for a company to continue operating. These legacy systems have to mesh with new systems somehow. We'll see that some VPN solutions offer better choices for supporting multiple protocols, for instance, making them better suited for integration with legacy networks. But, other solutions may require conversion to a suite of protocols only, and such changes have to be taken into account as you plan.

Another factor of great importance to network managers is the reliability of the product or service. For VPNs, reliability concerns focus on two different components—the hardware (and associated software) and the communications services (i.e., the Internet). Using standard components in the hardware—microprocessors, proven interface cards, and so on—is important, as is the maintainability of the hardware. Modular construction of a device is a plus, as is the capability to maintain some semblance of continued operation while the device is being maintained. Concerns about the reliability of the Internet as a data transmission channel have been frequently raised, but many ISPs have been working on ways to guarantee better reliability.

A related concern, especially for the Internet, is that of guaranteed performance. As a network manager, you want to ensure that data traffic goes through as expected, with the right amount of bandwidth assigned to high-priority and low-priority traffic. Delays should be minimized. *Service Level Agreements* (SLAs) with your network provider are a must; even now, SLAs are still evolving, as customers demand more services and assurances and providers roll out new features for improving their services. We'll see in later chapters that many of the methods used to secure data traffic can be computationally intensive, making it necessary to plan for the possible deleterious impact cryptographic processing may have on normal network flows.

Although there's a proven demand for Internet-based VPNs, the market is still in its relative infancy, as protocols and devices continue towards some semblance of standardization. A number of issues can impact both your design and deployment of an Internet VPN; we'll mention them briefly here and present more details in the following chapters of this book.

Security. An Internet VPN should be only one part of a company's security plan. Securing tunnels for private communications between corporate sites will do little if employee passwords are openly available or if other holes are in the security of your network. At the same time, VPN-related security management, of keys and user rights, for instance, have to be integrated into the rest of your company's security policies.

International operations also pose an added security problem. The export of advanced encryption software is restricted not only by the U.S. government but also by many other governments. Mobile workers using 128-bit encryption to secure transmissions in the United States are still largely restricted from using anything more than 56-bit encryption when traveling abroad.

Potential bottlenecks. Encryption and decryption can be computationally intensive processes that can lead to reduced throughput if your security gateway has insufficient computing horsepower. For high-bandwidth links, hardware-based encryption or at least a dedicated high-speed workstation running encryption software are likely solutions. Software-based encryption on shared hardware (a firewall or remote access server, for instance) can be sufficient for lower bandwidth connections, such as 56 Kbps or ISDN.

Packet encapsulation increases the size of the original packets, which may make them larger than the sizes normally based by routers and other network devices. In such cases, packets are fragmented, which can lead to poorer performance. One solution is to compress the original packets before encapsulation. VPNet Technologies offers this option in their products and the IPSEC Working Group is investigating ways to standardize this approach.

Interoperability. The current slate of protocols for tunneling and security are not interoperable. Yet, selection of a single protocol to meet all of your VPN needs is problematic, because protocols like PPTP and L2TP are better suited for client-initiated tunnels, while IPSec is best for LAN-to-LAN tunnels. The fact that most of the protocols are converging on IPSec for encryption improves interoperability, but you initially may find it necessary to use devices that support more than one tunnel protocol.

If your company has an existing WAN infrastructure, the costs of implementing a VPN will be lower if you can utilize much of the existing equipment. But, that may pose problems of interoperability with the new VPN equipment; for instance, some branch offices may not be able to upgrade their CPE to meet the requirements of a VPN.

IP address management.   If a corporate VPN is designed as one network with some special routed links called tunnels, full routing is possible between the parts of your network that are connected by tunnels, and you can use a single unified *Domain Name Service* (DNS) for resolving device names and IP addresses. This makes both reachability of hosts and routing more convenient and easier to manage.

But, the more common situation is one in which each part of the VPN is treated as a separate network, again with some tunneled and routed links. Unfortunately in this case, it's difficult to find a unified routing table, and the DNS also might be fairly fragmented, adding to the difficulty of managing the VPN.

Other management issues revolve around deciding which private IP addresses should stay private or be handled by NAT and how other DNS information is provided to parts of the VPN.

Reliability and performance.   Because Internet-based VPNs depend on the Internet, they are subject to the same performance problems that Internet traffic experiences. One solution is not to use the public Internet for your VPN but to employ a service provider's private IP network, although even these networks have not yet reached the reliability of traditional networks.

Furthermore, Internet VPNs can incur reliability and performance problems due to congestion, dropped packets, and other factors, which could cause problems for real-time applications, such as telephony and videoconferencing. Also, the encapsulated IP headers found in tunnels can cause problems for some QoS schemes, preventing them from allocating the appropriate network resources.

Multiprotocol support.   Even though many companies are switching to TCP/IP as the protocol suite of choice for their networks, other protocols are still important in legacy systems and networks. NetWare's IPX is one such example. Tunneling non-IP packets over IPSec is a problem, because IPSec is designed for encapsulating only IP packets. On the other hand, PPTP and L2TP include more multiprotocol support in their tunnels. If large enterprise VPNs are part of your design and neither PPTP nor L2TP can scale to your needs, you may have to include upgrading other services based on non-IP protocols to IP in order to create your VPN. Netware can now be run over IP instead of IPX, for example.

Integrated solutions.   Although a single-source solution in one device may sound like a good solution, especially from security and network management viewpoints, bear in mind that a single integrated device also can become a single point of failure—if it goes down, you've lost all of your VPN capabilities.

Summary

Private networks designed to link together a number of corporate sites have used a variety of technologies over the past 30 years. But, it's only been recently that alternatives to using dedicated leased lines, like frame relay, have seen more use. These newer technologies have enabled businesses to replace expensive leased lines with less expensive, dynamic links, or virtual circuits.

Internet VPNs go a step farther by offering businesses the opportunity to create these dynamic links over a variety of different transmission media, thus offering a single form of protected connectivity for both LANs at different sites and mobile workers. In addition to offering better flexibility and scalability, Internet VPNs can offer significant cost savings.

Being a relatively recent development, Internet VPNs still have some issues to deal with, such as guaranteed performance and security, but these issues are being actively addressed by the commercial providers as well as standards-setting bodies like the IETF.

3

A Closer Look at Internet VPNs

Using the Internet to create Virtual Private Networks presents considerable advantages to corporate users, as we saw in the preceding chapter. To provide a better understanding of the unique structure and processes of Internet VPNs, this chapter presents an overview of the tunneling and security features of the Internet, the protocols involved, and the various types of equipment available for building VPNs. The full details of many components are covered in following chapters.

The Architecture of a VPN

Two fundamental components of the Internet make VPNs possible. First, the process known as tunneling enables the virtual part of a VPN; second, various security services keep the VPN data private.

Tunnels: The "Virtual" in VPN

In VPNs, "virtual" implies that the network is dynamic, with connections set up according to the organizational needs. Unlike the leased-line links used in traditional VPNs, Internet VPNs do not maintain permanent links between the endpoints that make up the corporate network. Instead, a connection is created between two sites when it's needed. When the connection is no longer needed, it's torn down, making the bandwidth and other network resources available for other uses.

Virtual also means that the logical structure of your network is formed only of your network devices, regardless of the physical structure of the underlying network (the Internet, in this case). Devices such as routers or switches that are part of the ISP's network are hidden from the devices and users of your virtual network. Thus the connections making up your VPN do not have the same physical characteristics as the hard-wired connections used on your local area network (LAN), for instance. Hiding the ISP and Internet infrastructure from your VPN applications is made possible by a concept called *tunneling*.

Tunnels are used for other services on the Internet besides VPNs, such as multicasting and mobile IP. Tunneling creates a special connection between two endpoints. To create a tunnel, the source end encapsulates its packets in IP packets for transit across the Internet. For VPNs, the encapsulation may include encrypting the original packet and adding a new IP header to the packet (see Figure 3.1). At the receiving end, the gateway removes the IP header and decrypts the packet if necessary, forwarding the original packet to its destination (see Figure 3.2).

Tunneling allows streams of data and associated user information to be transmitted over a shared network within a virtual *pipe*. This pipe makes the routed network totally transparent to users.

Ordinarily, tunnels are defined as one of two types—permanent or temporary. But, *static tunnels,* as the first kind are often called, are of little use for VPNs, because they will tie up bandwidth even if it's not being used. Temporary, or dynamic, tunnels are much more interesting and useful for VPNs, because they can be set up as needed and then torn down after they're no longer needed (e.g., when a communications session is finished). Dynamic tunnels, therefore, don't require constant reservation of bandwidth. Because many ISPs offer connections priced according to the average bandwidth used on a connection, dynamic tunnels can reduce the bandwidth utilization and lead to lower costs.

Tunnels can consist of two types of endpoints, either an individual computer or a LAN with a security gateway, which might be a router or

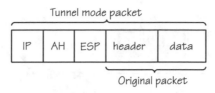

FIGURE 3.1 A packet prepared for tunneling.

firewall, for instance. Only two combinations of these endpoints are usually considered in designing VPNs, however. In the first case, LAN-to-LAN tunneling, a security gateway at each endpoint serves as the interface between the tunnel and the private LAN (see Figure 3.3). In such cases, users on either LAN can use the tunnel transparently to communicate with each other.

The second case, that of client-to-LAN tunnels, is the type usually set up for a mobile user who wants to connect to the corporate LAN. The client (i.e., the mobile user) initiates the creation of the tunnel on his end in order to exchange traffic with the corporate network. To do so, he runs special client software on his computer to communicate with the gateway protecting the destination LAN.

Security Services: The "Private" in VPN

Equally important to a VPN's use, if not more so, is the issue of privacy or security. In its most basic use, the "private" in VPN means that a tunnel between two users on a VPN appears as a private link, even if it's running over shared media. But, for business use, especially for LAN-to-LAN links,

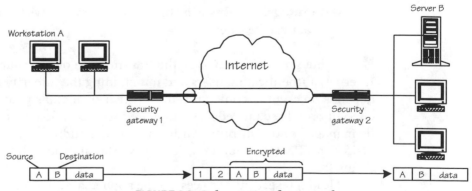

FIGURE 3.2 Schematic of a tunnel.

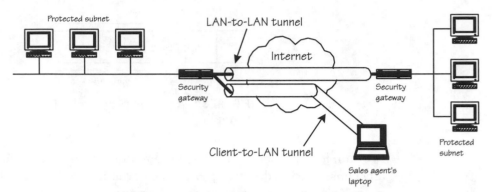

FIGURE 3.3 LAN and client VPN tunnels.

private has to mean more than that; it has to mean security, that is, freedom from prying eyes and tampering.

Today's Internet is a large cloud of interconnected networks, with most of its traffic being transmitted as open, or unencrypted, data. A prime requirement, then, for creating an Internet-based VPN is security.

VPNs need to provide four critical functions to ensure security for your data. These functions are as follows:

Authentication.   Ensuring that the data is coming from the source from which it claims to come.

Access control.   Restricting unauthorized users from gaining admission to your network.

Confidentiality.   Preventing anyone from reading or copying your data as it travels across the Internet.

Data integrity.   Ensuring that no one tampers with data as it travels across the Internet.

Although tunnels can ease the transmission of your data across the Internet, authenticating users and maintaining the integrity of your data depends on cryptographic procedures, such as digital signatures and encryption. These procedures use shared secrets called *keys*, which have to be managed and distributed with care, further adding to the management tasks of a VPN (see Chapter 4, "Security: Threats and Solutions," for more details).

Although security services can be applied at different layers of the communications stack, such as the Application layer, Session layer, and

VPNs and IP Addresses

In addition to hiding the underlying structure of the Internet between two endpoints, tunnels make preventing address conflicts that can arise when connecting two LANs easier.

Although the 4.3 billion addresses provided by the 32-bit IP address in IPv4 may seem adequate for most internetworking, companies may encounter a shortage of addresses if they want to communicate openly over the Internet. But, if a company wants to create its own private internet that does not connect to the global Internet, that company can use all of the 32-bit address range for its own network devices and computers. (Recommended practices reduce the available address space somewhat; see Chapter 14, "IP Address Management," for more details.) What happens when two previously isolated private IP networks want to connect and communicate with each other over the Internet? Even if we assume that the two networks are not using the same addresses, their private addresses are likely to conflict with other addresses used on the public Internet, which will cause routing problems. But, encapsulating packets to hide the privately assigned addresses relieves this problem. Part of the packet encapsulation process performed by a tunnel endpoint includes adding a new address to the packet; this address is the one corresponding to the other endpoint of the tunnel. Any forwarding of the encapsulated packet through the tunnel that must be done on the Internet is done using this address, not the address of the actual destination. Thus, only the addresses of the tunnel endpoints have to be IP addresses that are legitimate within the Internet IP address space, regardless of how many users with privately assigned IP addresses send data through the tunnel.

Network layer, our focus while describing Internet VPNs will be the services for authentication, encryption, and data integrity that are offered at layers 2 and 3 of the OSI model—that is, the Data-Link and Network layers. Deploying security services at the lower OSI layers makes much of the security services transparent to the user.

But, implementation of security at these levels can take two forms, which affect the individual's responsibility for securing his own data. Security can be implemented either for end-to-end communications (i.e., between two computers) or between other network components, such as firewalls or routers. This last case is often referred to as node-to-node security (see Figure 3.4).

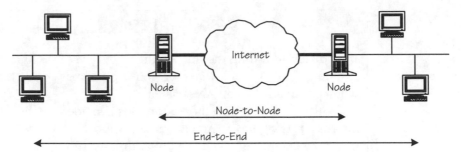

FIGURE 3.4 End-to-end versus node-to-node security.

Using security on a node-to-node basis can make the security services more transparent to the end-users and relieve them of some of the heavy-duty computational requirements, such as for encryption. But, node-to-node security expects—in fact, requires—that the networks behind the node must be trusted networks (i.e., secure against other attacks that unauthorized users might try). End-to-end security, because it involves each host, the sender and the receiver, directly, is inherently more sound than node-to-node security. End-to-end security comes with its own disadvantages; namely, it increases complexity for the end-user, and it can be more challenging to manage.

Now let's take a look at the way in which different network components fit together in an Internet VPN.

The Protocols behind Internet VPNs

Two major classes of protocols make VPNs possible on the Internet. First, there are the protocols that define how packets are encapsulated and tunnels formed, as well as how the packets are secured. Second, because the security protocols often involve the exchange of secrets between senders and receivers on the VPN, protocols are needed for handling the management of these secrets (i.e., cryptographic keys) and other authentication methods.

Tunneling and Security Protocols

Four protocols were originally suggested as VPN solutions. Three are designed to work at Layer2, the Link layer: the *Layer2 Forwarding* (L2F) protocol, the *Point-to-Point Tunneling Protocol* (PPTP), and the *Layer2 Tunneling Protocol* (L2TP). In an effort to improve interoperability and security while decreasing the proliferation of redundant, or near-redundant, protocols, the IETF is shepherding work on L2TP, which combines many of the features of L2F and PPTP. Because it's likely that L2F will soon be supplanted by L2TP, we'll focus on PPTP and L2TP as Layer2 solutions. The only VPN protocol for Layer3 is IPSec, which has been developed by the IETF over the past few years. (SOCKS is another protocol that can be used for VPNs, and it's handled at the application layer; we cover it briefly later) all the protocols are highlighted in Table 3.1.)

The details of each of these protocols are covered in later chapters; in the meantime, here's a quick run-down on their features:

- PPTP is a point-to-point tunneling mechanism originally created to support packet tunneling in Ascend's remote access server hardware and Microsoft's Windows NT software.
- The backers of PPTP combined efforts with Cisco and its L2F protocol to produce a hybrid Layer2 tunneling protocol called Layer2 Tunneling Protocol.
- IPSec is a standard created to add security to TCP/IP networking; it is a collection of security measures that address data privacy, integrity, authentication, and key management, in addition to tunneling.

All three VPN technology types that we consider here—PPTP, L2TP, and IPSec—support tunneling. PPTP and L2TP are strictly tunneling protocols. The tunneling mechanisms differ on what's done to the data (for instance, encryption and authentication), the headers that describe the data transmission and packet handling, and the OSI layer at which they operate.

Neither PPTP nor L2TP include encryption or key-management mechanisms in their published specifications. The current L2TP draft standard recommends that IPSec be used for encryption and key management in IP environments; future drafts of the PPTP standard may do the same. Although IPSec provides packet-by-packet encryption and authentication, it does not specifically cover management of the cryptography keys that would have to be exchanged (see the next section). Another working group in the IETF has been creating standards for key management in conjunction with IPSec; the protocol proposed for key management is called *ISAKMP/Oakley* (ISAKMP stands for *Internet Security Association and Key Management Protocol*), which is covered in detail in Chapter 5, "Using IPSec to Build a VPN."

TABLE 3.1 VPN Protocol Comparisons

Technology	Strengths	Weaknesses	Place in Network
IPSec	+Standards track protocol. +Works independently of higher level applications. +Built as part of IPv6. +Allows for network address hiding without Network Address Translation. +Will accommodate developing cryptographic techniques.	+No user management. +Little production interoperability among vendors. +Little desktop support.	+Best at edge of network domain to be secured or on individual LAN segments. +Software best on the user's computer for vendor proprietary solutions for dial-up remote access.
PPTP	+Runs from Windows NT, Windows95, and Windows 98 platforms. +Accommodates end-to-end and node-to-node tunneling. +Popular value-added feature for remote access. +Uses existing Windows user domains for authentication. +Provides multiprotocol capability. +Uses RSA RC-4 encryption.	+Does not provide data encryption from remote-access servers. +Largely proprietary, requiring a Windows NT server to terminate tunnels. +Uses only RSA RC-4 encryption.	+Best in remote-access servers for proxy tunneling. +Can be used between remote offices that have Windows NT servers running RRAS. +Can be used on Windows95 desktops or Windows NT workstations.
L2F	+Enables multiprotocol tunneling. +Supported by many vendors.	+No encryption. +Weak user authentication. +No tunnel flow control.	+Best for remote access at POP.
L2TP	+Combines PPTP and L2F. +Needs only a packet based network to run over X.25 and frame relay. +Uses IPSec for encryption.	+Not yet implemented in many products. +Final mile unsecured.	+Best for remote access at POP.
Socks v5	+Contains application-level security for tighter control over access to applications. +Provides desktop-to-server authentication and encryption.	+Socks server can be resource-intensive, hampering scalability. +Can be difficult to manage outside users, such as trading and development partners. +Requires modification to applications.	+Best on the edge of the network behind a firewall. +Can be used on internal networks for user control. +Anywhere strong user authentication is required.

IPSec is often considered the best VPN solution for IP environments, because it includes strong security measures, notably encryption, authentication, and key management, in its standards set. Because IPSec is designed to handle only IP packets, PPTP and L2TP are more suitable for use in multiprotocol non-IP environments, such as NETBEUI, IPX, and AppleTalk.

Another protocol, SOCKS, is occasionally mentioned as a protocol for forming VPNs. SOCKS is designed to permit a datastream to cross a firewall based on user authentication rather than on the characteristics of the IP packets, such as a destination's UDP port number, which is the way firewalls usually work. SOCKS operates at the TCP layer and above, which makes establishing application-specific tunnels easier. For more details, check out Chapter 6, "Using PPTP to Build a VPN."

Management Protocols

Maintaining the access rights of your users and the security information, such as cryptographic keys, that relates to them is a crucial management issue in VPNs. Two different sets of protocols are currently used according to the type of VPN that's being maintained. For dial-in or client-to-LAN VPNs—using PPTP and L2TP tunnels, for instance—a protocol called RADIUS can be used for authentication and accounting. For LAN-to-LAN VPNs, much of the management of IPSec focuses on key management using the ISAKMP/Oakley protocol. (Many of the details of these protocols are covered in Chapters 4 and 5.)

The most popular tool for managing authentication and accounting for remote access has been the *Remote Authentication Dial-In User Service* (RADIUS), and it's the preferred protocol for use with dial-in tunneling, such as in PPTP and L2F.

RADIUS supports the authentication and accounting with a database that maintains access profiles for all trusted users. The information in each user's profiles includes passwords (authentication), access privileges (authorization), and network usage (accounting). The network access equipment interacts with the RADIUS server securely, transparently, and automatically. When a user attempts to log on remotely, the network access switch queries the RADIUS server to obtain that user's profile for authentication and authorization. A proxy RADIUS capability lets the RADIUS server at a service provider access an organization's RADIUS server to obtain any necessary user information, which is necessary to secure Internet-based VPNs.

As mentioned before, many authentication and encryption methods used in VPNs require the determination and distribution of keys. For small systems, manual distribution of keys, such as face-to-face, over a secure phone conversation, or via a courier, will suffice, but more automated systems are needed for larger VPNs. Although no standard is required for manual key management, some standardization is required for automated systems, partly because all network access equipment must regularly and automatically interact with the key-management system. In the ISAKMP/Oakley protocol that's being standardized by the IETF, ISAKMP defines the method for distributing keys, while the Oakley part specifies how keys are determined. (See Chapter 5, "Using IPSec to Build a VPN," for more details.)

VPN Building Blocks

If you take a look at Figure 3.5, you'll see that there are four main components of an Internet VPN: the Internet, security gateways, security policy servers, and certificate authorities. Not all of these components are defined or used in every current VPN product, but for the moment, we'll describe the most general case to show what the components are and how they fit together.

The Internet

The Internet provides the fundamental plumbing for your VPN. Although a great deal of the work of an Internet VPN takes place behind the scenes, it's worthwhile to understand how the Internet works. This knowledge will help you understand not only what your ISP can provide, but also why certain techniques are required for the success of Internet VPNs.

A number of components and players are along the path of a message you send, for example. Different types of Internet Service Providers (ISPs) are available, ranging from small local ISPs to regional ISPs and national or supranational ISPs, all arranged in tiers according to their capabilities.

Tier One providers such as FiberNet, AT&T, IBM, GTE Internetworking, and PSInet own and operate private national networks with extensive national backbones. These independent networks meet and interconnect at the Internet *Network Access Points* (NAPs). Through peering agreements between these private companies, the orderly exchange of digital traffic is facilitated between the various networks. In other words, the networks interconnect and exchange traffic at the NAPs to form what is essentially the Internet.

There are six Internet industry-recognized NAPs in North America. They are the Chicago AADS NAP, which is managed by Ameritech; the Sprint NAP, which is managed by Sprint; the MAE East NAP, which is managed by MFS; the MAE West NAP, which is managed by MFS; the PAC Bell NAP, which is managed by Pacific Bell; and the CIX NAP, which is managed by The Commercial Internet Exchange.

A Tier Two provider is a company that buys its Internet connectivity from one of the Tier One providers and then provides residential dial-up access or World Wide Web site hosting or resells the bandwidth. It is important to note that none of the Internet NAPs provide Internet connectivity to the general public or to business and industry. The NAPs are only points for the orderly exchange of traffic between those organizations that maintain extensive national backbones. A NAP is not a point at which businesses or individuals can purchase Internet access. Additionally, connections to the Internet NAPs are made at a minimum of DS-3 speed (45 Mbps). The purpose of the Internet NAPs is to facilitate the orderly exchange of traffic from one network to another, not to sell Internet connectivity.

To become an industry-recognized NAP requires a substantial investment in Layer2 switching equipment and POP facilities. Typically, these facilities have redundant fiber optic cable paths to multiple carriers and can support circuit sizes up to and including OC-48 (2.4 Gbps).

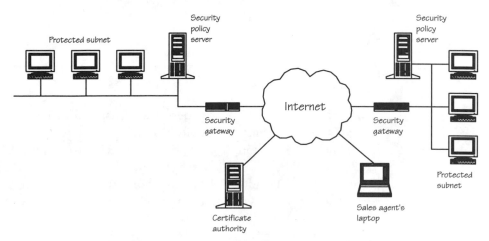

FIGURE 3.5 Components of an Internet VPN.

As an example of where your data is likely to travel, let's assume that you used a modem to dial your ISP's local Point-of-Presence to connect to the Internet and onto your corporate VPN (see Figure 3.6). The data travels from your laptop to the local POP and then on to the regional Internet network and probably over a few more POPs to the proper NAP before it's routed to another POP closer to the intended destination. There are two significant reasons why this all works: First, the different ISPs running the networks that make up the Internet cooperate with each other; second, the addressing features found in the IP protocol suite help tie all the networks together.

Whether you're an individual working at home or on the road and dialing into the Internet or a business with a full-time link to the Internet, the ISP's POP is an important cog in your use of the Internet. The POP is where the ISP handles the different types of media that its customers use for Internet access and forwards all the customer traffic to its backbone network, which connects to the rest of the Internet at some point (see Figure 3.7).

Some POPs contain different equipment for each transmission media they support, such as a modem bank for dial-in sessions and CSU/DSUs for frame relay and DDS; other ISPs have opted to leave support for the different media to the public network, instead running a leased line to their POPs. In addition to handling different media for customer traffic, the POP includes routers and/or IP switches to connect the POP's local LAN to the rest of the ISP's network as well as network management consoles. In some cases, the POP includes servers for hosting mail, news, Web sites, and RADIUS authentication servers for ISP's customers.

ISP or NSP?

Internet-related service providers are occasionally divided into two classes: Internet Service Providers (ISPs) and Network Service Providers (NSPs). Although ISPs offer Internet access only, NSPs offer dedicated IP bandwidth on private backbones, in addition to Internet access. UUNET and AT&T Worldnet are two examples of NSPs. Unless it's absolutely necessary to distinguish ISPs from NSPs, we use one term, ISP, to refer to both.

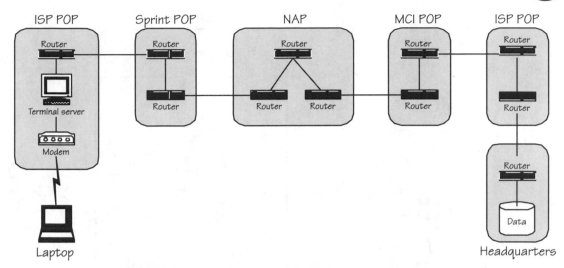

FIGURE 3.6 Communicating via ISPs, POPs, and NAPs.

Security Gateways

Take another look at Figure 3.5. Aside from the Internet cloud, which was just described, at least in part, the most significant components are those involving security. We not only have security gateways, but policy servers and certificate authority servers.

Security gateways sit between public and private networks, preventing unauthorized intrusions into the private network. They also may provide tunneling capabilities and encrypt private data before it's transmitted on the public network.

In general, a security gateway for a VPN fits into one of the following categories: routers, firewalls, integrated VPN hardware, and VPN software.

Because routers have to examine and process every packet that leaves the LAN, it seems only natural to include packet encryption on routers. Vendors of router-based VPN services usually offer two types of products, either add-on software or an additional circuit board with a coprocessor-based encryption engine. The latter product is best for situations that require greater throughput. If you're already using the vendor's routers, then adding encryption support to these routers can keep the upgrade costs of your VPN low. But adding the encryption tasks to the same box as your router increases your risks; if the router goes down, so does your VPN. For more details on the use of routers in VPNs, see Chapter 10, "Firewalls and Routers."

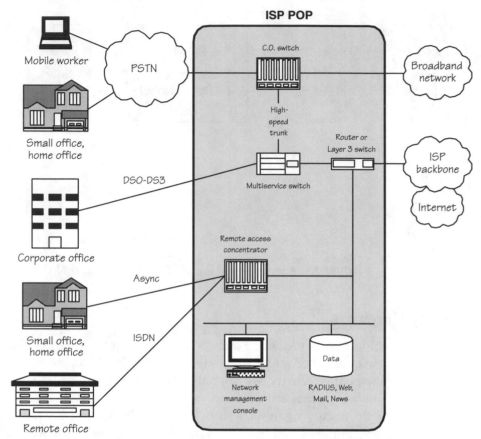

FIGURE 3.7 Schematic of a typical ISP POP.

Many firewall vendors include a tunnel capability in their products. Like routers, firewalls have to process all IP traffic—in this case, to pass traffic based on the filters defined for the firewall. Because of all the processing performed by firewalls, they're ill-suited for tunneling on large networks with a great deal of traffic. Combining tunneling and encryption with firewalls is probably best used only on small networks with low volumes of traffic. Also, like routers, firewalls can be a single point of failure for your VPN. For more details on firewall-based VPNs, see Chapter 10.

Another possible VPN solution is to use special hardware that's designed for the task of tunneling and encryption. These devices usually operate as encrypting bridges that are typically placed between the network's routers and WAN links. Although most of these hardware devices are designed for LAN-to-LAN configurations, some products also support

IP Addresses and the Internet

The routers that connect all networks that make up an IP internetwork, such as the Internet, forward traffic based on the IP address of the destination network. To help with the assignment of a large number of addresses, IP addresses are divided into three major classes: A, B, and C. A fourth class, D, is reserved for special uses such as multicasting. See Table 3.2. Each address consists of four octets, or sets of eight binary digits, separated by decimals. The first octet determines which class the IP address is in. Class A addresses use the last three octets to specify IP nodes; Class B addresses use the last two octets for this purpose; and Class C addresses use the last octet.

TABLE 3.2 Address Classes and Numbers of Nets and Hosts

Class	*Network ID*	*# Unique Networks*	*Host Address ID*	*# Unique Hosts*
A	7 bits	128	24 bits	16,777,216
B	14 bits	>16,000	16 bits	65,536
C	21 bits	>2 million	8 bits	256

Class A network addresses are the most desirable, because they are large enough to serve the needs of any size enterprise. But, because fewer than 128 Class A networks can exist in the entire Internet, they are very scarce, and no more Class As are being allocated. Only those organizations that were early users of the Internet (e.g., Xerox Corp., Stanford U., and BBN) are in possession of Class A network addresses.

The more than 16,000 possible Class B networks also have become scarce and are now difficult to obtain. A large supply (more than 2 million) of Class C network addresses exist, so they are still plentiful. The major problem is that for most organizations, a Class C network is too small (only 256 unique host IDs). Even a Class B network is not large enough for an enterprise with more than a thousand LANs.

client-to-LAN tunneling. See Chapter 11, "VPN Hardware," for more details.

Lastly, software VPN systems are often good low-cost choices for environments that are relatively small and don't have to process a lot of traffic. These solutions can run on existing servers and share resources with them, and they serve as a good starting point for getting familiar with

VPNs. Many of these systems are ideal for client-to-LAN connections and are covered in detail in Chapter 12, "VPN Software."

Other Security Components

Another important component of a VPN is the security policy server. This server maintains the access control lists and other user-related information that the security gateway uses to determine which traffic is authorized. For some systems, such as those using PPTP, access can be controlled via a RADIUS server; when IPSec is used, the server is responsible for managing the shared keys for each session.

Companies can choose to maintain their own database of digital certificates for users by setting up a corporate certificate server. For small groups of users, verification of shared keys may require checking with a third-party that maintains the digital certificates associated with shared cryptographic keys; these third parties are called *certificate authorities* (CAs). If a corporate VPN grows into an extranet, then an outside certificate authority also may have to be used to verify users from your business partners.

See Chapter 4, "Security: Threats and Solutions," for more details on cryptographic keys, digital certificates, and certificate authorities.

Summary

The Internet VPN depends on creating media-independent tunnels across the Internet to transmits packets between sites. Because the Internet is an open communications environment that can be subject to unauthorized interception and access, other measures have to be taken to keep corporate data on a VPN private. Encryption is thus an integral part of VPNs on the Internet.

At the moment, IPSec is the most complete protocol for VPNs, especially when coupled with ISAKMP/Oakley for managing cryptographic keys. Other protocols that have been proposed for VPNs, namely PPTP and L2TP, provide better support for multiprotocol networks but will probably still require deployment of IPSec's security features.

Securing an Internet VPN

A main component of Internet-based VPNs is security. The three major protocols proposed for VPNs—IPSec, PPTP, and L2TP—each provide differing degrees of security for your data and ease of deployment. Standardization efforts will make IPSec and L2TP the preferred protocols over the next few years.

When designing your VPN, you should take into account how the strengths and weaknesses of each protocol mesh with the business and data needs of your network. PPTP and L2TP are aimed more at remote access VPNs, while IPSec currently works best for connecting LANs.

4

Security: Threats and Solutions

One of the primary concerns of any corporation is protecting its data; fortunes can be made and lost, or reputations ruined, if information ends up in the wrong hands. Securing data against illegal access and alteration is even more of an issue on networks; transmitting data between computers or between LANs can make the data more vulnerable to snooping and interception than if it had remained on a single computer.

Many of the potential threats to transmitting data over today's networks are fairly well-known, and security experts know how to counter them. This chapter starts with a brief review of the common security threats in networked environments and then moves on to discuss the various cryptographic methods that enable you to protect your data on networks. With this background, we'll move on to the protocols and systems that implement these security solutions in the following chapters.

You should keep in mind that there's more to corporate security than what's covered in this chapter. A proper security framework for an organization includes seven different elements: authentication, confidentiality, integrity, authorization, nonrepudiation, administration, and audit trails (see Figure 4.1). The first three elements are the focus of this chapter, and

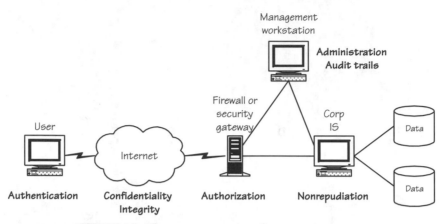

FIGURE 4.1 The components of a secure system.

we'll cover administration and auditing later in this book when we get to the section on VPN management. We'll leave it to other books, such as *Internet Security for Business,* by Terry Bernstein et al. (John Wiley & Sons, Inc., 1996) and *Computer Security Handbook,* edited by Arthur E. Hutt et al. (John Wiley & Sons, Inc., 1995), to cover some of the other details, such as configuring firewalls and setting up corporate security policies. Networking security is just one part—albeit an important part these days—of corporate security and should fit in with your corporate security policies.

Because the TCP/IP protocols were not designed with built-in provisions for security, many different security systems have been developed for applications and traffic running on the Internet. The software that's responsible for preparing data for transmission on a network offers a number of possibilities in which authentication and encryption can be applied. You could match each application of authentication and encryption to a specific protocol layer, using the 7-layer OSI Reference Model, for instance. But, for our purposes, it's sufficient to think of everything occurring in one of three layers: the application software, the network/transport stack, and the data link device and driver (see Figure 4.2). Some of the current-day cryptographic protocols for applications include *Secure MIME* (S/MIME) and *Pretty Good Privacy* (PGP) for e-mail and *Secure Sockets Layer* (SSL/TSL) and *Secure HTTP* (SHTTP) for Web applications. But, of greatest importance to the construction of VPNs is authentication and encryption at the Network and Data Link layers.

As we go through this chapter, recall that these methods can be applied to many different kinds of data and applications, but implementation in the Network layer is of primary importance to VPNs.

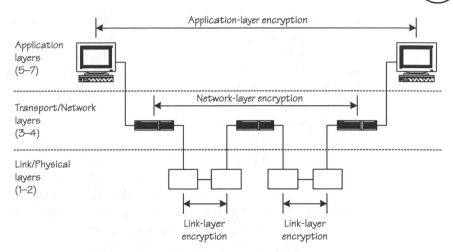

FIGURE 4.2 Network-layer versus Link-layer encryption.

Security Threats on Networks

In networked environments, the security of your data and communications depends on three things: authentication, confidentiality, and data integrity. Authentication means that the person with whom you're communicating really is that person; it's a step beyond identification because you're also verifying the identification. Maintaining the confidentiality of your communications is ensuring that no one can eavesdrop on your communications—that is, no one can read your data even if they intercept it. Lastly, guaranteeing the integrity of your data means that the data has not been altered in any way during transmission.

Unfortunately, as originally designed, the TCP/IP protocols and the networks built using these protocols, like the Internet, make it difficult to ensure that these three security features can be routinely provided. In the absence of proper security measures, data transmissions on IP networks can be subjected to a variety of threats. We'll review the more common types—spoofing, session hijacking, sniffing, and the man-in-the-middle attack—before moving on to the solutions that can defeat these attacks.

Spoofing

Like other networks, IP networks use a numeric address for each device attached to the network. The address of the source and intended recipient is included in each data packet transmitted on an IP network. *Spoofing* takes advantage of the fact that an attacker can use someone else's IP address and pretend to be the other respondent.

After an attacker identifies a pair of computers—A and B, for example—that are communicating with each other as a client-server pair, he attempts to establish a connection with computer B in such a way that B believes that it has a connection with A; in reality, the connection is with the attacker's computer.

The attacker accomplishes this by creating a fake message (i.e., a message from the attacker) but with A's address as the source address, requesting a connection to B. When it receives this message, B will respond with an acknowledgment, which includes sequence numbers for transmissions with A. These sequence numbers from server B are unique to the connection between the two machines.

To complete the setup of this session between A and B, B would expect A to acknowledge B's sequence number before proceeding with any further exchange of information. But, in order for the attacker to impersonate A, he has to guess the sequence numbers B will use, and he has to prevent A from replying. It turns out that, in certain circumstances, it's not too difficult to guess what the sequence numbers are.

In order to keep computer A from responding to any of B's transmissions (and thus denying that it had requested a connection in the first place), the attacker usually transmits a large number of packets to A, overflowing A's capacity to process them and preventing A from responding to B's message.

Even with automated tools, IP spoofing can be rather tedious to accomplish. Spoofing is relatively easy to protect against: Configure your routers to reject any inbound packets that claim to originate from a computer within your internal network, which prevents any external computer from taking advantage of session relationships within the internal network. If you have such relations that cross the network's borders, such as over the Internet, then guarding against IP spoofing is more difficult.

Session Hijacking

Spoofing is one level of attack; it makes possible another. In *session hijacking,* rather than attempting to initiate a session via spoofing, the attacker attempts to take over an existing connection between two computers.

The first step in this attack is for the attacker to take control of a network device on the LAN, either a firewall or another computer, so that he can monitor the connection. By monitoring the connection between the two computers, the attacker can determine the sequence numbers used by both parties.

After he's monitored the connection and determined the sequence numbers, the attacker can generate traffic that appears to come from one of the communicating parties, stealing the session from one of the individuals involved. As in IP spoofing, the attacker would overload one of the communicating computers with excess packets so that it drops out of the communications session.

The problems caused by session hijacking point out the need for a reliable means of identifying the other party in a session. The fact that you've identified the person with whom you're communicating once doesn't mean that you can depend on IP to ensure it will be the same person through the rest of the session. You need a scheme that authenticates the data's source throughout the transmission. Even the strongest authentication methods are not always successful in preventing hijacking attacks; the only true defense against such attacks is the widespread use of encryption.

Electronic Eavesdropping or Sniffing

Sniffing is another attack that's possible in shared-media networks like Ethernet-based IP networks. In most Ethernet LANs, packets are available to every Ethernet node on the network. The usual convention is for each node's *network interface card* (NIC) to only listen and respond to packets specifically addressed to it. It's relatively easy, however, to put many Ethernet NICs into what's called *promiscuous mode*—meaning that they can collect every packet that passes on the wire. Such a NIC cannot be detected from another location on the network, because the NIC doesn't do anything to the packets when it collects them.

A type of software colloquially called a *sniffer* (after the original network analysis tool designed to do this—Network General's Sniffer) can take advantage of this feature of Ethernet technology. Such tools can record all the network traffic going past them. As such, they are a necessary part of the toolkit of any network diagnostician working with Ethernets, allowing them to determine quickly what's going through any segment of the network. However, in the hands of someone who wants to listen in on sensitive communications, a sniffer is a powerful eavesdropping tool. For instance, an attacker can use a packet sniffer to record all login packets on a network and then use the login information to enter systems that he would otherwise be unauthorized to access.

Sniffing also can be used to collect company data and messages as they're transmitted on a network, for later analysis. For example, the attacker might perform a traffic analysis to learn who's communicating with whom, which could be competitive intelligence on secret partnerships or merger talks, for instance.

Strong authentication using one-time passwords or tokens is one way of keeping anyone with a sniffer from reusing a password that he's illegally obtained. Encrypting data is another way of protecting your data against sniffing, although even that isn't a foolproof solution; the attacker may have the resources to store the encrypted data and try decrypting the messages off-line.

Physical inspection of your networks is a good way to reduce the risk of sniffing, because sniffers have to be physically attached to your network to intercept packets. Also, on some computers, like those running Unix, you easily can check to see whether a NIC is set to run in promiscuous mode.

The Man-in-the-Middle Attack

Although it seems obvious that using encryption technologies to conceal and authenticate the data passed in IP packets is a solution to many of the IP security threats we've just discussed, encryption is not a foolproof solution. You still need to carefully manage your encryption system to guard against other attacks, such as *man-in-the-middle attacks*.

To use encryption, you first have to exchange encryption keys. But, exchanging unprotected keys over the network could easily defeat the whole purpose of the system, because those keys could be intercepted and open your data up to yet another type of attack—the man-in-the-middle attack. A sophisticated attacker employing spoofing, hijacking, and sniffing could actually work his way into such a key exchange, in a system that left the way open. He could plant his own key early in the process so that, while you believed you were communicating with one party's key, you actually would be using a key known to the man-in-the-middle.

Types of Authentication

Authentication can be divided into two types: weak and strong authentication. Weak, or simple, authentication mechanisms are "normal" mechanisms used by most systems, for example, the use of a password when a user logs in to a system. Strong authentication mechanisms are mechanisms where an entity does not reveal any secrets during the authentication process.

The bottom line is that you need to carefully deploy and maintain your security system, and check it regularly, to ensure that it's still effective against all kinds of threats. For VPNs, two important building blocks of secure systems are *authentication* and *encryption*. Let's start out exploring different methods for authenticating users and computers and then move on to encryption and some related aspects of modern-day cryptography.

Authentication Systems

Authentication is a vital part of a VPN's security structure. Unless your system can reliably authenticate users, services, and networks, you cannot control access to your corporate resources and keep unauthorized users out of your networks.

Authentication is based on one of the following three attributes: something you have (a key to a door or a token card); something you know (a password); or something you are (voiceprints, retinal scans). It's generally accepted among security experts that a single method of authentication, such as a password, is not adequate for protecting systems. Instead, they recommend what's called *strong authentication*, or using at least two of the preceding attributes for authentication.

The variety of VPN systems currently available depend on different methods of authentication or combinations of them. As background for the following chapters, in which we discuss the details of these systems, we'll review the more common authentication methods. They'll be classified in the following way: traditional passwords, one-time passwords (S/Key), other password systems (PAP, CHAP, TACACS, and RADIUS), hardware-based (tokens, smart cards, and PC cards), and biometric IDs (fingerprint, voice print, and retinal scans).

Traditional Passwords

It's generally recognized that the simplest form of authentication (i.e., user IDs and passwords) is inadequate for securing network access. Passwords can be guessed and intercepted during network transmissions.

Even when users are careful about guarding their passwords, they may not realize that different Internet services offer no protection for their passwords. For example, services such as FTP and telnet transmit user IDs and passwords as plaintext, making them easy to use when intercepted.

One-time password systems, which restrict the validity of a password to a single session, can be a good solution to some of the problems surrounding traditional password uses. We'll see shortly that some improved authentication methods choose to encrypt user IDs and passwords.

One-Time Passwords

One way to prevent the unauthorized use of an intercepted password is to prevent it from being reusable (i.e., restrict a password's use to a single communications session). As you'd expect from the name, one-time password systems aim to do just that, by requiring a new password for each new session. These systems, of which S/Key (originally developed by Bellcore) is the best example, relieves the user of the difficulty of always choosing a new password for the next session by automatically generating a list of acceptable passwords for the user. The IETF has taken on the task of standardizing S/Key; see their specifications for the One-Time Password (OTP) System in RFC 2289.

S/Key uses a secret pass-phrase, generated by the user, to generate a sequence of one-time passwords. The user's secret pass-phrase never travels beyond his local computer and does not travel on the network; therefore, the pass-phrase is not subject to replay attacks. Also, because a different one-time password is generated for each session, an intercepted password cannot be used again, nor does it give the hacker any information about the next password to be used.

A sequence of one-time passwords is produced by applying a secure hash function multiple times to the message digest produced in the initial step. (See the section, "An Introduction to Cryptography," later in this chapter for an explanation of hash functions and message digests.) In other words, the first one-time password is produced by passing the message digest through the hash function N times, where N is specified by the user. The next one-time password is generated by passing the message digest through the hash function $N-1$ times, and so on, until N one-time passwords are generated.

When a user attempts to log into a network, the network server, which is the S/Key-enabled host guarding the entrance to the network, issues a challenge consisting of a number and a string of characters, which is called the *seed*.

In responding to the network server's challenge, the user enters the challenge number and seed plus his own secret pass-phrase into the S/Key generator software that runs on his computer. The generator software then combines the secret pass-phrase with the seed and iterates a hash function repeating the operation for the number of times corresponding to the challenge number. The result of the calculation is a one-time password that takes on the form of six English words.

The one-time password is sent to the network server, which also iterates the hash function and compares the result with the stored one-time password that was used for the most recent login. If they match, the user is allowed to log in. The challenge number is decremented, and the latest one-time password is kept for the next login attempt.

One-time password systems like S/Key require that the server software be modified to perform the required calculations and that each remote computer have a copy of the client software. These systems may not be highly scalable because it's difficult to administer the password lists for a large number of users.

Other Systems

Aside from the traditional password method for authentication, which often includes sending the user ID and password in plaintext, a number of other important password-based systems have been developed for authentication, especially for remote access. Because many of the VPN systems use these methods for controlling remote access, it's worthwhile to review them briefly here. The methods are PAP, CHAP, TACACS, and RADIUS.

PASSWORD AUTHENTICATION PROTOCOL (PAP)

PAP, or the *Password Authentication Protocol,* was originally designed as a simple way for one computer to authenticate itself to another computer when *Point-to-Point Protocol* (PPP) is used as the communications protocol. PAP is a two-way handshaking protocol; that is, the host making the connection sends a user ID and password pair to the target system with which it's trying to establish a connection, and then the target system (the authenticator) acknowledges that the computer is authenticated and approved for communication.

PAP authentication can be used at the start of the PPP link as well as during a PPP session to reauthenticate the link.

When the PPP link is established, PAP authentication can be carried out over that link. The peer sends a user ID and a password in the clear to the authenticator until either the authenticator accepts the pair or the connection is terminated. PAP is not secure because authentication information is transmitted in the clear, and nothing protects against playback attacks or excessive repetition by attackers trying to guess a valid password/user ID pair.

CHALLENGE HANDSHAKE AUTHENTICATION PROTOCOL (CHAP)

CHAP was designed for the same uses as PAP, but CHAP is a more secure method for authenticating PPP links. CHAP is a three-way handshaking protocol. Like PAP, CHAP can be used at the start of a PPP link and then repeated after the link has been established.

CHAP is referred to as a three-way handshake protocol because it incorporates three steps to produce a verified link after the link is first initiated, or at any time after the link has been established and verified. Instead of a simple two-step password/approval process, such as that used by PAP, CHAP uses a one-way hashing function in a fashion similar to that used by S/Key. The actual process is as follows (see Figure 4.3):

1. The authenticator sends a challenge message to the peer.
2. The peer calculates a value using a one-way hash function and sends it back to the authenticator.
3. The authenticator can acknowledge authentication if the response matches the expected value.

The process can be repeated at any time during the PPP link to ensure that the connection has not been taken over or subverted in any way. Unlike PAP, which is driven by the client side, the server controls CHAP reauthentication. CHAP also removes the possibility, inherent in PAP, that an attacker can try repeatedly to log in over the same connection. When the CHAP authentication fails, the server is required to drop the connection. This complicates the attacker's task of guessing the password because he cannot try new guesses in a single connection.

PAP and CHAP do have some disadvantages. Both PAP and CHAP rely on a secret password that must be stored on the remote user's computer and the local computer. If either computer comes under the control of a network attacker, then the secret password is compromised. Also, with CHAP or PAP authentication, you cannot assign different network access privileges to different remote users who use the same remote host.

FIGURE 4.3 Challenge-response system using CHAP.

Because one set of privileges is assigned to a specific computer, everybody who uses that computer will have the same set of privileges. The next two protocols we'll discuss, **TACACS** and **RADIUS**, provide more flexibility for assigning access privileges.

Although **CHAP** is a stronger method than **PAP** for authenticating dial-up users, **CHAP** may not meet the scalability requirements of large organizations. Even though it doesn't transmit any secrets across a network, it requires a large number of shared secrets to be run through the hash function. Organizations with many dial-up users have to maintain very large databases to accommodate them all.

TERMINAL ACCESS CONTROLLER ACCESS-CONTROL SYSTEM (TACACS)

TACACS is one of the systems developed to not only offer authentication, but also add the other two As of remote access security—*authorization* and *accounting*. (Admittedly, **PAP** and **CHAP** also offer authorization or access control, but they're of limited flexibility.) Unlike the peer relations designed into **PAP** and **CHAP**, TACACS is designed to function as a client/server system, which affords it more flexibility, especially in security management. (We'll shortly see that RADIUS also is a client/server architecture.) Central to the operation of TACACS, and RADIUS, is an authentication server (see Figure 4.4).

Typically, a TACACS authentication server handles requests from authentication client software that's installed at a gateway or network entry point. The authentication server maintains a database of user IDs,

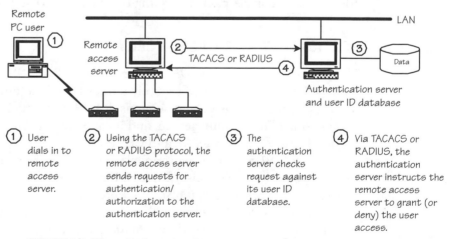

FIGURE 4.4 How authentication servers authorize remote access.

passwords, PINs, and secret keys, which it uses to grant or deny network access requests. All authentication, authorization, and accounting data is directed to the centralized server when a user tries to log in.

TACACS transmits all data in the clear between the user and the server, but a recent update from Cisco, TACACS+, adds a message-digest function to eliminate the plaintext transmission of passwords. TACACS+ also supports multiprotocol logins, meaning that a single user ID and password pair can authenticate a user for multiple devices and networks—for example, an IP network login and an IPX network login. Finally, TACACS+ also can handle PAP and CHAP authentication.

TACACS is currently best known as Cisco System's server-based security software protocol. All Cisco router and access-server product families use this protocol. Although TACACS has been described in an IETF RFC, and is freely available for other vendors to implement, most vendors view TACACS as proprietary and instead concentrate on RADIUS.

One advantage to TACACS is that it can act as a proxy server to other authentication systems, such as a Windows NT security domain, NDS, Unix-based NIS maps, or other security systems (such as the token-based systems we'll mention shortly). The proxy capabilities also make it easier for a corporate client to share VPN security data with an ISP, which is necessary when a VPN is outsourced; the ISP runs a proxy server to control dial-in access based on access rights managed by the corporate customer on its own secure server. But, transmitting authentication packets between the parent server and the proxy server across a public network poses a security risk. RADIUS and TACACS encryption is based on static keys; the user names, passwords, and authentication server info are conveniently contained in a single packet, making them easier to use if intercepted.

REMOTE AUTHENTICATION DIAL-IN USER SERVICE

The *Remote Authentication Dial-In User Service* (RADIUS) protocol also uses a client/server model to securely authenticate and administer remote network connection users and sessions. RADIUS is largely a way to make access control more manageable, and it can support other types of user authentication, including PAP and CHAP.

The RADIUS client/server model uses a *network access server* (NAS) to manage user connections. Although the NAS functions as a server for providing network access, it also functions as a client for RADIUS (see Figure 4.4). The NAS is responsible for accepting user connection requests, getting user ID and password information, and passing the information securely to the RADIUS server. The RADIUS server returns authentication status—approved or denied—as well as any configuration data required for the NAS to provide services to the end user.

RADIUS clients and servers communicate securely, using shared secrets for authentication and encryption for transmitting user passwords.

RADIUS creates a single, centrally located database of users and available services, a feature particularly important for networks that include large modem banks and more than one remote communications server. With RADIUS, the user information is kept in one location, the RADIUS server, which manages the authentication of the user and access to services from one location. Because any device that supports RADIUS can be a RADIUS client, a remote user will gain access to the same services from any communications server communicating with the RADIUS server.

Hardware-Based Systems

Earlier, when we wrote about the different methods for authentication, we mentioned that one class of methods focuses on using something that you have in your possession. This is where hardware devices come into play, such as smart cards, PC cards, and token devices.

SMART CARDS AND PC CARDS

Smart cards are devices about the size of a credit card but include an embedded microprocessor and memory. A smart-card terminal or similar reader for smart cards is required to communicate with a smart card so that information can be exchanged as needed. Many of these readers are now available for use with a PC floppy drive or are integrated into keyboards, making their use with PCs simpler than before.

Smart cards can store a user's private key along with any installed applications, which simplifies the authentication process, especially for mobile users. Some smart cards now include their own cryptographic coprocessors, making encryption of data easier and faster than with older smart cards. And, many software developers are now taking advantage of standardized APIs, like the CryptoAPI for use with Windows, to tie together smart cards and PCs.

The simplest systems for using digital certificates require the user to enter a PIN to complete the authentication process. In some cases, a PIN is stored on the smart card, and use of the PIN to authenticate the user is checked automatically by the smart card before any other communication with the rest of the system takes place. When a PIN isn't stored on the card, this method may not be secure enough (PINs can be guessed), so higher end systems combine the information stored in the smart card with biometric information. Using these systems, the card reader includes a biometric device, such as a fingerprint scanner. The scanned data then is compared with the data stored on the smart card to authenticate the card holder. This process soon may happen entirely on a smart card, as Verdicom and Lucent Technologies recently announced the development of a fingerprint scanner on a chip that can be installed on a smart card.

Although smart cards are seeing increasing use in security systems, it's also possible to use other types of electronic cards that can be inserted into a PC. One example is the PC card. PC cards, which used to be called PCMCIA cards, are those small circuit boards that can be inserted into special slots on desktop computers, and particularly laptops, to provide added functionality. These cards can offer some of the same functionality as smart cards but are restricted to use with PCs containing PCMCIA slots, making them less portable if a variety of access devices are to be used. However, PCMCIA cards do have the advantage of more memory, enabling them to store larger files for authentication purposes.

TOKEN DEVICES

Token-based systems usually are based on separate hardware (i.e., not built into a PC) that displays changing passcodes that a user then has to type into his computer for authentication.

Here's a quick rundown on how token-based authentication works. A processor inside the token card stores a series of secret encryption keys used to generate one-time passcodes. The passcodes are sent to a secure server on the network, which checks their validity and grants the user access. After the codes are programmed in, neither users nor administrators have access to them.

Before users are permitted to authenticate themselves, token devices request a PIN. They then use one of three different mechanisms to verify that users are who they say they are. The most widely implemented of these mechanisms is challenge-response (see Figure 4.3), in which the secure server issues a random number (called the *challenge*) when the user attempts to log in. The challenge appears on the screen of the user, who then types the numbers into the token card. The card encrypts the challenge with its secret key and displays the response on its LCD screen, and the user then types that response into the PC. Meanwhile, the server encrypts the challenge with the same key, and if the two results match, the user is allowed in.

Another scheme makes use of time synchronization. Here, the token displays a number encrypted with the secret key, which changes every 60 seconds. Users are prompted for the number when they try to log into the server. Because the clocks on the server and the token are synchronized, the server can authenticate the user by decrypting the token number and comparing results. (Users caught typing during the middle of a passcode change usually have to start again with the new code.)

The third scheme is event synchronization, a variation on time synchronization. Here, a counter records the number of login attempts made by a user. After every attempt, the counter is updated, and a different passcode is generated for the next login.

Problems with token-based systems stem from their use of extra hardware and the involvement of a human being to enter the authentication codes. This latter point not only can prove to be tedious for the user, but also makes authentication of unattended batch applications impossible.

Biometric Systems

Biometrics depends on using a unique personal trait to identify the user. You've probably seen a James Bond movie or other spy story in which voice prints, retinal scans, and hand images were used to identify (or misidentify) a main character of the film. Biometric technologies measure human characteristics such as fingerprints, voice recordings, iris and retinal scans, heat patterns, facial images, and even keystroke patterns. But, biometric systems have yet to see routine use in many environments because they've been expensive and usually are all-in-one security systems, making them difficult to interface with other security systems. That's likely to change, however, as newer, faster, and less expensive technologies come into play.

One approach that's likely to see widespread deployment is fingerprint scanning. Fingerprint scanners have dropped in price considerably and are being incorporated into PC keyboards in 1998. Also, as mentioned, a scanner-on-a-chip has been developed that enables fingerprint scanning to be directly incorporated into a smart card.

Some of the newer face analysis systems can operate on a PC with a low-cost, low-resolution camera such as is often used for videoconferencing. A central database stores images of authorized users and compares the image transmitted by the camera to the stored images to grant access.

Although the use of biometric systems appears to be on the rise, the lack of a standardized set of Application Programming Interfaces (APIs) for most of the biometric methods makes it difficult to readily incorporate biometrics into existing security systems. At least four different APIs have been proposed for developing security applications: the Biometric API (BAPI), backed by Japanese hardware manufacturers; the Human Authentication

API (HA-API), developed by National Registry Inc. for the Department of Defense; the Speaker Verification API (SVAPI), which has been proposed for voice recognition systems; and an API proposed by IBM. In an attempt to promote a common API for biometrics, Compaq Computer, IBM, Identicator Technology, Microsoft, Miros, and Novell formed the BioAPI Consortium in April, 1998.

An Introduction to Cryptography

Modern-day cryptographic algorithms coupled with today's powerful microprocessors now make possible the everyday use of powerful authentication and encryption methods. Cryptography covers a number of algorithms for encrypting and decrypting information, classified according the way secrets, or keys, are shared between correspondents, how the secrets are used to encrypt and decrypt information, and what form the algorithms take. For a complete review of cryptography, see *Applied Cryptography* by Bruce Schneier (2d edition, John Wiley & Sons, Inc., 1996); this chapter only covers a few cryptographic algorithms that are particularly pertinent to network security and VPNs.

What Is Encryption?

Encrypting or encoding information to prevent its being read by unauthorized parties has been the main use of cryptography since its early beginnings—Julius Caesar, for instance, used an alphabetical cipher when communicating with his field commanders.

For encryption to work properly, both the sender and receiver have to know what set of rules, called the *cipher*, was used to transform the original information into its coded form, often called *cipher text*. A simple cipher might be to add an arbitrary number of characters, say 13, to all characters in a message. As long as the receiving party knows what the sender did to the message, the receiving party can reverse the process (for example, subtract 13 characters from the message received) to extract the original text.

Encryption is based on two components: an algorithm and a key. A cryptographic algorithm is a mathematical function that combines plaintext or other intelligible information with a string of digits called a *key* to produce unintelligible cipher text. The key and the algorithm used are both crucial to the encryption.

Although some special encryption algorithms that don't use a key do exist, algorithms using keys are particularly important. (See the discussion of hash functions in the section, "What Is Public-Key Cryptography?," later in this chapter.) Basing encryption on a key-based system offers two important advantages. First, encryption algorithms are difficult to devise; you wouldn't want to come up with a new algorithm each time you want to communicate privately with a new correspondent. By using a key, you can use the same algorithm to communicate with many people; all you have to do is use a different key for each correspondent. Second, if someone does crack your encrypted messages, all you have to do is switch to a new key to start encrypting messages all over again; you don't have to switch to a new algorithm (unless the algorithm and not the key proved to be insecure—that can happen, but it's unlikely).

The number of possible keys each algorithm can support depends on the number of bits in the key. For example, an 8-bit key length allows for only 256 (2^8) possible numeric combinations, or keys. The greater the number of possible keys, the more difficult it is to crack an encrypted message. The level of difficulty is therefore dependent on the key length. It would not take a computer very long to sequentially guess each of the 256 possible keys (less than a millisecond) and decrypt the message to see whether it makes sense. But, if a 100-bit key were used, which equates to searching 2^{100} keys, and the computer could guess 1 million keys every second, it could actually take many centuries to discover the right key.

The security of an encryption algorithm correlates with the length of its key. Why? Because knowing that a key is n bits long only gives you an idea of how much time you'd have to spend to break the code. If security were dependent on such things as the secrecy of the algorithm, or the inaccessibility of the cipher text or plaintext, unauthorized persons could derive that information from publications or the pattern analysis of messages, or they could collect the information in other ways (traffic monitoring, for example). When the information is in hand, the unauthorized person(s) can use it to decrypt your communications.

The oldest form of key-based cryptography is called *secret-key* or *symmetric* encryption. In this scheme, both the sender and recipient possess the same key, which means that both parties can encrypt and decrypt data with the key (see Figure 4.5). But, symmetric encryption has some drawbacks: for example, both parties must agree upon a shared secret key. If you have n correspondents, then you have to keep track of n secret keys—one for each of your correspondents. If you use the same key for more than one correspondent, then they will be able to read each other's mail.

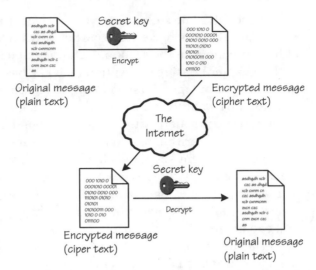

FIGURE 4.5 Symmetric encryption uses a single secret key to encrypt and decrypt messages.

Symmetric encryption schemes also have a problem with authenticity, because the identity of a message's originator or recipient cannot be proved. Because both Ann and Tim possess the same key, both of them can create and encrypt a message and claim that the other person sent it. This built-in ambiguity about who authored a message makes nonrepudiation impossible with secret keys. Proving that someone actually did send a message when he claims he didn't is called *nonrepudiation*. The way to solve the repudiation isssue is by using what is called public-key cryptography, which makes use of asymmetric encryption algorithms.

What Is Public-Key Cryptography?

Public-key cryptography is based on the concept of a key pair. One part of the key pair, the *private key,* is known only by the designated owner; the other part, the *public key,* can be published widely but is still associated with the owner. Key pairs have a unique feature: Data encrypted with one key can be decrypted with the other key in the pair (see Figure 4.6). You'll see some of the power of this in the next few pages.

These keys can be used in two different ways: to provide message confidentiality and to prove the authenticity of a message's originator. In the first case, the sender uses the recipient's public key to encrypt a message so that it will remain confidential until decoded by the recipient with

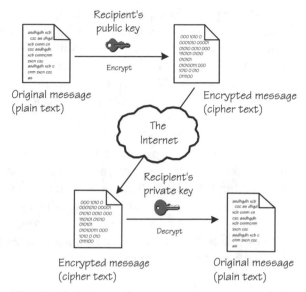

FIGURE 4.6 Using a key pair to encrypt and decrypt a message.

the private key. In the second instance, the sender encrypts a message using the private key, a key to which only the sender has access.

For example, in order to create a confidential message, Tim first would acquire Ann's public key. Then he uses her public key to encrypt the message and sends it to her. Because the message was encrypted with Ann's public key, only someone with Ann's private key (and presumably only Ann has that) can decrypt the message.

Although encrypting a message with part of a public key pair isn't very different from using secret-key encryption, public-key systems offer some advantages. For instance, the public key of your key pair can be readily distributed (on a server, for example) without fear that this compromises your use of your private key. You don't have to send a copy of your public key to all your respondents; they can get it from a key server maintained by your company or maybe a service provider.

Another advantage of public-key cryptography is that it enables you to authenticate a message's originator. The basic idea is this: Because you are the only person who can encrypt something with your private key, anyone using your public key to decrypt the message can be sure that the message came from you. Thus, your use of your private key on an electronic document is similar to your signing a paper document. The recipient then will be certain that the message came from you but cannot be sure that nobody else has read it as well.

Using public-key cryptographic algorithms to encrypt messages is computationally slow, so cryptographers have come up with a way to quickly generate a short, unique representation of your message, called a *message digest*, which can be encrypted and then used as your digital signature.

Some popular, fast cryptographic algorithms for generating message digests are known as one-way hash functions. A one-way hash function doesn't use a key; it's simply a formula to convert a message of any length into a single string of digits called a message digest. When using a 16-byte hash function, text processed with that hash function would produce 16 bytes of output. A message might result in the string, for example "CBBV235ndsAG3D67". The important thing to remember is that each message produces a random message digest.

Message digests on their own can prove useful as an indicator that data hasn't been altered, but digital signatures are even more reliable. If you encrypt the message digest with your private key, you've got a digital signature.

As an example, let's have the sender, Tim, calculate a message digest for his message, encrypt the digest with his private key, and send that digital signature along with the plain-text message to Ann (see Figure 4.7).

After Ann uses Tim's public key to decrypt the digital signature, she has a copy of the message digest that Tim calculated. Because she was able to decrypt the digital signature with Tim's public key, she knows that Tim created it, authenticating the originator. Ann then uses the same hash function, which was agreed-upon beforehand, to calculate her own message digest of Tim's plain-text message. If her calculated value and the one Tim sent her are the same, then she can be assured that the digital signature is authentic, which means that Tim sent the message and the message itself has not been tampered with.

The one problem with this approach is that a copy of the plaintext is sent as part of the message and, therefore, privacy is not maintained (i.e., someone could still read the data even if they couldn't alter it). If you want to maintain the data's privacy, you should encrypt the message. But, to reduce the computational overhead, use a symmetric algorithm with a secret key. This procedure further complicates matters, but it might be worth the added work.

Two Important Public-Key Methods

Although a wide variety of cryptographic algorithms exist for public keys, two public-key methods—Diffie-Hellman and RSA—account for the majority of public-key usage these days.

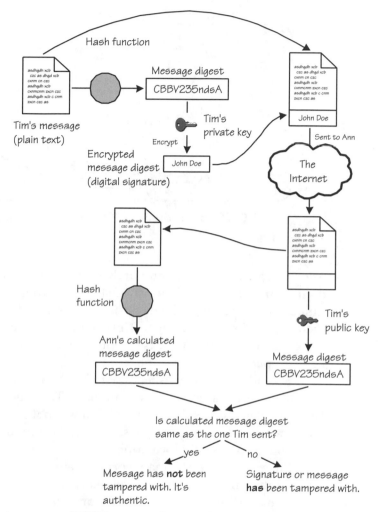

FIGURE 4.7 Verifying a digital signature.

THE DIFFIE-HELLMAN TECHNIQUE

The Diffie-Hellman technique was the first practical public-key cryptographic algorithm; in practice, Diffie-Hellman is very useful for key management. We'll see in the next chapter that the key exchange proposals for IPSec are each based on Diffie-Hellman.

On to the mechanics . . . Two correspondents can use Diffie-Hellman to produce a shared secret value that then can be used as a common key for a secret key encryption algorithm (see Figure 4.8). Let's have Tim and

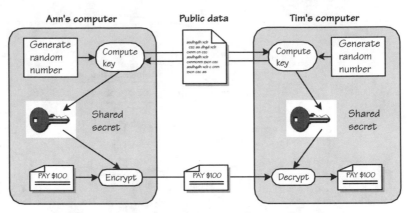

Ann's computer   Public data   Tim's computer

FIGURE 4.8 Producing a Diffie-Hellman shared secret.

Ann each generate a random number on their computers; these two random numbers become their private keys. In order to communicate, they first exchange some public data that is considered their public key. Ann then applies her private key to Tim's public key to compute the shared secret value. Tim does likewise, applying his private key to Ann's public key, computing the same value.

Should someone intercept the public values, they cannot easily compute the random secret values from them. The crucial point of the Diffie-Hellman algorithm is that Ann and Tim will both end up with the same numerical result, and nobody else can easily compute the same result from the publicly available information.

Basically, Diffie-Hellman works because you can apply exponentiation in different orders and still get the same result. In Diffie-Hellman, both Ann and Tim agree on a particular base number. That base number raised to the power of an individual's private key, a large random number, becomes the public key, say B^A (i.e., Base$^{\text{Ann's\_key}}$) for Ann. Tim's public key would be B^T. Now, when Tim receives Ann's public key, that is, B^A, he can raise it to the power of his private key to get the shared secret (i.e., $(B^A)^T$). When Ann receives Tim's public key, B^T, she can raise it to the power of her private key to get $(B^T)^A$, which is identical to the other result that Tim calculated.

The Diffie-Hellman technique can be particularly useful for creating temporary session keys, which are used only by the corresponding parties during an exchange of information and are deleted afterwards. Using a new key for each session reduces the risk of compromising your security.

> ## Perfect Forward Secrecy
>
> One of the reasons for continued interest in Diffie-Hellman is because it can be used to achieve perfect forward secrecy. The more often you use the same key to encrypt data, the greater the risk of having the key compromised. Longer keys help the situation somewhat, so picking some reasonable length that doesn't impose severe performance slowdowns and changing the keys frequently can reduce the risk. But, because each new key cannot be related to any previous keys (or an attacker will have more useful information to help crack the key), you need a method of generating a new key that's independent of the value of the current key. Diffie-Hellman makes that possible; cryptographers call the concept *perfect forward secrecy*.

RSA PUBLIC-KEY CRYPTOGRAPHY

The RSA public-key technique derives its name from its three developers: Ron Rivest, Adir Shamir, and Leonard Adelman. The security of this approach is based on the fact that it can be relatively easy to multiply large prime numbers together, but it is almost impossible to factor the resulting product. This technique produces public keys that are tied to specific private keys. This gives RSA the advantage of enabling the holder of a private key to encrypt data with it so that anyone with a copy of the public key can then decrypt it, much as we explained in the beginning of the section on public-key cryptography.

RSA keys consist of three special numeric values that are used in pairs to encrypt or decrypt data. The RSA public key consists of a public-key value (normally either 317 or 65,537) and a modulus. The modulus is the product of two large prime numbers, chosen at random, that are mathematically related to the chosen public key. The private key is calculated from the two prime numbers that were generated for the modulus and the public-key value.

In practice, the private key cannot be derived because there is no practical way to compute the values of the two selected prime numbers by factoring the modulus.

Selecting Encryption Methods

No one encryption system is ideal for all situations. Table 4.1 illustrates some of the advantages and disadvantages of each type of encryption.

TABLE 4.1 Advantages and Disadvantages of Cryptographic Systems

Encryption Type	Advantages	Disadvantages
Symmetric Key.	Fast. Can be easily implemented in hardware.	Both keys are the same. Difficult to distribute keys. Does not support digital signatures.
Public Key.	Uses two different keys. Relatively easy to distribute keys. Provides integrity and non-repudiation through digital signatures.	Slow and computationally intensive.

When selecting an appropriate algorithm to use, the general rule of thumb is this: First, determine how sensitive your data is and for how long it will be sensitive and have to be protected. When you've figured that out, select an encryption algorithm and key length that will take longer to break than the length of time for which your data will be sensitive.

One of the best discussions of key lengths and the efforts required to break a key is found in Chapter 7 of *Applied Cryptography* by Bruce Schneier (2nd edition, John Wiley & Sons, Inc., 1996). Table 4.2 is a condensation of his table estimating the cost of building a computer in 1995 to crack symmetric keys and the time required to crack certain length keys.

Remember that this is not a static situation. Computing power is always going up, and costs are falling, so it'll get easier and cheaper to break larger keys in the future. These estimates are for brute-force attacks—that is, guessing every possible key. There are other methods for cracking keys, depending on the ciphers used (that's what keeps cryptana-

TABLE 4.2 Comparison of Time and Money Needed to Break
Different Length Keys

Cost	Length of key in bits				
	40	56	64	80	128
$100 K	2 secs.	35 hrs.	1 yr.	70,000 yrs.	10^{19} yrs.
$1 M	.2 secs.	3.5 hrs.	37 days	7000 yrs.	10^{18} yrs.
$100 M	2 millisecs.	2 mins.	9 hrs.	70 yrs.	10^{16} yrs.
$1 G	.2 millisecs.	13 secs.	1 hr.	7 yrs.	10^{15} yrs.
$100 G	2 microsecs.	.1 sec.	32 secs.	24 days	10^{13} yrs.

Common Key Algorithms

DES (Data Encryption Standard).   A block cipher created by IBM and endorsed by the U.S. government in 1977. Uses a 56-bit key and operates one block of 64 bits. Relatively fast and used to encrypt large amounts of data at one time.

Triple DES.   Based on DES. Encrypts a block of data three times with three different keys. Being proposed as an alternative to DES, because it's been said that the potential of easily and quickly cracking DES is increasing every day.

RC2 and RC4.   Designed by Ron Rivest (the *R* in RSA Data Security Inc.). Variable key-size ciphers for very fast bulk encryption. A bit faster than DES, the two algorithms can be made more secure by selecting a longer key size. RC2 is a block cipher and can be used in place of DES. RC4 is a stream cipher and is as much as 10 times faster than DES.

IDEA (International Data Encryption Algorithm).   Created in 1991, it was designed to be efficient to compute in software. Offers very strong encryption using a 128-bit key.

RSA.   Named after Rivest, Shamir, and Adelman, its designers. Public-key algorithm supports a variable key length as well as a variable blocksize of the text to be encrypted. The plaintext block must be smaller than the key length. Common key length is 512 bits.

Diffie-Hellman.   The oldest public-key cryptosystem still in use. Does not support either encryption or digital signatures. System is designed to allow two individuals to agree on a shared key, even though they only exchange messages in public.

DSA.   Digital Signature Algorithm, developed by NIST and based on what's called the El Gamal algorithm. The signature scheme uses the same sort of keys as Diffie-Hellman and can create signatures faster than RSA. Being pushed by NIST as DSS, the Digital Signature Standard, although its acceptance is far from ensured.

Blowfish.   A 64-bit block cipher with a variable-length key designed by Bruce Schneier for implementation on large microprocessors. It's optimized for applications in which the key does not change often.

Skipjack.   The NSA-developed encryption algorithm designed for the Clipper and Capstone chips. The algorithm is an iterative 64-bit block cipher with an 80-bit key.

lysts employed), but estimates for brute-force attacks are commonly cited as a measure of the strength of an encryption method. For further details, see Bruce Schneier's Web site at www.counterpane.com.

Secret- and public-key ciphers use different key lengths, so the preceding table cannot be used for setting all of your security requirements. Table 4.3 compares the two systems for similar resistance to brute-force attacks.

TABLE 4.3 Secret-Key and Public-Key Lengths
for Equivalent Levels of Security

Secret-Key Length	Public-Key Length
56 bits	384 bits
64 bits	512 bits
80 bits	768 bits
112 bits	1,792 bits
128 bits	2,304 bits

When it comes to selecting software or hardware for your purposes, recall that more than one encryption system might be used in the product—that's a common practice because of the different computational requirements for secret-key and public-key algorithms. For example, basic implementations of IPSec use a keyed MD5 hash function for authentication of packets and DES for data encryption; other encryption techniques, such as RC4, can be negotiated between IPSec partners.

Public-Key Infrastructures

Although we've spent a lot of time describing how authentication and encryption can be used and what roles secret and public keys play, we've said very little about how these keys are generated and distributed. The security services that make this possible fall under the umbrella term Public Key Infrastructure (PKI). A PKI enables organizations to define the security domains in which they issue keys and the associated certificates, which are electronic objects used to issue and validate public keys. A PKI makes it possible not only to use keys and certificates, but also to manage keys, certificates, and security policies. Without such a system, use of public keys would be chaotic, inefficient, unmanageable, and most likely not secure.

We are not going to go into all the details of PKIs and the management of keys and certificates in this chapter but will leave the details for a later chapter in this book, Chapter 13, "Security Management." For the moment, we'll discuss the basic concepts of public-key certificates and key generation so that you can understand how VPN systems use keys.

PUBLIC-KEY CERTIFICATES

Public-key certificates (see Figure 4.9) are specially formatted data blocks that tell us the value of a public key, the name of the key's owner, and a digital signature of the issuing organization, called a *certificate authority* (CA). These certificates are used to identify the owner of a particular public key.

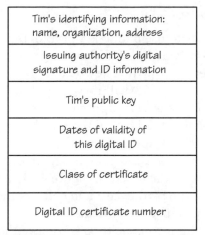

Tim's identifying information: name, organization, address
Issuing authority's digital signature and ID information
Tim's public key
Dates of validity of this digital ID
Class of certificate
Digital ID certificate number

FIGURE 4.9 Contents of a public-key certificate.

As long as you have a copy of the authority's public key, you can use it to check the certificates that it signed (see Figure 4.10). (We'll soon get to the procedures for dealing with validation of a certificate authority.) Any cryptographic software that you use must have a copy of the CA's public key in order to check a certificate's digital signature.

The primary standard for certificates is the X.509 standard designed by the *International Telegraph Union* (ITU). This standard not only specifies the format of the certificate but also the conditions under which certificates are created and used.

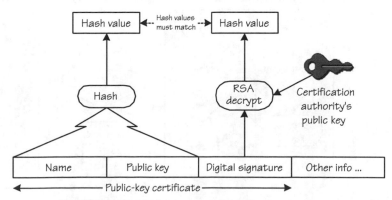

FIGURE 4.10 Validating a public-key certificate.

GENERATING PUBLIC KEYS

In order to use public-key cryptography, you need to generate a public key and a private key. After you've generated both keys, it's your responsibility to keep your private key secure and let no one else see it. Then you have to decide how to distribute your public key to your correspondents.

There are two approaches to generating public-key pairs: Some systems generate them on the host belonging to the key's holder, and others generate the keys as part of generating certificates.

First, you can generate them on the computer belonging to the key's holder, as illustrated in Figure 4.11. The user generates a public-key pair, retains the private key, and delivers the public key to the certificate authority to produce a certificate.

The second method is to have the certificate authority generate the public-key pair, produce the signed certificate, and then deliver both the key pair and the certificate to the user. Table 4.4 lists the trade-offs between these alternatives.

CERTIFICATE AND KEY DISTRIBUTION

Even though public keys are easier to distribute than secret keys, a trusted means of delivering public keys is necessary. Otherwise, it would still be possible to use a man-in-the-middle attack to trick a pair of public-key users into sharing a private communication. Aside from trusted manual distribution, the common method for delivering public keys is via digital certificates, or public-key certificates. (We'll call them certificates for short.)

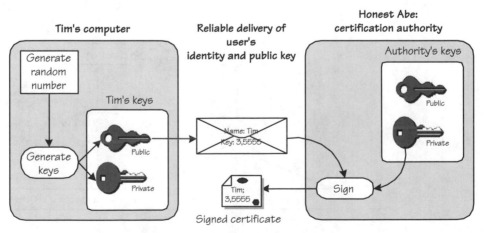

FIGURE 4.11 Generating a public key.

TABLE 4.4 Advantages and Disadvantages of Key Generation Schemes

Owner-Generated Keys	*Authority-Generated Keys*
– Users must deliver key to CA.	+ Fewer steps for users to perform.
+ Private key does not need to be copied.	+ Private key can be backed up.
+ Personal signature keys do not get backed up.	+ Key generation can be shared among users.

Certificates provide a safe method of distributing public keys via electronic media. After certificates are created, the next problem is to deliver the certificates to the hosts that need them. The techniques most often used in practice are transparent distribution and interactive distribution.

Transparent distribution involves either directory servers or key exchange protocols. The directory protocols for delivering public-key certificates evolved from the X.500 directory concept originally developed to support X.400 e-mail. Although large-scale master directories for certificates may be based on X.500, there's been a significant move to use another protocol, LDAP or Lightweight Directory Access Protocol, to utilize much of the structure of X.500, but over TCP/IP. Many certificate servers now offered for use at corporate sites are based on LDAP. We'll say more about key exchange protocols in Chapter 5, "Using IPSec to Build a VPN."

Interactive distribution usually consists of either e-mail requests, access to Web sites, or requests using the finger protocol. Many e-mail systems with support for cryptography provide a way to include a certificate with the messages they send; in some cases, a certificate server can be configured to accept e-mail requests for certificates.

CERTIFICATE AUTHORITIES

But from where does a CA get its authority? What makes it a trusted party in the scheme of things? Although there are two different types of certificate distribution systems—a hierarchical setup and a web of trust—we are going to concentrate on the hierarchical system because a web of trust isn't very scalable.

In a hierarchical system, a *root public key* exists at the top of the hierarchy, and it's used to sign for all top-level authorities, this root key might belong to a government agency, such as the DoD or the U.S. Postal Service, for example. CAs at the next lower level in the hierarchy have their certificates signed by the top-level CAs and sign for CAs below them in the hierarchy, and so on, down to the lowest level of the system.

The Lightweight Directory Access Protocol (LDAP)

Although the X.509 standard is designed for use with a globally distributed directory model, the X.500 directory standard was created for use with other ISO standards, and it's difficult to implement all of the client features on PCs using TCP/IP. The Lightweight Directory Access Protocol is a *lightweight* version of the X.500 client access *Directory Access Protocol* (DAP), which specifies how a client accesses a directory server.

LDAP can be mapped onto either proprietary services or X.500. LDAP has become a popular protocol for linking directories, and recent industry efforts have been adding many new features to LDAP, turning it into more of a directory protocol in its own right and making it less lightweight as time passes.

LDAP's extensible nature makes it appealing to use for key management, because an LDAP directory storing keys and certificates can be used both for authentication and for granting access rights based on the authentication.

To validate a user's certificate fully, you have to validate all the CAs in a hierarchy between your local CA and the issuing CA. That could include traveling up one branch of a CA hierarchy to the root and down another (see Figure 4.12).

In real life, CA hierarchies are not very deep—that is, they do not have many levels and sub-levels—so the time required to validate a key is short and does not seriously impact network usage. In fact, for a VPN, a corporation can serve as the CA without bothering to link to any national or international hierarchy. But, if you extend your VPN to include business partners, creating an extranet, you'll probably have to depend on some CA hierarchy for validating certificates. If the number of outside users of your VPN/extranet is small, they might agree to use your internal CA.

Using a CA hierarchy might not be a problem at the present time because the number of CAs is relatively small and hierarchies are shallow. But, as more and more uses for certificates are created and more certificates are issued, the number of CAs are bound to increase, and hierarchies will get more complicated.

Certificate authorities can offer ways to short-circuit the validation hierarchy by cross-certifying each other. If two CAs each agree to certify each other, a request for validating a certificate issued by one CA can

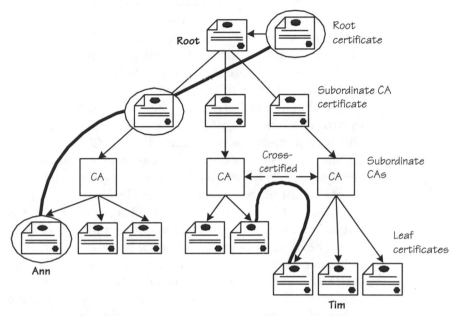

FIGURE 4.12 A hierarchy of certificate authorities.

be directly passed to the other CA without involving the rest of the CA hierarchy.

A better, trusted way of distributing public keys is to use a certificate authority. A certificate authority will accept your public key, along with some proof of your identity (it varies with the class of certificate), and serve as the repository of a digital certificate that others can request to verify your public key. The digital certificate acts like an electronic version of a driver's license. As an accepted method for distributing your public key, it provides you with a way for correspondents to verify that you are who you say you are.

Certificate authorities, such as VeriSign, CyberTrust, and Nortel, issue digital certificates. As shown in Figure 4.9, a certificate includes the holder's name, the name of the certificate authority, a public key for cryptographic use, and a time limit for the use of the certificate (most frequently, six months to a year long).

A digital certificate can be issued in one of four classes, indicating to what degree the holder has been verified. Class 1 is the easiest to obtain because it involves the fewest checks on the user's background; only the name and e-mail address are verified. For a Class 2 certificate, the issuing authority checks a driver's license, social security number, and date of birth. Users applying for a Class 3 certificate can expect the issuing authority to perform a credit check using a service such as Equifax in addition to the information required for a Class 2 certificate. A Class 4 certificate includes information about the individual's position within an organization, but the verification requirements for these certificates have not yet been finalized by certificate issuers.

Certificate authorities also have the responsibility of maintaining and making available a *Certificate Revocation List* (CRL), which lets users know which certificates are no longer valid. The CRL doesn't include expired certificates, because each certificate has an expiration date built-in. However, certificates may be revoked because they were lost, stolen, or because an employee left the company, for example.

In addition to commercial certificate authorities, such as VeriSign, CyberTrust, and Nortel, and government authorities, such as the U.S. Postal Service, corporations also can become a certificate authority by purchasing a certificate server from a vendor who has been certified by a certificate authority. Such arrangements are useful when a company needs to issue digital certificates to a number of employees for doing business, either within the company or with other companies. As more systems begin to use digital certificates to control computer access, corporate-maintained certificate servers will become more important. In the meantime, the U.S. government is trying to set up a Public Key Infrastructure for certificate authorities.

If a company creates its own internal CA, it has to be prepared to create key pairs, issue certificates, and manage these keys and certificates. Such a setup includes the following services:

Public-key certificates
A certificate repository
Certificate revocation
Key backup and recovery
Support for nonrepudiation of digital signatures
Automatic update of key pairs and certificates
Management of key histories
Support for cross-certification
Client-side software

Such an arrangement isn't overwhelming, although it is does require additional resources, and some organizations have chosen to outsource the PKI management. We'll cover more of the details of PKI management in Chapter 13.

Summary

Despite the variety of threats to networked data transmissions and access to networked devices, we've seen that the combination of authentication and encryption techniques can go a long way toward thwarting network attacks.

Using CHAP and/or RADIUS for authenticating remote access users is employed commonly for PPP links and therefore has significant bearing on some of the more important systems for dial-in VPNs, particularly PPTP and L2TP, which we'll cover in Chapters 6 and 7. Other authentication methods, particularly those using hardware tokens and/or biometrics, can be deployed with existing systems, such as RADIUS, to further improve the strength of authentication.

Encryption is fundamental to maintaining the privacy and integrity of data as it is transmitted on a network. Although secret-key encryption is easier to use and generally faster, the management of secret keys can be problematic as the number of corresponding parties grows. Public-key systems improve on the key management problem and offer additional advantages, particularly the capability to create digital signatures. However, when it becomes necessary to verify a public key or digital signature, outside organizations (certificate authorities) are required to provide validation information. Companies can serve as their own certificate authorities for VPNs because all users of the VPNs will be company employees. But, when creating an extranet, or communicating with outside correspondents that require verification, other certificate authorities likely will have to be involved.

5

Using IPSec to Build a VPN

Three major protocol suites have been proposed for building VPNs: IPSec, PPTP, and L2TP. This chapter, and the following two, concentrate on the details of these protocols and how they affect VPN design. With this coverage, you'll learn what the relative advantages and disadvantages of each technology are, which should help you pick the optimal solution for your corporation's VPN.

Each of the protocols covered in this book has some strengths and weaknesses when it comes to deploying it for VPNs. In cases like IPSec, it's more a question of being able to deploy all the features of IPSec and ensuring that all eventualities, such as key exchange, can be handled properly in the real world than it is a question of any deficiency in the protocol specifications. Plus, development continues on IPSec and related protocols as real-world examples point out what other features may need standardizing.

IPSec is the best starting point to discuss VPNs for three reasons:

1. Despite some specifications that leave implementation details up to the vendors and, therefore, leave the door open for possible

interoperability problems, it offers the most complete framework for VPNs.

2. The other protocols are leaning towards using parts of IPSec for their security services.

3. Because IPSec covers both LAN-to-LAN and client-to-LAN VPNs, other protocols can be described by comparing their features to IPSec.

This chapter starts out with an overview of IPSec's architecture and moves on to the details of how the protocol works. We've also included an extensive section on key management, since it's crucial to the operation of IPSec. Then, we move on to an overview of the types of products you can use to build a VPN using IPSec.

What Is IPSec?

As mentioned before, the original TCP/IP protocols did not include any inherent security features. In the early stages of the Internet, when many of the users were academic and research institutions, the need for securing data was much less than it is today with a wide variety of commercial uses taking place on the Internet. To address the issue of providing packet-level security in IP, the IETF has been working on the IPSec protocols within their IP Security Working Group. The first protocols comprising IPSec, for authenticating and encrypting IP datagrams, were published by the IETF as RFCs 1825 to 1829 in 1995.

These protocols set out the basics of the IPSec architecture, which includes two different headers designed for use in IP packets. The IP packet is the fundamental unit of communications in IP networks, including information on the source and destination as well as the type of data being carried in the packet (see Figure 5.1). IPSec defines two headers for IP packets to handle authentication and encryption: One, the IP Authentication Header (AH), is for authentication; the other, the Encapsulating Security Payload (ESP), is for encryption purposes.

Much of the development of IPSec took place during the development of the next generation of IP protocols, now called IPv6, and was intended for inclusion in IPv6. Because of the slow adoption of IPv6 and the current need for securing IP packets, IPSec has been modified to be compatible with the IPv4 protocols as well. Support for the IPSec headers is optional for IPv4 but mandatory for IPv6. Because IPSec is compatible with IPv4, current networking applications wanting to use IPSec can do so by using special TCP/IP stacks that have been written to include the IPSec proto-

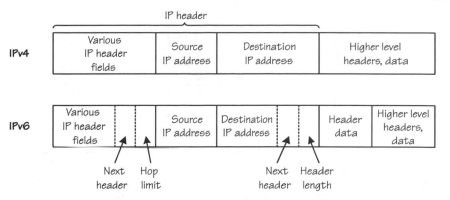

FIGURE 5.1 IPv4 and IPv6 packet headers.

cols. As more networks transition to IPv6 and as more IPv6 stacks become available and are deployed, the need for installing special IPSec-compatible stacks will be reduced.

IPSec is built around a number of standardized cryptographic technologies to provide confidentiality, data integrity, and authentication. For example, IPSec uses the following:

- Diffie-Hellman key exchanges to deliver secret keys between peers on a public net
- Public-key cryptography for signing Diffie-Hellman exchanges to guarantee the identities of the two parties and avoid man-in-the-middle attacks
- DES and other bulk-encryption algorithms for encrypting data
- Keyed hash algorithms (HMAC, MD5, and SHA) for authenticating packets
- Digital certificates for validating public keys

The use of all these technologies within IPSec have been carefully laid out in architectural documents like RFC 1825 and newer versions (currently the latest Internet draft is draft-ietf-ipsec-arch-sec-05.txt). Figure 5.2 displays a conceptualization of the IPSec architecture, showing the relationships between the different components of IPSec. The three main components are the AH protocol, the ESP protocol, and key management. The design of the AH and ESP protocols are modular in nature, allowing different cryptographic algorithms to be used as desired. If new algorithms are developed, such as the elliptic curve algo-

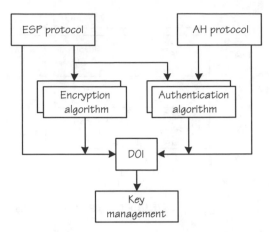

FIGURE 5.2 IPSec architecture.

rithms that are now becoming commercially available, the parameters for their use can be standardized and then used in conjunction with AH or ESP.

Because the security services offered by IPSec use shared secret values (cryptographic keys), IPSec relies on a separate set of mechanisms for putting these keys in place.

When two parties want to exchange secure communications, they need to be sure that they're reading the same page in the playbook. The two parties have to be using the same cryptographic algorithm, the same key length, and the same keys if they're going to successfully exchange secure data; this is handled via a *Security Association* (SA). Although IPSec specifies default algorithms for authentication and encryption, it also allows for other algorithms to be used. To help simplify and organize many of the parameters that need to be specified for a Security Association, IPSec uses a *Domain of Interpretation* (DOI) to standardize the expected parameters for a given protocol's SA.

The Domain of Interpretation groups related protocols that are required for negotiation of a security association. Thus, a DOI includes information on a security protocol, its related cryptographic algorithms (such as DES, for example), and the requirements for exchanging keys to make that algorithm work properly. The DOI further sets out the format of any data, such as the key format, that should be transferred in an SA. It's much like deciding which language you and your correspondent are going to use for communicating via e-mail, but in this case, a DOI is designed for security associations.

The Building Blocks of IPSec

Three main components are required for operating IPSec at its most basic level. These components are Security Associations, the Authentication Header, and the Encapsulating Security Payload.

Security Associations

Before we even get into the details of the protocols for authentication and encryption, we need to cover a very important concept in IPSec implementations, the Security Association. In order for two parties to exchange secured data (i.e., data that has been authenticated, encrypted, or both), both parties need to agree on which cryptographic algorithms they'll use, how to exchange keys, and then exchange the keys, if needed. They also may need to agree on how often they'll change the keys they're using.

All of these agreements have been bundled together in IPSec into a Security Association. Each secure communication between a sender and a receiver requires at least one SA and can require more than one because each IPSec protocol requires its own SA. Thus, authenticating a packet requires one SA, and encrypting that same packet requires another SA. Even if the same algorithms were used for authentication and encryption, two different SAs would be needed because two different sets of keys would be required.

A Security Association groups together all the things you need to know about how you communicate securely with someone else. An IPSec SA specifies the following:

- The mode of the authentication algorithm used in the AH and the keys to that authentication algorithm
- The ESP encryption algorithm mode and the keys to that encryption algorithm
- The presence and size of any cryptographic synchronization to be used in that encryption algorithm
- What protocol, algorithm, and key you use to authenticate your communications
- What protocol, encrypting algorithm, and key you use to make your communications private
- How often those keys are to be changed
- The authentication algorithm, mode, and transform for use in ESP plus the keys to be used by that algorithm

- The key lifetimes
- The lifetime of the SA itself
- The SA source address

You can think of the SA as your secure channel through the public network to a certain person, group of people, or network resource. It's like a contract with whomever is at the other end.

SAs are good for building multiple secure VPNs. Imagine that your company has its own VPN, and you develop a business relationship with another company that also has a secure VPN. You want to give them some access to your network by linking the two VPNs, but you don't want them to have full access to your network's resources. To accomplish this, you'd set up specific SAs between your VPN and theirs, controlling who has what access to which resources. And, you have a different set of specific SAs within your VPN for your employees, perhaps even broken down further by department.

SAs are good for only one-way communications—that is, they're defined for transferring data between a sender and a receiver but not for any exchanges in the opposite direction (i.e., from the sender back to the receiver). If two-way communications is necessary, two SAs must be agreed upon: one for data traveling from Ann to Tim, the other for data traveling from Tim to Ann.

The Authentication Header

In the IPSec system, a special header, the Authentication Header (AH), was designed to provide most of the authentication services for IP data. The AH contains a cryptographic checksum for the packet's contents. The Authentication Header is inserted into the packet between the IP header and any subsequent packets' contents (see Figure 5.3); no changes are made to the packet's data (the payload).

The Authentication Header contains five fields: the Next Header field found in all IP headers, a payload length, the Security Parameter Index, a sequence number, and authentication data. Two items are of particular note in the Authentication Header: first, the *Security Parameter Index* (SPI), which specifies to the device receiving the packet what group of security protocols the sender is using for communications; second, the authentication data itself, which is obtained by applying the cryptographic algorithm defined by the SPI to the packet's payload.

The new default methods for calculating the checksum are a relatively new cryptographic algorithm known as HMAC (for hash-based mes-

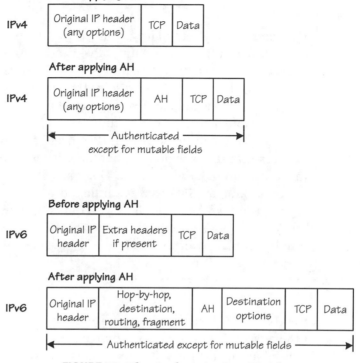

FIGURE 5.3 The Authentication Header.

sage authentication code) coupled with the MD5 hash function and HMAC coupled with the SHA-1 hash function. Both of these defaults are the result of recent changes to IPSec to improve the authentication mechanism, because the previous default, keyed MD5, was found to be susceptible to certain types of attacks called *collision attacks*, where a matching hash value is computed for two different messages.

The procedure for using either method (i.e., HMAC-MD5 or HMAC-SHA-1) is identical; SHA-1, however, is considered to be a stronger hash function than MD5. In both cases, the algorithm operates on 64-byte blocks of data. The HMAC-MD5 method produces a 128-bit authenticator value (or cryptographic checksum), while HMAC-SHA-1 produces a 160-bit authenticator. Because the default authenticator length specified in AH is only 96 bits, either of the authenticator values produced must be truncated before storing the value in the authenticator field of the AH.

Upon receiving the packet, the recipient then would calculate his own 128-bit or 160-bit authenticator value (depending on whether HMAC-MD5

AH in IPv4 versus IPv6

IPv6 is the next IP standard coming down the road. The IPv6 header is quite different from the existing IPv4 header. Among the more important changes, IPv6 headers carry 64-bit addresses instead of 32-bit addresses; IPv6 is expected to solve the problem of coming up with new IP addresses in an expanding Internet. It also is expected to enable a more flexible network architecture.

One of the difficulties with IPv6 headers and the host of optional headers that IPv6 specifies is that there is more in them that can change in transit through the network. This makes wrapping the AH's authentication around an IPv6 packet a little more complicated. However, the IPSec group has been developing AH in concert with IPv6 standards and has developed protocols for flexible ranges of authentication and intelligent placing of the AH in the IP packet so that it can work under either IPv4 or IPv6.

---

or HMAC-SHA-1 was used), truncate it according to the specified length of the authenticator field, and compare his authenticator value to the received authenticator value. As long as the two are identical, the data has not been altered in transmission.

Because it's possible for an attacker to intercept a series of packets and then retransmit, or replay, them at a later time, AH also offers an antireplay service that can be invoked at the discretion of the receiver to help counter denial-of-service attacks that would be based on these retransmissions.

Note that the Authentication Header does nothing to keep the data confidential. If an attacker were to intercept the packets on the network, say with a sniffer, he still could read the contents of the packet, although he could not alter the packet's contents and resend the packets without changing the hash value. In order to protect the data against eavesdropping, we need to turn to the second component of IPSec, the Encapsulating Security Payload.

ESP: The Encapsulating Security Payload

The second protocol in the IPSec scheme of things, the *Encapsulating Security Payload* (ESP), is responsible for encrypting a packet. Like the Authentication Header, the ESP header is inserted into the packet between the IP header and any subsequent packet contents (see Figure 5.4). However, because ESP is responsible for encrypting the data, the payload will be altered.

Like AH, the ESP header contains an SPI to indicate to the receiver what security association is appropriate for processing the packet. The sequence number found in the ESP header is a counter that increases each time a packet is sent to the same address using the same SPI. The sequence number indicates which packet is which and how many packets have been sent with the same group of parameters. The sequence number provides protection against replay attacks in which an attacker copies a packet and sends it out of sequence to confuse communicating nodes.

The remaining parts of the packet, except for the authentication data, are encrypted prior to transmission across the network. When unen-

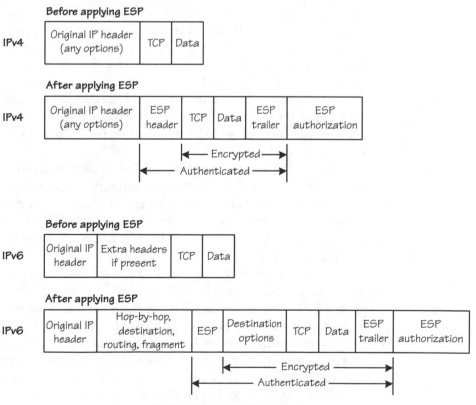

FIGURE 5.4 The ESP header.

crypted by the receiver, the new packet includes the payload data, up to 255 bytes of padding (to allow for the fact that certain types of encryption algorithms require the data to be a multiple of a certain number of bytes), and the pad length field, which specifies how much of the payload is padding as opposed to data.

ESP can support any number of encryption protocols; it's up to the user to decide which one to use. You can even use different protocols for each party with whom you're communicating. But, IPSec specifies a basic DES-CBC (DES with *Cipher Block Chaining*) cipher as its default, to guarantee a minimal interoperability among IPSec networks.

Using DES-CBC requires a 56-bit DES secret key, which is included as part of the security association. In order to use cipher block chaining, a 64-bit initialization vector is required, and the data is processed in 64-bit blocks; the packet's data is padded to create an integral number of 64-bit blocks if necessary.

ESP also can be used for authentication. The ESP authentication field, an optional field in the ESP header, contains a cryptographic checksum that's computed over the remaining part of the ESP (minus the authentication field itself). This checksum varies in length depending on the authentication algorithm used. It may also be omitted entirely, if authentication services are not selected for the ESP. The authentication is calculated on the ESP packet when encryption is complete.

The current IPSec standard specifies HMAC with hash functions SHA-1 and MD5 as mandatory algorithms for IPSec-compliant equipment and software to support as authentication procedures in the ESP packet's authentication field.

The authentication provided by the AH differs from that provided in the ESP in that the ESP's authentication services do not protect the IP header that precedes the ESP, although they do protect an encapsulated IP header in tunneling mode (see the next section). The AH services protect this external IP header, along with the entire contents of the ESP packet (see Figure 5.5).

If AH was already designed for authenticating packets, why include an authentication option in ESP? AH is meant for occasions when only packet authentication is needed. On the other hand, when authentication and privacy are required, it's best to use ESP, including ESP's authentication option. Using ESP for encryption and authentication, rather than ESP and AH together, reduces the amount of copying done during packet processing and requires only one "transform" operation, rather than one each for ESP and AH, so packet processing is more efficient.

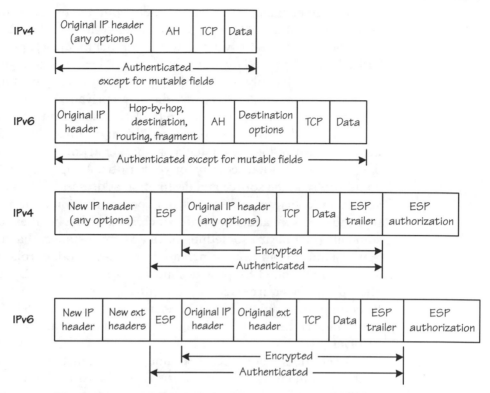

FIGURE 5.5 Authentication by AH versus authentication by ESP.

A Question of Mode

The IPSec specifications allow AH and ESP to be applied to an IP packet in two different ways, called modes. In *transport mode,* only the Transport-layer segment of an IP datagram is processed (i.e., authenticated or encrypted). The other approach, authenticating or encrypting the entire IP packet, is called *tunnel mode.*

Transport mode is applicable to either gateway or host implementations and provides protection for upper layer protocols, in addition to selected IP header fields.

In transport mode, AH is inserted after the IP header and before an upper layer protocol (e.g., TCP, UDP, or ICMP), or before any other IPSec headers that already have been inserted (see Figure 5.3), as described in the earlier section on AH. The IP address of the source and destination are still open to modification if the packets are intercepted.

In tunnel mode, the inner IP header contains the ultimate source and destination address, while the outer header contains other IP addresses (e.g., those of the security gateways). In tunnel mode, AH protects the entire inner IP packet, including the inner IP header (see Figure 5.6).

Because AH only protects the packet's contents against modification, other means are needed to ensure the data's privacy. In tunnel mode, the idea is to extend such protection to the IP header's contents, particularly the source and destination addresses. Although transport mode ESP is sufficient for protecting the contents of a packet against eavesdropping, it does not provide total security for your traffic. A sophisticated attacker could still read the source and destination addresses of the packet and apply traffic analysis to learn of your communication patterns. If new correspondents were added, or traffic increased with a business partner, someone might learn something of value—for instance, that a merger was being planned or inventory increased for a new product rollout.

Tunnel-mode ESP provides more security for each IP packet by encrypting the entire packet (see Figure 5.7). After the packet's contents (including the original header) are encrypted, tunnel-mode ESP generates a new IP header for routing the secured datagram from sender to receiver.

Even tunnel-mode ESP does not guard against all types of traffic analysis on the Internet, because the IP addresses of the sending and receiving gateways can still be determined by examining the packet headers. This could enable an eavesdropper to learn that two different businesses are talking to each other or that traffic between them has increased,

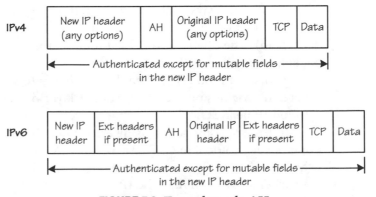

FIGURE 5.6 Tunnel-mode AH.

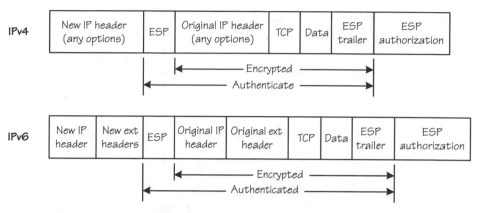

FIGURE 5.7 Tunnel-mode ESP.

but it doesn't give the attacker any clue as to the persons within the two companies who are talking to each other.

In addition to applying either AH or ESP to an IP packet in transport or tunnel modes, IPSec requires support for certain combinations of tunnel and transport modes (see Figure 5.8). Basically, the idea is to use tunnel mode to authenticate or encrypt a packet and its header (IP1 or *inner header*), then apply AH, ESP, or both in transport mode to further protect the newly generated header (IP2 or the *outer header*).

Note that tunnel-mode applications have one less permutation than transport-mode applications: AH and ESP aren't used together in tunnel mode. The main reason for this is that ESP has its own authentication option. It's recommended that this option be used if a tunnel-mode packet needs both encryption and authentication of the inner packet.

Key Management

With all the secret keys that have to be exchanged for different IPSec parties to communicate securely, it should be obvious that key management is an essential part of IPSec. Part of the procedure is handled by Security Associations and the SPI values that refer to them in each IPSec packet.

There are currently two ways to handle key exchange and management within IPSec's architecture: manual keying and *Internet Key Exchange* (IKE). Both of these methods are mandatory requirements of IPSec.

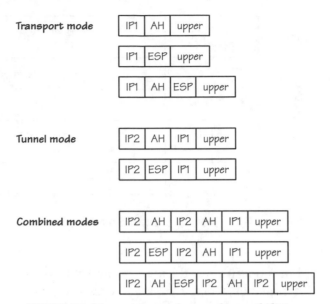

FIGURE 5.8 Transport and tunnel possibilities.

Key Exchanges Using SKIP

Another key distribution scheme, Simple Key Management for IP (SKIP), has been used by some companies for exchanging encryption keys. Instead of using session oriented keys, SKIP uses packet-oriented keys that are communicated in-line with the packets. Sun Microsystems, Novell and a few other companies currently offer security products that use SKIP for key distribution, but the IPSec Working Group has not pursued incorporating SKIP within its key management standards.

IPSec-compliant systems must support manual keying. In fact, for some time, this was the only way for vendors and other sites to exchange keys for interoperability testing. Face-to-face key exchanges, such as trading keys on paper or a floppy disk, can be used, or keys can be sent via a bonded courier or e-mail.

In 1996, RSA Data Security Inc., encouraged a group of product vendors to join together to test the interoperability of their IPSec products. This group, the S/WAN Initiative (S/WAN = Secure WAN), has run a number of interoperability trials since its formation. Prior to late 1997, almost all of the tests were run using the manual exchange of keys. To facilitate these exchanges, S/WAN published a recommended file format for the exchanges (see Figure 5.9).

Although manual keying is suitable for a small number of sites, scaleable, automated management is required to accommodate on-demand creation of SAs (e.g., for user- and session-oriented keying and to ease the use of the antireplay features of AH and ESP). The default auto-mated key management protocol for use with IPSec is IKE, which is the result of combining the *Internet Security Association and Key Management Protocol* (ISAKMP), which serves as a framework for authentication and key exchange, with the Oakley protocol, which describes various modes of key exchange. IKE is a relatively new name for ISAKMP/Oakley; you'll find many IPSec documents still refer to the key-exchange protocols as ISAKMP/Oakley. In this chapter, we'll use ISAKMP or Oakley as modifiers for concepts to emphasize the origin of a feature in IKE.

IKE is designed to provide four capabilities:

1. Provide the means for parties to agree on which protocols, algo-rithms, and keys to use.
2. Ensure from the beginning of the exchange that you're talking to the right person.
3. Manage those keys after they've been agreed upon.
4. Ensure that key exchanges are handled safely.

As you might expect, key exchange is closely related to the manage-ment of security associations. When you need to create an SA, you need to exchange keys. So IKE's structure wraps them together and delivers them as an integrated package.

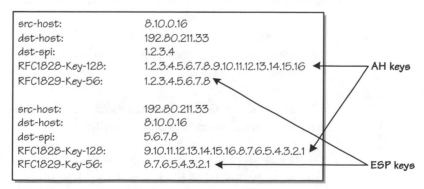

FIGURE 5.9 Recommended file format for manual key exchange.

ISAKMP's Phases and Oakley's Modes

IKE operates in two phases, as originally defined in ISAKMP. In phase one, two ISAKMP peers establish a secure channel for performing ISAKMP operations (called the ISAKMP SA). In phase two, those two peers negotiate general purpose SAs.

> NOTE   An ISAKMP peer is an IPSec-compliant node capable of establishing ISAKMP channels and negotiating SAs. It might be the computer on your desktop or a security gateway that negotiates security services for you.

Oakley provides three modes of exchanging keying information and setting up ISAKMP SAs: two for ISAKMP phase one exchanges and one for phase two exchanges.

1. *Main mode.* Accomplishes a phase one ISAKMP exchange by establishing a secure channel.
2. *Aggressive mode.* Is another way of accomplishing a phase one exchange. It's a little simpler and a little faster than main mode and does not provide identity protection for the negotiating nodes, because they must transmit their identities before having negotiated a secure channel.
3. *Quick mode.* Accomplishes a phase two exchange by negotiating an SA for general-purpose communications.

IKE also has one other mode, called new group mode, which doesn't really fit into phase one or phase two. The new group mode can only follow a phase one negotiation and is included to provide a mechanism for defining private groups for Diffie-Hellman exchanges.

> NOTE   When preparing for a Diffie-Hellman exchange, certain material is needed to generate the keys; this information is called a group and includes two numbers, a large known prime number and a seed.

To establish an IKE security association, the initiating node, a host or security gateway, proposes at least four items:

1. An encryption algorithm to protect data.
2. A hash algorithm to reduce data for signing.

3. An authentication method for signing the data.
4. Information about a group over which to do a Diffie-Hellman exchange.

A fifth item, a pseudo-random function used to hash certain values during the key exchange for verification purposes, also can be proposed in the Security Association. If it's not included, then the HMAC version of the hash algorithm specified in item 2 is used.

MAIN MODE

Main mode provides a mechanism for establishing the first phase ISAKMP SA, which is used to negotiate future communications. The steps are as follows:

1. Use main mode to bootstrap an ISAKMP SA for temporary communication.
2. Use quick mode within that ISAKMP SA to negotiate a general SA.
3. Use SA of step 2 to communicate from now until it expires.

The first step, securing an ISAKMP SA using Main mode, occurs in three two-way exchanges between the SA initiator and the recipient (see Figure 5.10). In the first exchange (steps 1 and 2 in the illustration), the two agree on basic algorithms and hashes. In the second exchange (steps 3 and 4), they exchange public keys for a Diffie-Hellman exchange and pass each other nonces—that is, random numbers that the other party must sign and return to prove their identity. In the third exchange (steps 5 and 6), they verify those identities and the exchange is completed.

In all of these steps, an ISAKMP header preceding the rest of the packet identifies the step being taken. Each of the items is carried in its own payload, but you can pack any number of these payloads into a single ISAKMP packet.

The parties actually use the shared key in three permutations, once they derive it. Both parties have to hash it three times: generating first a derivation key (to be used later for generating additional keys in Quick mode), then an authentication key, and, finally, the encryption key to be used for the ISAKMP SA.

A Main mode exchange protects the identities of the communicating parties. If it's not necessary to protect the identities, a faster exchange, the Aggressive mode, can be used.

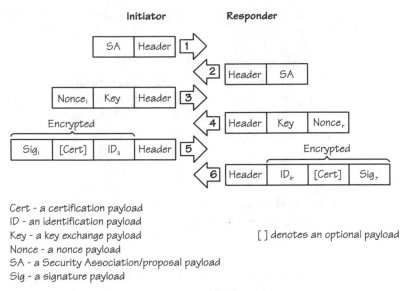

Cert - a certification payload
ID - an identification payload
Key - a key exchange payload
Nonce - a nonce payload
SA - a Security Association/proposal payload
Sig - a signature payload

[ ] denotes an optional payload

FIGURE 5.10 ISAKMP Main mode.

AGGRESSIVE MODE

Aggressive mode provides the same services as Main mode, that is, it establishes the original ISAKMP SA. Aggressive mode looks much the same as Main mode except that it is accomplished in two exchanges, rather than three, with only one round trip, for a total of three packets rather than six.

In Aggressive mode, the proposing party generates a Diffie-Hellman pair at the beginning of the exchange and does as much as is practical with that first packet—proposing an SA, passing the Diffie-Hellman public value, sending a nonce for the other party to sign, and sending an ID packet that the responder can use to check their identity with a third party. The responder than sends back everything needed to complete the exchange; this response combines all three response steps in Main mode, so that the only thing the initiator has to do is confirm the exchange (see Figure 5.11).

Since the Aggressive mode does not provide identity protection for the communicating parties, it's necessary that the parties exchange identification information prior to establishing a secure SA in which to encrypt it. So someone monitoring an aggressive exchange can actually identify who has just formed a new SA. The advantage of Aggressive mode, however, is speed.

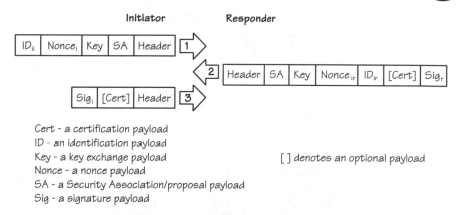

Cert - a certification payload
ID - an identification payload
Key - a key exchange payload   [ ] denotes an optional payload
Nonce - a nonce payload
SA - a Security Association/proposal payload
Sig - a signature payload

FIGURE 5.11 ISAKMP Aggressive mode.

QUICK MODE

After two communicating parties have established an ISAKMP SA using Aggressive mode or Main mode, they can use Quick mode.

Quick mode has two purposes: negotiating general IPSec security services and generating fresh keying material.

Quick mode is considerably simpler than either Main or Aggressive mode. Because it's already inside a secure tunnel (every packet is encrypted), it also can afford to be a little more flexible.

Quick mode packets are always encrypted and always start with a hash payload. The hash payload is composed using the agreed-upon pseudo-random function and the derived authentication key for the ISAKMP SA. The hash payload is used to authenticate the rest of the packet. Quick mode defines which parts of the packet are included in the hash.

Key refreshing can be done in one of two ways. If you don't want or need perfect forward secrecy (see Chapter 4, "Security: Threats and Solutions"), Quick mode can just refresh the keying material already generated in Main or Aggressive mode with additional hashing. The two communicating parties can exchange nonces through the secure channel and use these to hash the existing keys.

If you do want perfect forward secrecy, you can still request an additional Diffie-Hellman exchange through the existing SA and change the keys that way.

Basic Quick mode is a three-packet exchange, like Aggressive mode (see Figure 5.12).

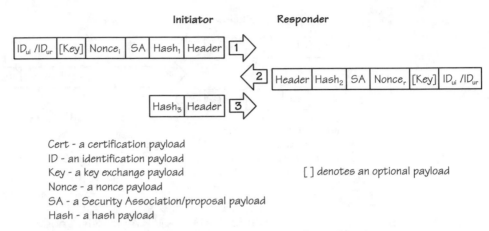

Cert - a certification payload
ID - an identification payload
Key - a key exchange payload
Nonce - a nonce payload
SA - a Security Association/proposal payload
Hash - a hash payload

[ ] denotes an optional payload

FIGURE 5.12 ISAKMP Quick mode.

If the parties do not require perfect forward secrecy, the initiator sends a packet with the Quick mode hash and a nonce. The respondent then replies with a similar packet but generating its own nonce and including the initiator's nonce in the Quick mode hash for confirmation. The initiator then sends back a confirming Quick mode hash of both nonces, completing the exchange. Finally, both parties perform a hash of a concatenation of the nonces, the SPI, and the protocol values from the ISAKMP header that initiated the exchange, using the derivation key as the key for the hash. The resulting hash becomes the new password for that SA.

If the parties do require perfect forward secrecy, the initiator first generates a public/private key pair and sends the public key along with the initiation packet (along with the hash and nonce). The recipient then responds with his or her own public key and nonce, and both parties then generate the shared key using a Diffie-Hellman exchange, again fully protected by the Quick mode hashes and by full encryption within the ISAKMP SA.

Negotiating the SA

Establishing a general purpose SA is relatively simple. To generate a new SA, the initiator sends a Quick mode message through the ISAKMP SA requesting the new SA. A single SA negotiation actually results in two SAs: one inbound, to the initiator, and one outbound. Each IPSec SA is one way; to avoid conflicting SPIs, the receiving node always chooses the SPI.

So, using Quick mode, the initiator tells the respondent which SPI to use in future communications with it, and the respondent follows up with its own selected SPI.

Each SPI, in concert with the destination IP address, uniquely identifies a single IPSec SA. However, in practice, these SAs are always formed in pairs—inbound and outbound—and these pairs have identical parameters, keys, authentication and encryption algorithms, and hashes, apart from the SPI itself.

Using IPSec

Returning to our original schematic of an Internet VPN that was introduced in Chapter 3 (reproduced in Figure 5.13), it should be obvious that there are three major locations for installing IPSec-compatible software: on security gateways, mobile clients, and hosts on your corporate subnets.

Not all of the devices pictured need to have IPSec software in order to create an effective VPN—it depends on your needs. For instance, if you're looking to create only a LAN-to-LAN VPN, IPSec security gateways will suffice. On the other hand, if you have mobile workers and small branch offices that will need to dial into the corporate net via an ISP, then IPSec client software has to be installed on the appropriate computers—laptops for the mobile workers, perhaps the branch office's desktop computers. Lastly, if you want to create a VPN in which every computer can communicate with every other computer via IPSec protocols, then you'll have to deploy IPSec software on every host.

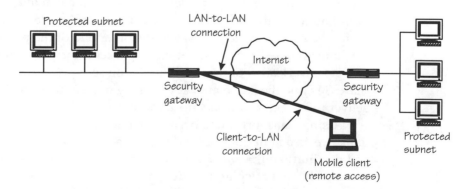

FIGURE 5.13 Components of an Internet VPN.

Security Gateways

We've already mentioned security gateways in describing VPNs. The security gateway is a network computing device, such as a router or firewall, that separates the internal, protected network from the external, unprotected network and performs cryptographic transforms on behalf of authorized users within the internal network.

Using IPSec on a security gateway means that the traffic of several hosts is funneled through a single encrypting host (i.e., the gateway) before it traverses the unprotected network. When constructing a VPN, you'd install a security gateway at each of your major offices and then establish security associations between each and every gateway.

Security gateways typically will establish and maintain individual security associations with each other. In other words, the gateways will use the same SA and related crypto keys regardless of whether Ann is communicating with Bill or Tim. If the three correspondents all had IPSec installed on their own computers, Ann would have to establish an SA to talk with each correspondent. Using security gateways reduces the complexity of key management, because only keys have to be assigned to the gateways. One fundamental requirement is that a network served by a security gateway should be internally secure (i.e., no "backdoor" unsecured entry points into the network exist, and it's understood that each individual is responsible for securing the data on his own computer).

Security gateways can transfer IPSec packets using either transport mode or tunnel mode. Selecting tunnel mode or transport mode for connections between your security gateways depends on your needs. For ultimate security, tunnel mode is preferred because it hides the IP addresses of the actual sender and receiver and guards against header cut-and-paste attacks. But, tunnel mode requires additional computation at the gateway and adds to the size of the packets, both of which can affect network throughput. Furthermore, packets at one end of an IPSec tunnel must always be routed to the gateway at the other end of the tunnel. There is no mechanism to redirect a tunnel-mode packet if the gateway at the destination gets overloaded or crashes. But, if you set up security gateways to share SAs and the associated keys among one another, the IP routing can deliver the packets to a backup gateway.

Using transport mode between gateways reduces the communications overhead but does not hide the IP addresses of the ultimate source and destination. If a *wild card* security association isn't used for all traffic destined for a particular security gateway, then key management becomes more complicated. Without wild card SAs, Ann has to maintain an SA for each correspondent on the network served by the other gateway.

Wild Card SAs

Wild card security associations are used to simplify communications between hosts that are protected by security gateways. Rather than associate an SA with a specific host's IP address, the wild card SA is associated with all hosts on the LAN served by the security gateway.

When reviewing the features and capabilities of security gateways, such as encrypting routers, here are a few things you should look for:

- Support separate network connections for plaintext and ciphertext.
- Available key sizes must be consistent with the sensitivity of the information you'll transmit across the data link.
- If you decide that the default crypto algorithms will not meet your needs, the device should support the accepted alternative algorithms.
- Both AH and ESP should be supported.
- Manual input of SAs, including wild card SAs, should be supported.
- Mechanisms for protecting secret and private keys should be included.
- A system for changing crypto keys automatically and periodically makes key management easier and more secure.
- A security gateway should include some support for logging failures when processing a header; even better, some kind of alarm for persistent failures should be included.

Remote Hosts

When you're on the road or in a small branch office that uses dial-in connections to the corporate VPN, it's unlikely that you'd have a firewall or router installed on your computer to serve as a security gateway. Security gateways are meant to protect LANs, not individual computers. This

Header Cut-and-Paste Attacks

If packets are encrypted, but not authenticated, an attacker can make copies of all packets transmitted between two parties and use those packets to forge a message or eavesdrop on an encrypted one. The attacker can copy the encrypted message from the original packets and send it to another correspondent with a new packet header. This correspondent (or co-conspirator, if you will) can decrypt the message as long as it's routed through the same security gateway.

means that IPSec-compliant client software has to be installed on your computer if you're going to connect to an IPSec-protected VPN. In most cases, this means that the TCP/IP stack running on your computer has to be modified to be IPSec-compliant, especially if you're running IPv4. (Recall that IPSec is an add-on feature for IPv4, although it's an integral part of IPv6.)

In IPv4 implementations, IPSec support can be inserted in one of two locations in the TCP/IP stack. In one case, the IPSec code can be inserted between the network and transport layers. In the second case, the necessary code can be inserted as a *shim* between the Data Link layer and the Network layer. The first case offers users more flexibility because it enables them to assign different security associations for different software; in other words, some traffic could be transmitted without IPSec because it's not needed, while other, more important traffic could be set to be transmitted with IPSec security. The shim approach can be easier to implement, but it can enforce security associations only at the IP address level and cannot enforce user identities.

One concern with handling remote client access is how to distribute the needed security associations. A practical approach is to have a central site generate all SA parameters and then send them to the clients, perhaps using the S/WAN format.

Another potential problem is handling the IP addresses for the remote clients. Because many mobile clients are likely to dial into the VPN via their local ISP, they'll often be assigned a variable IP address that's only good for that connection. Thus, the client's SA with the central site has to be able to work with a variety of IP addresses, some of which might not be known ahead of time. One solution is for the client not to make assumptions about its local address and to use a wild-card specification of central site addresses.

Just as we listed requirements for security gateways, here are some features to check when evaluating client software:

- Compatibility with other IPSec implementations; for example, match the site's encrypting server (transport and tunnel modes, key exchange protocol, crypto algorithms, etc.).
- Offers a clear indication of when IPSec is working.
- Supports downloading SAs (via paper or disks, for instance).
- Has to handle dynamically assigned IP addresses.
- Includes mechanisms to protect the keying material from theft (encrypt keys with passwords, for instance).
- Offers a mechanism to change the crypto key automatically and peri-

odically; includes dynamic assignment of new SPI numbers during rekeying; compatible with standard IPSec keying protocols; uses a cryptographically strong random-key procedure to generate its keys.

- Explicitly blocks non-IPSec traffic.

A large number of vendors already support IPSec (see Table 5.1 for a partial list). If you're already working with an installed base of network equipment that can be upgraded to support IPSec, but not all the equipment is from one vendor, be sure to check on the product's IPSec interoperability. The IPSec Working Group has published a series of suggested tests for IPSec interoperability (see web.mit.edu/tytso/www/ipsec/companies.html for details on vendor implementations and interoperability results). The *Automotive Network Exchange* (ANX) also has been pushing the implementation of IPSec and has been running its own interoperability tests (see www.aiag.org/anx/). Many products are interoperable at the level of AH and ESP headers but may not support all key management features, for example.

TABLE 5.1 Partial List of IPSec Products

Vendor	*Product*
3COM	Secure VPN/NetBuilder
Ascend Communications, Inc.	Secure Access
Bay Networks (New Oak)	NOC 4000 Extranet Access Switch
Bellcore	ERP IPSec
Cabletron/Network Express	NE-Secure
Check Point Software Technologies	Firewall-1
Cisco Systems	Cisco IOS
ftp Software	OnNet
Frontier Technologies Corp.	e-Lock VPN
Gemini Computers Inc.	Trusted Security Firewall-Guard
IBM	IBM SNG
Information Resources Engineering, Inc.	SafeNet
Lucent (Livingston Enterprises)	Livingston ComOS
Mentat Inc.	Mentat TCP
Network Associates, Inc.	Gauntlet
Network Systems	BorderGuard and Security Router
Raptor Systems	Eagle VPN
Secure Computing Corp.	BorderWare Firewall Server
TimeStep Corp.	PERMIT/Gate
TimeStep Corp.	PERMIT/Client
Toshiba Corp.	Network CryptoGate
V-One	V-ONE SmartWall
VPNet Technologies Inc.	VSU-1000 VPN Service Unit

In mid 1998, the International Computer Security Association (ICSA) also started certifying products for compliance with the IPSec protocol specifications. Check their Web site at www.icsa.net for more details.

Other details of IPSec software and hardware are presented in Chapters 10 through 12.

Tying It All Together

Admittedly, full-fledged implementations of IPSec involve a lot of different interactions: matching the security associations and keys to corporate security policies; negotiating security associations and exchanging keys between gateways and/or hosts; and the very important end-results of authenticating and encrypting the packets. Although IPSec itself doesn't define how security policies are to be formulated and distributed, many current industry efforts aim at using X.500 or LDAP-compatible directories to store security policies for users and/or devices. Figure 5.14 schematically represents how security policies fit into the rest of the IPSec operation for a session between two hosts.

Sample Deployment

To illustrate the use of IPSec in a corporate VPN, let's create a relatively simple VPN (see Figure 5.15) that's composed of two sites: the corporate headquarters and a regional office. Mobile workers also are given the capability to dial into the VPN via local ISPs. We'll use encrypting routers as the security gateways.

Traffic inside the corporate networks is transmitted as plaintext and would be protected from outside attackers with techniques other than IPSec, such as firewalls, access control lists on servers, and so on). Only traffic between sites, or between mobile workers and a main site, is protected with IPSec. This VPN design is likely to be one of the more common designs.

To secure this system, physical security should include ensuring that all hosts reside within the site's physical parameters and that all links to outside systems go through the encrypting routers. The connection between the site's internal networks and the external network(s) should be in a locked machine room with restricted access, and only authorized individuals (network managers, for instance) should have access to the encrypting routers.

Key assignment and management for the main sites should be fairly straightforward because only two static sites are involved, the main headquarters and the regional office. Both sites require a security association with each other's encrypting router, but that's all that is needed for users at either site to communicate with the other site.

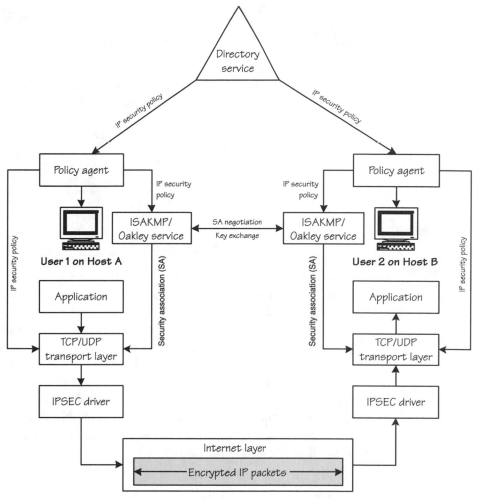

FIGURE 5.14 IPSec and security policies.

If the number of static sites grows, then it's probably best to use a central location for assigning SAs and keys. A hub-and-spoke topology may be needed in larger organizations as the relationships between different sites get more complicated. For example, each regional office might receive its SAs from the corporate headquarters, but a regional office could be responsible for issuing keys and SAs for the manufacturing plants or branch offices in its area. Some plants might also communicate with each other frequently, but not with other offices, so they could choose to set up an SA between themselves without the knowledge of the regional office.

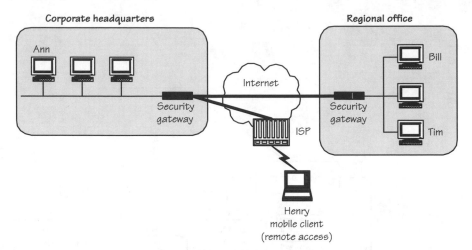

FIGURE 5.15 An example IPSec VPN.

In our example, key management for the mobile workers might demand the most attention. In this case, deciding between a centralized key-management system versus a distributed one depends on the number, and needs, of the mobile workers. If all the mobile workers only need to connect to either the corporate headquarters or the regional office, then that site should be responsible for issuing keys and SAs. In most companies, it's highly unlikely that many workers would need dial-in access to more than one site; in such cases, the keys probably should be assigned by what they call their "home office" and the appropriate keys and SAs disseminated to the other sites as needed.

Remaining Problems with IPSec

Although IPSec already incorporates many of the necessary features for deploying secure VPNs over the Internet, it's still a work in progress. Here's a brief rundown of some of the issues that may affect your deployment of IPSec. None of these are likely to be show-stoppers—keep in mind that various working groups in the IETF are working to solve many of these problems.

All IP packets processed with IPSec increase in size due to the addition of IPSec headers, which may lead to increased packet fragmentation and reduced throughput. It's been proposed that this problem can be addressed by compressing the packet's contents before encryption, but this has not been standardized yet. VPNet already offers compression in its IPSec hardware. Also, the overhead associated with key-management protocols like IKE will reduce the available bandwidth on a link.

IKE is still a relatively unproven technology. For example, much of the original interoperability work performed under the aegis of S/WAN in 1996 and 1997 used manual keying. This may not prove to be a problem if you're focusing on a limited number of security gateways, but manual keying is not a suitable procedure for handling host-based IPSec or large numbers of mobile workers.

Remember that IPSec is designed to handle IP traffic only; it cannot transform IPX, AppleTalk, or NETBEUI traffic. If you're running a multiprotocol network, you may have to deploy one of the other protocols that we'll be describing in subsequent chapters. Alternatively, you could plan to migrate your network just to TCP/IP protocols. Products like Novell's Netware have IP gateways and are being migrated to native support of IP as well.

The computational overhead associated with many of the cryptographic algorithms used in IPSec can still pose problems for older workstations and PCs, so deployment of IPSec at the desktop level can affect performance considerably (see Figure 5.16).

Distribution of cryptographic software and hardware is still subject to government restrictions (and not just in the United States). These restrictions may require additional management duties if you're running an international organization, because you'll have to set up one set of SAs and keys for use within the United States and at least one more set for your international branches.

Encrypting the original packets can cause problems if the network is to provide differentiated service classes because the pertinent data will be encrypted and hidden from routers on the path between the source and receiver. If service classes need to be implemented, host-level security rather than gateway-level security should be implemented. This is also less of a problem if IPv6 is used, because IPv6 headers include information for class of service that would not be encrypted.

Lastly, using IPSec for tunneling allows nodes to have illegal IP addresses (that is, ones meant only for internal use) and still communicate with each other. But, if you should switch to host-level security, the IP addresses for your various corporate subnets will have to be more carefully managed to ensure that they comply with each other.

Summary

This chapter dealt with many of the details of the IETF's favored system for creating VPNs and securing data over the Internet—IPSec. The system includes a great deal of flexibility in authentication and encryption algorithms, allowing it to meet the demands of both current and future net-

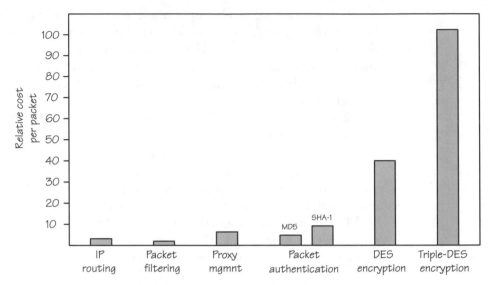

FIGURE 5.16 Computational cost per function.

working situations. The AH and ESP protocols can be applied either to authenticate and/or encrypt just the packet's payload (transport mode) or the entire IP header, including the IP addresses of the source and destination, as well (tunnel mode). The greatest degree of security is provided by applying authentication and encryption in tunnel mode.

In order to enable secure communications between two parties, a system for exchanging keys is required. IPSec's *Security Associations* (SAs) are created between correspondents to exchange keys as well as any pertinent details on the cryptographic algorithms that will be used for a session. Although manual exchanges of SAs and keys are possible for a small number of correspondents (or VPN sites), IPSec includes a fairly involved, but workable, framework for automatic key management called *Internet Key Exchange* (IKE) or ISAKMP/Oakley.

IPSec software can reside in stationary hosts, mobile clients, or security gateways. Only security gateways are needed if LAN-to-LAN tunnels need to be created. Mobile workers also would require IPSec client software if they wanted to connect to a VPN site. Should you want to maintain the identity of each correspondent (say for class-of-service differentiation), then installing IPSec on each and every computer may be necessary.

6

Using PPTP to Build a VPN

If you managed to work your way through Chapter 5, you now have an idea of just how complicated a Virtual Private Network can become. For someone planning an international VPN that provides the best security possible, supports both LAN-to-LAN tunnels and client-to-LAN tunnels, and still complies with national restrictions on cryptographic algorithms, IPSec's flexibility and numerous options are a must.

But, not all VPNs need to be so involved. Smaller businesses may only need a local or regional VPN with a limited geographic span. Some businesses may be more interested in supporting only their mobile workers and telecommuters with remote access via a VPN. These businesses could also benefit from using IPSec for their VPNs, but the market fragmentation has led to other solutions, such as PPTP (Point-to-Point Tunneling Protocol) and L2TP (Layer2 Tunneling Protocol), which are simpler and do not offer all the options, or protection, that IPSec does.

For those of you who have been following the VPN market in some detail, it may seem somewhat artificial to devote separate chapters to PPTP and L2TP and then to say nothing about L2F (Layer2 Forwarding). Originally, two simple tunneling protocols were proposed: PPTP by Ascend and Microsoft and L2F by Cisco. Because Microsoft has been actively supporting PPTP in its Windows NT Server (versions 4.0 and above) and because Ascend Communications (and other vendors) now include support for PPTP in hardware used by many ISPs, PPTP has become a popular method for constructing simple VPNs. On the other hand, L2F has stayed primarily a proprietary product from Cisco, and some of its features are being incorporated into L2TP. Because Microsoft's early support of PPTP makes it a current popular choice for VPNs, it should be covered in detail on its own, even if it will be superseded by L2TP, which is the plan of Microsoft and other vendors. L2F doesn't benefit from the same popularity, but its successor, L2TP, is likely to do so.

This chapter starts out with an overview of the architecture of PPTP and moves on to the details of how the protocol works. Then we move on to an overview of the types of products you can use to build a VPN using PPTP.

What Is PPTP?

The Point-to-Point Tunneling Protocol was first created by a group of companies calling themselves the *PPTP Forum*. The group consisted of 3Com, Ascend Communications, Microsoft, ECI Telematics, and US Robotics. The basic idea behind PPTP was to split up the functions of remote access in such a way that individuals and corporations could take advantage of the Internet's infrastructure to provide secure connectivity between remote clients and private networks. Remote users would just dial into the local number of their Internet Service Provider and could securely tunnel into their corporate network.

The most commonly used protocol for dial-up access to the Internet is the *Point-to-Point Protocol* (PPP). PPTP builds on the functionality of PPP to provide dial-up access that can be tunneled through the Internet to a destination site. As currently implemented, PPTP encapsulates PPP packets using a modified version of the *Generic Routing Encapsulation* (GRE) protocol (see Figure 6.1), which gives PPTP the flexibility of handling protocols other than IP, such as IPX and NETBEUI, for example.

Because of its dependence on PPP, PPTP relies on the authentication mechanisms within PPP, namely PAP and CHAP; since there's a strong tie between PPTP and Windows NT, an enhanced version of CHAP, MS-CHAP, is also used. This version utilizes information within NT domains for security. Similarly, PPTP can use PPP to encrypt data, but Microsoft also has

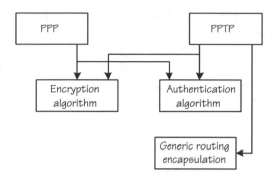

FIGURE 6.1 PPTP's architecture.

incorporated a stronger encryption method, *Microsoft Point-to-Point Encryption* (MPPE) for use with PPTP.

Aside from the relative simplicity of client support for PPTP, one of the protocol's main advantages is that PPTP is designed to run at Layer2, or the Link layer, as opposed to IPSec, which runs at Layer3. By supporting data communications at Layer2, PPTP can transmit protocols other than IP over its tunnels. IPSec, on the other hand, is restricted to transferring only IP packets over its tunnels.

Microsoft's inclusion of support for PPTP in its Windows NT Server and offering free clients for certain *Operating Systems* (OSs)—for NT and Windows95, for example—has made PPTP a popular method for creating dial-in VPNs. Microsoft's implementation of PPTP may not be a standard that's been ratified by a standards body like the IETF, and it may not even achieve the status of a *de facto* standard for VPNs due to its succession by L2TP. But, considering that so many of PPTP's features are tied to Windows NT and that Microsoft has tremendous influence in the PC world, it shouldn't come as a surprise that many of the initial products for PPTP have followed Microsoft's feature set. In fact, if your company is primarily a Windows shop, then setting up and using PPTP is fairly simple.

Because the *de facto* PPTP implementation is the one compatible with Microsoft's Windows NT version, this description of PPTP focuses on that implementation. As we go along, we'll note where the protocols and implementations differ from IETF standards or other documents that have been submitted to the IETF for consideration as standards.

Development of PPTP has proceeded in a number of different directions, leading to differing functionality among current and planned products. This means that you should exercise extra caution when selecting products and planning to use PPTP, because some products may not include the features you're planning for your VPN. For instance, Microsoft has included PPTP support in Windows NT 4.0 and released a *Dial-Up Networking* Pack (DUN) for Windows95 that includes PPTP, but these products support only client-to-LAN tunneling. LAN-to-LAN tunneling was introduced with the release of the *Routing and Remote Access Server* (RRAS) for Windows NT 4.0 in late 1997 and is planned for Windows NT Server 5.0.

The Building Blocks of PPTP

As mentioned earlier, PPTP depends on PPP for much of its basic functionality, as well as GRE for packet encapsulation. PPTP defines a number of tunnel types, based on the endpoints and control of authorization and authentication. For some of these tunnels, PPTP depends on RADIUS as a system for dynamic authentication of users. Also, to provide some form of data integrity, PPTP can use either PPP's encryption or MPPE, although these systems do not offer the robustness associated with IPSec.

PPP and PPTP

PPP has become the most common protocol for dial-up access to the Internet and other TCP/IP networks during the past few years. Working at Layer2 of the OSI protocol stack, the Data Link layer, PPP includes methods for encapsulating various types of datagrams for transfers over serial links. The PPP specifications also define two sets of protocols: a *Link Control Protocol* (LCP) for establishing, configuring, and testing the connection and a series of *Network Control Protocols* (NCPs) for establishing and configuring different network-layer protocols.

PPP encapsulates IP, IPX, and NETBEUI packets between PPP frames and sends the encapsulated packets by creating a point-to-point link between the sending and receiving computers (see Figure 6.2). To establish communications over a link, each end of the PPP link must first send LCP packets to configure and test the data link.

When a PPP link has been established, the user is usually authenticated. *This is an optional phase in PPP, but one that's likely to always be included by an ISP and certainly should be an integral part of any VPN.* Authentication must take place prior to starting the network-layer protocol phase. In PPP, authentication can be accomplished via either PAP or CHAP (see Chapter 4, "Security: Threats and Solutions").

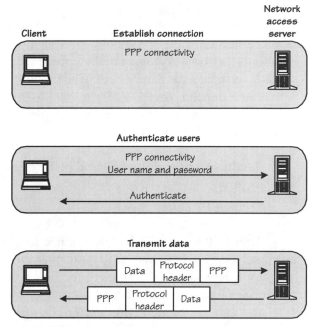

FIGURE 6.2 Dial-up networking using PPP.

Recall that in PAP, passwords are sent across the link in plaintext, and there is no protection from playback or trial-and-error attacks. CHAP is a more robust method of authentication, using a three-way handshake. CHAP protects against playback attacks by using a variable challenge value that is unique and unpredictable. Because CHAP can issue a challenge any time during and after the establishment of the link, the repeated challenges can limit the time of exposure to any single attack.

In an effort to accommodate better, more robust methods of authentication within PPP, the IETF has defined the PPP *Extensible Authentication Protocol* (EAP) in RFC 2284. EAP is a general protocol for PPP authentication that supports multiple authentication mechanisms. EAP does not select a specific authentication mechanism at the Link Control Phase, but rather postpones this until the Authentication Phase, enabling the authenticator to request more information before determining the specific authentication mechanism. This also permits the use of a back-end server that actually implements the various mechanisms while the PPP authenticator merely passes through the authentication exchange. By using EAP, you can integrate some of the systems we mentioned in Chapter 4, like one-time passwords and secure tokens, into the use of PPP; EAP also makes integration of PPP with RADIUS easier.

After the link has been established and various options negotiated as required by the LCP, PPP sends NCP packets to choose and configure one or more network-layer protocols. After each of the selected network-layer protocols has been configured, datagrams from each of the selected network-layer protocols can be sent over the link.

PPTP depends on the PPP protocol to create the dial-up connection between the client and a network-access server. PPTP expects PPP to perform the following functions:

> Establish and end the physical connection
> Authenticate the users
> Create PPP datagrams

After PPP has established the connection, PPTP takes over the role of encapsulating the PPP packets for transmission over a tunnel (see Figure 6.3).

In order to take advantage of the link created by PPP, the PPTP protocol defines two different types of packets—control packets and data packets—and assigns them to two different channels. PPTP then separates the control and data channels into a control stream that runs over TCP and a datastream that runs in an IP envelope, using GRE. A single TCP connection is created between the PPTP client and the PPTP server. This connection is used to exchange control messages.

Data packets contain the normal user data, that is, the datagram from the selected network-layer protocol. Control packets are sent as periodic inquiries about link status and manage signals between a PPTP client and the network server. Control packets also are used to send basic device

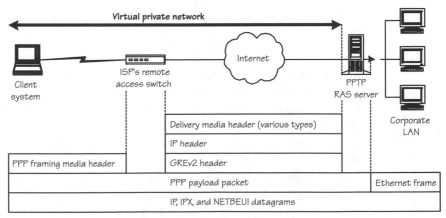

FIGURE 6.3 Example protocols used in a PPTP connection.

management and configuration information between tunnel endpoints. The control messages establish, maintain, and end the PPTP tunnel.

The control channel required for setting up a tunnel connects the PPTP client to the PPTP server. As we'll see in more detail later, the client can either be software on the remote user's computer or at the ISP's network access server. The location of the client determines the nature of the tunnel and the control that both the remote user and ISP have over the tunnel.

After the PPTP tunnel is established, user data is transmitted between the client and PPTP server. Data is transmitted in IP datagrams containing PPP packets. The IP datagrams are created using a modified version of the *Generic Routing Encapsulation* (GRE) protocol; the modified version includes information on the host's Call ID, which can be used to control access rights, and an acknowledgment capability, which is used to monitor the rate at which data packets are transmitted over the tunnel for a given session.

The GRE header is used to encapsulate the PPP packet within the IP datagram (see Figure 6.4). The payload packet is essentially the original PPP packet sent by the client, missing only framing elements that are specific to the media. Because PPTP operates as a Layer2 protocol, it must include a media header in the packet description to indicate how the tunnel is being transmitted. Depending on your ISP's infrastructure, this method might be by Ethernet, frame relay, or PPP links.

PPTP also includes a rate-control mechanism that limits the amount of data in-flight. This mechanism minimizes the need for retransmissions because of dropped packets.

Tunnels

PPTP enables users and ISPs to create a variety of different tunnel types based on the capabilities of the end user's computer and the ISP's support for PPTP. The end user's computer determines where the termination point of the tunnel is located—either on his computer if it's running a PPTP client or at the ISP's *remote access server* (RAS) if his computer supports only PPP and not PPTP. In the second case, the ISP's access server has to

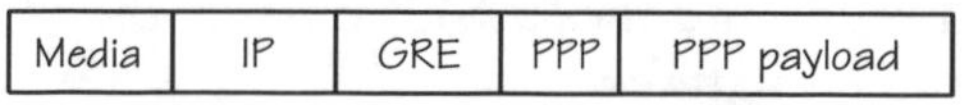

Media	IP	GRE	PPP	PPP payload

FIGURE 6.4 PPTP/GRE packet encapsulation.

support PPTP for this to work; no special ISP requirements are required if the end user has a PPTP client.

This dichotomy of end-user software capabilities and ISP support has resulted in a division of tunnels into classes, voluntary and compulsory. Voluntary tunnels are created at the request of the user for a specific use (see Figure 6.5). Compulsory tunnels are created automatically without any action from the user, and more importantly, without allowing the user any choice in the matter. Within the compulsory category are two sub-classes: static and dynamic. The static tunnels can be subdivided again, into realm-based and automatic classes.

Voluntary tunnels are just that, set up at the request of the end user. When using a voluntary tunnel, the end user can simultaneously open a secure tunnel through the Internet and access other Internet hosts via basic TCP/IP protocols without tunneling. The client-side endpoint of a voluntary tunnel resides on the user's computer. Voluntary tunnels are often used to provide privacy and data integrity for intranet traffic being sent over the Internet.

Because compulsory tunnels are created without the user's consent, they may be transparent to the end user. The client-side endpoint of a com-pulsory tunnel typically resides on a remote access server. All traffic origi-nating from the end user's computer is forwarded over the PPTP tunnel by the RAS. Access to other services outside the intranet would be controlled by the network administrators. PPTP enables multiple connections to be carried over a single tunnel.

Because a compulsory tunnel has predetermined endpoints and the user cannot access other parts of the Internet, these tunnels offer better access control than voluntary tunnels. If it's corporate policy that employ-ees cannot access the public Internet, for example, a compulsory tunnel would keep them out of the public Internet while still allowing them to use the Internet to access your VPN.

Another advantage to a compulsory tunnel is that multiple connec-tions can be carried over a single tunnel. This feature reduces the net-work bandwidth required for transmitting multiple sessions, because the control overhead for a single compulsory tunnel carrying multiple ses-sions is less that that for multiple voluntary tunnels, each carrying traffic for a single session. One disadvantage of compulsory tunnels is that the initial link of the connection (i.e., the PPP link between the end user's computer and the RAS) is outside the tunnel and, therefore, is more vul-nerable to attack.

Static compulsory tunnels typically require either dedicated equip-ment or manual configuration. These dedicated, or automatic, tunnels

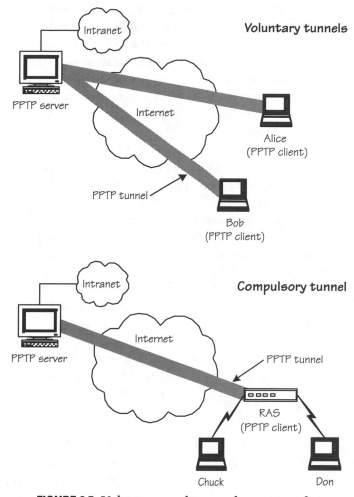

FIGURE 6.5 Voluntary and compulsory tunnels.

might require the user to call a special telephone number to make the connection. On the other hand, in realm-based, or manual, tunneling schemes, the RAS examines a portion of the user's name, called a *realm,* to decide where to tunnel the traffic associated with that user.

However, setup and maintenance of static tunnels increases the demands on network management. A more flexible approach would be to dynamically choose the tunnel destination on a per-user basis when the user connects to the RAS. These dynamic tunnels can be set up in PPTP by linking the system to a RADIUS server to obtain session configuration data on the fly.

Static tunneling requires the dedication of a *network access server* (NAS) to the purpose. In the case of an ISP, this restriction would be undesirable because it requires the ISP to dedicate an NAS to tunneling service for a given corporate customer, rather than enabling them to use existing network access servers deployed in the field. As a result, static tunneling is likely to be costly for deployment of a global service.

Realm-based tunneling assumes that all users within a given realm want to be treated the same way, limiting a corporation's flexibility in managing the account rights of their users. For example, MegaGlobal Corp. may desire to provide Jim with an account that allows access to both the Internet and the intranet, with Jim's intranet access provided by a tunnel server located in the engineering department. However, MegaGlobal Corp. may want to provide Sam with an account that provides only access to the intranet, with Sam's intranet access provided by a tunnel network server located in the sales department. Situations like these cannot be accommodated with realm-based tunneling.

Using RADIUS to provision compulsory tunnels has several advantages. For instance, tunnels can be defined and audited on the basis of authenticated users, authentication and accounting can be based on telephone numbers; and other authentication methods, such as tokens or smart cards, can be accommodated. When deployed in concert with roaming, user-based tunneling offers corporations the capability to provide their users with access to the corporate intranet on a global basis.

RADIUS

The RADIUS client/server model uses a network access server to manage user connections. Although the NAS functions as a server for providing network access, it also functions as a client for RADIUS. The NAS is

Roaming

Various ISPs have started to form strategic alliances—for example, the Stentor Alliance between MCI, British Telecom, and Bell Canada—that allow the partners to tunnel traffic across one another's networks. These agreements make it easier for your mobile workers to tunnel traffic to your corporate sites regardless of their location. If their work takes them to areas not serviced by your ISP, then they can call one of the partner ISPs in the area to use the VPN.

responsible for accepting user connection requests, getting user ID and password information, and passing the information securely to the RADIUS server. The RADIUS server returns authentication status, i.e., approved or denied, as well as any configuration data required for the NAS to provide services to the end user.

RADIUS creates a single, centrally located database of users and available services, a feature particularly important for networks that include large modem banks and more than one remote communications server. With RADIUS, the user information is kept in one location, the RADIUS server, which manages the authentication of the user and access to services from one location. Because any device that supports RADIUS can be a RADIUS client (see Figure 6.6), a remote user will gain access to the same services from any communications server communicating with the RADIUS server.

RADIUS supports the use of proxy servers, which store user information for authentication purposes and can be used for accounting and authorization, but they do not allow the user data (passwords and so on) to be changed. A proxy server depends on periodic updates of the user database from a master RADIUS server (see Figure 6.6). When corporations are looking to outsource their VPN to an ISP, they probably will arrange to have an ISP authenticate users of its PPTP server based on corporate-defined user data. In such cases, the corporation would maintain a RADIUS server and set user information on it, and the ISP would have a proxy RADIUS server that receives updates from the corporate server.

For RADIUS to control the setup of a tunnel, it has to store certain attributes about the tunnel. These attributes include the tunnel protocol to be used (i.e., PPTP or L2TP), the address of the desired tunnel server, and the tunnel transport medium to be used. In order to take further advantage of RADIUS' capabilities—namely, its capability to track network usage—a few more items are needed—the address of the tunnel client (the NAS) and a unique identifier for the tunneled connection.

When combining dynamic tunneling with RADIUS, at least three possible options are available for user authentication and authorization:

1. Authenticate and receive authorization once, at the RAS end of the tunnel.
2. Authenticate and receive authorization info once, at the RAS end of the tunnel and somehow forward the RADIUS reply to the remote end of the tunnel.
3. Authenticate on both ends of the tunnel.

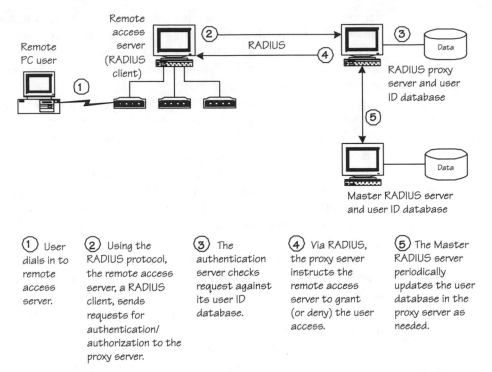

FIGURE 6.6 Interactions among a RADIUS server, proxy server, and clients.

The first model is a poor trust model because it requires the ISP alone to control access to the network, and the second is an adequate trust model but doesn't scale well, due to the way RADIUS authenticates replies. The third option is robust and works well if a RADIUS proxy server is used, which also supports the use of a single user name and password at both ends.

Let's look at the chain of events for creating a tunnel when using RADIUS this way (see Figure 6.7). First, the remote user dials into the remote access server and enters his password as part of the PPP authentication sequence (step 1 in the figure). The remote access server, acting as a RADIUS client, then uses RADIUS to check the password and receives tunnel information from the local RADIUS proxy server; this information would include attributes specifying which PPTP server is to be the endpoint of the tunnel that will be used for this particular user (steps 2 to 5). The remote access server will open the tunneled connection, creating a tunnel if necessary. *Recall that traffic from more than one user can be transmitted in the same compulsory tunnel at the same time.* The PPTP server

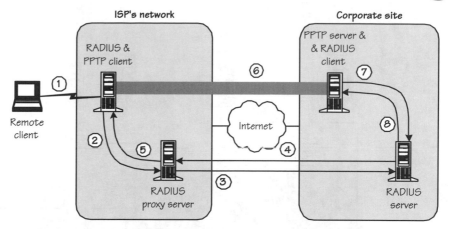

FIGURE 6.7 RADIUS authentication for dynamic tunnels.

would reauthenticate the user (step 6), checking the password against the same RADIUS server that was used in the initial exchange (steps 7 and 8). Upon authentication, the PPTP server will accept tunneled packets from the remote user and forward the packets to the appropriate destination on the corporate network.

Authentication and Encryption

Remote PPTP clients are authenticated by the same PPP authentication methods used for any RAS client dialing directly to a RAS server. Microsoft's implementation of RRAS supports CHAP, MS-CHAP, and PAP authentication schemes. MS-CHAP uses the MD4 hash for creating the challenge token from the user's password.

PAP and CHAP do have definite disadvantages when secure authentication is desired. Both PAP and CHAP rely on a secret password that must be stored on the remote user's computer and the local computer. If either computer comes under the control of a network attacker, then the secret password is compromised. Also, with CHAP or PAP authentication, you cannot assign different network access privileges to different remote users who use the same remote host. Because one set of privileges is assigned to a specific computer, everybody who uses that computer will have the same set of privileges.

In Microsoft's implementation of PPTP, data is encrypted via *Microsoft Point-to-Point Encryption* (MPPE), which is based on the RSA RC4 standard (see Figure 6.8). The *Compression Control Protocol* (CCP)

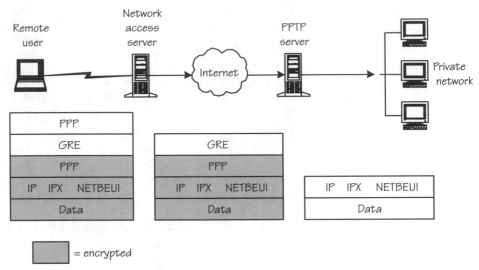

FIGURE 6.8 Packet encryption in PPTP.

used by PPP is used to negotiate encryption. MS-CHAP is used to validate the end user in a Windows NT domain, and an encryption key for the session is derived from the hashed user password stored on both the client and server. (A MD4 hash is used.) A 40-bit session key normally is used for encryption, but U.S. users can install a software upgrade to use a 128-bit key. Because MPPE encrypts PPP packets on the client workstation before they enter a PPTP tunnel, the packets are protected throughout the link from the workstation to the PPTP server at the corporate site. Changes in session keys can be negotiated to occur for every packet or after a preset number of packets.

LAN-to-LAN Tunneling

The original focus of PPTP was the creation of dial-in VPNs (i.e., to provide secure dial-in access to corporate LANs via the Internet). LAN-to-LAN tunnels were not supported at first. It wasn't until Microsoft introduced their Routing and Remote Access Server for NT Server 4.0 that NT Servers were able to support LAN-to-LAN tunnels. Since then, other vendors also have released compatible PPTP servers that also support LAN-to-LAN tunneling.

As implemented in Microsoft's RRAS, LAN-to-LAN tunneling occurs between two PPTP servers, much like IPSec's use of security gateways to connect two LANs. However, because the PPTP architecture does not make use of a key management system, authentication and encryption are controlled via CHAP, or via MS-CHAP. In effect, one site's RRAS, running PPTP, is defined as a user, with an appropriate password, at the other site's RRAS and vice versa (see Figure 6.9). To create a tunnel between the two sites, the PPTP server at one site is authenticated by the other PPTP server using the stored passwords, much as we described the process earlier for a dial-in user. One site's PPTP server thus looks like a PPTP client to the other server, and vice versa, so a voluntary tunnel is created between the two sites.

Because this tunnel can encapsulate any supported network-layer protocol (i.e., IP, NETBEUI, IPX), users at one site will have access to resources at the other site based on their access rights, defined for that protocol. This means that some form of collaboration between site managers is needed to ensure that users at a site have the proper access rights to resources at other sites. In Windows NT, for example, each site can have its own security domain and the sites would establish a trust relationship between the domains in order to allow users to access a site's resources.

Using PPTP

Because a major focus of PPTP is to provide secure dial-in access to private corporate resources, the components of a PPTP VPN are organized a bit differently from those of an IPSec VPN (see Chapter 5, "Using IPSec to Build a VPN"). The most important components are those that define the endpoints of a PPTP tunnel. Because one of these endpoints can be your ISP's equipment, this configuration can cut down on the software needed for your mobile clients but requires collaboration between you and your ISP for authentication of users.

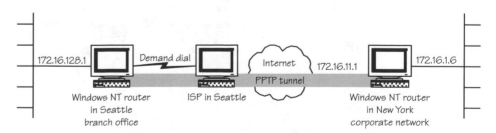

FIGURE 6.9 LAN-to-LAN PPTP tunnels.

In general, a PPTP VPN requires three items: a network access server, a PPTP server, and a PPTP client. Although the PPTP server should be installed on your premises and maintained by your staff, the network access server should be the responsibility of your ISP. In fact, if you choose to install PPTP client software on your remote hosts, the ISP doesn't even need to provide any PPTP-specific support.

Figure 6.10 illustrates few differences between the structure of an IPSec VPN and a PPTP VPN. One significant difference is that PPTP enables you to outsource some of the PPTP functions to the ISP. At a corporate site, a PPTP server acts like a security gateway, tying authentication to RADIUS or Windows NT domains. A PPTP client on a user's laptop or

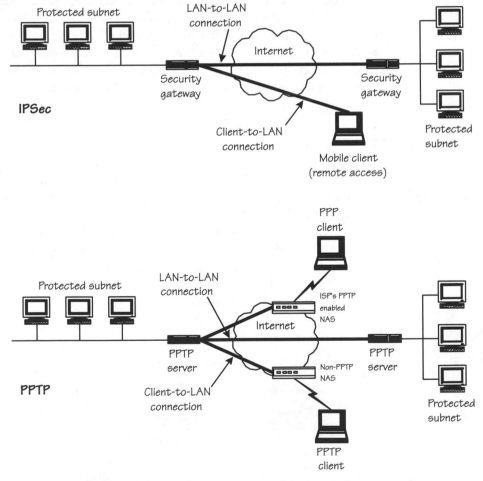

FIGURE 6.10 Comparing IPSec and PPTP architectures.

desktop computer performs many of the same functions as IPSec client software, although there are no key exchanges.

PPTP Servers

A PPTP server has two primary roles: it acts as the endpoint for PPTP tunnels, and it forwards packets to and from the tunnel that it terminates onto the private LAN. The PPTP server forwards packets to a destination computer by processing the PPTP packet to obtain the private network computer name or address information in the encapsulated PPP packet.

PPTP servers also can filter packets, using *PPTP filtering*. With PPTP filtering, you can set the server to restrict who can connect to either the local network or to the Internet. In systems like Windows NT 4.0 and RRAS, the combination of PPTP filtering with IP address filtering enables you to create a functional firewall for your network.

Setting up a PPTP server at your corporate site brings with it a few restrictions, especially if the PPTP server is to be placed on the private (i.e., corporate) side of the firewall. PPTP has been designed so that only one TCP/IP port number can be used for passing data through a firewall—port number 1723. This lack of configurability of the port number can make your firewall more susceptible to attacks. Also, if you have firewalls configured to filter traffic by protocol, you will need to set them to allow GRE to pass through.

A related device is the tunnel switch. Tunnel switches are relatively new devices, initially introduced by 3Com in early 1998. A tunnel switch is a combined tunnel terminator and tunnel initiator. The purpose of a tunnel switch is to extend tunnels from one network to another—extending a tunnel incoming from your ISP's network to your corporate network, for example (see Figure 6.11).

Tunnel switches can be used at a firewall to improve the management of remote access to private network resources. Because the tunnel switch terminates the incoming tunnel, it can examine the incoming packets for protocols carried by the PPP frames or for the remote user's name. The switch can use that information to create tunnels into the corporate network based on the information carried in the incoming packets.

PPTP Client Software

As pointed out frequently in this chapter, if the ISP equipment supports PPTP, no additional software or hardware is required on the client end; only a standard PPP connection is necessary. On the other hand, if the ISP

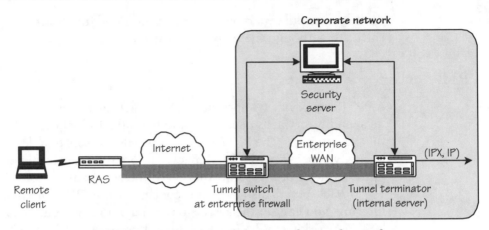

FIGURE 6.11 Example of the use of tunnel switches.

does not support PPTP, a Windows NT client (or similar software) can still utilize PPTP and create the secure connection, first by dialing the ISP and establishing a PPP connection, then by dialing once again through a virtual PPTP port set up on the client side.

PPTP clients already exist from Microsoft for computers running Windows NT, Windows95, and Windows 98. Network Telesystems also offers PPTP clients for other popular computers, including the Macintosh and computers running Windows 3.1. When selecting a PPTP client, compare its functionality to that of your PPTP server. Not all client software will necessarily support MS-CHAP for instance, which means they won't be able to take advantage of Microsoft's encryption in RRAS.

Network Access Servers

Unlike an IPSec VPN, there are many cases in which a PPTP VPN's design depends on the protocol support offered by the ISP. This support is particularly important if your mobile workers can use a PPP client but do not have PPTP clients installed.

Because ISPs can offer PPTP services without adding PPTP support to their access servers, this approach would require that all clients use a PPTP client on their computers. This approach has its advantages because it enables clients to use more than one ISP if the geographic coverage of a primary ISP isn't adequate. Also recall that remote hosts with a PPTP client can set up voluntary tunnels in the PPTP scheme of things; if you want to control employee access to Internet resources, then you'll have to resort to compulsory tunnels, which require the support of your ISP.

It's unlikely that you'll have any control over the PPTP hardware that your ISP uses, but you should be aware of its capabilities so that you can take the hardware's limitations into account in the design of your VPN.

Network access servers, which are also known as *remote access servers* or *access concentrators,* provide software-based line access management and billing capabilities and run on platforms that offer robustness and fault tolerance at ISP POPs. ISP network access servers generally are designed and built to accommodate a large number of dial-in clients. An ISP that provides PPTP service would have to install a PPTP-enabled network access server that supports PPP clients on a number of platforms, including Windows, Macintosh, and Unix.

In such cases, the ISP server acts as a PPTP client and connects to the PPTP server at the corporate network. The ISP access server thus becomes one of the endpoints for a compulsory PPTP tunnel, with the network server at the corporate site being the other endpoint.

The network access server would choose a tunnel that has not only the appropriate endpoint but also the appropriate level of performance and service. Network access servers can make tunneling choices based on calling number, called number, static port mappings, text-based "terminal server" login, user names (from PAP or CHAP authentication), user-name parsing through DNS, lookups to RADIUS or TACACS+, ISDN call type, or command-line tunnel requests.

Early versions of PPTP devices and software were designed to work with Microsoft's version of PPTP and for remote access only. For instance, it wasn't until the second quarter of 1998 that products other than Windows NT 4.0 could be used as PPTP servers. LAN-to-LAN PPTP tunneling wasn't supported until Microsoft released their Routing and Remote Access Server (RRAS) in late 1997.

A few vendors already support PPTP (see Table 6.1 for a partial list), with most of the initial equipment designed for ISPs. Since Microsoft's release of RRAS, other vendors also have started providing PPTP servers with similar features. If you're planning to install a PPTP VPN, you'll need to check the interoperability of your equipment with those of the ISP(s) you plan on using, because some features, like MS-CHAP, aren't supported on all devices and client software.

Sample Deployment

To illustrate the use of PPTP in a VPN, we'll create two different scenarios, one strictly for dial-in access (see Figure 6.12) and the second for a LAN-to-LAN VPN (see Figure 6.13). For simplicity's sake, we'll just have two

TABLE 6.1 Partial List of PPTP Products

Vendor	Product
3Com	AccessBuilder 5000, NETBuilder II
Ascend Communications	Max TNT
Bay Networks	Contivity Extranet Switches
Checkpoint Software Technologies	Firewall-1
ECI Telematics	Dial Access Concentrator
Extended Systems	ExtendNet VPN
Freegate Corp.	VPN Remote
Microcom	Access Integrator 1700
Microsoft Corp.	Windows NT Server, RRAS
Network Telesystems	Tunnel Builder
Shiva Corp.	LanRover Access Switch
US Robotics (now 3Com)	Total Control Enterprise Network Hub

sites—the corporate headquarters and a branch office—for the second example. In both cases, we'll concentrate on the exchange of data between endpoints and not worry about how the information is protected inside the corporate network (using firewalls, for example).

Just as with the IPSec example given in Chapter 5, physical security should include ensuring that all hosts reside within the site's physical parameters and all links to outside systems go through the PPTP server and an associated firewall. The connection between the site's internal networks and the external network(s) should be in a locked machine room with restricted access, and only authorized individuals (network managers, for instance) should have access to the encrypting routers.

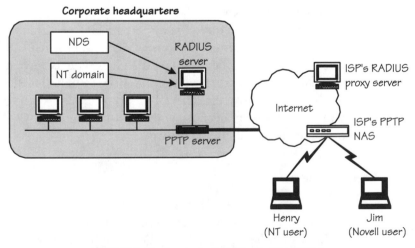

FIGURE 6.12 Sample PPTP dial-in VPN.

In the scenario diagrammed in Figure 6.12, MegaGlobal Corp. has decided to outsource much of the VPN work to its ISP. This means that the ISP providing MegaGlobal Corp.'s Internet connectivity has a RADIUS proxy server and PPTP-enabled network access servers. MegaGlobal Corp. still has to maintain a master RADIUS server and a PPTP server. Because the ISP is presumed to have PPTP-enabled access servers, you don't have to install special PPTP client software on the computers of your mobile workers.

Employing a RADIUS server to control authentication and access rights offers you the ability to centralize control of access, which can be particularly valuable if you're working in a multiprotocol environment. That's because many RADIUS servers have the capability to exchange information with other NOS-based directories, such as Windows NT and *Novell Directory Services* (NDS).

Now let's take a look at a VPN designed just for LAN-to-LAN connectivity, as in Figure 6.13.

In this example, a Windows NT server is installed at each site to serve as a router and PPTP server. In order for the two sites to communicate with each other over a PPTP tunnel, each PPTP server also will have to be configured to be a PPTP client of the other server. If the two sites connect via on-demand dialing, rather than through a permanent network link, the IP address of the ISP's network access server also has to be included in the configuration.

When any branch office traffic destined for the corporate site arrives at the branch office's PPTP server, the server will act as a PPTP client and will create a PPTP tunnel, if one doesn't already exist, to the corporate PPTP server in order to transfer the traffic. If traffic from the corporate site is destined for the branch office, the roles are reversed; the corporate PPTP server takes on the role of a PPTP client and creates a tunnel to the branch office's PPTP server.

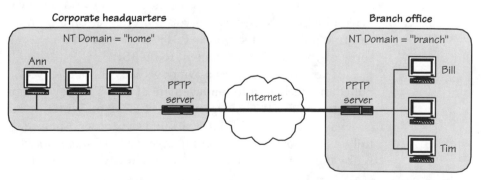

FIGURE 6.13 An example PPTP LAN-to-LAN VPN.

As mentioned earlier in this chapter, one of the primary concerns for managing LAN-to-LAN PPTP links is ensuring that users at one site have the appropriate access rights at the other sites. This access can be achieved in Windows NT either by creating a master domain covering all sites or by letting each site be its own domain. In the first case, or any similar situation in which a hierarchy of domains might be used, the tunnels will have to carry added traffic as rights are passed between sites to check a user's traffic. This added traffic might be undesirable; also, using a centralized domain increases the risk of losing authentication between two branch offices if the main domain is unreachable. If independent domains, one for each site, are deployed, then the domain managers will have to establish the appropriate trust relations between sites and exchange user rights accordingly.

Applicability of PPTP

As an interim solution for VPNs, PPTP has a lot going for it, especially if you're running a Windows-only shop. PPTP is an interim solution because most vendors are planning to replace PPTP with L2TP when the protocols are standardized. As you plan to create a PPTP VPN, it would pay to keep an eye on your vendors' plans for L2TP.

PPTP is also better suited for handling dial-up access by a limited number of remote users rather than LAN-to-LAN VPNs. One problem is the need to coordinate user authentication rights across LANs, either via NT domains or RADIUS. Also, the scalability of PPTP servers has often been called into question for large numbers of remote users and for large amounts of traffic, such as might be required for LAN-to-LAN links.

That said, PPTP can still be a good way for you to become familiar with VPNs. A VPN can still be a good cost-reduction measure, even if it's only focused on remote access costs. (Go back and review Chapter 2, "Virtual Private Networks," if you want to see some numbers.) Plus, if you can find an ISP that supports PPTP on its equipment, you can outsource some of your VPN management to the ISP.

If you're not running a Windows-only shop, then you'll have to bite the bullet and perhaps add management of an NT server to your list of tasks in order to use PPTP. The dependence of PPTP on Windows NT isn't likely to go away, especially with L2TP around the corner. Analyze this option carefully, as the cost savings accompanying an NT server may be more than offset by the support costs, if you're not already familiar with NT.

PPTP's security features aren't nearly as robust as those found in IPSec; see www.counterpane.com for some of the details. On the positive side, that means that security management is less complex for PPTP. But, the placement of the PPTP server with respect to any firewalls, as mentioned earlier, raises security concerns and opens possible holes for attackers.

PPTP's shortcomings make it a reasonable solution for remote access and multiprotocol traffic rather than LAN-to-LAN VPNs. Its popularity on the Windows NT platform and available clients for other popular PC platforms have given it a good headstart for dial-in VPNs. If you need to build a VPN that doesn't suffer from the restrictions of PPTP but aren't ready (or willing) to deploy IPSec, a better solution for VPNs is L2TP (Layer2 Tunneling Protocol), which will be covered in the following chapter.

Summary

We've just covered the details of how PPTP, a popular protocol for dial-up VPNs, works. PPTP systems are rather tightly tied to Windows NT, mainly because so many of the PPTP servers are run on NT servers. But, PPTP can be configured to support either PPP or PPTP clients, making it easier to support a variety of operating systems and clients among your mobile workers. Because it's based on PPP, PPTP is well-suited to handling multiprotocol network traffic, particularly IP, IPX, and NETBEUI protocols.

PPTP's design also makes it easier to outsource some of the support tasks to an ISP. By using RADIUS proxy servers, an ISP can authenticate dial-in users for corporate customers and create secure PPTP tunnels from the ISP's network access servers to your corporate PPTP servers. These PPTP servers then remove the PPTP encapsulation and forward the network packets to their appropriate destination on your private network.

C H A P T E R

7

Using L2TP to Build a VPN

Now that we're turning our attention to the *Layer2 Tunneling Protocol* (L2TP) in this chapter, we're almost finished with the three-letter and four-letter acronyms that make up the alphabet soup of VPNs.

L2TP should be considered the successor to PPTP; it combines many of the features originally defined in PPTP with those created for another protocol, *Layer2 Forwarding* (L2F) originally designed and implemented by Cisco. L2F has seen limited deployment; because L2TP combines the best features of the two protocols, it's been forecast that L2TP will supersede both PPTP and L2F as it becomes a standard sometime this year. Many vendors offering support for PPTP in their products either already include L2TP support as well or have plans to supersede PPTP with L2TP.

This chapter starts out with an overview of the architecture of L2TP and moves on to the details of how the protocol works, including its use of IPSec for encryption. Then we move on to an overview of the types of products you can use to build a VPN using L2TP.

What Is L2TP?

The Layer2 Tunneling Protocol was created as the successor to two tunneling protocols, PPTP and L2F. Rather than develop two competing protocols to do essentially the same thing—PPTP by Microsoft et al. versus L2F by Cisco—the companies agreed to work together on a single protocol, L2TP, and submit it to the IETF for standardization. Because we've already devoted a chapter to PPTP, we'll include a few words about L2F as background for our discussion of L2TP.

Like PPTP, L2F was designed as a tunneling protocol, using its own definition of an encapsulation header for transmitting packets at Layer2. One major difference between PPTP and L2F is that the L2F tunneling isn't dependent on IP and GRE, enabling it to work with other physical media. Because GRE isn't used as the encapsulating protocol, L2F specifications define how L2F packets are handled by different media, with an initial focus on IP's UDP.

Paralleling PPTP's design, L2F utilized PPP for authentication of the dial-up user, but it also included support for TACACS+ and RADIUS for authentication from the beginning. L2F differs from PPTP by defining connections within a tunnel, allowing a tunnel to support more than one connection. There are also two levels of authentication of the user: first, by the ISP prior to setting up the tunnel; second, when the connection is set up at the corporate gateway.

These L2F features have been carried over to L2TP. Like PPTP, the Layer2 Forwarding Protocol utilizes the functionality of PPP to provide dial-up access that can be tunneled through the Internet to a destination site. However, L2TP defines its own tunneling protocol, based on the work of L2F. Work has continued on defining L2TP transport over a variety of packetized media such as X.25, frame relay, and ATM. Although many of the initial implementations of L2TP focus on using UDP on IP networks, it's possible to set up a L2TP system without using IP as a tunnel protocol at all. A network using ATM or frame relay also can be deployed for L2TP tunnels.

Because L2TP is a Layer2 protocol, it offers users the same flexibility as PPTP for handling protocols other than IP, such as IPX and NETBEUI, for example.

Because it uses PPP for dial-up links, L2TP includes the authentication mechanisms within PPP, namely PAP and CHAP; like PPTP, L2TP supports PPP's use of the Extensible Authentication Protocol for other authentication systems, such as RADIUS. Many of the examples of RADIUS use given in Chapter 6, "Using PPTP to Build a VPN," also apply to L2TP.

We'll see later in this chapter that the designers of L2TP were concerned with the end-to-end authentication and data integrity of data passed from the end user to an L2TP server. Because of this concern, they devised ways to invoke IPSec-based authentication and encryption across the PPP link (see Figure 7.1). Using IPSec at the end user's workstation provides stronger security than simply relying on PPP-based authentication and encryption, as PPTP does.

Although Microsoft has made PPTP a popular choice for setting up dial-in VPNs by including support for the protocol within its Windows operating systems, the company also has plans to add support for L2TP within Windows NT 5.0 and Windows 98, which should make it easier for L2TP to become a widely used successor to PPTP. However, unlike PPTP, the feature set of L2TP is defined within the IETF's standards committees and is not necessarily being driven by the features found in Windows NT, as PPTP originally was.

The Building Blocks of L2TP

The components of an L2TP system are essentially the same as those for PPTP: the Point-to-Point Protocol, tunnels, and authentication systems like

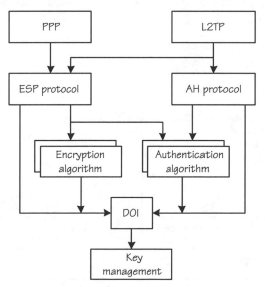

FIGURE 7.1 L2TP's architecture.

RADIUS. However, to increase the security of L2TP traffic, IPSec can be used to protect data, which brings key management into play following many of the procedures covered in Chapter 5, "Using IPSec to Build a VPN."

PPP and L2TP

PPP is the most common protocol for dial-up access to the Internet and other TCP/IP networks. Working at Layer2, the Data Link layer, of the OSI protocol stack, PPP includes methods for encapsulating various types of datagrams for transfers over serial links. PPP can encapsulate AppleTalk, IP, IPX, and NETBEUI packets between PPP frames and can send those encapsulated packets by creating a point-to-point link between the sending and receiving computers.

L2TP depends on the PPP protocol to create the dial-up connection between the client and a network access server. L2TP expects PPP to establish the physical connection, perform the first authentication phase of the end user, create PPP datagrams, and close the connection when the session is finished.

When PPP has established the connection, L2TP takes over. First, L2TP determines whether the network server at the corporate site recognizes the end user and is willing to serve as an endpoint for a tunnel for that user. If the tunnel can be created, L2TP takes on the role of encapsulating the PPP packets for transmission over the medium that the ISP has assigned to the tunnel (see Figure 7.2).

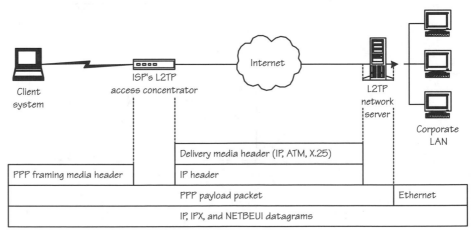

FIGURE 7.2 Example protocols used in an L2TP connection.

As L2TP creates tunnels between the ISP's access concentrator and the client's network server, it can assign more than one session to a tunnel. L2TP creates a *Call ID* for each session and inserts the Call ID into the L2TP header of each packet to indicate to which session it belongs.

It's also possible to create multiple simultaneous tunnels between an ISP's access concentrator and the client's network server. By choosing to assign a single user session to a tunnel rather than multiplex a series of sessions into a tunnel (as in the preceding paragraph), different tunnel media can be assigned to different users according to their *quality-of-service* (QoS) requirements. L2TP includes a tunnel identifier so that the individual tunnels can be identified when arriving from a single source, either an access concentrator or a network server.

Much like PPTP, the L2TP protocol defines two different types of messages—control messages and data messages—which it uses for setup and maintenance of the tunnels as well as the transmission of the data. However, unlike PPTP, L2TP transmits both the control messages and data messages as part of the same stream. If tunnels are being transmitted over an IP network, for instance, control and data are sent in the same UDP datagram.

The L2TP control messages are responsible for the establishment, management, and release of sessions carried through the tunnel, as well as the status of the tunnel itself.

In L2TP data messages, the payload packet is essentially the original PPP packet sent by the client, missing only framing elements that are specific to the media. Because L2TP operates as a Layer2 protocol, it must include a media header in the packet description to indicate how the tunnel is being transmitted (see Figure 7.3). Depending on your ISP's infrastructure, this might be Ethernet, frame relay, X.25, ATM, or PPP links.

L2TP also helps reduce network traffic and enables servers to handle congestion by implementing flow control between the network access server, an *L2TP Access Concentrator* (LAC), and the corporate network server, an *L2TP Network Server* (LNS) in L2TP terminology. Control messages are used to determine the transmission rate and buffering parameters that are used to regulate the flow of PPP packets for a particular session over the tunnel. To keep performance high, L2TP tries to keep overhead to a minimum—for example, by compressing packets headers.

FIGURE 7.3 L2TP packet encapsulation.

Tunnels

L2TP uses the same tunnel classes as PPTP (i.e., voluntary and compulsory tunnels) depending on whether the end user uses a PPP client or L2TP client to initiate the connection.

Voluntary tunnels are created at the request of the user for a specific use (see Figure 7.4). Compulsory tunnels are created automatically without any action from the user, and more importantly, without allowing the user any choice in the matter.

Voluntary tunnels are just that, set up at the request of the end user. When using a voluntary tunnel, the end user simultaneously can open a

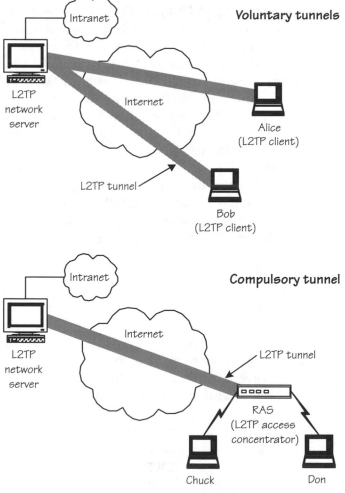

FIGURE 7.4 Voluntary and compulsory tunnels.

secure tunnel through the Internet and access other Internet hosts via basic TCP/IP protocols without tunneling. The client-side endpoint of a voluntary tunnel resides on the user's computer. Voluntary tunnels are often used to provide privacy and integrity protection for intranet traffic being sent over the Internet.

Because compulsory, or *mandatory*, tunnels are created without the user's consent, they may be transparent to the end user. The client-side endpoint of a compulsory tunnel resides on the ISP's LAC. All traffic originating from the end user's computer is forwarded over the L2TP tunnel by the LAC. Access to other services outside the intranet would be controlled by the network administrators. Keep in mind that L2TP allows multiple connections to be carried over a single tunnel, which improves L2TP's scalability and reduces the network's overhead for handling tunnels.

Because a compulsory tunnel has predetermined endpoints, and the user cannot access other parts of the Internet, these tunnels offer better access control than voluntary tunnels. If it's corporate policy that employees cannot access the public Internet, for example, a compulsory tunnel would keep them out of the public Internet while still allowing them to use the Internet to access your VPN.

Another advantage to a compulsory tunnel is that multiple connections can be carried over a single tunnel. This feature reduces the network bandwidth required for transmitting multiple sessions, because the control overhead for a single compulsory tunnel carrying multiple sessions is less than that for multiple voluntary tunnels, each carrying traffic for a single session. One disadvantage of compulsory tunnels is that the initial link of the connection (i.e., the PPP link between the end user's computer and the LAC) is outside the tunnel and, therefore, is more vulnerable to attack; this is one of the reasons why L2TP includes provisions for using IPSec to protect traffic, as we'll see in more detail shortly.

Although an ISP could choose to establish statically defined tunnels for its customers, this approach could tie up network resources unnecessarily if the static tunnels are unused or used infrequently. A more flexible approach, that of dynamically setting up the tunnel on a per-user basis when the user connects to the remote access server, or LAC, allows for more efficient use of the ISP's resources. One way to do this is for the ISP to store information about the end users, usually in a RADIUS server.

Using RADIUS to set up and control compulsory tunnels has several advantages. For instance, tunnels can be defined and audited on the basis of authenticated users; authentication and accounting can be based on telephone numbers; and other authentication methods, such as tokens or smart cards, can be accommodated.

In order for RADIUS to be able to control the setup of a tunnel, it has to store certain attributes about the tunnel. These attributes include the tunnel protocol to be used (i.e., PPTP or L2TP), the address of the desired tunnel server, and the tunnel transport medium to be used. In order to take further advantage of RADIUS' capabilities—namely, its capability to track network usage—a few more items are needed—namely the address of the tunnel client, the LAC, and a unique identifier for the tunneled connection. If the user information has to be linked with the customer's RADIUS (or other) database, then the interaction between the ISP and the customer would be the same as described in Figure 6.7 in the preceding chapter.

Authentication and Encryption

The authentication of a user occurs in three phases in L2TP: the first at the ISP and the second and optional third phases at the corporate site's network server.

In the first phase, the ISP can use the caller's phone number, the number called, or a user name to determine that L2TP service is required and then would initiate a tunnel connection to the appropriate network server. When a tunnel is established, the ISP L2TP Access Concentrator would allocate a new Call ID to identify the connection within the tunnel and would initiate a session by forwarding the authentication information.

PPP's Extensible Authentication

In an effort to accommodate better, more robust methods of authentication within PPP, the IETF has defined the PPP *Extensible Authentication Protocol* (EAP) in RFC 2284. EAP is a general protocol for PPP authentication that supports multiple authentication mechanisms. EAP does not select a specific authentication mechanism at the Link Control Phase but rather postpones this until the Authentication Phase, allowing the authenticator to request more information before determining the specific authentication mechanism. This also permits the use of a back-end server that implements the various mechanisms while the PPP authenticator merely passes through the authentication exchange. By using EAP, you can integrate some of the systems we mentioned in Chapter 4, "Security: Threats and Solutions," like one-time passwords and secure tokens, into the use of PPP; EAP also makes integration of PPP with RADIUS easier.

The corporate network server undertakes the second phase of authentication by deciding whether or not to accept the *call*. The call start indication from the ISP might include CHAP, PAP, EAP, or other authentication information; the network server would use this information to decide to accept or reject the call.

After the call is accepted, the network server can initiate a third phase of authentication at the PPP layer. This step would be similar to that used by a company to authenticate remote access users who are dialing in the old way (i.e., using a modem).

Although these three phases of authentication may guarantee that the end user, ISP, and network server are actually who they say they are, nothing up to this point has been done to protect the data against snooping or alteration. The rest of this section points out where encryption can be applied to protect your data.

The tunnel endpoints may authenticate each other during tunnel establishment. This authentication has the same security attributes as CHAP and offers reasonable protection against replay attacks and snooping during the tunnel establishment process. But, it is still fairly simple for an attacker to snoop and inject packets to hijack a tunnel after an authenticated tunnel has been successfully completed.

On their own, L2TP and PPP authentication and encryption do not meet the security requirements for a VPN. Although L2TP authentication can handle mutual authentication of an LAC and an LNS during tunnel setup, it does not protect control and data traffic on a per-packet basis. This lack of protection leaves tunnels open to a variety of attacks, including snooping data packets, modifying both data and control packets, attempts to hijack the tunnel or the PPP connection, or disrupting PPP negotiations to weaken any confidentiality protection or to gain access to user passwords.

PPP authenticates the client to the LNS, but it also does not provide per-packet authentication, data integrity, or replay protection. PPP encryption does meet confidentiality requirements for PPP traffic but does not address authentication, data integrity, and key-management requirements, making it a weak security solution, which does not assist in securing the L2TP control channel.

If L2TP tunnel authentication is desired, it's necessary to distribute keys. Although manual key distribution might be feasible in a limited number of cases, a key-management protocol will be required for most situations.

For L2TP tunnels over IP, IP-level packet security using IPSec provides very strong protection of the tunnel. This security requires no modification to the L2TP protocol. For L2TP tunnels over frame relay or other switched networks, current practice indicates that these media are much less likely to experience attacks on in-transit data.

Note that several of the attacks outlined may be carried out on PPP packets sent over the link between the dial-up client and the NAS/LAC, prior to encapsulation of the packets within an L2TP tunnel. Even though this is not strictly the concern of the L2TP specification (being a part of how PPP handles the link), L2TP can be a better VPN solution if it protects data from end-to-end. This led to the proposal of using IPSec for encrypting packets, at least for IP-based tunnels.

Because ESP functions are defined on the IP payload, excluding the IP header, the presence of an IP header is not a requirement for the use of ESP. Therefore, L2TP implemented on non-IP networks can transport ESP packets. But, key exchange and negotiation of security associations (see Chapter 5) is another matter. IKE, or *ISAKMP/Oakley* if you want to use the old term for the protocols, messages use UDP transport, which would require that non-IP media used for L2TP tunnels would have to support the transport of UDP datagrams. (Is this a problem?)

Let's look at how IPSec would be implemented within L2TP for compulsory and voluntary tunnels. In the case of a compulsory tunnel, the end user sends PPP packets to the LAC and isn't really aware of the tunnel that's created between the LAC and the LNS at the corporate site. A security association may be set up between the LAC and the LNS based on the end user's requirements and identity, and this association would be known to the LAC and LNS but not to the end user.

Because the end user wouldn't be aware of what security services are in place between the LAC and the LNS for his traffic, the best approach is for the end user to rely on IPSec starting on his computer. But, not all of the endpoints might be IPSec-capable, which might force renegotiations for using only PPP encryption (see Figure 7.5). In both cases, the ISP's LAC could apply the IPSec Authentication Header to traffic traveling through the tunnel it creates, but the encryption choice is left up to the end user— either ESP for IPSec-capable destinations or PPP's encryption scheme for non-IPSec destinations.

In the case of a voluntary tunnel, the end user serves as one endpoint of the L2TP tunnel and, therefore, can negotiate a security association with the LNS at his corporate site. But, negotiation of SAs and keys again depends on whether or not both endpoints are IPSec-capable (see Figure 7.6). Because the end user's computer serves as the endpoint for voluntary tunnels, the IPSec Authentication Header is applied at his workstation, not at the ISP's

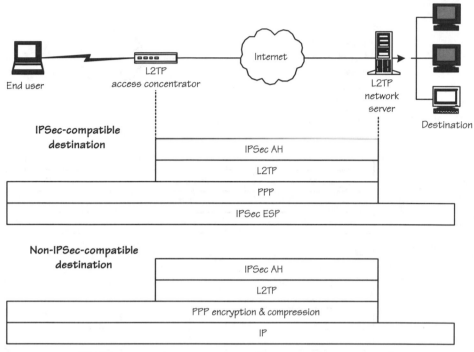

FIGURE 7.5 Packet encryption for compulsory tunnels.

device, which in this case is a network access server, not an L2TP access concentrator. If the destination is not IPSec-capable, then ESP encryption protects only the packets until they reach the LNS at the corporate site.

Although IPSec has been specified as the security system of choice for use with L2TP, it may not be suitable for all situations. Although ESP can be used to encrypt non-IP payloads, AH and ESP are designed to be inserted into IP datagrams. The proposed L2TP solution is to always use UDP datagrams for transporting L2TP packets regardless of the medium involved, such as frame relay or ATM. This solution offers the advantage of using only one protocol for securing L2TP traffic, whether it's over IP or non-IP networks.

Other alternatives for non-IP networks are still being investigated. One suggested approach has been to include the *Security Parameters Index* (SPI) (see Chapter 5, "Using IPSec to Build a VPN") for a security association and a cryptographic initialization vector of 128 bits in the L2TP header. In addition, control messages would be defined for negotiating a security association.

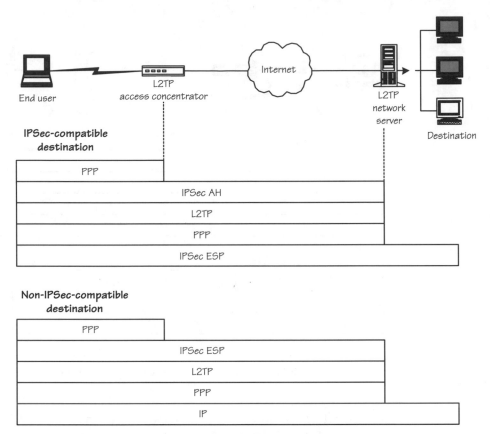

FIGURE 7.6 Packet encryption for voluntary tunnels.

LAN-to-LAN Tunneling

Although the primary focus of L2TP has been dial-up VPNs using PPP clients, it is possible to use L2TP for LAN-to-LAN links within a VPN.

The basic setup of LAN-to-LAN tunneling would occur between two L2TP servers with at least one having a dial-on demand link to their ISP, allowing them to initiate a PPP session whenever traffic is waiting for a destination at another VPN site. This type of arrangement would work best for branch offices that do not generate a great deal of traffic on their VPN links and do not need to stay connected to other VPN sites all the time.

In effect, each site serves as both an L2TP access concentrator and a network server, initiating and terminating tunnels as needed (see Figure 7.7). If this were a demand dial-in situation like the one we described for

Running L2TP on Non-IP Networks

Work has been proceeding in the IETF to define PPP framing for interfaces other than asynchronous ones (i.e., modem and serial lines) and ISDN. This work would allow PPP to work over ATM, using the AAL5 and FUNI interfaces of ATM, as well as frame relay, which means that VPN sites could create L2TP tunnels among themselves using dedicated links to their ISPs rather than depending only on dial-up links.

PPTP in Chapter 6, "Using PPTP to Build a VPN," authentication could follow the same three steps as for a remote client (i.e., first by the ISP, then by the LNS at the receiving site, and finally any further authentication of the PPP traffic is set up by the receiving site).

For LANs continually connected via the Internet (i.e., using frame relay, T1, etc., not a dial-up link), most likely a shortcut in the authentication process would exist because an ISP's remote access server would not be involved as a LAC.

Key Management

When two parties want to exchange secure communications, they need to be sure that they're processing the data in the same way. The two parties have to be using the same cryptographic algorithm, the same key length, and the same keys if they're going to successfully exchange secure data; this is handled via a *Security Association* (SA). Although IPSec specifies default algorithms for authentication and encryption, it also allows for other algorithms to be used.

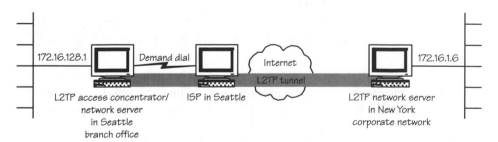

FIGURE 7.7 LAN-to-LAN L2TP tunnels.

A Security Association groups together all the things you need to know about how you communicate securely with someone else. An IPSec SA specifies the following:

- The mode of the authentication algorithm used in the AH and the keys to that authentication algorithm
- The ESP encryption algorithm mode and the keys to that encryption algorithm
- The presence and size of any cryptographic synchronization to be used in that encryption algorithm
- What protocol, algorithm, and key you use to authenticate your communications
- What protocol, encrypting algorithm, and key you use to make your communications private
- How often those keys are to be changed
- The authentication algorithm, mode, and transform for use in ESP plus the keys to be used by that algorithm
- The key lifetimes
- The lifetime of the SA itself
- The SA source address

Although security associations help two communicating parties define the cryptography they'll use to communicate, the procedures for exchanging and negotiating SAs as well as any keys involved in the communications are defined by IKE (or *ISAKMP/Oakley,* its older name). IKE is designed to provide four capabilities:

1. Provide the means for parties to agree on which protocols, algorithms, and keys to use.
2. Ensure from the beginning of the exchange that you're talking to the right person.
3. Manage those keys after they've been agreed upon.
4. Ensure that key exchanges are handled safely.

As you might expect, key exchange is closely related to the management of security associations. When you need to create an SA, you need to exchange keys. So IKE's structure wraps them together and delivers them as an integrated package.

Because IKE is IP-centric, it's easier to graft onto L2TP running over IP networks than over non-IP networks. Some question still exists concerning methods for negotiating security associations and managing keys when using L2TP over non-IP networks.

Using L2TP

Because a major focus of L2TP is to provide secure dial-in access to private corporate resources over the Internet, the components of an L2TP VPN are almost the same as for a PPTP VPN. (See Chapter 6 for more on PPTP.) The most important components are those that define the endpoints of an L2TP tunnel, the L2TP access concentrator, and the L2TP network server (see Figure 7.8). Because one of these endpoints can be your ISP's equipment, the software needed for your mobile clients can be reduced, which requires collaboration between you and your ISP for the first phase of authentication of users.

Although the LNS should be installed on your premises and maintained by your staff, the LAC should be the responsibility of your ISP. In fact, if you choose to install L2TP client software on your remote hosts, the ISP doesn't even need to provide any L2TP-specific support.

At a corporate site, an L2TP network server acts like a security gateway, tying authentication to RADIUS or Windows NT domains. An L2TP client on a user's laptop or desktop computer performs many of the same functions as IPSec client software, although there are no key exchanges.

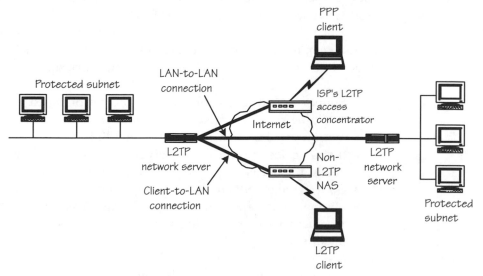

FIGURE 7.8 Basic L2TP components.

Like PPTP, L2TP offers you the advantage of outsourcing some of the VPN functions to the ISP.

L2TP Network Servers

As with PPTP, an *L2TP network server* (LNS) has two primary roles: it acts as the endpoint for L2TP tunnels, and it forwards packets to and from the tunnel that it terminates onto the private LAN. The L2TP server forwards packets to a destination computer by processing the L2TP packet to obtain the private network computer name or address information in the encapsulated PPP packet. Any computing platform capable of terminating PPP sessions can operate as an LNS.

Unlike PPTP, L2TP is not designed for filtering packets. Instead, the system's architecture leaves that task to your firewall.

When it comes to integrating network servers with your firewalls, L2TP has some advantages over PPTP. First, L2TP does not demand that only one specific port number can be assigned for the firewall to pass L2TP traffic, as PPTP does. (A default port number, 1701, is defined for L2TP, though.) Network managers have the option of selecting a different firewall port number for passing L2TP traffic, making it more difficult for attackers to take over L2TP tunnels or try other attacks based on a known port number. Second, because the L2TP data and control traffic pass over a single UDP channel, firewall setup is simpler. Because some firewalls are not designed to support GRE, compatibility between L2TP and firewall products is less of an issue than for PPTP.

Since IPSec can play a large role in the security of your data, you should keep in mind some of the features and capabilities that we mentioned in Chapter 5 when reviewing L2TP network servers, namely:

- Support separate network connections for plaintext and ciphertext.
- Available key sizes must be consistent with the sensitivity of the information you'll transmit across the data link.
- If you decide that the default crypto algorithms will not meet your needs, the device should support the accepted alternative algorithms.
- Both AH and ESP ought to be supported.
- Manual input of SAs, including wild card SAs, should be supported.
- Mechanisms for protecting secret and private keys should be included.
- A system for changing crypto keys automatically and periodically makes key management easier and more secure.
- A security gateway should include some support for logging failures

when processing a header; even better, some kind of alarm for persistent failures should be included.

L2TP Client Software

If the ISP equipment supports L2TP, no additional software or hardware is required on the client end; only standard PPP software is necessary. Note that this setup would not support data encryption via IPSec, which means that you may have to keep on the lookout for IPSec-enabled PPP clients to make the most of L2TP. On the other hand, if the ISP does not support L2TP, then an IPSec-compliant L2TP client can be used to create tunnels to the corporate LNS.

If you're concerned with proper IPSec support in either PPP or L2TP clients, here are some features to check when evaluating client software:

- Offers compatibility with other IPSec implementations; (i.e., match the site's encrypting server—key exchange protocol, crypto algorithms, etc.)
- Offers a clear indication of when IPSec is working
- Supports downloading SAs (via paper or disks, for instance)
- Has to handle dynamically assigned IP addresses
- Includes mechanisms to protect the keying material from theft (encrypt keys with password, for instance)
- Offers a mechanism to change the crypto key automatically and periodically; includes dynamic assignment of new SPI numbers during rekeying; is compatible with standard IPSec keying protocols; uses a cryptographically strong random-key procedure to generate its keys
- Explicitly blocks non-IPSec traffic

Network Access Concentrators

Unlike an IPSec VPN, in many cases an L2TP VPN's design depends on the protocol support offered by the ISP. This support is particularly important if your mobile workers can use a PPP client but do not have L2TP clients installed. It's also important when you consider what encryption methods to use for protecting your data.

Because ISPs can offer L2TP services without adding L2TP support to their access servers, this approach would require that all clients use an L2TP client on their computers. This approach has its advantages because it enables clients to use more than one ISP if the geographic coverage of a primary ISP isn't adequate. Also recall that remote hosts with an L2TP client can set up voluntary tunnels; if you want to control employee access to Internet resources, then you'll have to resort to compulsory tunnels, which require the support of your ISP.

An ISP that provides L2TP service would have to install an L2TP-enabled network access server that supports PPP clients on a number of platforms, including Windows, Macintosh, and Unix. The ISP access concentrator thus becomes one of the endpoints for a compulsory L2TP tunnel, with the network server at the corporate site being the other endpoint.

The L2TP access concentrator would choose a tunnel that has not only the appropriate endpoint (i.e., your network server) but also the appropriate level of performance and service. Network access servers can make tunneling choices based on calling number, called number, static port mappings, text-based terminal server login, user names (PAP or CHAP authentication), user-name parsing through DNS, lookups to RADIUS or TACACS+, ISDN call type, or command-line tunnel requests.

Your selection of an ISP partner for an L2TP VPN also may hinge on the degree to which you want to protect your data. If you want end-to-end encryption, for instance, you would install IPSec-compliant clients on your mobile workers' computers and expect the ISP to handle encrypted packets from clients all the way to your network server.

If lesser security can be tolerated and you only want to protect your data as it travels through the tunnel over the Internet, then you should deal with an ISP who's installed an L2TP access concentrator that supports IPSec and will encrypt your traffic between the LAC and your LNS.

A few vendors already support L2TP (see Table 7.1 for a partial list). If you're planning to install an L2TP VPN, you should check the interoperability of your equipment with those of the ISP(s) you plan on using.

Sample Deployment

To illustrate the use of L2TP in a VPN, we'll focus on a scenario designed strictly for dial-in access (see Figure 7.9). As with the scenarios in the previous chapters, we'll concentrate on the exchange of data between endpoints and not worry about how the information is protected inside the corporate network (using firewalls, for example).

Just like the IPSec example given in Chapter 5 and the PPTP examples in Chapter 6, physical security should include ensuring that all hosts reside within the site's physical parameters and that all links to outside systems go through the L2TP network server and an associated firewall.

TABLE 7.1 Partial List of L2TP Products

Vendor	*Product*
3Com	AccessBuilder, HiPer Access Router
Ascend Communications	SecureConnect, Pipeline Routers
Bay Networks	Contivity Extranet Switch 1000, 2000, 4000
Checkpoint Software Technologies	Firewall-1
Cisco	IOS
Extended Systems	ExtendNet VPN
Freegate Corp.	VPN Remote
Microcom	Access Integrator 1700
Microsoft Corp.	Windows NT 5.0
Shiva Corp.	LanRover Access Switch

The connection between the site's internal networks and the external network(s) should be in a locked machine room with restricted access, and only authorized individuals (network managers, for instance) should have access to the encrypting routers.

In the scenario we've diagrammed in Figure 7.9, MegaGlobal Corp. has decided to outsource much of the VPN work to its ISP. This means that the ISP providing MegaGlobal Corp.'s Internet connectivity has a RADIUS proxy server and an L2TP access concentrator (i.e., an L2TP-enabled network access server). MegaGlobal Corp. still has to maintain a master RADIUS server and an L2TP network server. Because the ISP is presumed to have L2TP-enabled access servers, you don't have to install

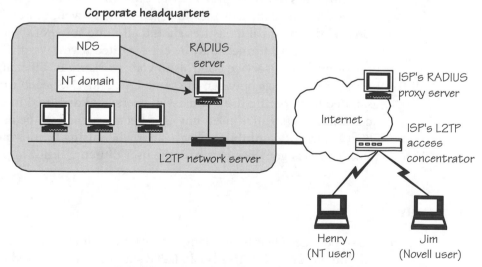

FIGURE 7.9 An example L2TP dial-in VPN.

special L2TP client software on the computers of your mobile workers (unless you want to provide IPSec encryption of the data).

Applicability of L2TP

L2TP will be the next-generation protocol for dial-in VPNs. It brings together the best features of PPTP and L2F, as well as supporting IPSec for improved data security. As a show of support for L2TP, most vendors of PPTP products are either offering L2TP-compatible products or will be introducing them before long.

Although a great deal of the initial development effort for L2TP has been focused on L2TP over IP, the capability to run L2TP over other networks, such as frame relay or ATM, should add to its long-term popularity. Plus, L2TP still has an advantage over IPSec, because it can transport protocols other than IP.

L2TP's support for non-IP networks also may prove to be a hindrance for some network planners, though. That's because IPSec's key-management scheme, IKE, is designed to work with IP, and translating IKE to other network protocols hasn't become a priority item. The PPPEXT Working Group of the IETF is still working on ways for securing L2TP traffic and managing keys over non-IP networks.

When we discussed PPTP, we mentioned that scalability concerns might arise if a large number of remote users need to be supported or if large amounts of traffic over LAN-to-LAN links might occur. Some of these same scalability concerns may apply to L2TP as well, but L2TP's congestion and flow-control measures should alleviate some of the problems.

Lastly, L2TP tunnels may be better-suited if you want to provide some type of quality-of-service controls to your workers. L2TP enables you to set up multiple tunnels between the same LAC and LNS; each tunnel can be assigned to a specific user, or class of users, and assigned to specific media according to QoS attributes that have been assigned to the user. Recall that IPSec's encryption of the packet header when using tunnel-mode ESP can make QoS assignments based on the user difficult, if not impossible.

Summary

We've now detailed the workings of L2TP, the third (and last) VPN protocol that we'll cover in this book. L2TP should be considered the next-generation VPN protocol, particularly for dial-in VPNs; most vendors already have plans to supplant PPTP-based products with L2TP products.

L2TP offers a number of the advantages of PPTP, particularly for handling multiple sessions over a single tunnel as well as assigning QoS parameters of different tunnels to the same site. In addition, L2TP's capability to run over media like X.25, frame relay, and ATM, while handling multiple network layer protocols, in addition to IP, affords users and ISPs a great deal of flexibility in designing VPNs. L2TP also provides stronger security for your data, because it uses IPSec's ESP for encrypting packets, even over a PPP link between the end-user and the ISP.

$\mathcal{8}$

Designing Your VPN

The planning and design of a VPN should be done with care, because it not only affects the connectivity between different parts of your organization and the security of your data, but it can also affect network traffic at each site. It doesn't make any difference if you're designing a small two- or three-site VPN, a dial-up VPN for hundreds or thousands of remote users, or a huge international VPN; proper planning will help you prepare yourself and your fellow users for deployment and use of the VPN. Proper design, one aligned with your current and future needs, will also help you deal with any problems that might come up along the way.

Although it's difficult to anticipate the special requirements of each type of network, this chapter attempts to cover as many VPN design issues as possible. To achieve that goal, you'll find that we often focus on problems and issues that only larger installations are likely to face. Although these issues may not be especially pertinent to those of you building smaller VPNs, they can prove useful if you're planning to increase the size of your network in the future. What may seem like a small, inconsequential problem on your network now can easily become a monstrous problem as your network grows. Considering that network usage and technologies often grow by leaps and bounds and are often unpredictable, it's nice to have some idea of what to expect down the line.

To help you deal with the issues surrounding the design of a VPN, we'll break down the process into three groups of issues and suggestions. First is the needs analysis: what are the requirements for your VPN—for bandwidth, connectivity, applications, users, and so on? Then, we'll move on to many of the issues actually affecting VPN design, such as selecting an ISP, managing addresses, and security options. Finally, we'll cover some steps for deploying your VPN.

Armed with the information and questions presented in this chapter, you should be well-prepared for the following four chapters, which lay out many of the connectivity and product options that have become available for creating VPNs.

Determining the Requirements for Your VPN

In order to design a usable VPN, you need to have some idea of the demands that will be placed on the VPN; in other words, what kind of traffic will be transmitted, what applications will be used, how often will the network be used, and so on. Also since one of the major components of a VPN is security, you have to factor in the type of security you'll require—for data, applications, and computers, as well as users. Many of the questions and answers are interrelated, but we'll attempt to keep them categorized in some logical fashion.

Let's take a look at site-related network needs first. Some of the questions you'll need to answer for each site include the following:

How many users are there at each site?

What kind of connection to the Internet will the site require? Will it be a full-time or on-demand (i.e., dial-up) connection?

How much network traffic does this site generate? How does the traffic vary hourly and daily?

If a full-time Internet connection is required, what's the minimum uptime the site can tolerate? Might a second connection be required as backup?

If an on-demand connection is required, how often will it be
required? What kind of reliability is needed? (That is, can busy
signals be tolerated? How often?)

Will the site have to support remote users? How many?

You've probably guessed from some of the questions we raised that
network capacity planning is an important issue for VPNs. Actually, it's an
important step for just about any major change in your network, whether
it be setting up a new WAN link or upgrading servers or routers.

To take capacity planning a step further, you need to know more
about the type of traffic generated on your network and the applications
that generate the traffic. Let's review some of the pertinent details about
different types of applications and the traffic they generate before continuing with our VPN needs analysis.

It's often been the case that corporate LANs have sufficient bandwidth to handle most types of traffic and applications. That was especially
true when mainframes and minicomputers held the majority of the data
that users required. Accessing that data via terminals or client-server applications led to fairly predictable traffic patterns on networks.

But, that's changed considerably as the World Wide Web and other
collaborative applications have become more dominant on many networks. Traffic patterns have become more chaotic and less predictable,
with more and more traffic crossing organizational boundaries and their
associated subnets, both within and between businesses.

To further complicate the analysis of network capacity, the usage of
new types of applications has started to grow. In particular, applications
that depend on real-time interactions, such as video conferencing, IP
telephony, and other multimedia applications, are becoming more popular.
And, they put new demands on both network bandwidth and latency.

Even as you get a handle on these applications and their network
demands for your corporate LANs, you have to factor in how this traffic
can be accommodated by your WAN links. This probably will have the
greatest effect on your VPN plans, because the architectures of your WAN
and VPN are likely to be largely the same, at least for LAN-to-LAN VPNs.

WAN links traditionally have less bandwidth than LAN pipes, partly
because less traffic is expected to flow between sites on a WAN. Since your
WAN links are likely to be a determining factor in the efficiency of your
VPN, it's crucial to know what kind of traffic travels on your WAN. With
that information in hand and knowing what kind of uses will be reserved
for the VPN, you can determine whether existing WAN bandwidth will be

Applications and Traffic Types

Because the Internet is a massive conglomeration of different circuits managed by a variety of corporate and academic entities, there's a wide range in the performance of traffic on the Internet. Your traffic may not only be competing with other traffic for the same bandwidth or other network resources at some points in the internetwork, but it also may be subjected to delays that can affect the performance of your applications. Just as nature abhors a vacuum, users will always find ways to use any available bandwidth on a network. Even as new technologies like Gigabit Ethernet make it easier to provide more bandwidth, applications are gobbling up more bandwidth and placing restrictive demands on such data-delivery parameters as network latency and jit-

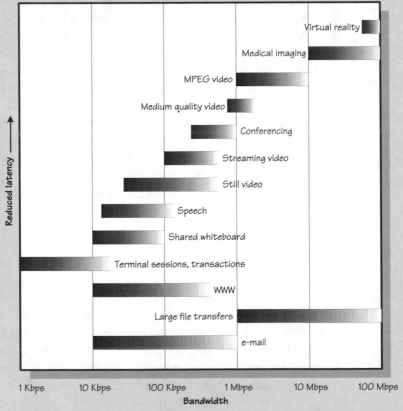

FIGURE 8.1 Bandwidth and latency requirements for different classes of applications.

ter. Thus, real-time data requires some kind of bandwidth reservation based on quality of service as well as priorities related to mission-critical situations.

Some of the simpler multimedia data, such as text combined with graphics, or animation files, do not pose special transmission problems on networks. These files may be larger than the norm, but they don't require synchronization of different parts of the data. But, more complex multimedia data, such as that used in interactive applications—videoconferencing and streaming video, for example—impose special restrictions on networks beyond demands for more bandwidth (see Figure 8.1).

Although bandwidth is the crucial factor when precise amounts of data must be delivered within a certain time period, latency affects the response time between clients and servers. Latency is the minimum time that elapses between requesting and receiving data and can be affected by many different factors, including bandwidth, an internetwork's infrastructure, routing techniques, and transfer protocols. Real-time interactive applications, such as desktop videoconferencing, are sensitive to accumulated delays, usually less than 0.2 seconds end-to-end. Interactive traffic, such as a TELNET terminal session or legacy protocols like SNA, can stand slightly longer latencies, on the order of one second or less. Bulk transfer traffic (an FTP file transfer, for example) can deal with any latency because the services have built-in measures for dealing with the acknowledgment of lost packets, rearranging packet sequences, and so on, but are not time-dependent.

sufficient for your VPN or whether you'll need to upgrade some of the WAN connections. (We'll see later how bandwidth management and QoS enter into the picture.)

Concerns about the bandwidth of the links to your ISP aren't restricted to LAN-to-LAN VPNs. Bandwidth can become an issue even if you're creating a dial-in VPN, because you'll need adequate bandwidth between your ISP and the VPN server site to handle the anticipated number of simultaneous tunnels from your remote users.

Let's move from site-related data to consider your entire VPN or corporate network. Unless you're planning a dial-in VPN that connects to only one central site, your VPN is going to connect a number of sites together. As you plan your VPN, you should not only have a list of the sites that will be served by the VPN, but you'll need to know their geographic distribution as well. Also, determine whether all the sites will need to interact with each other or if some sites can serve as satellites of other sites. Even though the Internet enables you to create a mesh between all sites, a hierarchy of site functionality and communications capabilities can lead to better traffic control than if you treat each site as the equal of all other sites (see Figure 8.2). Depending on your ISP's capabilities and POP locations, you may find that one architecture is less expensive than the other.

Geography also plays a role in the security of your VPN. If you're creating a multinational VPN, you'll no doubt run into some export restrictions

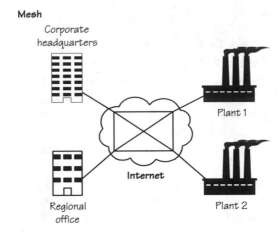

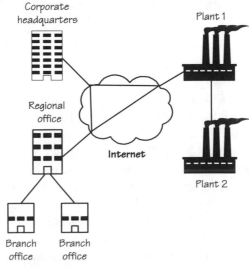

FIGURE 8.2 Mesh versus hierarchy.

on the cryptographic algorithms and key lengths that you can use for authentication and encryption. The U.S. government may eventually change its stance on restricting the export of long key lengths; some VPN products have been granted export licenses by the United States. In the meantime, be prepared to use systems that support at least two different key lengths and can pick between the two based on the destination of the traffic.

While we're on the subject of security, you can improve your understanding of the security needs surrounding your enterprise's data by ranking the relative importance of the different data sources within your company and the effect unauthorized access would have on company operations. It should be obvious that not all data is of equal importance to your company, but it may be less obvious that not all the data from one source (the CEO, for instance) is always of the same importance. *Warning: this is not a trivial exercise!* But, it could be important to help you decide what data needs to be encrypted for the VPN and what can travel in the clear. Ranking the relative importance of corporate data also can help mold corporate security policies.

Not only should the relative importance of the data be determined, but try to determine the timeliness of the data. Should two-year-old sales data be treated the same as last month's sales data? Probably not. And, it's unlikely that today's purchase orders need to be protected from eavesdropping and alteration for longer than it normally takes to fill those orders and receive payment. When you know the time period for which data needs to remain secret, or at least protected, then you can knowledgeably pick appropriate key lengths and cryptographic algorithms to protect that data. Not all of your data needs to be protected for 20 years, for example.

As you collect all of this data to lay the foundation for the specifics of your VPN, don't forget to try and get a feeling for how the corporation and its data needs will change in the future. Very few of us have crystal balls that work, but certain details in corporate plans can affect how you design your VPN. For example, it's worth knowing that the company plans to increase electronic communications with its business partners or suppliers; a logical course of action then would be to anticipate building an extranet using the VPN as a base. In fact, some writers and business people like to use the words extranet and VPN interchangeably. As we mentioned earlier in this book, we consider an extranet to be a special extension of a company's intranet; it doesn't have to be the same as a VPN.

One last note about extranets. (We'll cover extranets in more detail in Chapter 16, "Extending VPNs to Extranets.") If an extranet is part of the network plans, you'll eventually need to know the networking capabilities of your partners and what applications will be used, which means that someone will have to obtain information from your partners similar to what we've described in this chapter.

Some Design Considerations

You're likely to run into a number of common situations and caveats as you design your VPN. We've broken them down as follows: current network issues, security-related issues, and ISP issues.

Network Issues

We're assuming that you're not building your entire network from scratch; if you are, you're lucky! But, in most cases, you have to take into consideration previous network infrastructure decisions and equipment purchases that cannot be easily changed.

One of the network issues you should take into account in your design is the capabilities of your current routing and security devices. As we'll see in later chapters, it's possible to add hardware and/or software to your routers and firewalls so that they can serve as security gateways for your VPN. But, if your routers and firewalls are already maxed out and have no computational horsepower to spare for VPN functions, it'd be a mistake to plan on adding these functions to your existing equipment. If that's the case, you have three choices:

1. Upgrade your routers or firewalls so that they can support VPN functions.
2. Replace routers or firewalls with newer, more capable equipment.
3. Use a different type of device to provide your VPN services.

The range of hardware and software you can use for this last option is covered in Chapters 11, "VPN Hardware," and 12, "VPN Software." The network locations for devices supporting VPNs are shown in Figure 8.3.

Encryption is a computationally intensive process, but it varies according to algorithm, as Figure 8.4 shows. The strongest encryption available takes the most resources, which may make it unsuitable for many of your existing network devices. But, that doesn't automatically mean that your routers and firewalls cannot do the job; some vendors offer special cryptographic coprocessor cards for routers or firewalls to give them the extra horsepower they would need for a VPN.

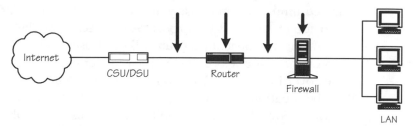

FIGURE 8.3 Locations on network for VPN functions.

Other equipment you have to consider are your remote access servers and modem banks. One of the current driving forces behind VPNs is the desire to move the management, support, and equipment requirements of remote access from the corporate premises to an ISP. Some of you may well be planning a dial-in VPN only to achieve this, while others will be looking at hybrid VPNs that support both LAN-to-LAN traffic as well as remote tunnels to LANs. In either case, you've got some remote access equipment hanging around. Unfortunately, most of it will be of little use to your VPN. Some remote access servers can be upgraded to support VPN tunnels, but that has to be handled on a product-by-product basis.

You may want to maintain a remote access server even as you deploy a VPN. If your company supports a large number of telecommuters who dial in via local, rather than long-distance lines, a VPN is not a cost-effective option. It will cost you more to set up ISP accounts for your

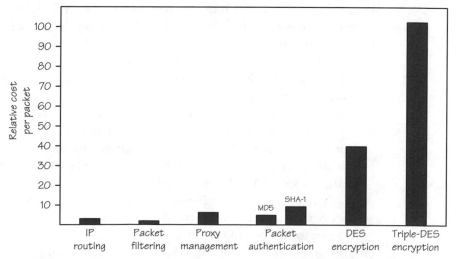

FIGURE 8.4 Computational requirements of cryptographic algorithms.

telecommuters than to use your modem bank and remote access server to provide them access to corporate resources from their homes.

One component that can still be of use to your VPN is the authentication system you've been using for your remote users. Many VPN devices we cover in Chapters 10 through 12 can use such popular remote access authentication systems as RADIUS, TACACS+, and token-based authentication systems like Axent and SecurID. This compatibility enables you to continue using the same authentication systems as you convert from your current remote access servers to a VPN. In fact, many VPN vendors have recognized that many potential customers are reluctant to change from their existing remote access authentication systems and, therefore, need to support those systems in their products; more and more vendors are adding support for many of the authentication systems we just mentioned.

Keep in mind that your users' computers will be somewhat affected by the VPN. If you're planning a LAN-to-LAN VPN using security gateways, the encryption and decryption of VPN traffic will occur at the gateways, relieving the source and destination computers of that task. But, the encryption/decryption process may introduce some latency that will be noticed by some time-dependent applications. No general agreement exists on the amount of latency that security gateways introduce. If this is likely to be a factor for building your network, it's likely that many of the hardware products covered in Chapter 11, "VPN Hardware," will produce shorter latencies. The cryptographic coprocessors for routers and firewalls that we mentioned earlier will most likely keep latencies low as well.

Remote users are most likely to be affected by the tunneling protocols and encryption algorithms you pick for your VPN. In most cases, those users have nothing to rely on except their laptop to perform encryption and decryption, and their sessions on a VPN are likely to seem somewhat slower than when they don't use a VPN. The weak encryption provided by PPTP and IPSec (only when using short key lengths) might be preferable for remote users, but remember to factor in the importance of the data they're transmitting when making your decision on protocols and key lengths.

Multiplatform issues also can arise when picking the software for your remote clients. Most products support the more recent Windows operating systems (NT 4.0 and 95), for example, although not all support Windows 3.x or the Macintosh OS.

Two very important issues that need to be resolved in your VPN network design are how the network is to handle routing and name resolution. You can follow one of two directions. First, you can view the network as a single network covering all of your sites. Or, you might choose to consider each site of the VPN as a separate network, joined together by tunnels.

In the first case, you can employ full routing between the different parts of the network connected by tunnels, plus you can set up a single unified name space for the entire corporate DNS. But, your own enterprise network structure may prevent you from implementing such an approach. Much of the problem stems from allocations of IP addresses and the use of *Network Address Translation* (NAT). Companies cannot often acquire a large set of contiguous IP addresses when they want to connect to the Internet, due to the allocation procedures for different classes of IP addresses and the scarcity of IPv4 addresses on the Internet. As an alternative, they could privately assign any addresses they pleased for the internal IP networks and use NAT (see Figure 8.5) to handle translation between the private addresses and a smaller range of addresses that were allocated for public (i.e., Internet) use.

You already may see the problem this approach causes for VPNs. When you attempt to connect these sites with tunnels, it's highly likely that two (or more) networks may have the same addresses, which will break routing services and other network functions.

We'll cover NAT and address management in more detail in Chapter 13, "Security Management," but it's enough to say that there are no simple solutions for combining two or more sites that have privately allocated IP addresses that overlap.

A related issue is that of DNS. It's not unusual to shield DNS entries for internal resources from external uses, but you'll need a way to provide this information to other sites connected via your VPN tunnels. One approach is to limit the number of hosts that can be reached by other

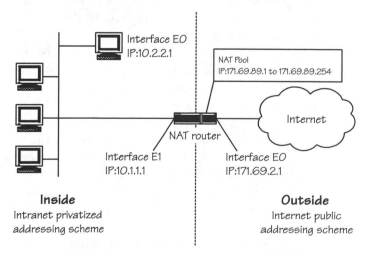

FIGURE 8.5 Example network using NAT.

parts of the VPN, but this means maintaining dual DNS entries, one set for internal site usage, the other for VPN usage. If NAT is used for translating private addresses, you may have to use DNS spoofing as well. Fortunately, some firewall and VPN products support DNS spoofing, which will make your job a little easier.

As part of the solution to potential addressing problems, particularly for larger enterprises and internetworks, you should consider your company's plans for upgrading networks to IPv6, because its large address space can solve many VPN-related problems. Demand for this next generation of IP is slowly growing, and vendors are offering a smattering of products that support IPv6. This migration is likely to be more of a long-term effort rather than something that can be accomplished within the next year. You might not be able to use IPv6 today, but it's something to keep in mind; remember that IPv6 implementations also will include built-in support for IPSec, which may simplify your deployment of client and host software later.

Security Issues

Protecting your data as it travels across a VPN is only one part of ensuring its security. VPN security design, therefore, has to be treated as part of the broader issue of corporate security policy. In general, a corporate security policy should focus on determining who has access to what resources. A good starting point is RFC 2196, the *Site Security Handbook*.

Portions of your existing corporate policy (assuming you have one) may directly impact how you handle your VPN. For instance, policies on user passwords—how often they're changed and so on—already may be enforced for remote access and can be directly translated to VPN access rights and their maintenance.

Access rights is another issue that needs to be extended for VPNs, because you'll have users gaining access to subnets and devices they probably otherwise would not see on the network. In general, a tunnel lets a user onto the network without any restricted access. Depending on which tunnel protocol and which network operating system you're using, you can allocate access rights to the tunnel's user as the tunnel is set up. For instance, many tunnel servers and security gateways use NT user domains for access control, which enables you to control access to Windows network resources. As policy-based management for all types of networks becomes more widespread, this sort of control will extend to all systems and networks.

If you want to control tunnel traffic according to source and destinations or applications, then you should design your VPN so that all decrypted incoming traffic passes through a firewall before entering the destination network. As you'll see in Chapters 10–12, some VPN products can be easily installed before the firewall to make this kind of control possible. Also, some VPN hardware products (see Chapter 11) include a firewall as part of the integrated product so that you can apply access controls as you desire.

A popular security solution for companies wanting to share some information with Internet-based users or customers, while protecting the rest of their resources, involves setting up what's often called a *demilitarized zone* (DMZ). See Figure 8.6. The DMZ is delineated by two firewalls: one between the Internet and the company's shared resources and the second located between the shared resources and the rest of the corporate network.

Servers in the DMZ act as secondary storage of data so that if they're compromised, little harm is done. For example, a Web server in the DMZ might store copies of Web pages, and the originals are located in the corporate intranet. Whenever changes to the Web pages are made, they're relayed to the DMZ Web server. If dynamic data must be passed to or from the DMZ server—from html forms, for instance—the data is processed on the DMZ server first, reducing the chances of propagating an attack and then passed to the intranet.

If a DMZ is an integral part of your corporate security, you may find yourself having to install your VPN security gateways within the DMZ. Should this be the case, the firewalls defining the DMZ will have to be reconfigured. In particular, the exterior firewall (i.e., the one between the Internet and the DMZ) will have to pass the encrypted tunnel traffic to your security gateway. The interior firewall (i.e., the one between the DMZ and the rest of your corporate network) may not need to be altered, unless you want to add new access controls for VPN traffic.

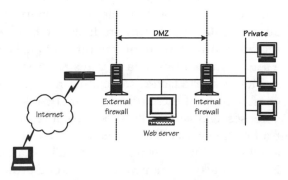

FIGURE 8.6 A sample DMZ.

Two important components of security that may be new to you as you implement a VPN are key management and digital certificates. As we've discussed in Chapters 4, "Security: Threats and Solutions," and 5, "Using IPSec to Build a VPN," key management is crucial to the proper operation of today's cryptographic systems, so much so that special procedures and protocols had to be developed. And, all the bugs have yet to be worked out, as we'll see later.

As you design your VPN, you'll have to decide how you want to exchange keys between security gateways, for example. Many of the first IPSec-compatible devices were tested using manual key exchanges, using the S/WAN-recommended file format or similar means. If your VPN has a small number of gateways, manual key exchange is still a reasonable procedure. But, you might not be able to perform all the key exchanges yourself, especially if the VPN sites are scattered around the country or the globe. In such cases, you might have to resort to secure e-mail (which may be a chicken-and-egg problem, because it, too, involves exchanging keys) or using a bonded courier to deliver the keys.

When you review the range of products in the marketplace, you'll find that some products can be centrally configured and managed, making distribution of the initial keys easier. *Keys required for subsequent sessions are usually generated from the initial set of keys.* After the keys are distributed, they should be protected from unauthorized access. In fact, anything involving a security gateway should be protected against unauthorized access. The equipment should be stored in a secure location, preferably a locked room to which only a few network managers have access. When you are comparing products, be sure that any connections, whether by LAN or modem, that are used for remote management of the gateway are strongly secured by the product—a dial-in line with password-controlled access won't do, for instance. Two-factor authentication would be preferable.

For maximum security of your VPN traffic, it's wise to implement automatic rekeying; many devices support this function. The keys used to authenticate and encrypt products can be changed according to the following rules: After a particular number of packets have been transmitted, after a set amount of time has passed since session initiation, whenever a new session is started, after some other manually set parameter is met, or a combination of these rules. Automatic rekeying helps strengthen your defenses against attackers, because it reduces the time they have to collect traffic and crack a key to read or alter your packets; it also reduces the amount of time for which a cracked key can be used. Automatic rekeying is particularly useful if you want strong protection but have to use shorter key lengths, due to export restrictions, for example.

If you recall our description of public-key cryptography in Chapter 4, one step in the process of using a public key pair is verifying the validity of the key. The accepted tool for verifying validity is the digital certificate, which is a small block of data that contains the public key and an endorsement made by someone else's digital certificate. These certificates serve to bind a public key to a named entity, either a person or a computer. If you're setting up a LAN-to-LAN VPN, then you might only be concerned with issuing certificates for the security gateways, for instance. On the other hand, any individuals wanting remote access to the VPN would probably need their own digital certificates for authentication purposes.

We'll cover more of the details of digital certificates in Chapter 13, "Security Management." Although the use of digital certificates has not yet become widespread, your company already may be using them for other, non-VPN-related uses. For instance, many Web browsers use digital certificates, particularly for secure communications with servers using the *Secure Sockets Layer* (SSL) protocol for electronic commerce. Many e-mail systems offering encryption capabilities (using S/MIME, for instance) also depend on digital certificates and the technologies used to distribute them—the *certificate authorities* (CAs) and *public key infrastructures* (PKIs). These systems will only see more use in the future.

Whether or not your VPN will be the first corporate use of digital certificates, it's important to decide on a single method for handling digital certificates. You don't want to duplicate past efforts nor unnecessarily multiply PKIs, so see how a single PKI can be used to support your VPN as well as other applications that require digital certificates or that may require them in the future. One step in the right direction is to use standards, such as the X.509v3 standard for digital certificates.

Some companies have decided that the installation and management of a PKI require more resources than they are prepared to commit. This is particularly true if they expect to issue thousands of digital certificates. This could be the case if your VPN has to support many remote users or will eventually depend on host-to-host tunnels. These companies have turned to outsourcing the key management tasks to another party, such as GTE Entrust or VeriSign.

Another factor affecting your choice of running a CA in house or outsourcing it is your plan for dealing with business partners via an extranet. An in-house CA may prove ideal for issuing digital certificates and keys to your employees, and it also may be suitable if a small number of extranet partners are involved. But, if the extranet involves larger corporate partners, these partners may have their own CAs, and you'll have to find a way of getting the CAs to work together. An outsourced CA may make this easier, but you also can choose to have your internal CA certified by another, external CA, making cross-certification and validation of digital certificates possible outside of your company (see Chapter 4).

The choice between in-house maintenance of a CA versus outsourcing this function underscores an issue that will come up again later in our discussion of ISPs: Who manages your security? Does your company feel that it alone can maintain proper security of its resources? Does it have the appropriate personnel and sufficient resources? Or, is it willing to entrust some of its security to a second party—in this case a certificate authority? Admittedly, the major CAs have spent millions of dollars and large amounts of time to protect their systems, which should make their services quite trustworthy. But, selecting either option comes down to a question of control.

One last note about key management: Be sure to include some type of key recovery mechanism when selecting a key management system. There are good reasons for having a key recovery system in place. As long as critical data is going to be encrypted using public-key systems, situations will arise in which your company may have to recover old data when the original key is no longer available. This situation might happen when employees leave the company, either voluntarily or otherwise, or when someone dies, for instance. In such cases, having a third key that can be used in place of the "lost" public key enables you to recover older protected data.

ISP Issues

It may seem obvious, but you cannot overlook the capabilities of your ISP when you're designing your VPN. After all, we've been talking solely about private networks that are using the Internet as the "plumbing" for the networks in this book. If you don't have a connection to the Internet, you can't have a VPN, at least using the definitions we've adopted for this book.

ISPs can be involved in a VPN in a number of ways. Using PPTP and L2TP for tunneling enables ISPs to offer value-added services as tunnel initiators and proxies for user authentication for your VPN. Other ISPs also are offering full-fledged outsourced VPNs, including security management and installation of the appropriate VPN equipment on your premises (see Chapter 9).

Bear in mind that your current ISP doesn't have to be your VPN provider; you can use two or more ISPs to handle your Internet traffic, and you could use one for open traffic, with a second for your encrypted traffic.

One reason for using different ISPs might be their geographical coverage. If you're designing a VPN for a multinational corporation, you may need POPs in some countries that very few ISPs service. This issue becomes more important if you're more concerned with LAN-to-LAN tunneling than remote access to a VPN. Multinational remote access to a VPN can be set more easily now, thanks to the new roaming services that have been instituted.

Basically, a roaming service lets travelers or other remote users access the Internet via a local ISP rather than dialing long distance to log on through the corporate ISP. A broker service manages the settlement charges between ISPs and provides client-based access software, including a phone book with a list of local POPs. Initial services have concentrated on PPTP and, to a lesser degree, L2F; future expansion is aimed at IPSec and L2TP.

If you have a large number of remote users to support on your VPN, then roaming services offer you a reasonable alternative to selecting only one ISP for remote access. These services also give you and the VPN users more flexibility as new sales areas and branch offices open up in previously uncovered regions.

Another step to increased flexibility, as well as reliability, is to use more than one ISP for your Internet connections, even for the main sites of your VPN. Although it doesn't happen everyday, ISPs have been known to loose Internet connectivity, sometimes for a day or so. If you're planning to transmit mission-critical data on your VPN, running all your traffic through a single ISP without any backup connection isn't wise. We'll see in the next chapter that *Service Level Agreements* (SLAs) can be negotiated with ISPs to provide refunds when service is lost, but you would rather not lose the connection in the first place.

If you're planning to use PPTP or L2TP to construct a VPN in conjunction with an ISP, then you'll need to know the capabilities of their equipment and how they handle security. (Many of questions revolving around these issues are covered in the next chapter.) If an ISP is going to maintain a proxy RADIUS server for your users, then you want to be sure that the service is secure against unauthorized access, both from outside the ISP and within the ISP—either from ISP staff or other customers of the ISP. We earlier raised the issue of who controls security, in reference to CAs and digital certificates. That question now comes up again, in the context of other forms of user authentication. The recommended approach is for your corporation to maintain a RADIUS (or similar) server for authentication of its employees and to let the ISP's proxy server obtain its database of access rights from that server.

Depending on the uses planned for your VPN, performance can have a number of meanings. At the very least, performance is providing the required bandwidth as needed, when it's needed. Many applications, such as e-mail, FTP, and Web browsing, can function properly with this minimal definition. But, if you're planning to run transactional data or real-time interactive applications over your VPN, then network latencies can become an issue as well. Many of the details surrounding SLAs and monitoring ISP performance are presented in the next chapter.

Providing quality of service on the Internet is still relatively new (see Chapter 15, "Performance Management"). In fact, it's not something you expect on many parts of the Internet and probably won't get for a few more years. ISPs willing to provide some type of QoS and bandwidth management as part of their performance guarantees will do so only for the traffic that flows on their network. That may not be a problem for your VPN if it's based on a single ISP that runs its own network and can segregate its customers' traffic from other Internet traffic.

But, if you're planning on expanding your VPN to an extranet and your applications require performance guarantees and QoS, you'll most likely be out of luck for the next few years. You could construct an extranet with guaranteed performance if you and your extranet partners are all using the same ISP. At the moment, no one has proposed a way of guaranteeing performances for traffic transmitted over multiple ISP networks. The first agreements of this kind probably will occur between large ISPs that own and control their own networks, such as AT&T and UUNET.

Planning for Deployment

Although we haven't yet discussed the details of the different devices you'll use to make your VPN an actuality—that's left to Chapters 9 through 12—you can do a few things to prepare for the installation of your VPN.

First, there's the question of the current state of your business's security. It'll do little good if you create a VPN for the secure transmission of corporate data across the Internet if you leave open other ways for attackers to acquire or alter your data. In other words, you need to make sure that your corporation is secure against outside attacks even before you open up any access via a VPN. It's a good idea to initiate a security audit of your corporate security practices, usually by an outside firm, before you install your VPN. If there are weak spots, try to correct them before your VPN is operational. (Another hint: Have these security audits performed periodically. If you don't know where to start with security audits, look at Bernstein et al., *Internet Security for Business*, John Wiley & Sons, Inc., 1996.)

Deploying the various components of your VPN can be a particularly complex task, depending on the number of sites and users comprising the VPN. As we've mentioned previously, some VPN products allow for centralized configuration of all VPN security gateways, which at least ensures that the configuration files will be correct before distribution.

As much as possible, try to treat your branch offices alike. You can use a cookie cutter approach to the VPN products for each site as well as for much of the configuration. This approach not only simplifies the deployment of the VPN, but troubleshooting as well. You may find it difficult to use this approach, however, if each of the VPN sites have very little in common regarding network hardware and capabilities and if you find yourself purchasing different VPN equipment for each site—the real world doesn't always cooperate with your plans. On the other hand, maybe you can use the VPN as an excuse for making each site's network depend on common equipment and configurations.

We've already written much about the distribution of keys and digital certificates, and we'll have more to say in later chapters, but you should consider how users will store and use their digital certificates and how that will affect deploying certificates. You might want to combine your PKI with smart-card technology to provide a personal, flexible, and secure means of identifying people and their capabilities. Some systems are already available for combining smart-card readers with desktop and portable PCs. The combination of smart cards and digital certificates may well prove popular alternatives to other token-based security systems, like SecurID, as more uses for digital certificates make their way into the mainstream.

We're firm believers in pilot projects; before you roll out a corporate-wide VPN, you should plan on trying a smaller test network. If possible, this network should still function under normal operating conditions but should not include much, if any, mission-critical information. Use this test network to work out the bugs in your configuration and management of the VPN before it becomes an integral part of the rest of the company.

It's also a good idea to change corporate traffic over to the VPN in stages. Bulk traffic, such as e-mail and file transfers, should be shifted first, while transactional and other real-time traffic should be done later once the characteristics of your VPN are known. We started this chapter with a discussion of network capacity planning and performance analysis, and we end the same way. Learn what are the effects of your VPN on your applications, and vice versa, before transferring all intersite traffic to the VPN.

Summary

VPN design needs to take into account not only security issues, but also the bandwidth and latency requirements of your applications as well as national restrictions on cryptographic key lengths.

Deciding between adding software to existing network devices, such as routers and firewalls, and purchasing new devices specifically designed for VPNs depends on the need for performance as well as cost constraints, because encryption is a computationally intensive process. Be sure to factor in the importance of the data being transmitted to determine the period over which it must be protected; not all data has to be secure for years, for instance.

Even if new VPN devices are installed, some existing services, such as authentication servers for remote users, can be adopted for use on the VPN.

One of the most important issues in deploying VPNs and the authentication of users and security gateways is the selection of the infrastructure for distributing digital certificates. Companies can choose to set up their own certificate authority in-house or outsource the operation to a recognized CA. Expect that more uses for certificate-based authentication will arise, making the certificate authority a more important part of your security system as the years pass.

Building Blocks of a VPN

A VPN consist of two main components: The Internet connectivity provided by an ISP and the hardware and software that protects your data by encrypting it for transmission over the Internet. VPN functions can be performed in firewalls, routers, and specially-designed hardware, making deployment of VPN devices relatively easy.

Since a VPN is mission-critical to your business, you should ensure the best possible performance from your ISP, by a guaranteed Service Level Agreement (SLA). While the SLA should define the expected throughput and maximum delays tolerated, you need to plan how your company will monitor network performance to ensure compliance. Also, when selecting the devices that will perform encryption and tunneling for your VPN, you should match your expected WAN throughput with the capabilities (such as speed of encryption) of the devices.

9

The ISP Connection

Whatever the design of a Virtual Private Network, its success depends greatly on one element—your *Internet Service Provider* (ISP). Because your ISP is responsible for the transmission of your data over the Internet once it leaves your sites, it's important that you have a good working relationship with an ISP that you can trust. Establishing a good working relationship with a service provider depends not only on knowing what your network needs, but also knowing what the service provider can deliver.

But, you can't run your company on gentlemen's agreements alone, so a documented agreement regarding service provider performance, reliability, and liability helps keep relations and expectations on business-like terms. These agreements, *Service Level Agreements* (SLAs), help define what both parties—your ISP and your company—expect of a VPN and, most importantly, the Internet portion of the VPN.

This chapter will cover the different aspects of an ISP's role in VPNs. We'll start out discussing the details of an ISP's capabilities for handling Internet traffic and the requirements that an ISP should be able to fulfill for VPNs. This discussion will be broken down according to the customer's desire to either outsource most, if not all, of the VPN or do most of it in-house. Then we'll go over the details of SLAs, including how they can be monitored and enforced. The last part of the chapter will include an overview of some of the current VPN services offered by ISPs and NSPs, both here in the United States and internationally.

ISP Capabilities

Before we discuss what services an ISP can provide, let's review the way that ISPs are classified according to their capabilities and hierarchy within the Internet structure.

Types of ISPs

The service providers whose networks make up part of the Internet are classified in tiers according to the capabilities of their networks and the type of Internet connectivity that they provide (see Figure 9.1).

Tier One providers, such as AT&T, GTE Internetworking, IBM, MCI, PSInet, and UUNET, own and operate private national networks with

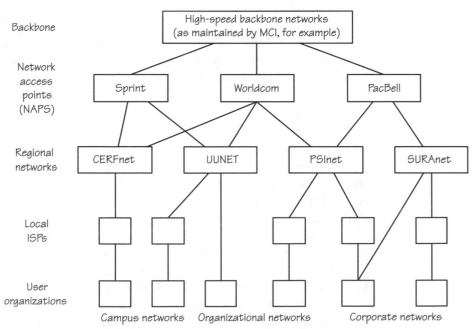

FIGURE 9.1 The hierarchy of Internet providers.

extensive national backbones, often architected like the schematic network shown in Figure 9.2. These independent networks meet and interconnect at the Internet *Network Access Points* (NAPs). In other words, the networks interconnect and exchange traffic at the NAPs to form what is essentially the Internet.

The independently created national networks set up by companies like PSInet and UUNET, among others, mostly tie into the NAPs. Some

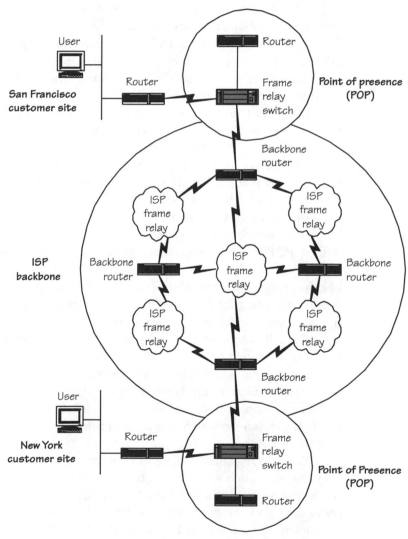

FIGURE 9.2 Typical ISP backbone design.

service providers have made their own arrangements for exchanging Internet traffic by sidestepping the NAPs, which can be bottlenecks. These *peering points* help relieve some of the load at the NAPs. The independently created national networks also give these multiservice providers an added advantage when offering services like VPNs to their customers because they can control the traffic that runs on their network and the reliability of the network better than if a series of networks were be used to handle your traffic. (We'll see later that service providers will often offer guarantees of bandwidth and latency as long as traffic is restricted to their network.)

Note that none of the Internet NAPs provide Internet connectivity to the general public or to business and industry. The NAPs are only points for the orderly exchange of traffic between those organizations that maintain extensive national backbones; a NAP is not a point-to-purchase Internet access. Additionally, connections to the Internet NAPs are made at a minimum of DS-3 speed (45 Mbps).

A Tier Two provider is a company that buys its Internet connectivity from one of the Tier One providers and then provides residential dial-up access, provides World Wide Web site hosting, or resells the bandwidth. These regional providers typically operate backbones within a state or among several adjoining states. They also may be connected to a NAP, but usually no more than one NAP.

Below Tier Two providers are the individual Internet Service Providers, which can be anything from two or three persons running a dial-up POP to much larger operations supporting as many as 100,000 dial-up customers, for example. These providers generally don't operate a backbone or even a regional network of their own. If they offer national service, they use the POPs and backbone structure of a larger backbone operator with which they're associated.

For a business with a full-time link to the Internet or an individual working at home or on the road and dialing into the Internet, the ISP's POP is an important cog in the use of the Internet. The POP is where the ISP handles the different types of media that its customers use for Internet access and from where the ISP forwards all the customer traffic to its backbone network, which connects to the rest of Internet at some point (see Figure 9.3).

Some POPs contain different equipment for each transmission media they support, such as a modem bank for dial-in sessions and CSU/DSUs for frame relay and *Digital Data Service* (DDS); other ISPs have opted to leave support for the different media to the public network, instead running a leased line to their POPs. In addition to handling different media for customer traffic, the POP includes routers and/or switches to connect

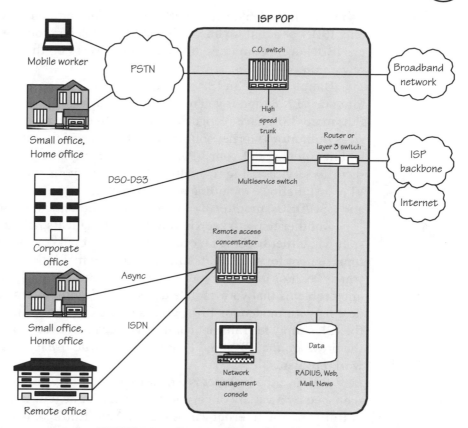

FIGURE 9.3 Schematic of a typical ISP POP.

the POP's local LAN to the rest of the ISP's network as well as network-management consoles. In some cases, the POP will include servers for hosting mail, news, and Web sites, and RADIUS authentication servers for an ISP's customers.

The fundamental service of an Internet Service Provider is connectivity to the Internet. This connectivity can take the simple form of providing dial-up access for individual users with a modem or ISDN line, or it can be dedicated lines (T1 or T3, for instance) running from your corporate LAN to the ISP's *Point-of-Presence* (POP) and then to the rest of the Internet.

The entire range of connectivity options offered by an ISP is important to your VPN design because you're likely to have a range of requirements that differ from site to site and user to user. For example, a large corporation would most likely want high bandwidth connections, such as a T3 line, for its corporate headquarters or main computing center, regional offices could get by with T1 lines, and branch offices might need only ISDN or a dial-up line with a modem. Telecommuting workers might use ISDN or modem lines at home, and workers on the road would likely rely on dial-up access.

Simply having an ISP provide the "pipes" to the Internet may suffice for your VPN design if you're planning on doing everything else in-house. But, many ISPs have recognized the benefit of offering value-added services built atop Internet connectivity. These services can make the design and maintenance of your VPN easier; for example, ISPs offer managed security services using firewalls for protecting your sites as well as full VPN installations, including all necessary CPE equipment such as routers and CSU/DSUs, monitoring software, and authentication servers.

Another thing to keep in mind is that the ISP's help desk and support staff will either become an extension of your own corporate help desk or a replacement for some of its functions as you meld the ISP's services into your VPN. For instance, you should expect the ISP's help desk to handle any problems that your mobile users and telecommuters may have when dealing with modem or ISDN access to the Internet. Plus, whether you use the ISP simply for Internet connectivity or outsource more of your VPN to the provider, the ISP should have a tiered structure for dealing with network problems.

Because the Internet is a massive conglomeration of different circuits managed by a variety of corporate and academic entities, the performance of traffic on the Internet varies greatly. Your traffic may not only be competing with other traffic for the same bandwidth or other network resources at some points in the internetwork, but it also may be subjected to delays that can affect the performance of your applications.

Even as new technologies like Gigabit Ethernet make it easier to provide more bandwidth, applications are gobbling up more bandwidth and placing restrictive demands on such data-delivery parameters as network latency and *jitter*, the variation in latency. Thus real-time data requires some kind of bandwidth reservation based on quality of service as well as priorities related to mission criticality.

With the ever-expanding move to multimedia, more applications now require control of the quality of service they receive from the networks. To support the different latency and bandwidth requirements of multimedia and other real-time applications, networks can use QoS parameters to accept an application's network traffic and prioritize traffic relative to other QoS requests from other applications. QoS provides network services that are differentiated by their bandwidth, latency, jitter, and error rates.

Even if your current application needs do not include a guaranteed latency or prioritization, keep these requirements in mind because they're likely to become more important in the future as applications change. Even though ISP treatment of QoS is in its infancy, provisioning QoS will become a fact of life among ISP offerings in the near future. We'll cover some of the details in Chapter 15, "Performance Management."

What to Expect from an ISP

If you're shopping for an ISP for your VPN, you should use a few criteria right at the beginning of the selection process before we get into more detailed requirements. Not all of you will have the same requirements of an ISP; because different businesses have different Internet requirements, they can be met by different levels of ISPs.

As for the initial screening criteria, first there's the issue of geographical coverage offered by the ISP. For instance, a multinational corporation probably would find its requirements met by a global service provider, but not by a local or regional ISP. On the other hand, a company with offices only in California or Texas might find that all its needs are met by a regional or local ISP.

Second, there's the type of access your company requires. If you're planning only a dial-in VPN, you'd like to be sure that the prospective ISP can provide both sufficient modem ports and POPs for your workers and have POPs in the areas from which your workers are likely to call. In some cases, this latter requirement is not a severe constraint: Some companies like GRIC Communications and iPass offer a roaming service that allows a series of ISPs to cooperate to offer wider dial-in access. In other words, you can have an account with one ISP but use the POPs of other ISPs in the roaming service when local coverage from your original ISP isn't available. Roaming services can be especially valuable for overseas travellers because they not only keep dial-in costs down for calls back to the United States, but also usually offer more reliable connectivity than many long-distance lines in foreign countries (even among those countries in Europe that have modern, reliable PTTs within their own country).

Third, are you planning to design and implement your VPN entirely with in-house support, or do you want to outsource some, if not all, of the VPN to a service provider? If you're planning on an IPSec-based VPN, any ISP can provide you the connectivity to the Internet that you require (assuming, of course, that they can meet your bandwidth, latency, and location requirements). Not all ISPs have the equipment to handle PPTP or L2TP systems, though. And, only a few ISPs can offer you a turnkey VPN customized to your needs, although the number is growing. We'll get into more details about outsourced VPNs later in this chapter.

Fourth, what are the future plans for your business and the VPN? If your business grows and adds more sites, can your prospective ISP accommodate your growth? Does the ISP cover the geographic areas you're expanding into? Or, perhaps you're planning to open your VPN to partners, distributors, and suppliers, forming an extranet. We'll see later in this chapter that ISP performance guarantees currently cover only traffic serviced by a single ISP and not cross-ISP traffic. If guaranteed performance is important to your partnerships and the extranet, then your choice of ISP may be influenced by which one you and your partners can use.

These initial selection criteria should help you pare down your list of possible ISPs to a select few that you can investigate in detail. The following section lists many of the details about an ISP that you should include in your investigations as you narrow down your search for the appropriate business partner for constructing your VPN.

Learning an ISP's Capabilities

This section contains a fairly extensive (although by no means exhaustive) list of issues that should be raised with any prospective ISP when setting up your VPN. If your company is like most medium- and large-sized businesses in the United States, you already have an ISP that provides you with connectivity to the Internet. If so, you might choose to quickly skim the following set of issues. On the other hand, if you're unhappy with your present ISP or plan to use a different ISP for your VPN, you probably should look over the rest of this section. Although many of the items listed here are applicable to any ISP service and not just VPNs, they do impact the provisioning of value-added services. As you'll see, only a few issues specifically address VPNs or security.

ISP INFRASTRUCTURE

Your first concern should be the ISP's network backbone, because it's going to determine how well your network traffic is handled. The best designs are a full mesh with multiple redundant paths between transfer points; redundant routers and/or switches also should be installed at each of the major transfer points in the network. Each router or switch location in the network should meet data-center quality for environmental controls, including such items as redundant backup power and air conditioning.

Maintainability is improved if standard equipment is used, not equipment that is custom-designed and may be hard to replace quickly.

Although the current state of the Internet is such that you'll receive the best VPN services from an ISP with its own national or international network, some VPNs (such as dial-in VPNs and those not requiring low latencies for their applications) can be created to handle traffic that crosses ISP boundaries. Furthermore, you may need to balance VPN traffic with other nonsecure traffic that involves your business on the same ISP, requiring that the reach of your communications involves more of the public Internet. Whatever the reason, moving beyond a single-network situation means that you should pay attention to how your ISP exchanges traffic with other providers. For instance, does the ISP's network extend to all the major NAP peering points and does the ISP have full peering rights with the other major providers?

NETWORK PERFORMANCE AND MANAGEMENT

Aside from the backbone's design, you should understand how the service provider has provisioned bandwidth and how your bandwidth requirements will be treated. For example, how much bandwidth has the service provider already committed to other customers? Also, is the bandwidth you require maintained throughout the system? For example, if you buy a 10-Mbps circuit, does the traffic become aggregated onto higher bandwidth lines? Is the bandwidth always available? Is it available as a burst speed, which lets you occasionally transmit more traffic than the average load? Ask whether the service provider publishes statistics on the network's traffic loads as well as its reliability statistics.

It's a fact of life that all ISPs occasionally have outages. Find out how long an ISP's outages have lasted and what percentage of the systems and users were affected.

Quality of Service or guarantees of prioritized delivery of different traffic classes can be important when you want to ensure that important traffic always makes it through your network, even if other, lower-priority, traffic doesn't. But, providing QoS on the Internet is a relatively new service that's still largely being handled as an experiment by ISPs. Again, an ISP can more readily guarantee QoS for traffic that is transmitted only on its own network rather than over multiple ISPs. That will no doubt change in the future as policies for defining QoS among ISPs are ironed out. But, if you're interested in differentiating your corporate traffic for different delivery priorities, you should check whether the prospective ISP offers any QoS guarantees.

Proper operation of a service provider depends on an efficient *Network Operations Center* (NOC) that is fully staffed 24 hours a day, 7 days a week (24 × 7). Again, like the transfer points of the network, the NOC should be housed in an environmentally sound facility, including backup power and air-conditioning as well as earthquake protection. It should also be a secure facility and have written plans for dealing with detection of security breaches and procedures for dealing with breaches. A standard system, such as HP Open View or Sun's SunNet Manager, is a good start for monitoring the network but it's also nice to see whether the NOC has developed other tools for monitoring and troubleshooting. Check and see whether the facility has undergone any form of recognized audit.

CONNECTIVITY OPTIONS

Most ISPs specializing in business-to-business services sell a full range of connectivity options, with bandwidth products ranging from 56 Kbps through T3 speeds being common. When planning for a particular bandwidth connection, determine how the connection is actually handed off to you. For example, some ISPs supply a T1 line in an Ethernet format, allowing easy integration into your network. Others present the T1 link in a raw serial format, requiring gateway equipment to transform it into a protocol you can use.

To ensure that your connection has an adequate continuous bandwidth throughout the network system, ask your ISP for a network schematic, with bandwidths listed on each network segment.

Confirm what is included in the standard service price. Some ISPs require that you purchase the routers and CSU/DSU devices, while others will supply and manage them for you. The ISP-supplied equipment normally is configured, monitored, and diagnosed for problems via the ISP's NOC.

Most ISPs have three costs in their access service: installation charges, basic connection bandwidth service you subscribe to, and the local loop charges required to connect your location to the ISP's *Point-of-Presence* (POP).

Find out what assistance the ISP will provide in addressing user connection issues, especially for your dial-in users. Also determine whether they have a tiered support system for their help desk.

SECURITY AND VPNS

On the security side of things, a professional security officer should be a member of the staff, and the ISP should have a written set of security policies. The ISP should have active monitoring tools protecting its own systems and have experts on the staff capable of configuring firewalls and monitoring devices.

Firewall-management services should include firewall selection, installation and setup according to your policy criteria, as well as round-the-clock monitoring of the firewall for attempted security breaches. An ISP should have a written escalation procedure for handling security breaches and guaranteed response times for emergency security breach notification. Reports should cover inbound traffic with attempted break-ins as well as outbound sites visited. Because the service provider will be responsible for the firewall, he should be responsible for updating the software when new vendor releases come out; this should be handled automatically whenever possible. But, because your company is responsible for setting the policies that the firewall is enforcing, you should have the freedom to periodically change the policy rules.

Turning to VPNs, the details of the ISP's operations that you'll need to know will depend on how much of the VPN you want the ISP to handle. In other words, if the ISP is simply providing the pipe, many issues surrounding encryption keys and certificate authorities aren't pertinent. If the ISP is to handle a dial-in VPN for you, then questions about RADIUS proxy servers and authentication updates become more important.

Some of the important ISP issues you should resolve include: The encryption algorithms supported by the ISP's system, whether the system can switch between algorithms automatically, whether the system conforms to IPSec, and whether the ISP uses a system that is approved for use and export outside the United States. If you're going to use a system that follows IPSec protocols, then you should determine whether key exchanges are only handled manually or if they can be done automatically and how rekeying is handled (automatic rekeying is preferred).

Authenticating legitimate users of your VPN is always important, but the ISP's role in authentication is most important when you're supporting dial-in users, say with PPTP or L2TP as we discussed in Chapters 6 and 7. In such cases, you'll want to know what types of authentication the ISP supports. If you plan on using RADIUS, for example, then will the ISP's server act as a proxy server to your master RADIUS server? The ultimate management of security rights should rest in your company's hands, not those of the ISP. Even if you outsource your entire VPN to a service provider, you should determine and manage the access rights of your employees.

If you choose to use digital certificates to authenticate users and devices, you might want to use the ISP as a *certificate authority* (CA) for managing the certificates. Certificate management would include issuing the certificates and managing revocation lists, as well as maintaining a certificate server for verification of the certificates. Another option is to outsource the certificate management to another firm, other than the ISP. The issues for evaluating certificate management capabilities are the same regardless of the type of firm being reviewed.

If the ISP or another service company acts as a certificate authority, check to see whether your company can act as a backup or concurrent CA to further guard against failures. Be sure that the ISP treats the maintenance of its certificate server with the same care as you'd expect for other crucial network resources. In other words, the certificate server should be located in a secure environment that includes backup power and backup data facilities (usually located at another site).

We've already mentioned in other chapters that encryption methods can have an adverse effect on throughput because they're computationally intensive. Software-based encryption can often be slower than hardware-based encryption, for example, and neither may be able to keep up with the demands of a high-bandwidth pipe. Find out how the ISP implements encryption and what's the maximum throughput the system can handle; ask for some benchmark data.

Security breaches and breakdowns can happen at any time. Check with the ISP to determine whether the NOC provides around-the-clock monitoring of the entire encryption system. Also find out who's responsible for changing any system firmware—you or the NOC?

One of the advantages of a VPN is supposed be its flexibility; you should be able to easily and quickly add new sites to your VPN, for example. Find out how easy it is to add offices to a VPN. How long does it take for the ISP to add a new site? Are there any written guarantees on maximum times for establishing a new link?

Even though one of your primary concerns in designing a VPN is securing all of its traffic, you also might want to let your users communicate in the clear with other sites that are not a part of the VPN. See whether the ISP's architecture allows that; if so, can users distinguish between plaintext and secured communications easily, and can they switch between the two modes easily?

As always, reports and accounting are important to monitoring the VPN. See whether the ISP provides throughput reports for VPN traffic, and with what frequency (daily, weekly, monthly?). What type of accounting and billing reports does the ISP offer? Does the ISP provide reports on a user-by-user basis or site-by-site basis, for example?

Service Level Agreements

Whenever you're planning to outsource part of your network's operations to another firm, you need some way of ensuring that your expectations regarding network performance, maintenance, and problem resolution are met. An increasingly popular method for documenting your expectations and what a service provider is willing to provide is the *Service Level Agreement* (SLA). Service Level Agreements are a relatively new development in the telecommunications world. SLAs originally were designed for private voice networks and later extended to frame relay data services. Now we're seeing SLAs applied to the world of Internet VPNs, with good reason—everyone needs a way of determining what kind of performance guarantees they're getting for their VPN dollar.

The SLAs that document service-level guarantees have one main purpose: They help keep conflicts between you and your service provider to a minimum by setting reasonable expectations of service. SLAs benefit you, the client, by providing effective grading criteria and protection from poor service. They benefit the service provider by providing a way of ensuring that expectations are set correctly and will be judged fairly. Remember, SLAs include some kind of monetary reimbursement for lost or poor service, but that's a last resort; you'd really rather have good service than compensation for poor service.

Three basic items should be covered in every SLA: availability, effective throughput, and delay. Other items to consider include the mean time to respond to problems and the mean time to repair or restore service.

Network availability is a simple measure of the uptime of the network links available to you, complicated only by the fact that it's measured over all your sites. If you measured network availability over a month's time, the formula would look like this:

$$\frac{(24 \text{ hours} \times \text{days in month} \times \text{number of sites}) - \text{network outage time}}{(24 \text{ hours} \times \text{days in month} \times \text{number of sites})}$$

Even for so simple a measure as network availability, check to see what's included in the service provider's definition. Availability guarantees should include all components of the provider's network, the local loop to the network, and any CPE equipment provided by the service provider (such as a CSU/DSU and router). Excluded items may include a customer-provided CSU/DSU, router, or other access device; the local loop when provided by the customer; network downtime caused by the carrier's scheduled maintenance; customer-induced outages; dial-in links; and *acts of god*.

Note that there's an important distinction between network-based availability and site-based availability. For a network consisting of 10 sites, an average network availability of 99.5 percent would allow 36 total hours of downtime in a 30-day month. If the SLA is written around a site-based availability instead of being network-based, then any one site can be down for only 3.6 hours in the month. The distinction can be very important when computing downtime.

When dealing with measurements of throughput, traffic load and delay should be measured when the impact is at its highest (i.e., at times of peak traffic load). Because service providers will often exclude certain data, such as data loss during provider maintenance, dial-up lines, or new circuits added during the month, be sure that you understand which data has been included in any measurement so that your own cross-check measurements will correspond to those performed by the service provider.

Unfortunately, as this book was being written, no standards had been created for Internet SLAs, so you'll have to compare what each ISP offers. Even in the frame-relay world, where SLAs are a more mature feature, no standards exist, although many of the metrics quoted in SLAs are the same from provider to provider.

Any of the SLAs currently offered by service providers covers only single-ISP traffic, because that's really the only traffic that the service provider can hope to control. It'll probably be some time before we see SLAs that cover multiple-ISP traffic, because both policies and technologies have to be developed further before the ISPs can routinely work together on guaranteeing reserved resources that affect such things as latency and other QoS parameters. To start, all service providers will have to agree on how to measure availability, delay, and packet loss.

Many service providers are now offering SLAs for their services, but most of these SLAs are not negotiable unless your company is linking more than one or two sites; frame-relay carriers are usually willing to negotiate when a customer has 10 or more sites, and this rule-of-thumb probably is applicable to ISPs as well. But, whatever you do, if you're in the position to negotiate an SLA, don't attempt to negotiate unless you have some background on your network's performance and needs and what level of WAN service is needed for your users.

Preparing for an SLA

As you prepare your company for a Service Level Agreement, you can follow some steps to see that you get the best possible SLA. (These steps are based on similar ones detailed for frame-relay SLAs in a white paper developed by TeleChoice and Visual Networks.)

1. Continuously determine what WAN service levels are needed.
2. When service levels are established, verify them. You need to monitor performance in real-time, review historical performance, and assess any quality-affecting trends that you find.
3. Baseline your network. Understand your applications, peak times, and areas of concentration.
4. Negotiate SLAs if at all possible. Read the fine print and do the calculations. If the negotiated network availability guarantee is 99.5 percent, how many hours of down-time does that mean for the network per month?
5. Formulate a plan for monitoring your service provider.
6. Analyze your network's performance and reliability on a weekly basis.
7. Compare your own measurements of the network's statistics with your service provider's reports every month.

Monitoring ISP Performance

Whether you accept a standard ISP-provided SLA or spend a great deal of effort negotiating a custom SLA, an SLA will mean little if you don't have some means of monitoring the service levels specified in the SLA.

A network management system has many components, as shown in Figure 9.4, but four are particularly important for verifying your provider's performance:

1. Monitoring devices located at the edge of the provider's network.
2. A database to gather information on performance.
3. Applications designed to analyze data and issue reports specific to each customer's use of the network.
4. Web-accessible HTML versions of the reports.

A few key implementation issues have a direct impact on the usefulness of SLAs to the network manager. The first issue is where the measurements are taken: end-to-end or just within the ISP's network cloud (see Figure 9.5). The local loop can have a profound impact on network perfor-

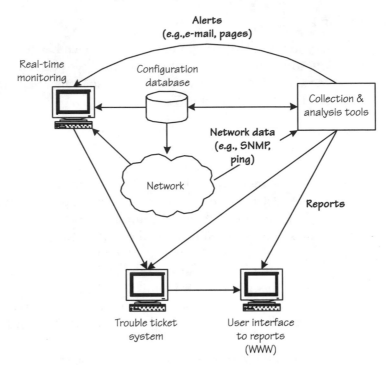

FIGURE 9.4 Network management and monitoring.

mance, but it is ignored in a switch-to-switch implementation. Performance measurements and troubleshooting must be performed end-to-end.

The second issue is utilizing a measurement system that is independent of the network you are measuring. Use an objective system that is not biased towards either switch or router architectures. Also keep in mind that how this information is presented is almost as important as the information itself.

Agreeing on definitions of measured parameters and how they're measured is an important task, but one that's not easy to accomplish, particularly because there's no standardization of these metrics among ISPs. Although it'll be some time before standardized metrics for IP network performance and availability are agreed upon, check out the work of the IETF's working group on *Internet Provider Performance Metrics* (IPPM) to see the latest efforts.

Many of the service providers offering guaranteed service will often locate measurement devices at your CPE. For comparison's sake, you should try to locate your own measuring devices in parallel with those installed by your ISP. You also may find that, before long, ISPs offer direct

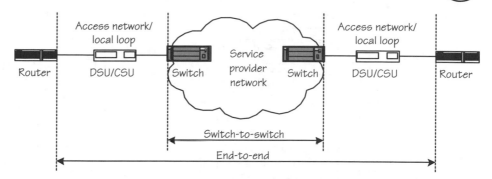

FIGURE 9.5 Measurement areas for SLAs.

connections between their management and monitoring environment and customer-management environments (see Figure 9.6), allowing customers direct access to the data that relates to their VPN.

Just as there are no standards for Internet SLAs and performance metrics, there's no standard format for the reports that ISPs provide to show that they're complying with an SLA. Whenever possible, see that the reports are delivered regularly, perhaps every week, that they contain information on any gaps the ISP may have had in gathering the data, and that they include an explanation of the process for gathering the data. Their interpretation of the data is also welcome, especially if it includes any warnings about possible future degradation of performance before users are affected.

There are more than 4,500 Internet Service Providers in the United States. Obviously, attempting to describe their services and fee structures in any detail on an individual basis is beyond the scope of this book. Nor would it necessarily provide timely information for your benefit because mergers and changing technologies keep the market in near-constant flux. If you're shopping for an ISP, a good place to start looking for likely candidates is the *Directory of Internet Service Providers* published by Boardwatch Magazine at different times throughout the year, which provides a fairly complete listing; also check out the Boardwatch Web site at www.boardwatch.com and TheList at thelist.internet.com. Then apply the selection criteria we've listed in this chapter to help select an ISP that will meet your needs.

In-House or Outsourced VPNs?

As we mentioned in Chapter 8, "Designing Your VPN," part of the VPN design process is to decide how much of the implementation effort is to remain in-house and how many tasks are outsourced to the service

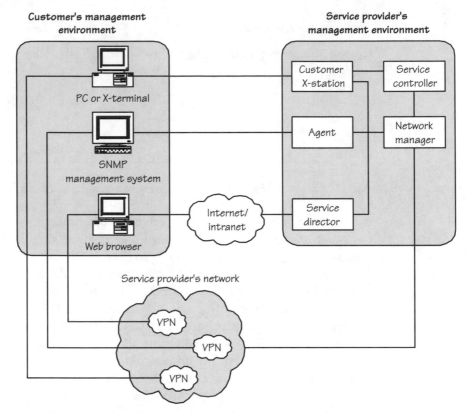

FIGURE 9.6 Integrating corporate and ISP network management.

provider (see Figure 9.7). Obviously, the more of the VPN operations that you outsource to your ISP, the stronger your need for an SLA.

There are a variety of reasons for outsourcing your VPN. For instance, you may not have enough staff to maintain the CPEs and manage security. Or, you may find that the cost of maintaining your own remote access servers and modem banks is prohibitive and you would be better served with a dial-in VPN.

As Figure 9.7 illustrates, there's no simple dividing line between an in-house VPN and an outsourced one. You'll find that ISPs are willing to offer a variety of services that can be tailored to your needs, ranging from straight connectivity to full installation, configuration, and management of your VPN.

Consider two key areas of operational requirements when dividing the responsibilities between the service provider and your company: administration and configuration management.

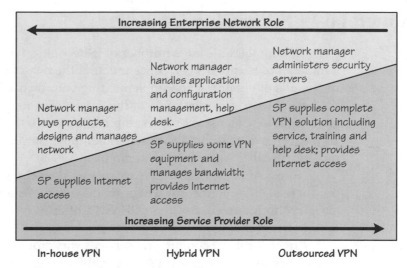

FIGURE 9.7 Outsource efforts versus in-house.

Administrative requirements include such items as account management, help desk, and troubleshooting assistance. Just as important is how you'll coordinate support between the provider and your enterprise. As corporations and service providers move into the shared network architecture that characterizes VPNs, it will be important to create an effective support chain that permits the two-way flow of information.

Another administrative factor to consider is managed access, or the management architecture that will support the public architecture of the Internet and mediate the interconnection between the provider's network and your private enterprise networks. Managed access has a role to play in determining both where monitoring tools and servers are located and how problems are resolved. Finally, there are various billing, usage tracking, and analysis factors to consider. For example, dial-up access servers should allow both enterprise accounts and/or user accounts to be debited for their access time. Network utilization reports should be accessible electronically and dynamically (preferably via the Web); allowing for custom-built reports is also a useful option.

Under configuration management, the key task is that of managing security. Under all circumstances, your corporation should hold primary responsibility for the policy and configuration of security services.

Commercial VPN Providers

Even though there's a huge number of ISPs, only a few are prepared to handle an outsourced VPN. Since much of the rest of this book is about the details of designing and implementing your own VPN, this seems like the best place to describe some of the typical outsourced VPN services that are available. This list is only a sampling, although the VPN market is young, it is growing rapidly as both potential customers and service providers realize what they may gain from VPNs.

Note that many of the services are based on firewalls, often with product-specific client software for mobile users. Figure 9.8 sketches a typical VPN architecture, based on UUNET's offerings, which we'll describe later in the section.

Prices for these commercial services vary from $750 to $5,000 per month per site, depending on such variables as the speed of the connection, the hardware installed at the site, the desired network availability and latency, and, in some cases, the strength of security desired and the number of remote users.

ANS VPDN Services

Advanced Network Services (ANS) has been offering its *Virtual Private Data Network* (VPDN) service to corporations for a few years, using its own proprietary encryption and tunneling technologies. The VPDN services include SureRemote for remote dial-in access, InterManage for managed security, and InterLock for firewalls.

ANS' proprietary system uses 128-bit RC2 for encryption at domestic sites, but also offers 64-bit RC4 for either domestic or foreign sites. Tunneling is accomplished via a proprietary system based on UDP, and key management and exchange is performed via a proprietary extension to the *Open Shortest Path First* (OSPF) routing protocol. With changes in the market and technology, ANS has announced plans to support open standards as they're finalized, which includes IPSec and digital certificates, perhaps before the end of 1998.

Monitoring and management of the VPN is handled through the ANS Network Operations Center located in Ann Arbor, Michigan. Reports delivered on a weekly basis include bandwidth usage, security logs, and dial-in line availability.

ANS's Service Level Agreement commits to 99.5 percent availability for each site connected to the VPDN, with a network latency of 70 milliseconds or less. This availability covers the CPE at each customer location,

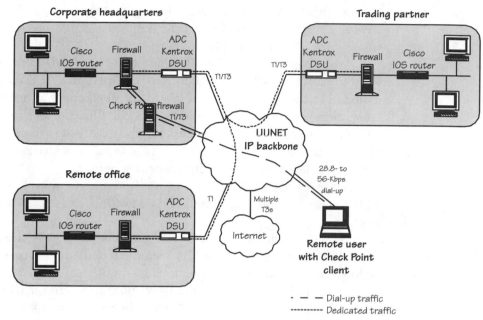

FIGURE 9.8 Typical commercial VPN architecture.

the local loop, and the router configuration. In an effort to promote the flexibility of VPNs and accommodate new sites, ANS promises to turn on your VPDN within 32 business days; this process includes hardware procurement, on-site installation, and end-to-end network testing. This time period is measured from the day the contract is signed to the day the sites are reviewed.

AT&T WorldNet VPN

AT&T first started offering its WorldNet VPN services in late 1997. The network includes more than 300 POPs and 800/888 service for dial-in access, with international access (dial-in or ISDN) in 35 countries.

The first two bundles offered in WorldNet VPN are a firewall-based service, using Check Point Software's Firewall-1 running on Sun's Netra servers, and a dial-in service using Bay Networks' Instant Internet Access Server with a built-in firewall. Like many of the other services profiled in this section, AT&T can manage the firewalls for the customer or let the customer manage the firewalls themselves. AT&T also will arrange to manage any other optional network equipment, such as routers and CSU/DSUs, or deploy Cisco routers for its customers as needed, upon request.

As this book went to press, AT&T had plans to expand its WorldNet VPN offerings to include IPSec tunneling with digital certificates as well as support for PPTP and L2TP.

WorldNet VPN uses RADIUS based on Novell NDS servers for authentication via CHAP for dial-in users. Proxy RADIUS servers weren't included in the initial rollout of WorldNet VPN, but they are planned for a later release, perhaps by the middle of 1998. Closed user groups also can be defined to restrict dial-in access for groups of users to particular sites. The firewalls are configured to protect internal IP addresses via NAT and include packet filters to prevent address spoofing.

The WorldNet VPN system is monitored and maintained on a full 24×7 basis. Remote users can access a hotline for support at any time of any day.

AT&T includes a Service Level Agreement as part of the service contract. The main points of the SLA include: if dedicated access connection is down for 10 minutes or more during any single day, AT&T will credit the customer for 5 percent of the monthly connection charge (up to a maximum of 25 percent in one month, with the annual maximum credit no more than one full month of service); network uptime is guaranteed to be at least 99.7 percent; and the network latency will be 150 milliseconds or better between any two AT&T-managed customer sites.

For customers who purchase optional router service, the end-to-end guarantee covers the total AT&T IP backbone, the access router, and the local access service that connects the customer's premises to AT&T. Without the router option, the guarantee covers the AT&T IP backbone from entry port to exit port.

CompuServe IP Link

CompuServe may be well-known for its international bulletin board services and dial-up Internet access for individuals, but its Network Services Division also offers VPN services for corporate clients, called IP Link and IP Link Plus.

IP Link and IP Link Plus are aimed primarily at dial-in VPNs and only differ from each other in the number of users they support; IP Link is limited to 100 users, while IP Link Plus covers businesses seeking to support more than 100 users.

IP Link uses a Cisco router at the customer's site and leverages CompuServe's extensive network of POPs to provide dial-up access for VPN users. Mobile users are required to have a PPP client on their computer because IP Link is based on L2TP.

CompuServe uses its own authentication system, the CompuServe Authentication Service, which can be configured for event, challenge-response, or time-based authentication. Event and challenge-response systems are based on Secure Computing's SafeWord system, which also allows use of standard authentication protocols like TACACS+ and RADIUS. The time-based system uses Security Dynamics' ACE/Server as an authentication server and SecurID cards as password generators on the user's computer. VPN traffic is encrypted using the DES algorithm.

GTE Internetworking

The VPN services offered by GTE Internetworking also are based around managed firewall services. This service, called Site Patrol, can be set up with either the Gauntlet firewall from Network Associates Inc. or Firewall-1 from Check Point Software. To accommodate dial-up users, GTE Internetworking uses V-ONE's SmartGate product in conjunction with the site's firewall; SmartGate can be used for authentication, encryption, and authorization of remote users.

Geographic coverage includes 550 local dial-in numbers in the United States, with 240 locations scattered throughout the United States and 79 countries around the world.

Site Patrol's managed firewall services for the VPN include 24 × 7 security monitoring and assistance, and a predefined, three-stage escalation procedure for security breaches. Policies for dealing with security events are worked out as a collaborative effort between GTE security personnel and the customer's staff.

One of the unique features of Site Patrol is that it's not restricted to traffic carried only by GTE Internetworking. Even for cases in which connectivity is provided by an ISP other than GTE Internetworking, the Site Patrol service monitors security and pinpoints security breaches on the other networks.

Summary reports of usage, traffic, and security incidents are delivered to customers on a monthly basis. In addition, GTE Internetworking maintains an archive of historical data that the customer can access to review past performance or incidents to review and formulate new policies when needed.

InternetMCI VPN

MCI (now a part of Worldcom) offers a firewall-based VPN service called InternetMCI VPN, which also supports dial-in access via a firewall-specific client. MCI also can secure corporate data at each site with its managed firewall services, which includes installation, configuration, and monitoring of each site's firewalls.

MCI employs the Firewall-1 product from Check Point Software for both its managed firewall and VPN services. Firewall-1 offers users IPSec with either manual key exchange or Sun's SKIP automatic key exchange, as well as a proprietary encryption scheme called FWZ. More details on Firewall-1 will be presented in Chapter 10, "Firewalls and Routers."

The remote client, Firewall-1 SecuRemote, also is provided by MCI for mobile users wanting dial-in access to corporate sites protected by Firewall-1. User authentication can be based on one-time passwords using S/Key, the SecurID token cards from Security Dynamics, the user's operating system password, or a RADIUS account.

As part of its support for mobile users, MCI maintains a global directory of dial-in numbers that users can access from any country that MCI services. InternetMCI VPN support is handled on a 24 × 7 basis, including coverage of security and global dial-in access problems.

InternetMCI's help desk support can be configured in one of two ways. If your company wants to maintain its own help desk for VPN support, then MCI will provide support directly to your network managers only. On the other hand, if you don't want to provide in-house support for VPN users, then InternetMCI will offer help desk support to all of your users.

Clients can set up and administer user accounts for their VPN via a Web-based interface.

UUNET ExtraLink

UUNET (also a part of Worldcom) offers its ExtraLink and ExtraLink Remote VPN services based on encrypting routers rather than firewalls. Data within corporate sites is protected by Check Point's Firewall-1, which is managed by UUNET as part of the service. ExtraLink Remote enables mobile users to dial into the VPN via UUNET's worldwide network of more than 845 POPs.

Each site must have a Cisco router installed, because traffic is encrypted by the 56-bit DES algorithm that ships with Cisco's IOS. Access lists also can be created on each router to block sites from communicating with each other, if necessary. The Firewall-1, also installed at each VPN site, is used to handle user authentication; remote clients use Check Point's SecuRemote client software to access the VPN.

UUNET also installs a PC-based network management system as part of each site's CPE. The system monitors performance by collecting packet throughput information and relating that information to a central UUNET management site. Reports on performance and availability are provided to customers on a monthly basis.

UUNET's Service Level Agreement promises 99.6 percent availability for VPNs consisting of 3 to 5 sites and 99.9 percent availability for VPNs that consist of 12 sites or more. Latency is guaranteed to be 150 milliseconds or better. If UUNET misses the guarantee in a month, the company promises to refund 25 percent of the total network charge.

Other VPN Providers

The number of VPN service providers is likely to grow as this book goes to press. Some of the current providers we haven't covered in detail include the following:

> Concentric Network Corp., whose Enterprise VPN uses VPNet Technologies' VPLink products for hardware encryption at each LAN site
>
> Netcom On-line Communication Services Inc., which uses Livingston's IRX Firewall Router and Milkyway's Black Hole firewall as part of its NETCOMplete for Business service
>
> Pilot Network Services Inc., with its Secure Road Warrior service, which includes 128-bit key encryption
>
> TCG CERFnet, whose Enterprise-Quality VPN offers IPSec tunnel mode and either 4-Mbps or 10-Mbps encryption devices

Future Trends in ISPs

Internet Service Providers in general are looking at value-added services like VPNs as a way to expand their business and get new corporate customers. This shift towards managed services over the Internet means that the ISPs have to deploy more intelligence at their network's edge (i.e., the interface between the customer's LAN and the ISP) and that they have to maintain closer relations with their customers, acting more as partners than simply a business providing a service.

Most of the VPN services offered by ISPs today should be considered first-generation VPNs. Look to the future for improved handling of different classes of traffic, either through classes of service or other QoS approaches such as *ReSource reserVation Protocol* (RSVP) over IP or ATM's built-in QoS classes. As devices become available for automatic mapping of RSVP classes to ATM classes, expect ISPs to deploy them as part of their effort to provide QoS services.

Also look for ISPs to come together over the next few years and reach agreement on how to measure network availability and latency so that SLAs can be extended to traffic that spans multiple ISPs. Both this issue and that of QoS support depends on the ISPs cooperating on various issues, relating to both technologies and policies. It'll happen, but not overnight. Both the work of the IPPM working group to create standard metrics for network performance and efforts by the *Automotive Industry Action Group* (AIAG) to qualify ISPs for what may be the world's largest extranet are leading the charge forward.

Summary

The ISP is an important cog in the design and success of your VPN. The design of your VPN will determine the involvement of your ISP and may limit the ISP to simply providing the pipe to the Internet or might utilize the ISP as a full-fledged designer and maintainer of an outsourced VPN.

When evaluating an ISP for your VPN, you should consider many details, but they generally fall into the following categories: ISP infrastructure, network performance and management, connectivity options, and security.

As you plan the relationship between your company and an ISP for the construction of your VPN, look at using a Service Level Agreement (SLA) to set expectations for the network's performance and how the ISP will handle troubleshooting and network repairs, among other issues of mutual concern. If you do use a SLA, keep in mind that you should track your ISP's performance in parallel with the provider's own measurement systems in order to ensure that the terms of the SLA are being met.

If you choose to outsource your VPN to a service provider, a growing number of companies are capable of doing the job, including ANS, AT&T WorldNet, internetMCI, GTE Internetworking, and UUNET, among others.

10

Firewalls and Routers

After you have a connection to the Internet, the important network devices for your VPN are the ones that control the access to your protected LAN from an external, Internet-based source—the security gateways as we've called them in past chapters. The external source might be another of your corporate LANs tunneling to your site, a mobile worker with a laptop using an ISP-created tunnel, or a business partner tunneling through the Internet to your LAN. Ideally, VPN devices should be able to handle all of these situations equally well; many do, but not all are equally adept at handling the different connectivity situations.

Just as the market definition of VPNs has been fairly confusing, so too has been the classification of the hardware and software required for creating Internet VPNs. Each vendor has his own idea of what a VPN is and how his products fit into the scheme of things (and some of them are right!).

Since each vendor has his own idea of what a VPN device is, classifying VPN hardware and software can be somewhat problematic. As this market begins to mature, we're seeing not only new classes of products, but also a move towards integrating many of what had been individual

VPN devices into a single product. This integration inevitably leads to the time-honored argument of whether buying *best-of-breed* individual products or an integrated solution is a better course of action. The information in this and following chapters should help you determine whether modular or integrated solutions will best meet your needs.

VPN hardware and software can be placed at various locations in the network. Consider for the moment how the corporate site of your VPN would be connected to the Internet via an ISP (see Figure 10.1). Starting at the link from the ISP's POP, you would have a CSU/DSU followed by a router, a firewall, and then the corporate LAN. VPN devices can be placed at various locations along this path from ISP to corporate LAN.

Recall that a full-fledged VPN depends on encryption, authentication, and tunneling services. Devices that add these services can be inserted between the CSU/DSU and the router or between the router and the firewall. Other products offer VPN services as part of either the firewall or the router. Some products integrate all of the network services between the ISP and your LAN, bundling WAN links, routing, firewalls, and VPN services into a single device. Lastly, some of the Network Operating Systems (NOS) such as NT Server and NetWare are integrating VPN support into their software.

To start with, we'll concentrate on using firewalls or routers to create VPNs in this chapter, then go on to dedicated VPN hardware, including stand-alone encryptors and integrated devices, in the next chapter. Chapter 12, "VPN Software," will focus on how NOSs and other software have evolved to support VPNs.

A Brief Primer on Firewalls

Firewalls have long been used to protect LANs from other parts of an IP internetwork by controlling access to resources on the basis of packet type, application type, and IP address. Deployment of firewalls has increased

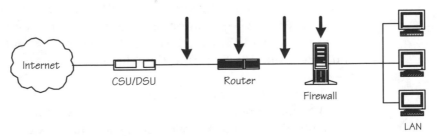

FIGURE 10.1 Locations for VPN functions.

> ## Firewalls and Security Policies
>
> A firewall is an integral part of your organization's security policy, because it determines what traffic passes between your internal networks and the Internet. (Firewalls also may be used to protect sensitive or restricted subnets from the rest of your corporate network.) In addition to your firewalls, the corporate security policy should include password policies for sensitive systems, data encryption, data backup, and user account management.

tremendously since the Internet has become more commercialized and as businesses seek to attach their networks to the Internet. If your corporate network is connected to the Internet, you probably already have at least one firewall to control traffic from the Internet.

Before we discuss how firewalls can be used to support VPNs, let's spend a few pages reviewing some of the salient features of firewalls. If you're already familiar with firewalls, you might choose to skip the rest of this section and go right to the section on firewalls and VPNs.

Types of Firewalls

There are three main classes of firewalls: packet filters, application and circuit gateways (*proxies*), and stateful inspection (or smart filter) firewalls.

PACKET FILTERS

Packet filtering firewalls were the first generation of firewalls. Packet filters track the source and destination address of IP packets permitting packets to pass through the firewall based on rules that the network manager has set (see Figure 10.2).

Two advantages of packet filter firewalls are that they are fairly easy to implement and they're transparent to the end users, unlike some of the other firewall methods we'll discuss shortly. However, even though packet filters can be easy to implement, they can prove difficult to configure properly, particularly if a large number of rules have to be generated to handle a wide variety of application traffic and users.

Packet filtering often doesn't require a separate firewall because it's often included in most TCP/IP routers at no extra charge. Of course, if

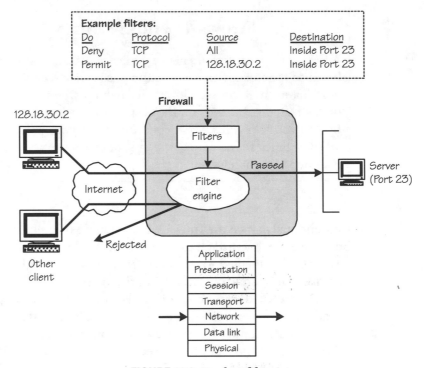

FIGURE 10.2 Packet filtering.

you're planning to use packet filtering in a router as part of your security policy, you should ensure that the router itself is secure.

But, packet filtering is not the best firewall security you can get. One of its deficiencies is that filters are based on IP addresses, not authenticated user identification. Packet filtering also provides little defense against man-in-the-middle attacks (see Chapter 4, "Security: Threats and Solutions,") and no defense against forged IP addresses. Also, packet filtering depends on IP port numbers, which isn't always a reliable indicator of the application in use; protocols like *Network File System* (NFS) use varying port numbers, making it difficult to create static filtering rules to handle their traffic.

Packet filters can be used as a part of your VPN, because they can limit the traffic that passes through a tunnel to another network, based on the protocol and direction of traffic. For example, you could configure a packet filter firewall to disallow FTP traffic between two networks while allowing HTTP and SMTP traffic between the two, further refining the granularity of your control on protected traffic between sites.

APPLICATION AND CIRCUIT PROXIES

Since they're based on address information, packet filters look exclusively at some of the lower layers of the OSI model. Better, more secure firewalls can be designed if they examine all layers of the OSI model simultaneously. This principle led to the creation of the second generation of firewalls: application and circuit proxies. These firewalls enable users to utilize a proxy to communicate with secure systems, hiding valuable data and servers from potential attackers.

The proxy accepts a connection from the other side and, if the connection is permitted, makes a second connection to the destination host on the other side. The client attempting the connection is never directly connected to the destination. Because proxies can act on different types of traffic or packets from different applications, a proxy firewall (or *proxy server*, as it's often called) is usually designed to use proxy agents, in which an agent is programmed to handle one specific type of transfer, say FTP traffic or TCP traffic. The more types of traffic that you want to pass through the proxy, the more proxy agents need to be loaded and running on the machine.

Circuit proxies focus on the TCP/IP layers, using the network IP connection as a proxy (see Figure 10.3). Circuit proxies are more secure than packet filters because computers on the external network never gain information about internal network IP addresses or ports. A circuit proxy is typically installed between your network router and the Internet, communicating with the Internet on behalf of your network. Real network addresses can be hidden because only the address of the proxy is transmitted on the Internet.

Circuit proxies do not examine application data; application proxies, which we'll get to next, do that. When a circuit proxy establishes a circuit between a user and the destination, the proxy doesn't inspect the traffic going through the circuit, which can make the proxy more efficient than an application proxy, but may compromise security.

On the other hand, circuit proxies are slower than packet filters because they must reconstruct the IP header to each packet to its correct destination. Also, circuit proxies are not transparent to the end user, because they require modified client software.

As we mentioned earlier, application proxies examine the actual application data being transmitted in an IP packet (see Figure 10.4). This approach thwarts any attackers who spoof IP packets to gain unauthorized access to the protected network. Because application proxies function at the Application layer of the OSI model, they also can be used to validate other security keys, including user passwords and service requests.

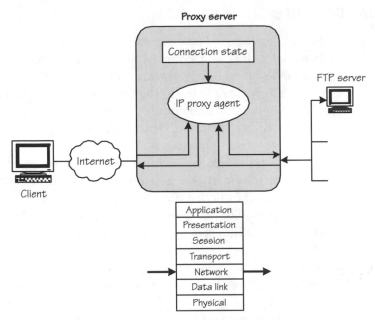

FIGURE 10.3 A circuit proxy.

Proxy firewalls often require two copies of an agent running for each service: one copy to communicate with the internal hosts and one to communicate with the external hosts. Thus, an application proxy may have two copies each of FTP, HTTP, and telnet agents. A circuit proxy operates in a similar fashion; it may have one copy of TCP for the internal network and one copy for the external network.

Because application proxies operate as one-to-one proxies for a specific application, you have to install a proxy agent for every IP service (HTTP/HTML, FTP, SMTP, and so on) to which you want to control access. This leads to two of the disadvantages of application proxies: a lag usually exists between the introduction of new IP services and the availability of appropriate proxy agents; and the application proxy requires more processing of the packets, leading to lower performance. Furthermore, many of the application proxies require modified client software, although the firewall's operation is becoming transparent to end users in many of the newer application proxy firewalls.

One important differentiating feature of application proxies is their capability to identify users and applications. This identification can enable more secure user authentication, because digital certificates or other secure token-based methods can be used for identifying and authenticating users.

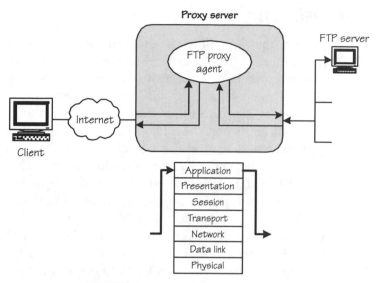

FIGURE 10.4 An application proxy.

SOCKS   Since circuit-level proxies can offer adequate security for many networks and because some users don't want to pay the price of lower performance found in application-level proxies, a standard for circuit proxies, called *SOCKS,* has been developed. The SOCKS proxy is designed to pass only SOCKS-related traffic, so SOCKS client software has to process all traffic being passed to the proxy for the traffic to be recognized. No other proxies are included in a SOCKS proxy firewall.

SOCKS was designed for TCP-based client/server applications, using a proxy data channel to communicate between the client and the server. In a SOCKS environment, an application client makes a request to SOCKS to communicate with the application server. This request includes the application server address and the user's ID. SOCKS then establishes a proxy circuit to the application server and relays information between client and server. With SOCKS version 5, authentication and support for UDP relay have been added. SOCKS is commonly implemented as a circuit-level proxy that has enhanced features, such as auditing and alarm notifications, so that it offers many of the features expected of a firewall.

The downside to SOCKS is that client applications must be specially coded for SOCKS or application-level proxies. Aventail, one of the main vendors of a SOCKS-capable firewall, tries to address this problem by including a DLL with its Windows client.

STATEFUL INSPECTION

The optimal firewall is one that provides the best security with the fastest performance. A technique called *Stateful Multi-Layer Inspection* (SMLI) was invented to make security tighter while making it easier and less expensive to use, without slowing down performance. SMLI is the foundation of a new generation of firewall products that can be applied across different kinds of protocol boundaries, with an abundance of easy-to-use features and advanced functions.

SMLI is similar to an application proxy in the sense that all levels of the OSI model are examined. Instead of using a proxy, which reads and processes each packet through some data manipulation logic, SMLI uses traffic-screening algorithms optimized for high-throughput data parsing. With SMLI, each packet is examined and compared against known states (i.e., bit patterns) of friendly packets (see Figure 10.5).

One of the advantages to SMLI is that the firewall closes all TCP ports and then dynamically opens ports when connections require them. This feature allows management of services that use port numbers greater than 1,023, such as PPTP, which can require added configuration changes in other types of firewalls. Stateful inspection firewalls also provide features such as TCP sequence-number randomization and UDP filtering.

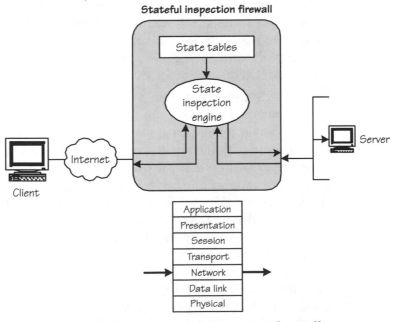

FIGURE 10.5 A stateful inspection firewall.

Firewalls and Port Numbers

Each TCP/IP application is assigned a unique port number used to establish a connection. For a client/server pair, both the client and the server have unique port numbers. Almost all TCP/IP client applications use a randomly assigned port number greater than 1,023 for their end of a connection. If a client/server pair is going to communicate over a firewall, then the firewall has to be configured to open port numbers higher than 1,023, or the client will be unable to establish a connection. But this can cause configuration problems, since some services such as NFS, NIS, and Netware/IP also use ports greater than 1023. If these ports were already opened at the firewall to enable communications between client/server applications, an attacker could disrupt the other services depending on ports greater than 1023.

Stateful inspection firewalls are highly secure, which explains why they're being used in more and more VPN bundles. However, these firewalls have to be supplemented with proxies in order to support other important functions, such as authentication.

General Points

It's not possible to say that any one firewall type is always better than another. That's why firewall vendors these days are starting to blend approaches—mixing stateful inspection and proxies, for instance. When deciding on which firewall to select, try to determine what level of protection you need for your traffic based on what part of the packet a firewall processes (see Figure 10.6); also, keep in mind how your firewall is likely to interact with your VPN protocols, which we'll cover in more detail in the next section.

Many of the ISPs offering VPN services (see Chapter 9, "The ISP Connection") either include managed firewalls as part of their VPN offerings or as separate services, giving you the option to outsource your firewall management and monitoring. But, if you're going to manage your own firewalls, one of the best places to gets security updates and advisories is the CERT Coordination Center at www.cert.org, located at Carnegie Mellon University's Software Engineering Institute. Another organization to check is the *International Computer Security Association* (ICSA) at www.icsa.net, which certifies firewall products and can audit your site security.

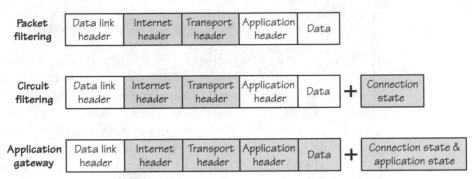

FIGURE 10.6 What firewalls inspect.

Firewalls and VPNs

Although firewalls should be considered part of your corporate security solution, they are not sufficient on their own for creating a VPN. That's because a firewall cannot monitor or prevent changes to data that may occur as a packet crosses the Internet (data integrity), nor does a generic firewall include encryption.

Furthermore, even if you installed host-based encryption on all your computers (using IPSec, for instance), you'd still need firewalls in your organization. Internet firewalls enforce an enterprise network security policy and are part of a perimeter defense. IPSec on every desktop provides for privacy and authentication but does not ensure that the corporate network security policy is enforced (what services are allowed, when to force virus scanning, etc.). Firewalls are able to enforce a policy that requires private links between networks even if desktop users cannot or do not use an encrypted connection.

Firewalls are often considered to be logical VPN termination points because you can manage your entire network security policy through that single point. However, firewalls are complex devices to install and manage because of the possibility of conflict between rules if you are not careful in establishing or modifying the rule base. Additionally, having firewalls perform VPN services increases your risk in case the firewall fails or is compromised. If you lose your firewall, your VPN goes with it.

Firewalls between busy networks, as on a WAN connection, carry a heavy load just processing the traffic passing through them. Adding encryption and key management may significantly hurt performance, especially when several VPNs are running. Some firewalls, such as Cisco's PIX, move data encryption off the processor and onto a card within the box to improve performance. Check Point Software is making similar arrangements, planning to offer a bundle of the Chrysalis accelerator board (for faster encryption) with its Firewall-1 software later in 1998. Other companies also are bundling firewalls into their hardware. For example, Timestep has ported Check Point's Firewall-1 software to the operating system that's part of their PERMIT security gateway.

IPSec traffic can be handled in two different ways, either as unfiltered packets or as filtered packets (see Figure 10.7). In the unfiltered approach, the IPSec traffic is handled the same way it is in a router—that is, the IPSec-protected data is transferred directly to the internal network without any filtering or controls on its contents. In the filtered approach, the firewall's filter and proxy controls are applied to the IPSec traffic before it is allowed into the internal network. Filtering IPSec traffic can be particularly useful if your security policy is to pass only certain types of traffic between VPN sites, say e-mail and FTP. Filtering also can be useful for controlling the traffic exchanged with business partners if you expand your VPN to an extranet.

It's always a challenge to maintain consistent security policies across different sites. It's particularly important to maintain consistency for the firewalls at all sites, because they control the access to and from each site. Configuration and access rules should be the same for every firewall in the entire enterprise. But, many firewalls require that such consistency be achieved by hand, with administrators at each site carefully updating their own copy of the global rules. Fortunately, some firewalls do maintain their security rules and configuration in a set of files that can be copied from one firewall to another, making your management job easier. But, remember that, if the firewall's configuration files can be transported and installed in the other firewalls, then your next problem is to deliver these files safely. This might have to be done by face-to-face exchanges, a bonded courier, or even secure e-mail, but you should do your best to ensure the security of the exchange and the handling of those files.

Firewalls and Remote Access

Because many firewalls already have strong user authentication mechanisms, they can offer additional functionality by serving as the focal point for dial-in users. Quite a few firewall products can verify the user's identity and establish an encrypted session between the firewall and the dial-in user's computer to protect confidentiality, forming the basis of a dial-in VPN.

In order to make this work, your remote users will have to install appropriate client software on their computers. If you're planning a fire-

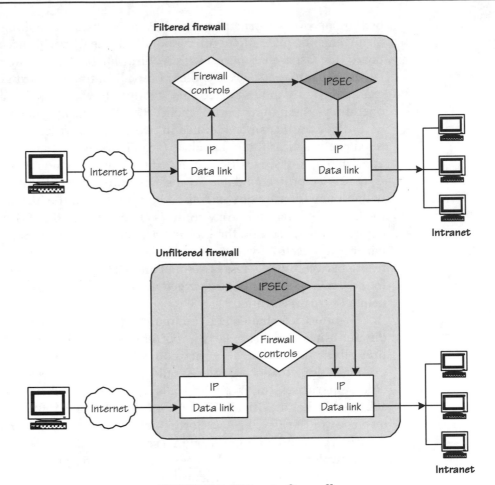

FIGURE 10.7 IPSec in firewalls.

wall for terminating PPTP or L2TP, then all your users need is a PPP client for dialing into their ISP. Recall, though, that a PPP client doesn't provide the strongest security for any data transferred between the client and your corporate site; if you want stronger encryption, you'll need to install either a PPTP or, preferably, a L2TP client on the remote user's computer.

As we've mentioned before, the current market trends emphasize PPTP and L2TP for dial-in VPNs and IPSec for LAN-to-LAN VPNs. But, IPSec is just as well-suited for dial-in VPNs. A number of firewall vendors offer remote client software that uses IPSec. Because IPSec has no standardized way for authenticating users, IPSec remote clients are usually vendor-specific. This means that you'll have to match the IPSec remote client software to your vendor's firewall and that, at least for the near future, you should stick with a single vendor to avoid interoperability problems. This could become particularly important if your mobile workers routinely access more than one VPN site. In such cases, each site should have the same firewall installed, with the same VPN options. Of course, having the same firewall at each site can simplify security policy management as well.

Product Requirements

If you're going to use a firewall as a security gateway for your VPN, let's review the main issues that you need to consider. We'll review the common requirements first, then discuss IPSec-related requirements, finally touching on issues surrounding PPTP and L2TP.

COMMON REQUIREMENTS

Regardless of which protocol is used for your VPN, you need to consider how the firewall integrates with the rest of your security and network management systems. For example, many of the PPTP and L2TP systems depend on RADIUS or token-based systems for user authentication; if you're already using a particular system for authenticating remote users, then you can simplify the transition by installing a firewall that's compatible with your current system. Alternatively, you may feel the need to improve the security of your authentication systems by installing a two-factor system like SecurID (see Chapter 4, "Security: Threats and Solutions") as you roll out your VPN services. *A firewall's authentication method may become less of a distinguishing factor as more firewall vendors have been bundling stronger authentication systems with their products.* Whatever the reason, system compatibility is important. The same suggestions hold for IPSec implementations as well, even though IPSec has not standardized on a particular authentication method, and most solutions are vendor-specific.

If you're planning to use an authentication system based on digital certificates, then you should give some thought to how the certificates will be distributed and verified. We'll get into this in more detail in the chapter on security management (Chapter 13), but some of the factors to consider include whether a certificate authority should be maintained in-house or outsourced and how will certificates be linked to other services (through a directory service, for example).

Looking ahead, the need to integrate management of the increasing number of user privileges, such as bandwidth, QoS, remote access, and access to servers and other network resources, will drive further use of policy-based management. Policy-based management depends on having a distributed system for identifying and authenticating users that can be managed easily. Directories are thus fast becoming a cornerstone technology for policy-based management, particularly X.500 directories and *Lightweight Directory Access Protocol* (LDAP). It's worth keeping an eye on how the firewall vendors are tying their products, particularly authentication services, to LDAP and X.500 directories, as a first step towards deployment of policy-based management, even if you don't think you will be using such systems for a few more years.

Last, but perhaps just as important, remember that you're most likely going to be installing firewalls at more than one site. You'll be able to maintain a more consistent security policy if the firewall product you pick supports synchronized administration of multiple sites. This administrator might involve file exchanges, as we discussed earlier, or some other form of remote management. If remote management capabilities are included in a product, be sure that remote access to the firewall is secure.

IPSEC

Since much of IPSec revolves around the use of cryptographic functions, either for encryption or packet authentication, it is important to ensure that a firewall not only supports the proper algorithms, but also the ancillary processes, such as rekeying and security associations. Also, since the IPSec standards are currently undergoing revisions to version 2, you should carefully investigate each product's compatibility with the version 2 specifications, which provide added flexibility and security.

The most secure devices support separate network connections for unencrypted and encrypted traffic, which enables you to provide connectivity for both kinds of traffic (it's highly unlikely that all of your traffic needs to be encrypted) and to maintain a physical separation between your encrypted networks and more open networks. Secure devices should reject all packets without a proper header (an IPSec header, for example) that arrive on the encrypted side, except perhaps for key-exchange protocols.

Check which cryptographic algorithms the VPN firewall supports. For those uses considered to be medium risk, the default DES CBC algorithm for encryption and HMAC-MD5 or HMAC-SHA-1 hash algorithms for authentication will suffice; if your traffic is higher risk, then be sure that automatic rekeying is supported.

On a related matter, even though manual keying is the minimum required by the IPSec specs, you should look for products that allow the cryptographic keys to be changed automatically and periodically or whenever a new connection is established. If interoperability will become a concern, don't settle for a proprietary key-exchange system, but insist on the systems described in IKE (see Chapter 5, "Using IPSec to Build a VPN"). Automatic rekeying further strengthens the security of your traffic by increasing the difficulty of cracking a key when it's intercepted (i.e., the key expires before it can be cracked).

Also be sure which IPSec headers the firewall employs. Although the original IPSec standards did not require the support of both AH and ESP headers, it's preferable to apply both headers to each packet. Some IPSec-compliant devices support only the Authentication Header.

Because security associations are crucial to the operation of IPSec, you should be able to manually input security associations, usually from a file similar to that recommended by S/WAN (see Chapter 5), and, if possible, specify wild card security associations to simplify configuring proxies.

The firewall always has to be treated as a secure device, which includes protecting the secret and private keys used by the device. Personnel with incidental access to the firewall should not be able to obtain the keys, for example.

In the original IPSec specifications, there was no system for countering replay attacks in which an attacker intercepts a series of packets and then retransmits, or replays, them at a later time. However, the revised IPSec standards that were passing through the IETF standards process in late 1998 included an antireplay service in the new Authentication Header; this service can be invoked at the discretion of the receiver to help counter denial-of-service attacks that would be based on these retransmissions. To provide added security to your VPN, see whether the vendor's products supports the new IPSec antireplay system rather than using a nonstandard variant.

As we've said, every security device should have a way of logging security events (*incidents*) and reporting them. If possible, be sure that the system can generate some kind of alarm if some persistent activity takes place, as this may indicate a systematic attempt at breaching the site's security.

Although you may feel that the IPSec transport mode is sufficient to protect your data, there will inevitably come a time when you'll need the stronger protection afforded by tunnel mode. A proper IPSec-compliant firewall should support both modes.

PPTP AND L2TP

Because PPTP and L2TP expect tunnels to be terminated at a network server, firewalls aren't usually used as the termination points for these tunnels. Instead, any firewall you install on your network should be configured to pass the traffic from PPTP or L2TP using the properly assigned port number. PPTP traffic uses TCP port 1723, which cannot be changed, and the default port for L2TP is 1701. L2TP does not demand that one specific port number be assigned for the firewall to pass L2TP traffic. Network managers have the option of selecting a different firewall port number for passing L2TP traffic, making it more difficult for attackers to take over L2TP tunnels or try other attacks based on a known port number.

Microsoft's implementation of its PPTP server for Windows NT (the *Routing and Remote Access Server*, or RRAS) does permit packet filtering to be enabled as part of the configuration. If packet filtering is enabled on a server running RRAS, then only PPTP packets will be passed.

AN OVERVIEW OF THE PRODUCTS

Because firewalls often seem to be the logical location for terminating VPN tunnels and enforcing security policies, there are currently more VPN-compatible firewalls than any other class of VPN device. As you'll see in Table 10.1, some of these firewalls are software products designed to run on a variety of operating systems, such as Unix and Windows NT, and a few are hardware devices that can be configured via most of the popular workstations.

Does the operating system for a firewall make a difference? As far as security is concerned, it's becoming less of an issue. The most secure firewalls have traditionally been those written with their own operating systems, and various security holes were found in the more common workstation and server OSs, like Unix and Windows NT. But, vendors offering firewall software that runs on the more common OSs now usually include added code that patches any of the known security holes in the OS. If performance is an issue, Unix might be preferred to Windows NT, but that's an issue we'll leave for others to address in any detail, because benchmarks can change almost every day.

When you're reviewing this list of products to help you pick likely candidates for your own VPN, bear in mind that the market doesn't stand still, and newer versions of some of these products will either include modified features or new features that were introduced since this book was put together. In other words, use the table as a guide, not the "last word."

Note that many vendors of routers and other VPN hardware have started to bundle firewalls with their products; the two most notable bundled firewalls are Check Point Software's Firewall-1 and Network Associates' Gauntlet.

Despite the relatively large number of firewall-based products for VPNs, a major continuing concern is the performance of these products. Even to perform their normal operations, firewalls—especially those that investigate packet contents (application proxies, for instance)—have a lot of computations to perform to get their job done. Add to that the overhead associated with encryption, and many systems will be severely taxed. For example, benchmarks run by Network World indicate that firewall-based VPNs often delay traffic anywhere from 1.3 to 3.3 times that expected without the VPN processing.

Using firewalls to create VPNs is a workable solution for some networks. Firewall-based VPNs are probably best suited to small networks that transfer small amounts of data (on the order of 1-2 Mbytes/sec over a WAN link) and remain relatively static (i.e., don't require frequent reconfiguration). If you're looking for higher performance, there are other, better solutions.

Some companies, like Check Point Software, are now pushing the idea that traffic control, including such tasks as bandwidth management and QoS, should be part of the definition of a VPN. That's a step beyond the definition of VPN that we adopted in this book, but it's a reasonable next step that will most likely gain more support in the future. After all, if you want to treat the tunnels transporting your data over the Internet as your network—whether they're virtual or not—shouldn't you have the same control and policies as you have on your own physical network?

Integrating traffic control with authentication and access control also makes sense over the long run, as policy-based network management becomes more prevalent (and useful). We're only beginning to see the first steps in integrating various management functions and implementations of policy-based management for enterprise networks, and it'll probably be a few more years before we start to see widespread deployment.

TABLE 10.1 Firewalls for VPNs

Product (Company)	AIX Firewall (IBM)	BorderGuard (StorageTek)	BorderWare Firewall Server (Secure Computing)	Eagle (Raptor)	Firebox II (Watchguard Technologies)	Firewall-1 (Check Point Software)	Gauntlet (Network Associates)
Price	$4,495–$16,495	$3,000 +	$4,000–$13,000	$6,500+	$4,995	$18,990	$11,500 (50–250 users)
Platforms—server	AIX, OS/2, Windows NT	N/A	Unix	Windows NT 4.0, Solaris, Unix	Windows95, NT, Linux	AIX, DEC Unix, HP-UX, Solaris, Windows95, NT	BSDI, Solaris, HP-UX, Windows NT
Platforms—remote access	Windows95, NT, OS/2 Warp	Windows95, NT	Windows NT, DOS, Unix	Windows 3.11, Windows95, NT	Windows95, NT	Windows95	Windows95, NT
Tunneling protocol	IPSec, L2TP	proprietary	IPSec	IPSec, swIPe	IPSec, PPTP	PPTP, L2TP, L2F	swIPe, IPSec
Protocols supported	IP, IPX	IP	IP	TCP, UDP, ICMP	TCP, UDP	IP	TCP, UDP, ICMP
Encryption type	IPSec, DES, CDMF	IDEA, NSC1, DES, Triple Des	DES, Triple DES, RC4,	DES, Triple DES, RC2, IPSec AH	RC4 (40 bit or 128 bit)	DES, Triple DES, IPSec, FWZ-1	56 bit DES
User authentication	—	software or hardware tokens	CryptoCard, SecurID, S/Key	S/Key, NT Domain, RADIUS, TACACS+, Cryptocard, SecurID, Assurenet	CHAP	S/Key, SecurID, Axent	—
Access controls	Source, destination, protocol, IP address, port, user, time	Source, destination, IP address, service, user, time	Source, destination, protocol, user, port, time	Source, destination, IP address, service	LAN segment	Source, destination, service, user, time	User group, service group, IP address, host name
User management integration	—	—	—	Firewall users, NT user domains	NT User domains	RADIUS	NT Domains
Key management	Manual, proprietary	Proprietary	Manual	Proprietary	Manual	IKE, SKIP, FWZ, Manual IPSec	IKE
# tunnels supported	—	—	—	Unlimited	64	—	99 trusted links
# nodes supported	—	—	—	Unlimited	Unlimited	—	Unlimited
Remote management	Yes	Yes	Yes	—	Yes	Yes	Yes
Certificates	—	—	—	—	—	Yes	Yes
Remote access client	Yes	Yes	Yes	Yes	Yes	Yes	Yes
NAT	Yes	—	Yes	—	—	Yes	Yes
Product type	software	software	software	software	firewall appliance	software	software

TABLE 10.1 *(Continued)*

Product (Company)	Mobile VPN (Aventall)	PERMIT 2505, 4504 (TimeStep)	PIX Firewall (Cisco)	Proxy Server (Microsoft)	SecurIT FIREWALL (Milkyway)	SmartWall (V-One Corp.)	Sunscreen EFS (Sun Microsystems)
Price	$4,995–$11,995	$4,995–$10,995	$9,000 (64 connections) $15,000 (256 connections)	$995	$1,900–$14,500	$20,000 +	$4,995
Platforms—server	Windows NT, Solaris, AIX, IRIX, BSD/OS, Linux, ScO OpenServer	N/A	N/A	Windows NT	Suns/OS	HP-UX, Solaris, Windows NT, BSDI	Solaris, Windows95
Platforms—remote access	Windows 3.x, Windows95, NT, Solaris, Linux, BSD/OS, IRIX, SCO OpenServer	Windows95	—	Windows95, NT	Solaris, Sun/OS, Windows95, NT	Windows 3.x, 95, NT, Mac	Solaris, Windows95, NT
Tunneling protocol	SOCKS 5.0, PPTP, IPSec	PPTP, L2TP, L2F	IPSec (ESP)	PPTP	IPSec	PPTP	SKIP
Protocols supported	TCP, UDP	TCP, UDP	TCP, UDP	TCP, UDP	TCP, UDP	TCP, UDP	TCP, UDP
Encryption type	DES, Triple DES, MD4, MD5, SHA-1, RC4	DES, Triple DES, IPSec, FWZ-1	DES	MPPE, PPP	CAST, MD2, MD5, DES	DES, Triple DES, RSA	RC2, RC4, DES, Triple DES, 128-bit SAFER OBO
User authentication	Username & password, CHAP, RADIUS, SecurID, SSL	S/Key, SecurID, Axent	RADIUS, TACACS+	RADIUS	Username & password, group ID	Smart cards, Fortezza	SKIP, Password, SecurID
Access controls	Source, destination, IP address, application or service, user identity	Source, destination, service, user, time	RADIUS, TACACS+	IP address, source, destination	Source, destination, IP address, user identity, application type, time of access	Destination host name, port, URL IP address	Source, destination, IP address, application
User management integration	NT User domains, Unix password files, SecurID, RADIUS, NDS	RADIUS	NT user domain, LDAP, RADIUS	NT User domains	LDAP, X.500	—	Unix password, SecurID
Key management	RSA B-Safe	IKE, SKIP, FWZ, Manual IPSec	Manual	N/A	Entrust	Manual	SKIP
# tunnels supported	Unlimited	—	256	—	not given	—	—
# nodes supported	Unlimited	—	—	—	not given	—	—
Remote management	No	Yes	Yes	Yes	Yes	—	Yes
Certificates	No	—	—	No	X.509	X.509	No
Remote access client	Yes	Yes	No	Yes	Yes	Yes	Yes
NAT	—	—	Yes	—	—	Yes	Yes
Product type	software	firewall appliance	hardware	software	software	software	software

233

Routers

If firewalls seem like a logical place for installing VPN functions, then routers are even more so. After all, routers have to examine and process every packet that leaves the LAN, so why not let them handle the encrypting as well?

We've already mentioned one way that routers can be used to protect your LAN from outside attackers, and that's with packet filtering. (Just remember that relying on a router's packet filtering for part or all of the firewall protection means that the router itself must be secure.) But, packet filtering isn't sufficient to secure against many kinds of attacks on your network, which is one of the reasons why other types of firewalls have been developed. Within the context of VPNs, the type of routers in which we're most interested are encrypting routers.

Product Requirements

Many of the requirements for an encrypting router are the same as the ones for firewalls that we presented earlier in this chapter. After all, they're performing the same functions, it's just that the auxiliary network functions differ (routing versus security perimeter defense). Because the requirements are similar, we just briefly list them here.

Encrypting routers are appropriate for VPNs if they do the following:

- Include separate network connections for encrypted and unencrypted traffic
- Support at least the default IPSec cryptographic algorithms (DES CBC, HMAC-MD5, and HMAC-SHA-1)
- Support a cryptographic key length that best matches your security needs
- Allow manual security association configuration
- Restrict access by operations personnel to keys
- Support automatic rekeying at regular periods or for each new connection
- Support the antireplay mechanism of IPSec version 2
- Log failures when processing headers and issue alerts for repeated disallowed activities
- Support both transport mode and tunnel mode IPSec

You've probably noticed that there's a distinct IPSec slant to the preceding list—that's in keeping with the opinion, mentioned previously in this book, that IPSec offers the most secure VPN systems possible. Some routers support either PPTP or L2TP for tunneling, in which case the requirements for interoperability are fewer. Because L2TP defers to IPSec for encryption, L2TP-capable routers should be judged using the same requirements as for IPSec-capable routers.

Because routers are generally designed to investigate packets at Layer3 of the OSI model and not authenticate users, you'll most likely have to add an authentication server in addition to your encrypting router to create a secure VPN. If you're not already using an authentication system, say for remote access, review some of the systems we described in Chapter 4. PAP or CHAP, such as provided in a typical PPTP installation or in Intel's ExpressRouter, is weak authentication. The strongest authentication is a two-factor system, such as that provided by SecurID or CryptoCard. Many of these systems are designed to work with encrypting routers, but you'll have to check with the vendors to be sure of their compatibility.

TABLE 10.2 VPN-Capable Routers

Product (Company)	IntelExpress Router VPN (Intel)	IOS 11.3 (Cisco)	MicroRouter Series, RISC Router 3500, 3800 (Compatible Systems)	2210 Nways Multiprotocol Routers (IBM)	Pipeline 220 w/ SecureConnect option (Ascend)	NetBuilder II Routers (3Com)	VPN500 Series (Bay Networks)
Price	$1,299–$5,999	$500–$7,000 acc. to router (not including router)	Microrouters $1,895–$2, 695 RISC Routers: $3,995–$4,495	$2,800–$3,800	$6,495	$10,000+	500n: $3,995 550n: $4,995
Tunneling protocol	proprietary	L2F	IPSec, GRE	L2TP, IPSec	PPTP, L2TP, L2F	PPTP, L2TP	IPSec
Protocols	TCP, UDP, IPX	TCP, UDP IPX	TCP, UDP, IPX	TCP, UDP, IPX	TCP, UDP, IPX	TCP, UDP, IPX	TCP, UDP
Encryption type	144-bit Blowfish	DES	RSA, DES	IPSec	IPSec	IPSec, MPPE	DES, 3DES
User authentication type	PAP, CHAP	RADIUS, TACACS+	CHAP, PAP, RADIUS	—	PAP, CHAP, RADIUS, h/w token cards	PAP, CHAP, RADIUS, ACE, NT domains	ACE, RADIUS, CHAP
Integrated firewall	Yes	Yes	Yes	—	Optional	Yes	No
Compression	Yes	—	Yes	—	No	Yes	Yes
NAT	Yes	—	—	Yes	Yes	Yes	Yes

AN OVERVIEW OF THE PRODUCTS

If you compare the two product tables, Tables 10.1 and 10.2, in this chapter, you'll see that the number of encrypting routers is much smaller than that for VPN-capable firewalls. One reason for this disparity is that many of the integrated hardware devices for VPNs, which we'll be covering in the next chapter, often incorporate a router into the box.

Although most of the products listed in Table 10.2 support one or more of the standards we've discussed in this book (i.e., PPTP, L2F, L2TP, and IPSec), note that the Intel router uses a proprietary scheme for tunneling. It also uses the Blowfish algorithm for encryption, which, although a good algorithm, isn't included in any of the other standards. Because the Intel router is proprietary, it cannot be used with any other routers to create a VPN; all of your sites would have to have Intel Express routers installed to form a VPN.

As we've said before, the feature sets of these products should not be taken as the last word, because companies are always adding and changing features. As an example, although the IBM routers initially supported L2TP as a tunneling protocol, the company has publicly announced that these routers will also support IPSec in the near future.

Just as with firewalls, routers can take a performance hit when having to perform the added functions of a VPN, particularly encrypting packets. Cisco's *Encryption Service Adapter* (ESA) is one way of dealing with such performance hits; the ESA is a coprocessor-based encryption engine that relieves the router's regular processor of this task.

Routers are being expected to perform more tasks in current-day networks. Not only might they be expected to handle VPN tunnels and encryption, but they have to handle quality-of-service provisioning as well, for example. These new tasks place new loads on the router, so you should choose carefully when deciding which functions need to be installed on your routers; otherwise, new functionality, such as QoS-based routing and VPNs, may well reduce the performance of your networks rather than enhance them. Routers continue to be logical devices for managing these many different tasks, so you'll need to balance a router's computational power, and that of add-on hardware like Cisco's ESA, against the new tasks you want the router to perform.

Because routers cannot handle all the functions of a VPN, such as user authentication, it's becoming increasingly common for vendors to bundle firewall software with their routers. For example, Bay Networks has embedded the INSPECT engine from Check Point's Firewall-1 into version 11.02 of the Bay Router Services OS so that a router and stateful inspection firewall can be shipped in the same box.

Summary

The three main types of firewalls—packet filters, proxies, and stateful inspection systems—each differ in the security they provide, their performance, and the difficulty of configuration. In general, the more secure a firewall is, the slower it is. And, because any one type of firewall does not cover all the bases for securing your LAN, you'll often find that firewall vendors are integrating the different methods into a single product for maximum security.

Both firewalls and routers can be used as key components for creating a firewall. A wider variety of VPN-capable firewalls than routers is available currently, and this probably will continue, because the idea of adding one security function (i.e., VPN tunneling and encryption) to another (i.e., perimeter security) makes sense to many buyers. But, beware that there may be high performance penalties for combining these two functions, and the available throughput may be inadequate for your higher speed links. Adding encryption coprocessor cards to the firewall/VPN computer can help solve the performance problem.

A small number of stand-alone encrypting routers are available for creating VPNs. They usually have to be supplemented with other products, such as authentication servers, in order to make a complete VPN. Furthermore, as we'll see in the next chapter, many integrated hardware devices, which include routing functionality, are now available for VPNs.

11

VPN Hardware

The preceding chapter covered many of the products that focus on using either a firewall or a router as the main building block for creating a VPN. And, as we've already mentioned, each of these classes of products suffers from certain shortcomings. For instance, although many of the products are suitable for small networks with low- to medium-sized bandwidth requirements, very few of the products mentioned in Chapter 10 can handle Ethernet speeds or T3 (44.736 Mbps) WAN links. Furthermore, many products have to be bundled with other companies' products in order to provide all the functions needed for VPNs, particularly authentication as well as encryption and tunneling.

If you'll recall our discussion of classifying VPN products in the beginning of Chapter 10, we mentioned that a number of locations in a network are suitable for performing the basic functions of a VPN, particularly if you have to use different products for different functions. One of the fastest-growing market segments seeking to provide VPN solutions consists of vendors offering integrated VPN hardware, in which a single box includes all of the required VPN functionality, replacing the need for adding software and hardware to an existing firewall or router and, in some cases, any hardware for the WAN link (see Figure 11.1).

One of the purposes of these VPN products is to offload the VPN functions from a firewall or router that doesn't have the computational horsepower to handle functions like encryption. Many of the systems mentioned in this chapter utilize custom-designed ASICs and, in some cases, special cryptographic chips to give them as much of a performance edge as possible.

Not all of the products mentioned in this chapter offer the same features. Some products are aimed at providing a turnkey solution for security, including a firewall. Other VPN hardware ranges from boxes that focus on encryption to turnkey systems that handle all aspects of an Internet connection, including WAN connections, routing, VPNs, DNS, and e-mail services, among others.

Types of VPN Hardware

One of the main differences among the products is their focus on the device that initiates a tunnel. Either a security gateway can create a tunnel to connect the LAN it serves to another gateway, or a single remote host can create a tunnel to connect to a gateway and the LAN it serves; in the past, we've referred to these as LAN-to-LAN VPNs and dial-in VPNs, respectively. We'll continue to use the term VPN gateway to describe products that can handle LAN-to-LAN VPNs and, in most cases, remote access

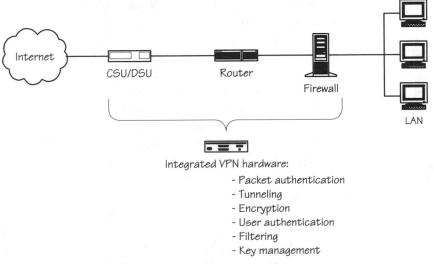

FIGURE 11.1 Integrating VPN functions.

by individuals. But, to emphasize that some gateways are designed specifically to handle dial-in tunnels, we'll refer to those products as *remote VPN gateways*. We've shied away from using dial-in as a modifier here because the user never dials into the gateway directly, as he would for a remote access server; the only dial-in connection is between the user and his ISP.

The function of a remote VPN gateway is pretty much what you would expect from the name; it is the termination point for tunnels from remote clients. Generally, these products concentrate on PPTP and L2TP, but a few, like the Bay Networks Contivity Extranet Switch, also support IPSec remote hosts using IPSec ESP as the tunneling protocol. Some vendors currently shipping PPTP/L2TP gateways have also committed to adding IPSec support as the standards are approved this year.

One class of products that we won't cover in this book are the remote access concentrators used by ISPs to provide tunneling services such as those used by PPTP and L2TP (see Chapters 5, "Using IPSec to Build a VPN," and 6, "Using PPTP to Build a VPN"). Our focus throughout is on products that you would use to create your corporate VPN.

The Price of Integration

Integrating various functions into a single product can be particularly appealing to businesses that do not have the resources to install and manage a number of different network devices and also don't want to outsource their VPN operations. A turnkey installation can certainly make the setup of a VPN much easier than installing software on a firewall and reconfiguring a router as well as installing a RADIUS server, for example. Of course, this presumes that the configuration software for an integrated VPN box simplifies VPN configuration as well—unfortunately, that's not always the case with the products we've seen.

Aside from differences between LAN-to-LAN and dial-up VPNs, some vendors have two different views on how to extend integrated VPN devices. For some, an integrated device is the ideal location for adding any network service that users may access from other locations. Thus, they bundle Web caching, e-mail servers, and DNS caching with their VPN device. Other vendors, on the other hand, see the VPN device as an appropriate location for controlling the network connection, offering bandwidth management and resource reservation as part of the package.

Integrating many functions into a single box can be too much of a good thing, because that box now becomes a single point of failure. It may be one thing to accept that all security functions controlling communications with the Internet may fail when a single device goes down; at least, a broken communications link means attackers cannot get into your intranet over that link. But, it's another thing entirely to put an e-mail server or a Web server in the same box as your security and external communications link; if it fails, your employees can lose some internal services as well.

One of the biggest problems in dealing with all these devices, at least for most of 1998, is their lack of interoperability. It's rare to find a vendor whose VPN product line can cover the needs for all your sites—corporate, regional, and branch offices—so interoperability can become very important as you attempt to purchase different-size devices for different sites.

But, expect this situation to change in the near future. We should see IETF approval of the second version of IPSec as a standard sometime in 1998, and many vendors already have promised IPSec-compliant products after the standards are settled. One of the obstacles to prior deployment of IPSec has been the lack of a key-management standard, and that's now being handled in version 2 with IKE. Version 2 will make it easier to find interoperable products before long.

Different Products for Different VPNs

Consider that the important functions of any VPN, as we've mentioned throughout the book, are tunneling, encryption, authentication, and key management. Depending on which protocol you're planning to use for your VPN—PPTP, L2TP, or IPSec—there's a different relative emphasis on each of these functions. PPTP, for example, focuses on tunneling and includes weak encryption, and L2TP supports stronger user authentication and relies on IPSec for strong encryption; IPSec, on the other hand, handles encryption and key management well, but still needs work to be used with strong user authentication.

Depending on a product's features, gateways either can be used in place of some existing network devices, like firewalls, or they may be deployed as additional equipment. In either case, where you put a gateway affects not only ingress to and egress from your network but also the amount of traffic on your network. Another thing to keep in mind is that, although a VPN gateway may well integrate a number of functions and thereby simplify the management of the integrated functions, installing a gateway might force you to reconfigure your existing network devices, such as routers and firewalls.

If a VPN gateway includes a WAN port, you can install it in two ways on your network. In one case, you can place the gateway between the ISP's

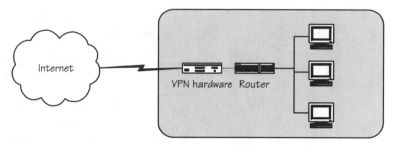

FIGURE 11.2 Placing the gateway before the router.

connection and your intranet (see Figure 11.2), in which case the gateway will process all traffic into and out of your network. This placement minimizes the need for reconfiguring any of your existing devices, because the gateway will provide transparent encryption and decryption services to the entire site, and existing routers and firewalls on your LAN will see ordinary TCP/IP packets.

You should look carefully at the control that a product like this offers; if you want to encrypt all the traffic that is sent to the Internet, then this type of product does not pose any problems. On the other hand, if you want to encrypt only some traffic, perhaps that associated with certain applications (e-mail and FTP file transfers, but not HTTP, for example), then you should ensure that the product offers such application-specific control over encryption. If not, you would have to set up two different connections to the Internet: one for encrypted traffic and the other for unencrypted traffic (see Figure 11.3).

This second configuration for a WAN-capable VPN gateway takes special care, because the two access devices you use—a VPN gateway for encrypted traffic and a router for unencrypted traffic, for example—must contain rules that ensure that the proper traffic is directed to, and passed by, the correct device.

When a VPN gateway doesn't include a WAN port and simply has two or more Ethernet ports, three different configurations should be noted: placing the unit between an access control device (a router, for instance) and the rest of the LAN (see Figure 11.4A), placing the gateway in front of the access device (see Figure 11.4B), or as another node on the LAN.

In the first two cases, your control of the traffic differs. If you place the gateway between the Internet and the router, then the router can be used to filter both VPN and non-VPN traffic with the same rules. Also, the router doesn't need to be reconfigured to pass special tunnel traffic, which is the case when a gateway is installed behind the router. One caution: If the gateway is on the public, or untrusted, side of the network, you need to

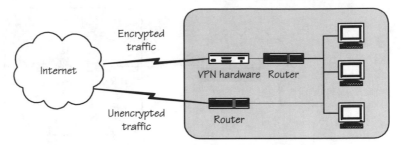

FIGURE 11.3 Parallel encrypted and unencrypted links.

ensure that management of the gateway cannot be compromised from someone on the untrusted net. If this link is handling both VPN and non-VPN traffic, then the VPN gateway needs to be configured to pass non-VPN traffic.

When you locate the gateway behind an access-control device, the control device would have to be configured to pass VPN traffic without filtering. Although this configuration increases the security of the gateway (it's less susceptible to compromising the management port, for instance), it also means that you have less control over the traffic entering the LAN after decryption by the gateway. If you want to filter VPN traffic by destination, time-of-day, or application type, for instance, then you either have

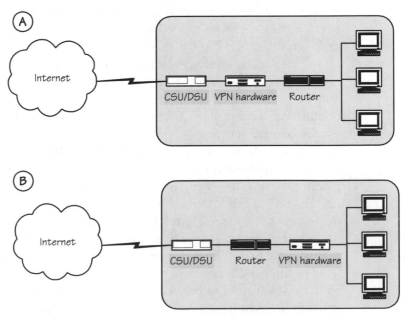

FIGURE 11.4 Differing gateway-router configurations.

to duplicate the filters from your router or use the configuration described earlier (see Figure 11.4A).

Installing the VPN gateway as another node on the LAN (see Figure 11.5), usually called a *one-armed* configuration, forces all VPN traffic to travel on the LAN twice: once to the gateway for processing and once from the gateway after processing. You may not care to add traffic to your net this way, but this configuration allows for better load balancing (especially if you have multiple links from the Internet) and can be especially useful when you have to handle hundreds or thousands of simultaneous sessions with remote clients.

For many systems, particularly those employing IPSec, keys have to be generated for sessions and verified that they're legitimate (see Chapter 4, "Security: Threats and Solutions"), which brings up the need for some kind of *certificate authority* (CA). In those systems using public-key pairs, private keys are usually generated on the VPN and stored in the device's memory, but the public key has to be made available to the other devices on the VPN. This is typically done in one of two ways: Either the keys are distributed to every device in the VPN, which is adequate if the number of devices is small, or the public keys can be stored in a centralized directory, a certificate server.

If you have a large number of keys and digital certificates to manage, then you might already be considering outsourcing the CA responsibilities; some of the companies offering CA systems, such as CyberTrust and VeriSign, also will manage your CA system for you. But, most of the prod-

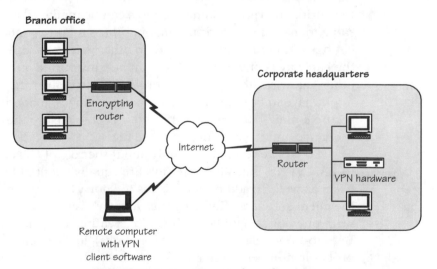

FIGURE 11.5 A *one-armed* configuration.

ucts discussed here expect that you'll be running a CA in-house, either on a Windows or Unix computer or as a sealed piece of dedicated hardware. We'll cover more of the issues surrounding key management in Chapter 13, "Security Management."

The last important feature of a VPN that we listed earlier was user authentication. For many network managers, authentication and access control aren't likely to be new tasks. If your company already is supporting remote users via dial-up modems, then you probably already have some user-authentication system in place. And, any company with more than a handful of employees probably has some policy in place for restricting access to files, servers, and other network resources.

The point is this: In order to integrate a VPN into your existing internetwork, you'll need to consider what links these devices provide to your existing security systems, especially for user authentication and access control.

For example, RADIUS is a particularly popular standard for authenticating remote users, and it can be used as a centralized authentication database in conjunction with two-factor authentication methods like SecurID. Although many of the products covered in this chapter can use RADIUS for user authentication as a RADIUS client (see Chapter 4), a few, like the Bay Networks Contivity Extranet Switch, go a step further and include a RADIUS server as part of the product.

It's always a challenge to maintain consistent security policies across different sites. It's particularly important to maintain consistency for the gateways at all sites, because they control the access to and from each site. Configuration and access rules should be the same for every gateway in the entire enterprise. Some products can be managed centrally from the same management workstation, but others require generating a common configuration file that's installed on other gateways. But, remember that if the gateway's configuration files can be transported and installed in the other gateways, then your next problem is to deliver these files safely. This might have to be done by face-to-face exchanges, a bonded courier, or even secure e-mail, but you should do your best to ensure the security of the exchange and the handling of those files.

So far, we've written mainly about the role of VPN gateways in LAN-to-LAN VPNs. But, VPN gateways are equally adept at handling remote users as well. To add remote access to your VPN, you only need to obtain the client software offered by the gateway's vendor and install that software on your remote hosts. If you're creating a hybrid VPN (i.e., one with LAN-to-LAN links as well as remote links), just remember to factor in the probable number of remote users into your calculations when you're determining how many simultaneous tunnels your gateway needs to support.

VPN gateways make no distinction between a tunnel from another LAN and one from a remote user with a laptop. (Remember that remote VPN gateways, as we've called them, deal entirely with dial-in tunnels, not LAN-to-LAN tunnels, so the number of simultaneous tunnels supported by a product should also correspond to the number of simultaneous remote users you're expecting to support.)

Recall that if you're planning to use one of the devices covered in this chapter for terminating PPTP or L2TP, then all your users need is a PPP client for dialing into their ISP. Remember that this doesn't provide the strongest security for any data transferred between the client and your corporate site; if you want stronger encryption, you'll need to install either a PPTP or L2TP client on the remote user's computer.

Product Requirements

If you're going to use one of the hardware devices in this chapter as a security gateway for your VPN, you need to consider a few main issues.

To start out, are you going to transfer only IP traffic across your VPN, or will you also have to support IPX and NETBEUI? Many gateways support only IPSec, which is fine for IP-only networks, but that doesn't help if you're running NetWare over IPX, for instance. If you choose not to migrate NetWare to the IP version, don't want to use an IPX-IP gateway, or don't want to replace NetWare entirely to create an IP-only network, then you'll have to use a gateway that supports either PPTP or L2TP, which handle multiple protocols.

Regardless of which protocol is used for your VPN, you need to consider how the product integrates with the rest of your security and network-management systems. For example, many systems depend on RADIUS or token-based systems for user authentication; if you're already using a particular system for authenticating remote users, then picking a gateway that's already compatible with your current authentication system will simplify configuration and management of the gateways.

Alternatively, you may feel the need to improve the security of your authentication systems by installing a two-factor system like SecurID (see Chapter 8) as you roll out your VPN services. Whatever the reason, system compatibility is important.

If you're planning to use an authentication system based on digital certificates, then you should give some thought to how the certificates will be distributed and verified. We'll get into this in more detail in the chapter on security management (Chapter 13), but some of the factors to consider include whether a certificate authority should be maintained in-house or out-sourced and how certificates will be linked to other services (through a directory service, for example). Some of the devices covered in this chapter include *Lightweight Directory Access Protocol* (LDAP) links that can be used with certificate servers and, in a few cases, their own LDAP server, for instance.

Looking to the future, network management involves integrating an increasing number of user privileges, such as bandwidth, QoS, remote access, and access to servers and other network resources. This evolution of network management will drive further use of policy-based management. Policy-based management depends on having an easily managed distributed system for identifying and authenticating users. Directories are thus fast becoming a cornerstone technology for policy-based management, particularly X.500 directories and LDAP. It's worth keeping an eye on how the vendors are tying their products, particularly authentication services, to LDAP and X.500 directories as a first step towards deployment of policy-based management, even if you don't think you will be using such systems for a few more years.

Bear in mind that you're most likely going to be installing these products at more than one site. You'll be able to maintain a more consistent security policy if the product you pick supports synchronized administration of multiple sites. This might involve file exchanges, as we discussed earlier, or some other form of remote management. If remote management capabilities are included in a product, be sure that remote access to the product is secure. One product even bothers to encrypt any requests for log files as well as the reports it creates as a result of those requests.

Check which cryptographic algorithms the product supports. The IPSec default algorithms, the DES CBC algorithm for encryption and HMAC-MD5 or HMAC-SHA-1 hash algorithms for authentication, should suffice for those uses considered to be medium risk; if your traffic is higher risk, then be sure that automatic rekeying is supported.

On a related matter, even though manual keying is the minimum required by the IPSec specifications, you should look for products that allow the cryptographic keys to be changed automatically and periodically or whenever a new connection is established. If interoperability will become a concern, don't settle for a proprietary key-exchange system but insist on the systems described in IKE (see Chapter 5, "Using IPSec to Build a VPN"). Automatic rekeying further strengthens the security of your traffic by increasing the difficulty of cracking a key when it's intercepted (i.e., the key expires before it can be cracked).

Much of key management depends not only on the reliability and security of a certificate authority or certificate server, but also how products react when one part of the key-management process fails or a key is canceled. Some products drop the session immediately when a canceled key is detected, and others will wait until the session is completed; the most secure systems are those that drop the session immediately. Also, to provide additional backup for keys in the case of a CA failure, you can purchase dedicated hardware that stores the appropriate keys for a VPN gateway.

If the gateway supports IPSec, be sure which IPSec headers the product employs. Although the original IPSec standards did not require the support of both AH and ESP headers, it's preferable to apply both headers to each packet. Some IPSec-compliant devices support only the Authentication Header. Because security associations are crucial to the operation of IPSec, you should be able to manually input security associations (usually from a file similar to that recommended by S/WAN; see Chapter 5) and, if possible, specify wild card security associations to simplify configuration. To provide added security to your VPN, see whether the vendor's products support the new IPSec antireplay system rather than using a nonstandard variant.

The gateway always has to be treated as a secure device, which includes protecting the secret and private keys used by the device. Personnel with incidental access to the gateway should not be able to obtain the keys, for example.

As we've said in the past, every security device should have a way of logging security events (*incidents*) and reporting them. If possible, be sure that the system can generate some kind of alarm if some persistent activity takes place, as this may indicate a systematic attempt at breaching the site's security.

Last, if you're considering a product that includes a router, find out what its routing capabilities are. Some of the available products offer limited routing (they may not route IPX protocols, for instance) and need to be deployed in conjunction with routers that already are in place in your network.

An Overview of the Products

At least 17 different VPN hardware products were available as of mid 1998. By the time you're reading this, no doubt even more are available. We've chosen to categorize the products in Tables 11.1 and 11.2 according to their support of LAN-to-LAN VPNs versus remote VPNs.

When you're reviewing this list of products to help you pick likely candidates for your own VPN, bear in mind that the market doesn't stand

TABLE 11.1 VPN Gateways

Product	ADI (Assured Digital)	ciPro-VPN (Radguard)	Fort Knox Policy Router 5000 (Internet Devices)	Infocrypt Enterprise (Isolation Systems/ Shiva)	LanRover VPN Gateway (Shiva)	Multiservices Internet Gateway (Freegate)	NetFortress VPN (Fortress Technologies)	NetScreen (NetScreen)
Price	ADI-500: $995 ADI-1000: $1,295+ ADI-2000: $1,595 ADI-4500: $20,000	$6,450	$3,000–$11,000	$6,200	$9,250	$5,395	$5,995–$45,995	NS-10, $3,995 NS-100, $9,995
Platforms—remote access	Windows	Windows95, NT (Unix)	Windows	Windows95, NT	Windows95, NT	Windows	Windows95, NT, 3.11	
Tunneling protocol	IPSec, PPTP	IPSec	IPSec	IPSec	IPSec	PPTP, L2TP	proprietary	IPSec
Protocols supported	IP, IPX	TCP/IP		TCP, UDP, ICMP	TCP, IP	IP	IP, IPX	IP
Encryption type	DEs, Triple DES, IPSec	DES, RSA, MD5	DES, Triple DES, IPSec	DES, Triple DES	DES, Triple DES	MPPE, IPSec, DES	IDEA, DES, Triple DES	DES, Triple DES, IPSec MD5, DSS,
Packet authentication	MD5, SHA-1	IPSec AH	IPSec AH source,	RSA	RSA source,	PPTP	checksums	SHA-1
Access controls		source, destination, application, time of day	destination, port, application, URL	source, destination, port IP address, LAN segment	destination, port, IP address, LAN segment	source, destination, IP address, application		Source, destination, IP address, protocol, time
User authentication	—	X.509, SecureNet	none	X.509, username/password, SecurID	NT user domain, RADIUS, SecurID, X.509	CHAP	none	RADIUS, local user directory
Key management	IKE	IKE	IKE	Diffie-Hellman, RSA	IKE	—	Diffie-Hellman	manual
# tunnels supported	1000 dial-up or 400 hi-speed (max for ADI-4500)	—	—	1024	1024	200	1024	NS-10: 16,000 NS-100: 32,000
# nodes supported	—	—	—	unlimited	unlimited	—	—	—
Integrated firewall	No	Yes	Yes	Yes	Yes	Yes	No	Yes
Firewall type	—	packet filter, application proxy	application proxy, packet filter	application proxy, packet filters	application proxy, packet filters	packet filter, proxy	—	packet filter
Remote management	—	Yes	Yes	Yes	Yes	Yes	Yes	—
Certificates	X.509	X.509	—	X.509	X.509	No	No	—
Remote access client	Yes	No	No	Yes	Yes	Yes	Yes	No
Management platform	—	HP OpenView for Windows	Java, Web browser	Windows95, NT	Windows95, NT	Web browser	—	Java
Compression?	—	No	No	Yes	No	MPPC	Yes	No
Rekeying?	—	auto	—	auto	auto	—	auto	manual
Other features	ADI-2000 incl. 8-port Enet hub; ADI-500 = PCI card for server	traffic monitor, event logging, certificate authority, VPN topology discovery	Web cache, URL filter, e-mail server, DNS cache, RAS		load balancing, fallover btw. multiple units	IP router, Web server, e-mail, FTP, DNS, DHCP		DHCP server, traffic control (via TCP windowing), URL filter
WAN Ports	varies with model	None	None	—		ISDN, 56k DDS, T1	None	None
NAT	—	Yes	Yes	—	Yes	Yes	—	Yes
Other products		Certificate Server, $6,500		SecureToken PCMCIA card, ExtremePCI coprocessor card, CA management s/w ($2,400)	CA management s/w ($2,400)	PPTP (Remote, $495), IPSec (Branch, $995)		

TABLE 11.1 (Continued)

Product	PERMIT/Connect (Timestep)	PN7 (Unified Access)	Ravlin (Redcreek)	SafeNet/LAN (IRE)	Secure Domain (Cylink)	SecureVision (ADC Kentrox)	TunnelBuilder (Network Telesystems)	VSU-1000, VSU-1010 (VPNet)
Price	$7,995 (shared secrets), $14,395 (Entrust PKI)	$4,995	Model 4: $1,300 Model 10: $3,500 Model 100: $11,500	$4,995	$5,500+	$4,395	$10,000 (250 users), $15,000 (1,000 users), $2,500 (25-user s/w only)	VSU-1000, $3,995; VSU-1010, $4,995
Platforms—remote access	Windows95, NT		Windows95	Windows 3.11, 95, NT	Windows 3.x, 95, NT	Windows95, NT	Windows, Mac	Windows95
Tunneling protocol	IPSec	proprietary	IPSec (ESP)	IPSec & proprietary	proprietary	IPSec	PPTP, L2TP	IPSec
Protocols supported	IP, IPX	IP	IP, IPX	IP	IP, IPX	IP	IP, IPX	IP
Encryption type	IPSec, DES	DES, Triple DES, 112-bit RC2	DES, Triple DES	IPSec (ESP), DES	DES, proprietary	DES, Triple DES	—	DES, Triple DES
Packet authentication	MD5, RSA	RSA	IPSec AH	IPSec AH	MD5, SHA-1	MD5	—	MD5
Access controls	LAN segment	source, destination, port, IP address	RADIUS, LAN segment	source, destination, IP address, port, protocol	—	—	—	IP address
User authentication	X.509, NT user domain	groups	NT user domain, LDAP, RADIUS, X.509	ANSI X9.26 one-time password	—	CHAP, SecurID	NT user domain, SecurID	X.509, CHAP, RADIUS, SecurID
Key management	RSA, proprietary	RSA	IKE	ANSI X9.17, IKE	Diffie-Hellman	SKIP	—	IKE, SKIP
# tunnels supported	200	—	10,000 +	—	—	—	1,000	600
# nodes supported	5,000 +	—	unlimited	—	—	—	—	unlimited
Integrated firewall	Yes	Yes	No	Yes	No	No	No	Yes
Firewall type		application proxy, packet filters	N/A	packet filter, proxy	N/A	N/A	N/A	
Remote management	Yes	Yes	Yes	Yes	—	Yes	Yes	Yes
Certificates	X.509	None	X.509		Yes	X.509	—	X.509
Remote access client	Yes	—	Yes	Yes	No	Yes	Yes	Yes
Management platform	Windows NT, 95	Windows NT	Windows NT, 95	Windows	Windows	Windows95, NT	Windows, Java	Java
Compression?	No	No	No	No	—	Yes	—	Yes
Rekeying?		auto	auto	auto	—	—	Yes	auto
Other features								DNS redirection, load balancing
WAN Ports		None	None			No	Yes	—
NAT		—	—	Yes	—	N/A	Yes	
Other products	PERMIT/Gate 2520 IPSec 2-port gateway (4 Mbps), PERMIT/Gate IPSec 2-port gateway (10 Mbps)		Ravlin 45/PCI coprocessor card	SafeNet/Security Center (s/w & workstn) $15,995+; SafeNet/Soft (host-to-host IPSec s/w) $79; SafeNet/Smart (smartcard & reader), $125+	Management software, $10,000	SecureVision Administrator, $4,395		VPN Management Tool Suite, $3,995

TABLE 11.2 Remote VPN Gateways

Product (Company)	ExtendNet VPN (Extended Systems)	Contivity Extranet Switch (Bay Networks)	Intraport VPN Access Server (Compatible Systems)	Riverworks (Indus River)
Price	$2,999 (10 connections) $5,999 (25 conn.) $9,999 (50 conn.)	ES1000: $2000 ES2000: $20,000 ES4000: $50,000	Intraport 2: $3,995 Intraport 2+: $9,995 Intraport Enterprise: $35,000	$25,000
Platforms— remote access	Windows95, NT	Windows95, NT	Windows95, NT, Mac, Linux GRE, IPSec	Windows95, NT
Tunneling protocol	PPTP	PPTP, L2F, L2TP, IPSec		PPTP, IPSec
Protocols supported	IP, IPX	TCP/IP, IPX	IP, IPX	IP, IPX
Encryption type	MPPE	DES, Triple DES, RC4	STEP, MD5, IPSec, DES, Triple DES	IPSec, DES, Triple DES
Packet authentication	PPTP	IPSec AH	IPSec AH, MD5, SHA source, destination,	PPTP
Access controls	—	source, destination, IP address, port, service, user	IP address, port, service, user	—
User authentication	CHAP, MS-CHAP, PAP, RADIUS, NT user domain	RADIUS LDAP, NT Domains, Axent, SecurID, LDAP	RADIUS	CHAP, RADIUS, SecurID
Key management	MS RAS shared secret	IKE	Diffie-Hellman	—
# tunnels supported	50	ES1000: 50 ES2000: 200 ES4000: 2,000	Intraport 2: 64 remote, 16 site-to-site Intraport 2+: 200 rem, 32 s-s Intraport Enterprise: 2,000 rem, 64 s-s	2,000
# nodes supported	unlimited	unlimited	unlimited	unlimited
Integrated firewall	optional	Yes	Yes	No
Firewall type	—	packet filter	limited packet filter	
Remote management	Yes	Yes	Yes	Yes
Certificates	No	X.509	No	No
Remote access client	Yes	Yes	Yes	Yes
Management platform	Windows	Windows	Windows	Windows
Compression?	Yes (MPPC)	No	—	Yes
Rekeying?	Yes	Yes	Yes	None
Other features	—	bandwidth management, LDAP	—	Remote access server
WAN Ports	No	Optional		T1, T3
NAT	No	Yes	No	No

still, and newer versions of some of these products will either include modified features or new features that were introduced since this book was put together. In other words, use the table as a guide, not the last word.

In both categories, the main differences among the products are the number of simultaneous tunnels they can support and the added services that are bundled into the products. For instance, the number of tunnels can range from 8 to 2,000. Some products include bandwidth management and extensive support for user-authentication systems, and other products have included Web and e-mail servers in the same box as the dial-in server.

Some of the products listed here are bundles of more than one product. If you don't need all of the service listed for a particular product, it's a good idea to check with the vendor to see whether he offers unbundled solutions, because we chose to emphasize complete solutions in the list. For example, Radguard offers separate encryption and firewall units.

For key management, many of the products depend on a certificate server that's installed on either a Windows or Unix workstation and should be secured against any tampering and have very restricted access by internal staff. For even greater security, an additional piece of dedicated hardware, such as that offered for use with cIPro, can be installed for key management, allowing the VPN to continue running even if the Certificate Authority isn't.

While we're on the question of reliability, it's also worth noting that some of the products we've covered allow multiple devices to be run in parallel and can have one device take up the load from another in case of the device's failure. Bay Networks' Contivity Extranet Switches and Shiva's LanRover VPN gateway include such *failover features.*

It's generally to be expected that these hardware solutions will perform VPN functions, especially encryption, faster than their software counterparts. But, determining the actual performance of these products is difficult. Many vendors will quote throughput values ranging anywhere from 22 Mbps to 60 Mbps in their product literature, for example; use these values only for the roughest comparisons.

Quoted throughput values are usually measured with large packet sizes (1,450 bytes), although normal network traffic often includes many more small packets, which reduces throughput values. Also keep in mind that session initialization places a heavy burden on the processor as the device is calculating session keys and that more sessions lower performance. The products that list support for thousands of sessions cannot set all of them up simultaneously. Just as some vendors have installed special ASICs in their hardware for some of the VPN functions, a few companies also use a dedicated RSA chip for any computations involving public-key cryptography. Cryptographic processing speed will become increasingly important if you're looking for highly secure systems and switch from DES to the slower Triple DES algorithm.

Although many of the hardware devices covered in this chapter are likely to offer you the best performance possible for your VPN, you'll still need to decide how many functions you want to integrate into a single device. Small businesses or small offices without large support staffs, especially those experienced in network security, will benefit from products that integrate all the VPN functions as well as a firewall and perhaps one or two other network services. Some products—usually the more expensive ones—include dual power supplies and failover features to ensure reliability. But, you need to decide which network services are crucial to your company's minute-to-minute operation; after prioritizing those services, you can make the decision whether they should be installed in a single product.

Should you purchase VPN hardware instead of installing additional software and/or hardware on your routers or firewalls? That depends. If you're looking for a low-end solution that doesn't have to process a large amount of traffic, then the products we discussed in Chapter 10, may do the trick. If you don't have a firewall or if you're planning on adding VPN capabilities to branch offices, then some of the integrated boxes described in this chapter will fit the bill; they also can reduce your need for an on-site security specialist or at least reduce some of your network management tasks.

It's hard to beat many of the products in this chapter for throughput and handling large numbers of simultaneous tunnels, which should be crucial to larger enterprises. Some of the products listed in this chapter may seem expensive, but recall when you're making price comparisons that the software prices we mentioned in Chapter 10, "Firewalls and Routers," (and those we'll cover in the next chapter) do not include the prices of the machine on which they run.

Also, don't overlook the importance of integrating the control of other network-related functions, such as resource reservation and bandwidth control (see Figure 11.6). Some companies already include these features in their products, and it's a step that will most likely gain more support in the future. Integrating traffic control with authentication and access control also makes sense over the long run, as policy-based network management becomes more prevalent and useful. We're only beginning to see the first steps in integrating various management functions and implementations of policy-based management for enterprise net-

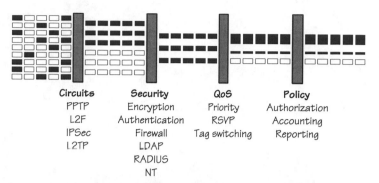

FIGURE 11.6 Integrating VPNs and QoS.

works, and it'll probably be a few more years before we start to see widespread deployment.

Summary

If you're looking for performance, VPN hardware products usually can offer better throughput than their software counterparts. The most basic versions of these products include packet authentication, tunneling, encryption, and key management as well as links to user-authentication systems. More advanced products often package more services into a single box, such as RADIUS and LDAP servers, and support for thousands of simultaneous tunnels.

12

VPN Software

We now come to the last group of VPN products that we'll cover in this book—software. This group is somewhat of a diverse collection because it covers any software that isn't specifically aimed as an addition to either firewalls or routers, which we covered in Chapter 10, "Firewalls and Routers." Many of the software products covered in this chapter parallel the hardware we covered in Chapter 11, "VPN Hardware," in which a number of different VPN and network services are provided in a bundled product. As you go through this chapter, you'll see that it includes some of the major Network OSs (NOS), such as NetWare and Windows NT, as well as products specifically created for forming and maintaining secure tunnels (AltaVista Tunnel and F-Secure VPN), along with software that can be used for host-to-host tunnels without the need for an intervening security gateway.

It's true that some of the products covered previously, particularly certain firewall products, are also software-based, in which the buyer gets to select the computing platform. But, these products easily fit into the category of firewalls; whereas the products we'll discuss in this chapter cannot be easily categorized. In many ways, this chapter covers a grab-bag of different software products but ones that may be important enough to play a role in the construction of your VPN.

Different Products for Different VPNs

Two classes of software are worth mentioning here. One is composed of the products that provide VPN services for a LAN, much like the hardware that was discussed in Chapter 11. The second class of products are those that can be used for host-to-host tunneling without the need for a security gateway.

The products that provide VPN services for a LAN cover the full gamut of tunneling and VPN approaches, some offering support for the protocols we've covered in this book, and others using proprietary approaches to tunneling and key management.

The evolution of VPN standards, their requisite infrastructures (for digital certificates, for instance), and the current networking marketplace have made LAN-centric solutions a higher priority than host-to-host solutions, which has made the choices for host-to-host software rather small in number so far. Although a few shrink-wrapped products can be used for secure host-to-host connections, some commercially available *software development kits* (SDKs) let developers create their own IPSec-compatible programs.

Tunneling Software

Earlier in this book, when we described tunneling, we pointed out that tunneling was nothing more than encapsulating one packet inside another. In some cases, like with the MBone, the experimental multicasting backbone on the Internet, no effort is made to protect the encapsulated packets. And, with PPTP for example, the amount of protection offered by encryption is rather weak because of the methods employed. IPSec, on the other hand, creates tunnels by applying strong encryption methods to the encapsulated packets.

Now, with VPN software, we see that encrypting encapsulated packets to form tunnels can be done in other ways as well. Of the products covered in this chapter, four use their own proprietary methods for tunneling. And, of course, not one of the methods is compatible with any of the others.

There's much to be said for standards and interoperable products, such as we're seeing with IPSec. Being able to pick and choose among vendors enables you to purchase the best products for your needs without feeling tied to a single vendor; these days, it's highly unlikely that any one vendor has a *lock* on the best networking technology. (Of course, you still have to worry about configuring and managing these different devices if you buy from more than one vendor. Businesses often will go with a single vendor to avoid management and maintenance hassles.)

With the strong move to standardize VPNs using IPSec and L2TP (and PPTP, to a lesser extent), is it wise to use proprietary solutions like the ones mentioned in this chapter? In general, little advantage is gained by using proprietary solutions. A few of these products were some of the first ones created for Internet-based VPNs and thus precede many of the standards efforts. Although we'd much rather use standards-based solutions, we're including the proprietary products for the sake of completeness.

Also keep in mind that vendors change their products over time in response to market pressures. At least two of the products covered here—AltaVista Tunnel and Borderguard—are supposed to include IPSec support before long. Starting out with a proprietary product doesn't keep you from being interoperable with other standards later.

It's also possible to use standard protocols other than IPSec and L2TP to create VPNs. Aventail's use of SOCKS v5 is one such example (see Chapter 10). Another example is DataFellows' use of *Secure SHell* (SSH) in their F-Secure product. SSH is familiar to Unix system administrators for securing communications and has been used on a variety of networks (by NASA and some banks, for instance) for securely transmitting data. Unlike the protocols we've discussed in this book, however, SSH works at the transport layer.

VPNs and NOS-Based Products

Although there will come a time when the authentication and encryption functions of VPNs will be included in each computer as part of the operating system, we're currently forced to rely on using security gateways or remote client software to create VPNs. As a first step to provide VPN support in some of the Network Operating Systems, companies like Microsoft and Novell have started to provide security gateway functions in their NOS software.

We've already mentioned that Microsoft was the first to provide a tunnel server for PPTP in their *Routing and Remote Access Server* (RRAS) product for Windows NT 4.0. Although RRAS is designed to serve as a tunneling server for PPTP (and eventually L2TP) tunnels, either for LAN-to-LAN or host-to-LAN VPNs, it's not a bundling of security services like some other products. For example, RRAS has a very limited packet filtering system—you either pass PPTP packets or nothing at all. To add the security of a firewall to control access with a finer granularity, you need to add Microsoft's Proxy Server to your server machine. (The Proxy Server was covered in Chapter 10.)

Novell's Borderguard is a series of software modules that can either be used separately or as a unit. Of particular interest to our discussion here are the firewall and VPN modules. The firewall is a fairly generic packet filtering and application proxy type. Borderguard's VPN services use Novell's own tunneling technology to encrypt TCP packets (using the RC2 bulk encryption algorithm). The product also utilizes *Simple Key Management for IP* (SKIP) to exchange keys, although the implementation apparently does not interoperate with key-management servers from other vendors.

Although Borderguard may not be suitable for all VPNs, it's an ideal product for companies currently using Netware and IPX, but who want to set up a VPN. Since Borderguard includes an IPX-to-IP gateway, you can set up your VPN without converting your internal IPX networks to IP. And, should you decide to convert to IP, Borderguard could continue to serve as the VPN software as you convert different portions of your network from IPX to IP, because it supports both protocols. However, since only Borderguard installations can take part in the VPN, you wouldn't be able to tie non-Netware sites into the VPN very easily.

Borderguard, RRAS, and Conclave all emphasize the same dilemma: How many different network services should you install on a single computer? There are actually two issues here. First, there's the single-point-of-failure argument, which we discussed in Chapter 11, "VPN Hardware": How many of your network services can you afford to lose if the computer fails? Second, there's the issue of performance: Will installing too many services on a single computer seriously impair the performance of important services? This issue doesn't come up as often for the integrated hardware we discussed in Chapter 11, because many of those products use customized operating systems and hardware for better performance. But, running a variety of network services on a single computer using an OS designed for a variety of computing tasks, which may not be optimized for your network services, could lead to poor performance. (For example, it's often recommended not to install all of Borderguard, especially the Web-caching module, on a single machine.)

Host-to-Host VPNs

Throughout most of this book, we've written about either LAN-to-LAN VPNs or dial-in VPNs, both of which involve some kind of security gateway. But, another kind of VPN involves communications between each individual host; this host-to-host (or end-to-end) VPN doesn't require any security gateways to create tunnels or encrypt packets, because all encryp-

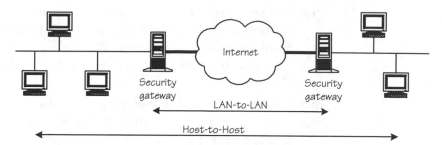

FIGURE 12.1 LAN-to-LAN versus host-to-host connections.

tion is done at the host (See Figure 12.1). Rather than use tunnel-mode IPSec, as security gateways would, host-to-host connectivity is set up using transport-mode IPSec (see Chapter 5, "Using IPSec to Build a VPN").

Although the IPSec standards provide for host-to-host connectivity, the majority of products currently available for IPSec VPNs have focused on the use of a security gateway for a number of reasons. First, the market is relatively young, and deployment of security measures at the edges of your network (i.e., routers, firewalls, and VPN gateways) makes it easier to discover the vagaries of VPNs. Second, key management is considerably easier when a limited number of security gateways are involved, rather than the more numerous individual hosts on all your LANs. (Although managing keys for remote hosts using dial-in VPNs might be comparable to taking care of all the hosts on your network.) Third, the performance penalty for encrypting or decrypting packets can be considerable for many existing computers and is likely to slow down an individual workstation's operations too much to be usable on a routine basis.

All of the preceding factors may lead to slower deployment of encryption at the level of individual hosts, but they don't present insurmountable obstacles to setting up host-level VPNs. Another thing to keep in mind is that IPSec originally was developed in parallel with efforts to define the next version of IP, IPv6, and is a mandatory feature of IPv6, meaning that all IPv6 protocol stacks and drivers will contain IPSec. On the other hand, IPSec is an optional feature in IPv4, and TCP/IP stacks have to be modified in order to use IPSec.

Product Requirements

When selecting VPN software for a LAN, the product requirements are much the same as the ones we've mentioned in the past two chapters. We'll briefly review them here.

Protocol support.   First, consider which protocols will be transmitted across your VPN—IP only or IPX and NETBEUI as well? Many gateways support only IPSec, which is fine for IP-only networks, but that doesn't help if you're running NetWare over IPX, for instance.

Integration with existing systems.   You also need to consider how the product integrates with the rest of your security and network management systems. For example, many systems depend on RADIUS or token-based systems for user authentication; if you're already using a particular system for authenticating remote users, then picking a gateway that's already compatible with your current authentication system will simplify configuration and management of the gateways.

Digital certificate issues.   If you're planning to use an authentication system based on digital certificates, then you should give some thought to how the certificates will be distributed and verified. We'll get into this in more detail in the chapter on security management (Chapter 13), but some of the factors to consider include whether a certificate authority should be maintained in-house or outsourced and how will certificates be linked to other services (through a directory service, for example). Some of the devices covered in this chapter include LDAP links that can be used with certificate servers and, in a few cases, their own LDAP server, for instance.

Multisite maintenance.   Keep in mind that you're most likely going to be installing these products at more than one site. You'll be able to maintain a more consistent security policy if the product you pick supports synchronized administration of multiple sites. This might involve file exchanges, as we discussed earlier, or some other form of remote management. (VTPC/Secure, for example, creates a floppy disk with the required configuration for each VPN gateway; these disks are then taken to the gateway computers to complete the installation of the software.) If remote management capabilities are included in a product, be sure that remote access to the product is secure.

Cryptographic algorithm support.   Check which cryptographic algorithms the product supports. The IPSec default algorithms, DES CBC algorithm for encryption and HMAC-MD5 or HMAC-SHA-1 hash algorithms for authentication, should suffice for those uses considered to be medium risk; if your traffic is higher risk, then be sure that automatic rekeying is supported. Automatic rekeying further strengthens the security of your traffic by increasing the difficulty of cracking a key when it's intercepted (i.e., the key expires before it can be cracked). Even some of the systems mentioned in this chapter, which do not use IPSec, support some kind of automatic rekeying procedure.

If the software supports IPSec, be sure you know which IPSec headers the product employs. Although the original IPSec standards did not require the support of both AH and ESP headers, it's preferable to apply both headers to each packet. Software for host-to-host communications should support transport-mode IPSec, although security gateways are more likely to require only tunnel-mode IPSec.

Because security associations are crucial to the operation of IPSec, you should be able to manually input security associations (usually from a file similar to that recommended by S/WAN; see Chapter 5) and, if possible, specify wild card security associations to simplify configuration. To provide added security to your VPN, see whether the vendor's products support the new IPSec antireplay system rather than using a nonstandard variant.

Incident logging.   Every security gateway should have a way of logging security events (*incidents*) and reporting them. If possible, be sure that the system can generate some kind of alarm if some persistent activity takes place, as this may indicate a systematic attempt at breaching the site's security.

Turning to host-based software, as transport-mode IPSec is deployed to individual computers in the future, it's likely that certificate servers, perhaps using LDAP, also will become more widely deployed (see Figure 12.2). Couple that with the increased usage of digital certificates in general—for electronic commerce and secure e-mail, for instance—and a centralized policy for creating and managing certificate servers will be needed. Try to factor that into your planning as you review these products. Much of the work on implementing *Public Key Infrastructures* (PKIs) is still under development.

An Overview of the Products

The bulk of the products in Table 12.1 is software for creating and managing tunnels, either between a pair of security gateways or between a

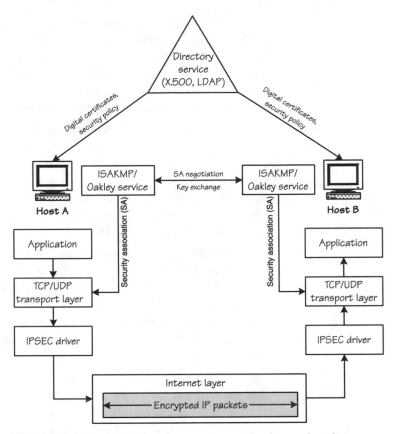

FIGURE 12.2 Interactions between two hosts and a directory server.

remote client and a security gateway. E-Lock can be used for host-to-host VPN connections; other host-to-host products are part of systems mentioned in Table 11.1.

It's not possible for a book to include completely up-to-date information on products, especially considering the pace of networking products' introductions and modifications. This table should serve as a guide of what's available, but not as the final word on either the entire marketplace, a vendor's product line, or a particular product's feature set.

In particular, don't make price comparisons using only the data included in the table. Only prices for the server and client portions of the software are given, and client prices frequently change with the number of users. Also, look out for different pricing schemes; for example, Conclave is priced on the basis of the number of users, not the number of sites.

TABLE 12.1 VPN Software

Product	AltaVista Tunnel 98 (Compaq)	BorderManager (Novell)	Conclave (Internet Dynamics)	E-Lock (Frontier Technologies)	F-Secure VPN (DataFellows)	Omniguard/ PowerVPN (Axent)	PrivateWire (Cylink)	RRAS/NT Server (Microsoft)	SmartGate (V-ONE)	VTPC/Secure (InfoExpress)
Price	$995+	$2,495+	$2,495 (25 users, no CA) $3,995 (25 users, CA)	Desktop: $249, Director: $1,000	$2,495+	$2,995	$19,000+	free*	$4,995 (Windows), $6,495 (Unix)	$1,495
Platforms— server	Windows NT, Digital Unix	Solaris, SunOS, NetWare, Windows95, NT	Windows NT, Netware, Unix	Windows NT, 95	NetBSD kernel	Windows NT, Solaris, BSDI, HP/UX, Linux	Windows NT, Solaris	Windows NT	BSD Unix, Solaris, HP-UX, Inix, Windows NT	Windows NT, Unix
Platforms— remote access	Windows95, NT	Windows95, NT	Windows, Unix, Mac	Windows NT, 95	No	Windows 3.x, 95, NT	Windows 3.x, 95, NT	Windows95, NT	Windows 3.x, 95, NT, OS/2, Mac (MaXVPN Windows 05, NT only)	Windows 3.x, 95, NT, Solaris, Linux, Mac
Tunneling protocol	proprietary	proprietary	IPSec, PPTP	IPSec	SSH	PPTP	proprietary	PPTP	tunnel-independent	proprietary
Protocols supported	IP	IP, IPX	IP	IP	IP	IP	IP	IP, IPX, NetBEUI	IP	IP, NetBios
Encryption type	128-bit RC4	128-bit RC2	DES, Triple DES, RC2, RC4	DES, Triple DES	RSA, Triple DES, Blowfish	DES, Triple DES	DES, Triple DES, RC4	RC4	DES, RSA	DES, Triple DES
User authentication	SecurID, LAN segment	RADIUS	SecurID	—	TACACS+, SSH	RADIUS certificates, SecurID	CHAP, PrivateCard	token or MSCHAP, PAP	software ACE, RADIUS, smartcard	TACACS+
Access controls	none	source, destination, protocol	document-level, source, destination	none	none	none	—	PPTP filtering	destination, port, URL	source, destination, protocol, port, user, group
User management integration	NT user domain	NDS	Windows ID, X.509	digital certificates, LDAP	—	Defender software tokens	proprietary directory	NT user domain	proprietary	—
Key management	RSA	SKIP	SKIP	manual, Diffie-Hellman, DNS, LDAP, PKIX	proprietary (RSA)	—	Diffie-Hellman	Diffie-Hellman	—	Diffie-Hellman
# tunnels supported	2,000 (on Unix server)	—	—	—	100	—	—	256	—	unlimited
# nodes supported	unlimited	—	—	—	—	—	—	—	—	unlimited
Integrated firewall	No	packet filter, application proxy	packet filter, application proxy	No	No	No	Yes	No (incl. with NT server)	No	Yes
Remote management	Yes	Yes	Yes	Yes	Yes	Yes	Yes	Yes	Yes	Yes
Certificates	Yes		X.509	X.509	—	—	Yes	No	X.509 (optional)	Yes
Remote access client	Yes	No	Yes	Yes	Yes	Yes	Yes	Yes	Yes	Yes
Compression?	Yes	No	No	(planned)	Yes	Yes	—	Yes	—	Yes

Some of the products listed here are bundles of more than one product. If you don't need all of the service listed for a particular product, it's a good idea to check with the vendor to see whether he offers unbundled solutions. For example, Novell has decided to offer some of the modules in Borderguard as separate products.

As we've said before in this chapter, be sure to balance your network's requirements with a product's performance, especially if you're planning to install multiple network services on a single computer. If you find that the best performance is achieved by distributing applications across a few computers, consider how you're going to keep them all secure from both physical and electronic tampering—in such cases, a single piece of hardware, picked from the list in Chapter 11, "VPN Hardware," might be a better choice.

Given that we've said that VPN hardware is likely to provide the best throughput of any VPN products, why would you bother with some of the software-based products we're covering in this chapter?

First, there's the cost. Some of these products are relatively cheap, or even free in the case of Microsoft's RRAS as long as you already have Windows NT. If you already have an appropriate computer on which to install the software, the cost of deploying a VPN is reduced even more.

Second, you already may be familiar with the operating system or NOS on which the software runs, which may make management of the VPN more appealing. Conversely, installing a new OS just to create your VPN may not make sense; if you're a Unix shop, for instance, you may not want to go through the trouble of buying Windows NT and installing RRAS or Conclave.

Lastly, the services and performance that these products provide may be all you need. If you're building a small VPN or handling small amounts of traffic, you may not require the performance (and price) found in many of the hardware products we've covered in Chapter 11.

Summary

Many of the software products for creating VPNs use proprietary tunneling protocols and nonstandard methods for key exchanges, limiting their interoperability. But, some of those same products are likely to become IPSec-compatible this year, improving their interoperability.

If interoperability isn't an issue, some of these products do a good job of filling certain market niches. For example, Microsoft's RRAS is a good PPTP tunnel server for Windows NT servers (and it's free); Novell's

Borderguard is especially useful if you're dealing with IPX as well as IP protocols.

Moving from security gateways to networks on which each computer manages its own VPN sessions and keys is likely to happen more frequently in a few years. In the meantime, a limited number of products support host-to-host VPNs using IPSec transport mode.

Managing a VPN

VPN management consists of three main areas: security, IP address allocation, and network performance. Security management includes not only authenticating users from other locations and controlling their access rights but also managing the cryptographic keys associated with VPN devices. VPNs often link together previously isolated networks, which entails extending IP addressing and name management across the entire enterprise and can lead to numbering conflicts.

You should be able to link your VPN's security and address management to existing corporate policies and services. But you will probably have to deploy new technologies to provide performance management on the WAN links usually used for VPNs. You'll not only have to decide how to differentiate network services according to business needs but also how to implement policies for the network to provide different performance for different classes of traffic. Lastly, you'll have to match your performance requirements with what your ISP can provide.

13

Security Management

Entire books have been written about securing computers and networks and the data that either is stored on devices or flows through them. But, that's not our mission here. Although we'll say a few things about corporate security policies in general, our concern here is covering the issues surrounding the management of VPN-related security. To that end, we'll focus on selecting encryption algorithms and key lengths, distributing keys and associated information in IPSec security associations, as well as user authentication and the control of access rights. Because of the importance of authenticating users and devices with digital certificates, we'll spend some time discussing the details of in-house management of certificates.

As we've discussed in previous chapters, IPSec offers the widest range of options for securing data of any of the protocols and includes perhaps the most complex architecture for negotiating and supporting those options. Because of those options and complexity, much of what we have to say about managing security for VPNs in this chapter will focus on IPSec; coverage of PPTP and L2TP also is included where pertinent.

Corporate Security Policies

There's much more to corporate security than what's covered in this book. A proper security framework for an organization includes seven different elements: authentication, confidentiality, integrity, authorization, nonrepudiation, administration, and audit trails (see Figure 13.1). Networking security is just one part—albeit an important part these days—of corporate security and should fit in with your corporate security policies.

A solid security policy should do the following:

Look at what you're trying to protect

Look at what you need to protect it from

Determine how likely the threats are

Implement measures that will protect your assets in a cost-effective manner

Review the process continually

Improve things every time a weakness is found

A traditional security policy identifies all of the assets in the corporate information infrastructure that are being protected, corporate databases and computer hardware, with overall policies on how to protect these assets. This policy should include everything from physical access to the property, general access to information systems, and specific access to services on those systems.

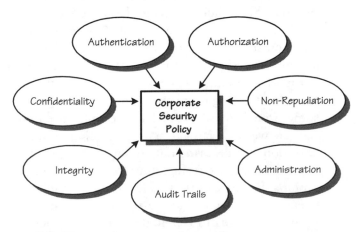

FIGURE 13.1 The components of a secure system.

But, as information systems have become more distributed, corporate security policies have had to include guidelines governing department LANs as well. This means adding policies on who has access to resources belonging to different departments: Can Sales access the R and D servers, for instance, or who can read the divisional manager's e-mail?

As you define security policies for your network, identify every access point to your information system and define policy guidelines to protect that entrance/exit point. Don't overlook all those modems that employees may have in their offices, which can become inviting access points for hackers as users dial into on-line services.

Some of the questions you should ask when formulating a security policy include the following:

- Which Internet services does the organization plan to use?
- Where will the services be used? Are they to be used on a LAN or via remote access?
- What additional needs (e.g., encryption) may be supported?
- What risks are associated with providing these services and access?
- What is the cost, in terms of control and impact on network usability, of providing protection?
- What assumptions are made about security versus usability?

Integral to your security plan is the capability to monitor compliance and respond to incidents involving violations. As part of your security policy, an emergency response procedure should be defined.

One of the new issues in security policy that arises from VPNs is that of key management. In the past, if a leased-line VPN was used, link-layer encryption may have been used, which didn't require exchanging cryptographic keys. But, the more dynamic nature and added flexibility of Internet-based VPNs requires a wider distribution of keys and more frequent rekeying, which in turn requires more complicated systems for key management. This is especially true when remote users are involved.

Even though we've said very little about the content of traffic passed between hosts, securing content against attacks, such as from computer viruses, also should be an important part of your security policies. Viruses are here to stay, so to prevent costly infections from spreading, antiviral scanning software should be included in your security implementation.

Now let's turn to some of the details of VPN security management.

Selecting Encryption Methods

As you set up your VPN, you'll find that there are two major constraints on securing your data to the desired degree (after you've selected the VPN protocols you'll use). First, even though some protocols like IPSec support a variety of encryption protocols in the specifications, not all products include every encryption algorithm. Second are the country-specific restrictions on exportable key lengths. For instance, here in the United States, you're usually restricted to using 40-bit or 56-bit key lengths with DES for export, although you can use 128-bit key lengths within the United States.

After you've collected and analyzed the corporate data we outlined in Chapter 8, "Designing Your VPN," and selected the products for your VPN from Chapters 10–12, you should be able to select the appropriate algorithms and key lengths.

Protocols and Their Algorithms

Each of the VPN protocols we've discussed in this book—IPSec, PPTP, and L2TP—specify their own list of allowed algorithms for encrypting data.

Although PPTP can use PPP and its negotiable encryption options (including DES and Triple DES) to encrypt data, Microsoft has incorporated an encryption method called *Microsoft Point-to-Point Encryption* (MPPE) for use with PPTP tunnels. MPPE uses the RC4 algorithm with either 40-bit or 128-bit keys, depending on export restrictions. Similarly, L2TP can use PPP to encrypt data, but the preferred method is to use IPSec for this task.

Within IPSec, the default encryption algorithm for use in ESP is DES with an explicit initialization vector. IPSec allows alternative algorithms to be used. These include Triple DES, CAST-128, RC5, IDEA, Blowfish, and ARCFour (a public implementation of RC4).

The choice of supporting algorithms other than DES is left to vendors, so you may find that a vendor's products do not support the alternative algorithm you had planned on using. DES and Triple DES seem to be the most common algorithms supported thus far. There's a definite benefit to having a choice of encryption algorithms: Would-be attackers not only must break the cipher, but they also must determine which cipher they are attempting to break.

Recalling the Oakley modes used in IPSec (Chapter 5), main mode negotiates the encryption method, hash, authentication method, and Diffie-Hellman group between VPN endpoints. The Diffie-Hellman group determines the strength of the keying material; there are 4 Diffie-Hellman groups. Diffie-Hellman Group 1 is strong enough for DES, and Groups 2 and 3 should be used for Triple DES. Because main mode might require six packets, if you're using high-latency satellite connections, for example, it would be better to use the stronger Diffie-Hellman group, even for DES.

Oakley's quick mode also negotiates the algorithms and lifetimes for IPSec. These lifetimes determine how often, based on time or data, another quick-mode negotiation is required. The main-mode lifetime controls the Oakley SA, and the quick-mode lifetime controls the IPSec SA. As an example, the quick-mode lifetime could be set to 15 minutes, or 10 MB, and the main mode lifetime set to 1 hour, or 40 MB, when DES is being used for IPSec. These lifetimes would be increased for Triple DES, because it's more secure than DES, or decreased for ARCFour, because it's less secure than DES. The idea is to balance the strength of the IPSec services and the strength of the underlying cryptographic algorithms against the cost of ISAKMP/Oakley packet overhead; too many changes in keys could affect the efficiency of your network.

Key Lengths

Back in Chapter 8, "Designing Your VPN," we suggested that you determine the sensitivity of your data so that you could calculate how long it will be sensitive and how long it'll have to be protected. When you've figured that out, you can select an encryption algorithm and key length that should take longer to break than the length of time for which your data will be sensitive.

As a starting point, take a look at Table 13.1, which is a condensation of information from Bruce Schneier's book, *Applied Cryptography*, which we also used in Chapter 4, "Security: Threats and Solutions." The table does a good job of illustrating that many of the key lengths currently in use can be broken with a relatively small outlay of funds. This table also helps

TABLE 13.1 Comparison of Time and Money Needed to Break Different Length Keys

| Cost | *Length of key in bits* | | | | |
	40	*56*	*64*	*80*	*128*
$100 K	2 secs.	35 hrs.	1 yr.	70,000 yrs.	10^{19} yrs.
$1 M	.2 secs.	3.5 hrs.	37 days	7000 yrs.	10^{18} yrs.
$100 M	2 millisecs	2 mins.	9 hrs.	70 yrs.	10^{16} yrs.
$1 G	.2 millisecs	13 secs.	1 hr.	7 yrs.	10^{15} yrs.
$100 G	2 microsecs	.1 sec.	32 secs.	24 days	10^{13} yrs.

emphasize this point: know your attacker. If you expect that highly skilled and well-funded industrial spies will be attempting to intercept and decrypt your data, then long key lengths and frequent rekeying are an absolute necessity.

These estimates are for brute-force attacks, that is, guessing every possible key. There are other methods for cracking keys, depending on the ciphers used, which is what keeps cryptanalysts employed, but estimates for brute-force attacks are commonly cited as a measure of the strength of an encryption method.

Remember that this is not a static situation either. Computing power is always going up and costs are falling, so it'll get easier and cheaper to break larger keys in the future. Off-the-shelf processing power (costing around $500 thousand) can crack the 56-bit DES code in 19 days; hackers choosing to invest in custom chips could break the code in a few hours. A student at UC Berkeley used a network of 250 workstations to crack the 40-bit RC5 algorithm in three and a half hours.

Key Management for Gateways

A number of keys are usually required for secure communications between two gateways. First is the key pair that identifies two gateways to each other; these keys might be hard-wired, exchanged manually, or transmitted via digital certificates. Second are the session keys required for authentication and encryption of the packets transmitted between the gateways, using IPSec's AH and ESP headers, for instance. Different keys are required for each IPSec header and are negotiated via security associations (see Chapter 5). If both AH and ESP are used to process packets, for instance, then two SAs are negotiated between the gateways or hosts.

Identification of Gateways

Before a secure tunnel can be established between two security gateways, or between a remote host and a gateway, these devices have to be authenticated by each other and agree on a key. First, let's look at exchanges between two gateways. This authentication is not the same as the authentication of packets using the AH header; here, we are authenticating the devices themselves.

Gateways using public-key pairs can be authenticated manually. In such cases, the key pairs are usually hard-wired into the device before it's shipped. The network manager then registers the new device with other security gateways on the VPN, giving those gateways the public key so that they can exchange session keys.

If a security gateway isn't shipped with hard-wired keys, the gateway would be set to randomly generate its own key pair. A digital certificate then would be signed with the private key and sent to the appropriate certificate authority, either an in-house certificate server or a third-party CA like VeriSign. When the certificate is approved, that certificate is available from the CA for use by other security gateways and remote clients to authenticate the site before any data is exchanged (see Figure 13.2).

Although these certificates do not need to be standardized (using the X.509 standard, for instance) if only one vendor's products are used for the VPN, interoperability between products is possible when X.509 certificates are employed. More vendors are adopting this approach, which also makes it easier to utilize an outside certificate authority for storing the necessary certificates. This might be a necessity if you're expanding your VPN to include partners in an extranet.

Other gateways and remote hosts usually will obtain the appropriate certificate from a CA to authenticate the destination gateway by using mechanisms such as LDAP or HTTP to retrieve certificate information through a *public key infrastructure* (PKI) Existing PKIs also require checking *certificate revocation lists* (CRL) to ensure the validity of an existing certificate. However, because the CA hierarchy for verifying certificates that we described in Chapter 4, "Security: Threats and Solutions," can

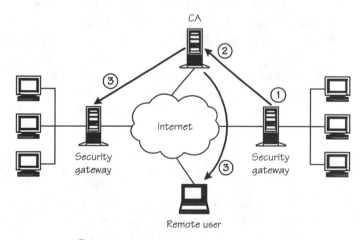

① Generate key pair
② Register public key with CA
③ Deliver public key in digital certificate upon request

FIGURE 13.2 Key exchanges between gateways.

become ungainly, and CRLs can become complicated to handle, other mechanisms for verifying certificates are being developed and most likely will become available starting in 1999. In particular, the IETF PKIX working group has been working on definitions for an interoperable PKI and *Online Certificate Status Protocol* (OCSP). OCSP aims to provide an efficient method for handling compromised or revoked certificates (see "Hardware-Based Security" later in this chapter).

These systems are based on assigning a public-key pair to each security gateway, and the public key is published in a directory that's accessible to all VPN sites. At the start of each encrypted session, the session key is scrambled by combining the security gateway's private key with the recipient's public key.

Handling Session Keys

If key exchange (such as in IPSec and L2TP) is required between sites, the most basic method is to exchange keys manually. An initial session key is randomly generated by one security gateway and then the network manager has to deliver the key to the administrator of the second device, by telephone, registered mail, or bonded courier, for instance. The second administrator inputs the key to the second security gateway, and a secure session between the two gateways can take place. New keys are generated as required (perhaps once a week) and distributed in the same fashion as before.

This approach is rather cumbersome and not particularly secure; phone lines can be tapped and mail can be intercepted. Dynamic key management, using IKE for instance, is much easier and better suited to frequent key changes and large numbers of sites. Session keys are randomly generated, either by the initiating security gateway or a key-management server, and distributed over the network. The session key itself is scrambled using the recipient's public key before transmission on the net.

Hardware-Based Security

Hardware-based encryption products are less vulnerable to physical attack, which reduces the chances of compromised device keys and, therefore, the need to exchange new keys between gateways. Whether keys are hard-wired or entered from a management workstation, most hardware encryptors are strongly sealed against physical prying and usually erase any stored keys when disturbed.

If session keys are compromised, you'll need a way to revoke a key pair and assign a new one. The procedures for key revocation vary from product to product. How security gateways respond to a revoked key also varies among products. The best, most secure method is to drop the session and log the failed attempt as soon as a revoked key is detected. Some products wait for a session to be completed before denying any further access with that key.

If you're in a situation where your VPN is restricted to shorter length keys than you would like (due to export restrictions, for example), then you should try to improve the security of your VPN sessions by increasing the frequency of rekeying. If keys are used for shorter lengths of time, then any attacker will have less time to acquire the information he needs to break a key; also, the amount of data that could be obtained with a compromised key will be reduced.

Key Management for Users

Generating and distributing keys for LAN-to-LAN VPNs can be a relatively simple process to manage when the number of sites is not very large. Even if the number of sites is in the hundreds, a dynamic system using an outside certificate authority or in-house certificate server should not involve a great deal of management overhead. On the other hand, managing keys for remote users, if they number in the thousands, needs to be as scalable and automated as possible. An automated system also is required if you plan to use the antireplay protection in IPSec. Distribution of the keys and associated information, in particular, may be especially tedious and time-consuming.

Back in Chapter 5, "Using IPSec to Build a VPN," we pointed out that a pair of IPSec devices has to establish a security association with each other in order to communicate. If you're planning to support a large number of remote users with a security gateway, then you'll need to generate the client security associations centrally and probably in large numbers. The most practical way is to set up a central site to generate all IPSec SA parameters needed and to provide a mechanism to import them into the client. For example, a central site could generate SA data in S/WAN format and send the appropriate information to each client user.

The IPSec architecture is based on the assumption that hosts assign the *Security Parameter Index* (SPI) for inbound IPSec headers, but the essential requirement is simply that inbound SPIs be unique. If you set up a central site for generating keying material and assigning the SPIs to use

Protecting Clients Against Theft

Because laptops are particularly susceptible to theft, they pose a special security risk to your VPN because the keys stored on a stolen laptop could be used to access corporate resources via the VPN.

There are essentially three techniques for protecting keys from theft:

1. Store the keys on a removable device like a disk or smartcard and carry it separately from the clients.
2. Encrypt the keys with a secret password or phrase and require the client to verify the password before IPSec can be used (some smartcards can do this as well).
3. Encrypt the keys with a secret password or phrase and let IPSec processing fail if the wrong password is used.

Of these options, the third is the most secure. But, it also can be the most annoying to a legitimate user if he accidentally enters the wrong password because he may not be able to discern the reason for a communications failure.

them, then the client software can use those SPIs for communications without having to generate any on their own.

Remote VPN users have to be authenticated by security gateways in much the same way as security gateways have to identify themselves to each other and be authenticated. The number of options for authenticating users are greater, though, and will be covered in the following section. Since the use of digital certificates for user identification is becoming more popular and is now being supported by more VPN products, we'll discuss the details of managing certificates for users in "Managing an In-House CA" later in this chapter.

Authentication Services

As we discussed in Chapter 4, a variety of ways exist to authenticate users: simple passwords, one-time passwords, challenge/response systems using RADIUS or TACACS+, or two-factor systems using tokens, as well as digital certificates. If you're already supporting remote access via a modem bank and remote access server, for instance, then you already may have an authentication system in place and you'll just need to link it to your security gateway to control the authentication and access rights of your VPN users.

If you're using PPTP, L2F, or L2TP to create tunnels, you might be using your ISP as a tunnel endpoint, as we discussed in Chapters 6, "Using PPTP to Build a VPN," and 7, "Using L2TP to Build a VPN." Should that be the case, the ISP should be running its own authentication server, which, in turn, is a proxy to your authentication server (see Figure 13.3). This enables you to maintain control over setting authentication parameters and access rights but lets the ISP use that information to provide access to your remote users.

Assuming that you may be setting up an authentication system for the first time as you roll out your VPN, you can choose from any of the different approaches we mentioned earlier. (See Chapter 4, "Security: Threats and Solutions," for more details.) The better systems are RADIUS, token-based authentication, and digital certificates.

RADIUS has three advantages. It's been standardized by the IETF, and many vendors offer products that interoperate. RADIUS also is used by the majority of ISPs for authenticating their customers. Lastly, RADIUS can act as a centralized authentication database, drawing on rights defined for users from various network operating systems such as NT's user domains and NDS trees, making it a good platform for integration.

Both RADIUS and TACACS+ let you define how to authenticate and pass session variables, such as protocol types, addresses, and other parameters. An important feature in both of these systems in the capability to define server-based access control policies. These policies can include time-of-day restrictions, usage quotas, simultaneous login controls (each user can use only one session at a time), and login threshold violations (accounts are locked after *X* number of consecutive failed logins). RADIUS also can be used for accounting purposes, although quota enforcement

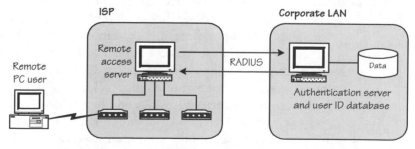

FIGURE 13.3 Main and proxy authentication servers.

requires constant tracking of each user's time online and can become a relatively complex task.

A RADIUS server usually consists of three main files: a database of authorized users, a file of client access servers that are authorized to request authentication services, and a set of customized options, called *dictionaries,* for each remote access server or security gateway. If you were configuring RADIUS for use with an ISP and PPTP, for instance, you would add the name or address of the ISP's proxy server to the file of client access servers and define a new dictionary for that server, describing any special authentication and authorization features for the server. (TACACS+ does not include dictionaries in its architecture.)

Token-based authentication usually requires using a special reader attached to the workstation or laptop and a token card that generates special passcodes that are checked by a secure server on the network before access is granted to the user. Before users are permitted to authenticate themselves, token devices request a PIN. Two of the more popular mechanisms for verifying users are a challenge-response system (see Chapter 4) or time synchronization, which depends on synchronized clocks and a frequently changing secret key that the user has to enter when logging in. Although tokens are a very secure method for authentication, because they use a two-factor method (i.e., something the user has—the token card— and something the user knows—the PIN), they can prove to be awkward to use because of the additional hardware that's required.

It's also possible to use digital certificates for authenticating users, although these systems aren't nearly as widespread as RADIUS servers. That's likely to change with time. Some of your employees already may be using personal digital certificates with their Web browsers or e-mail clients. If you're already sending secure e-mail that requires digital certificates and a public-key infrastructure (see Chapter 4), then you could use the same system for issuing and storing the digital certificates required for authentication on the VPN. If not, you'll have to set up an appropriate certificate authority for your users; this could be either a commercial CA like Verisign or an in-house certificate server that you maintain.

Using a third-party certificate authority can make certificate management easier, because it'll be accessible via the Internet and would be more readily accessible to any extranet partners. But, if you're supporting only internal users (i.e., corporate employees), an in-house CA should work just fine. Since your security gateways will be performing authentication of the VPN's users, outside access to the digital certificates isn't necessary. But, you'll still need to secure the computer used for issuing and storing digital certificates, as well as any backup files or tapes (see the next section).

Whichever course you choose, you'll need a way to initially distribute to each user the approved digital certificates and the private keys they contain. Outside CAs normally handle certificate distribution via e-mail or HTTP. If you're running your own certificate server, you can do the same, but you also might choose a physical means, such as a floppy disk or smart card. Many companies are employing smart cards for distributing and storing digital certificates because of their portability and the fact that they also can be further secured with a user-specific PIN that makes the card useless if lost or stolen. Plus, these cards shut down after a series of failed login attempts.

Managing an In-House CA

Digital certificates have a limited lifecycle (see Figure 13.4); after they're issued, they should be expired after a reasonable period of time (6 months, for instance) or may be revoked if the owner changes jobs or his private key is compromised. Certificates also can be renewed and need to be backed up in case keys need to be recovered at a later date. If you want to run your own certificate authority in-house, managing the system will involve not only creating key pairs and issuing certificates but also managing those keys and certificates. Certificate management includes maintaining a certificate repository, revoking certificates as needed, and issuing *certificate revocation lists* (CRLs). Key management involves key backup and recovery, automatic updates of key pairs (and their certificates), and management of key histories.

As you plan the deployment of a private certificate server, keep in mind that the infrastructure for digital certificates and certificate manage-

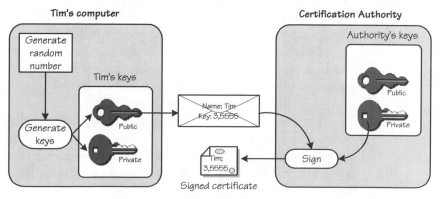

FIGURE 13.4 The lifecycle of digital certificates.

OCSP: A Dynamic Way to Track Certificates

There currently is no practical way to revoke a certificate if the password that unlocks a user's certificate is breached or when the user's private key is compromised. The only solution certificate servers offer right now is the CRL. Ultimately, we'll be looking to the PKIX standard and OCSP for a real solution.

The only way you can use CRLs is by laboriously matching up two lists (the list in your local storage and the one in the CRL) and deleting certificates by hand. OCSP moves away from this static-list model toward a more dynamic one. OCSP defines LDAP and HTTP status queries that are designed to provide fast response time and high availability. In response to a client query, an OCSP server sends a simple status message—valid, invalid, revoked, not revoked, or expired. Using this model, the load is balanced between the client and the server, and it becomes possible to do real-time certificate checking on a per-transaction basis.

ment is still in a relatively early stage of development. The use of CRLs for monitoring revoked certificates is also inadequate for dynamic situations, such as you're likely to encounter with remote users accessing a VPN. But, new solutions, like Online Certificate Status Protocol (OCSP), are also under development. Furthermore, commercially available certificate servers still need improvement of their support for administrative tasks. In-house CA systems can be purchased from Certco Inc., Entrust Technologies Inc., GTE CyberTrust Inc., Microsoft Corp., Netscape Communications Corp., Security Dynamics Technologies Inc., and Xcert Software Inc. Some VPN product vendors include a CA as an option, although many of these products are software-based CAs installed on a workstation. Radguard offers a sealed hardware-based CA for use with cIPro.

Despite these problems, a private certificate server can be installed and managed within your corporation to authenticate both security gateways and users on your network. Let's take a look at some of the features that a useful certificate system should include.

The basic task of a certificate server is to accept requests for new certificates, queue them for their review by the system administrator, and issue the certificates for client retrieval (see Figure 13.5). In general, certificate servers accept certificate requests from a certificate-management workstation, when an administrator is performing batch issues of certificates, or from individuals themselves via HTTP or e-mail. Whenever new requests for certificates are received, they should be matched against certificates held in the directory to prevent accidental obsolescence of valid public keys. The user's certificate can be presented to its owner via HTTP or e-mail as well, or transferred to a disk or smart card for manual distribution.

The private keys of each public-key pair that's issued should be stored within a central repository that's secured against unauthorized access. This repository also should be backed up in a secure fashion (usually as encrypted files), because it becomes part of the key-recovery system should older messages need to be decrypted if a key is lost or compromised and revoked. Backup tapes must be carefully guarded and strictly accounted for.

Since you'll be signing all issued certificates as a certificate authority, a special, dedicated workstation will need to be set up for storing the private keying material (your *root certificate*, as it's called); this same workstation also will include any of the software (and any special hardware, if it's required) for collecting, signing, distributing, and revoking certificates. This workstation should be physically secured against unauthorized access; it should not be treated as a multipurpose computer.

Because one of the purposes of digital certificates is to distribute a public-key pair, the certificate system needs a way of making the public key available to those who need it. The usual method is to store the public keys in a directory. Although large-scale master directories for certificates may be based on X.500, there's been a significant move to use another protocol, *Lightweight Directory Access Protocol* (LDAP), to utilize much of the structure of X.500, but over TCP/IP. Many certificate servers now offered

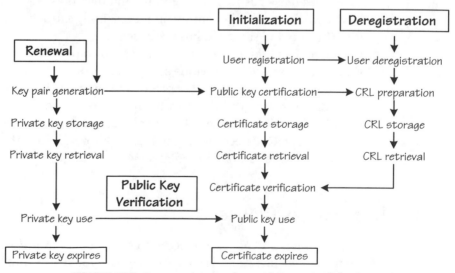

FIGURE 13.5 Generating and certifying a public key.

for use at corporate sites are based on LDAP. The increasing popularity of LDAP for directory access also will make it easier for you to link other directory-based services to your digital certificates.

Certificate servers also have to maintain and make available a Certificate Revocation List which lets users know which certificates are no longer valid. Certificates may be revoked because they were lost, stolen, or because an employee left the company, for example.

For small numbers of digital certificates, a single centralized certificate server will most likely suffice. But, if the number of certificates that the company requires is large, using multiple certificate servers arranged in some sort of hierarchy (perhaps based on departments) will be more manageable and more reliable because the system no longer has a single point of failure. Some certificate servers support multiple levels of administration; one group can perform certificate approval and revocation tasks, for instance, and another group can perform these functions as well as assign certificate authority to subordinate CAs. This makes it possible to set up distributed administration by assigning responsibility for a portion of the directory tree to another CA and set of administrators.

You also should be able to set certain parameters for the clients from your central system; these parameters should include defaults such as approved directory servers and certificate signers.

The task of supporting user access to certificates will become much easier if your system can support more than one method for requesting and receiving a certificate. At a minimum, clients should be able to perform these tasks using HTTP, e-mail, and disk files. As we've said before, smart cards are also becoming an increasingly attractive alternative for distributing and storing digital certificates.

Users should be informed of the need to properly store and protect their certificates. The previous sidebar on protecting clients against theft includes some suggestions for protecting their certificates.

Lastly, expect the client software to provide automatic checking of a certificate's validity using CRL downloads (in the background, for offline use). When OCSP becomes available, look for software that supports it so that certificates can be immediately verified online.

Controlling Access Rights

Even though a VPN is architected to provide communications between hosts and security gateways, it's likely that you'll still want to maintain some control over the access that each VPN user has to network resources.

For instance, if sales department personnel are not allowed access to R and D resources when they're on a hard-wired LAN, they should still be restricted from that access if they dial into the VPN while they're on the road. This means that you'll have to merge the control of the new access routes provided by your VPN with the access controls currently programmed into your routers and firewalls.

VPN traffic can be handled in two different ways by a firewall, either as unfiltered packets or as filtered packets (see Figure 13.6). In the unfiltered approach, the VPN traffic is handled the same way it is in a router; that is, the protected data is transferred directly to the internal network without any filtering or controls on its contents. In the filtered approach, the firewall's filter and proxy controls are applied to the VPN traffic before it is allowed into the internal network. Filtering VPN traffic can be particu-

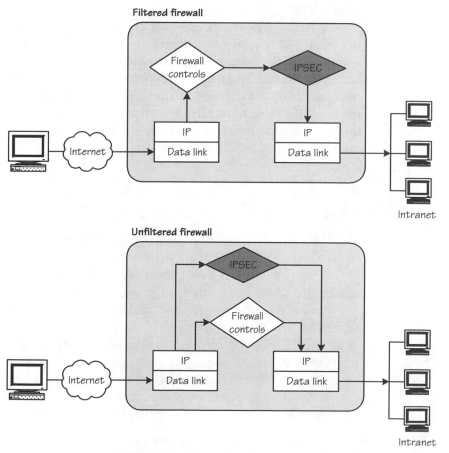

FIGURE 13.6 Firewalls filtering VPN.

larly useful if your security policy is to pass only certain types of traffic between VPN sites, say e-mail and FTP. Filtering also can be useful for controlling the traffic exchanged with business partners if you expand your VPN to an extranet.

If you place the gateway between the Internet and the router, then the router (and subsequent firewalls) can be used to filter both VPN and non-VPN traffic with the same rules; the gateway will provide transparent encryption and decryption services to the entire site. Also, the router doesn't need to be reconfigured to pass special tunnel traffic, which is the case when a gateway is installed behind the router. One caution: If the gateway is on the public, or untrusted, side of the network, you need to ensure that management of the gateway cannot be compromised from someone on the untrusted net. If this link is handling both VPN and non-VPN traffic, then the VPN gateway needs to be configured to pass non-VPN traffic.

When you locate the gateway behind a router or firewall, the control device would have to be configured to pass VPN traffic without filtering. Although this increases the security of the gateway (it's less susceptible to compromising the management port, for instance), it also means that you have less control over the traffic entering the LAN after decryption by the gateway. If you want to filter VPN traffic by destination, time-of-day, or application type, for instance, then you have to duplicate the filters from your router or firewall on the gateway.

Summary

Much of the management of security for VPNs is a straightforward extension of standard corporate security policies, especially for authentication of users and control of their access to network resources. However, VPNs do require added knowledge of the strengths and weaknesses of different encryption algorithms and associated key lengths so that the data transmitted on a VPN is properly protected.

The distribution of keys to authenticate security gateways and remote hosts on a VPN is an important part of VPN management, with many systems employing digital certificates for this task. Either commercial certificate authorities or a private in-house certificate server can be used to issue and control distribution of the digital certificates.

14

IP Address Management

The explosive growth in the use of IP for data communications, both within and among enterprises, has led to a number of problems in the allocation and management of IP addresses. Although the original 32-bit address space of IPv4 may have seemed sufficient to handle any network's requirements when it was first described, there is a growing concern that IPv4's address space will soon prove inadequate, at least for the public Internet. (Private internetworks are another matter, as we'll see shortly.) The next generation of IP, version 6 or IPv6, features a 128-bit address space, which should be suitable for some time, but until it's deployed globally, other short-term solutions to address shortages have been put into place. Unfortunately, although these short-term solutions help network managers deal with current-day addressing and routing problems, they can cause problems for those of us deploying VPNs.

Although IPSec, as well as many other protocols, may be best suited for use with IPv6, most of us have to deal with the current situation surrounding the continued use of IPv4 and the added complexity that various short-term solutions bring with them. Because IPv4 is likely to stay around for the next few years, VPN design and deployment has to accommodate the complexities surrounding address management even as network engineers look for other solutions that will make addressing easier to use within VPNs.

To help point out some of the addressing problems VPN designers and managers face, this chapter covers the current methods for allocating addresses to network devices, both on public and private networks, as well as the related task of naming network entities via the Domain Name Service (DNS). As we go along, we'll point out some of the special problems VPNs may incur. Wherever possible we'll also discuss some of the current solutions proposed to counter these problems.

Address Allocation and Naming Services

For large enterprises, allocating IP addresses among thousands of workstations and servers and configuring these addresses in TCP/IP software is often a daunting task. In the past, adding, moving, or changing workstations and servers required manual assignment of new IP addresses. Simplistic approaches to tracking addresses, such as a notebook or electronic spreadsheet, may work for small networks, but these approaches quickly prove to be inadequate as networks get larger. Automated servers and related tools have to be employed to ensure that the networks run smoothly. Foremost among these for IP networks are Dynamic Host Control Protocol (DHCP) for address management and DNS for name management; and now, using Dynamic DNS to link the two makes network management easier, although not foolproof.

A variety of problems can result from inadequate tracking of network addresses. Without proper tracking, addresses can be lost during equipment changes or moves just when network growth is leading to address scarcity. Not knowing which addresses are assigned can lead to mistakenly assigning the same address to two different machines, which leads to loss of connectivity and routing problems.

Another difficult task is allocating addresses for mobile users. Roaming sales reps with laptops may have to be provided with multiple network addresses, one for each router or remote access server that they might access via a dial connection leading to a waste of addresses and further tracking nightmares. Multiple addresses aren't needed when you convert the users of your remote access servers to a VPN, but you may still want to dynamically assign an address rather than use static allocations.

The current state of allocating addresses to companies also causes problems. Companies requiring addresses for more than 1,000 devices cannot obtain Class A or B network addresses and usually are forced to use *Classless Inter-Domain Routing* (CIDR) to combine available Class C addresses. But, using CIDR requires contiguous network numbers, leading to grouping networks by region so that all network numbers within a given region can be represented by a single entry in the routing tables of other regions (see Figure 14.1). If addresses for devices in a given region are not allocated contiguously, then routing table aggregation cannot be performed, and router performance will be reduced.

Static and Dynamic Address Allocation

In the past, an IP address was usually allocated by hand to a network device such as a router, server, or workstation when the device was attached to the network. (Printers and other devices using BOOTP are exceptions.) These addresses corresponded to the subnet in which the device was located—172.52.X.X for Human Resources versus 172.53.X.X for R and D, for instance—and had to be changed if the computer was relocated to another subnet. Furthermore, a device's address was static and didn't change unless someone (usually the network manager) changed the device's configuration file.

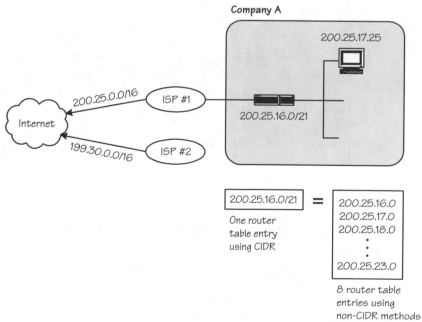

FIGURE 14.1 CIDR and routing table aggregation.

Allocating IPv4 Addresses

IP addresses are divided into three major classes: A, B, and C. (A fourth class, D, is reserved for special uses such as multicasting.) Each address consists of four octets, or sets of eight binary digits, separated by decimals. The first octet determines the class of the IP address. Class A addresses use the last three octets to specify IP nodes; Class B addresses use the last two octets for this purpose; and Class C addresses use the last octet.

Class A network addresses are the most desirable, because they are large enough to serve the needs of any size enterprise (see Table 14.1). But since fewer than 128 Class A networks can exist in the entire Internet, they are very scarce, and no more Class As are being allocated. Only those organizations that were early users of the Internet (e.g., Xerox Corp., Stanford U., BBN) are in possession of Class A network addresses.

TABLE 14.1 Properties of IPv4 Address Classes

Class	Network ID	# Unique networks	Host address ID	# Unique hosts
A	7 bits	128	24 bits	16,777,216
B	14 bits	>16,000	16 bits	65,536
C	21 bits	>2,000,000	8 bits	256

The more than 16,000 possible Class B networks also have become scarce and are now difficult to obtain. There is a large supply (over 2 million) of Class C network addresses, so they are still plentiful. The major problem is that for most organizations, a Class C network is too small (only 256 unique Host IDs). Even a Class B network is not large enough for an enterprise with more than a thousand LANs.

But, networks are far from static: Equipment gets changed or upgraded; people and equipment are moved; and networks rearchitected. Manually assigning static IP addresses is time-consuming when any changes are necessary; it also can be an error-prone process. To help deal with this continuing problem, a dynamic method for allocating addresses, the *Dynamic Host Control Protocol* (DHCP) was developed. And, since users normally are more comfortable with names rather than numeric addresses for network devices, the standard naming service, *Domain Name Service* (DNS), also was modified so that it could dynamically link with DHCP and track any changes made by DHCP.

DHCP is designed to provide a centralized approach to the configuration and maintenance of an IP address space, allowing the network administrator to configure various clients on the network from a single location. DHCP permits IP address leases to be dynamically assigned to workstations, eliminating the need for static IP address allocation by network and systems management staff. Pools of available IP addresses are maintained by DHCP servers.

DHCP operation is fairly straightforward. When a DHCP client workstation boots, it broadcasts a DHCP request asking for any DHCP server on the network to provide it with an IP address and configuration parameters. A DHCP server on the network that is authorized to configure this client will offer an IP address by sending a reply to the client. The client can either accept it or wait for additional offers from other servers on the network. Eventually, the client selects a particular offer notifying the proper server. The selected server then sends back an acknowledgment with the offered IP address and any other configuration parameters that the client might have requested.

DHCP servers aren't restricted to assigning only dynamic addresses. A set of addresses can be set aside as static network addresses for assignment to specific clients, such as file and mail servers. The DHCP server treats the lease periods for each of these static addresses as infinite.

The IP address offered to the client by a DHCP server has an associated lease time, which dictates how long the IP address is valid. During the lifetime of the lease, the client usually will ask the server to renew. If the client chooses not to renew or if the client machine is shut down, the lease will eventually expire, and the IP address can be given to another machine.

The *Domain Name Service* (DNS) is the Internet's official naming system and is designed to name various network resources, including IP addresses. DNS is a distributed naming system—the database that translates names to objects is scattered across many thousands of host computers.

Domain name requests (i.e., requests to convert a network name into its corresponding network address) are handled by a hierarchy of DNS servers (see Figure 14.2). Requests are sent first to the local (i.e., lowest level) nameserver in the network hierarchy, with the IP address of this nameserver typically configured in each workstation's TCP/IP software. If this nameserver cannot answer the query, it sends the request to a higher level nameserver. This higher level nameserver can either resolve the name request itself or obtain information from a lower level nameserver that's unknown to the original requester. For example, the marketing and sales subdomains at **Big Company** may have nameservers at the same level in the DNS hierarchy, but the only way that users in marketing can obtain name information from the sales nameserver would be to request it via the bigcompany.com higher level nameserver.

In the past, DNS was designed to work with static IP addresses. A relatively new feature, Dynamic DNS (DDNS), has been defined by the IETF (RFC 2136) and now is provided by some vendors for their DHCP servers to automatically pass IP address lease-assignment information to DNS servers. This permits workstations with addresses assigned dynamically by DHCP to be tracked by DNS servers; workstations are then reachable by a name without manually maintaining the DNS database (see Figure 14.3).

Even though DHCP and Dynamic DNS can simplify IP address management, DHCP's dynamic allocation of IP addresses can cause other problems. Some firewalls and other Internet security products track IP addresses on the assumption that an IP address uniquely identifies a computer. If these products cannot map a DHCP-assigned address back to a specific user, an unauthorized user may gain access to the network because the address is authorized to go beyond the firewall, but the user is not.

Similarly, any attempt to debug problems on a live network relies on being able to translate an IP address to a particular user's computer. Other problems that can arise from dynamic IP address assignments might include control of content filtering (i.e., restricting Web browsing to certain sites), as well as billing and chargeback.

Dynamic address assignments can create problems for your security setup unless you're prepared for them. Because firewalls often match

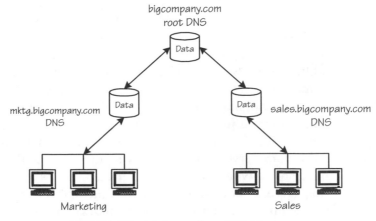

FIGURE 14.2 A hierarchy of DNS servers.

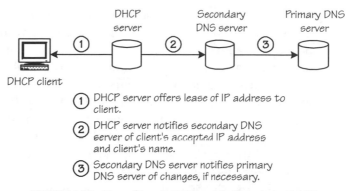

FIGURE 14.3 Coupling DHCP and dynamic DNS.

access rights to IP addresses, systems supporting DHCP should allow for the reservation of a batch of IP addresses for a specific group of users (a specific named team or department, for instance). As long as those same IP addresses are the ones allowing firewall traversal, use of the firewall can be controlled on a group basis, even when IP addresses are dynamically assigned.

Although DHCP and DDNS are a nice fit, you can use DHCP without DDNS. In that case, not all devices on your net should have their addresses assigned dynamically. When assigning IP addresses to the file, mail, and other important servers on your net, static address assignment should be used. This makes it possible to use DNS to directly map network names to network addresses. Similarly, workstations that assume server functionality (e.g., personal Web servers) will normally also need static addresses so that they can be tracked by DNS.

Internal versus External DNS

When you're protecting external access to your intranet, say with a firewall or a security gateway, you have to take extra steps to protect your Domain Name Services while still allowing your users to access outside resources when necessary (and allowed). This usually involves setting up what is often called a double DNS scheme.

For a private IP network, your corporate DNS server would have sufficed, because it could take care of all address-name translations for the network, and the lack of a connection to the public Internet would help keep outsiders from discovering the names of corporate computing resources.

The first problem arises when you have a connection to the Internet and some corporate employees need access to resources on the outside. To properly map names to addresses, your corporate DNS server has to communicate with an external DNS server, presumably one hosted by your ISP. But, because you don't want outsiders to access your internal resources, you need to protect your internal DNS server (along with other network resources), so you install a firewall. Since the ISP's DNS server is outside the firewall, and your corporate DNS server is inside the firewall, they cannot readily communicate, which keeps employees from accessing outside resources as well as the reverse.

The solution is to install two corporate DNS servers: one on the outside of the firewall and one inside it. This is the double DNS scheme. The next step is to separate the hosts that had been on your sole DNS server into two groups. The first group lists those hosts that you want anyone on the Internet to find, such as your e-mail gateway, public Web site, and anonymous FTP server, for instance; it'll also include the name of the firewall's external interface. The second list contains the set of hosts that only your internal network users will be able to find. Don't forget that the second list also should include the external hosts that your internal users must be able to find.

As you might expect, the external DNS server stores the first list, and the internal DNS server stores the second list. The external DNS server is advertised to the Internet as the authoritative DNS server for your domain, which means that requests from Internet-based hosts will reach the external DNS server, but not the internal DNS server.

The hosts on your internal network use the internal DNS server as their primary DNS server. When they want to access external hosts, the internal DNS server will forward DNS resolution requests to the external DNS server outside the firewall. This is accomplished because the internal DNS server would be configured with a *forwarders entry* telling it where to find the external DNS server. Because the requests have to pass through the firewall, a DNS proxy service is set up on the firewall, allowing it to make a separate connection to the external DNS server on behalf of the internal DNS server (see Figure 14.4).

You may encounter similar situations with your VPN. If you're using an internal DNS server and shielding your DNS entries from the rest of the world, then you'll need a way to provide this information to the other sites and remote users of your VPN so that they can complete connections to appropriate resources. If you intend to allow access to a limited number of hosts on your VPN, then you could try maintaining dual DNS entries: one set for internal usage and the second for VPN use.

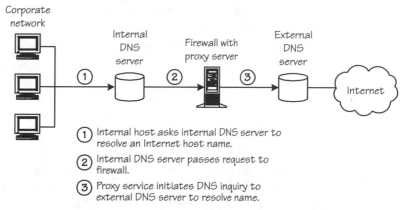

(1) Internal host asks internal DNS server to resolve an Internet host name.

(2) Internal DNS server passes request to firewall.

(3) Proxy service initiates DNS inquiry to external DNS server to resolve name.

FIGURE 14.4 Linking internal and external DNS.

Private Addresses and NAT

The blocks of IP addresses allocated by the IANA are meant for use on the public Internet. If your company had no intention of using the Internet, but would transmit only IP traffic on its own internetwork, then any range of addresses can be used. Even then, the IETF recommends that only certain ranges be used so that Internet routers would not be confused if the addresses were inadvertently advertised on the Internet. These blocks, which are defined in RFC 1597, "Address Allocation for Private Subnets," are as follows:

Class A	10.0.0.0–10.255.255.255
Class B	172.16.0.0–172.31.255.255
Class C	192.168.0.0–192.168.255.255

It's possible to use these private addresses for an internal internetwork and still connect to the Internet. To do so, you need to be allocated a block of registered addresses and use a firewall or router that performs *network address translation* (NAT).

NAT converts your inside addressing schemes into the registered addresses prior to forwarding the packets to the public Internet. The translation is fully compatible with standard routing functionality and features; NAT needs to be applied only on the router or firewall that is connected physically to both inside and outside addressing schemes.

NAT is interface independent, meaning that NAT can be applied to any interface on the router that links inside to outside addressing schemes.

In Figure 14.5, the host system is using a privatized IP address of 10.2.2.1 as part of the intranet. When the packet reaches the router, NAT translates the 10.2.2.1 address into another address from the NAT IP pool allocated, say 171.69.89.2. It is as if that machine is virtually moved to the outside network segment for outside communication purposes. This network segment resides within the NAT router box itself for this example.

The NAT IP pool is considered part of the outside addressing scheme and not part of the inside addressing scheme.

Remember that NAT requires the capability to translate any part of the headers and packets that reference the addressing scheme. IP and TCP checksums need to be accessible, limiting the encryption of these areas. When the data is encrypted within the IP packets, it is impossible for NAT to perform the internal packet address translations. Thus, hosts using encryption should be assigned legally registered, outside addresses, exempted from NAT.

One significant disadvantage is the loss of end-to-end IP traceability. It becomes much harder to trace packets that undergo numerous packet changes over multiple NAT hops.

If an enterprise uses the private address space, then DNS clients outside of the enterprise should not see addresses in the private address space used by the enterprise, because these addresses would be ambiguous. One way to ensure this is to run two servers for each DNS zone containing both publicly and privately addressed hosts. One server would be visible from the public address space and would contain only the subset of the enter-

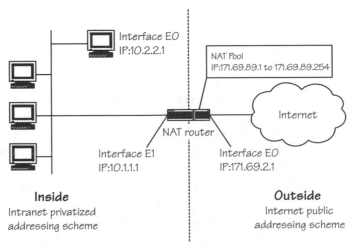

FIGURE 14.5 NAT at boundary router.

prise's addresses that were reachable using public addresses. The other server would be reachable only from the private network and would contain the full set of data, including the private addresses and whatever public addresses are reachable from the private network.

NAT configuration can become particularly complex for VPNs, so much so that various working groups within the IETF are still looking for the best solutions to typical uses of NAT and how they affect VPN design.

Multiple Links to the Internet

If you want to increase the reliability of your Internet connections for a VPN, one approach is to use redundant Internet connections (i.e., maintaining two, or more, connections) each served by a different ISP. But, redundant connections do pose problems of their own when configuring routers and firewalls.

The simplest method for supporting a second Internet connection is to connect both links to the same router and utilize the *Border Gateway Protocol* (BGP) on the router to decide which of the two ISPs should receive traffic (see Figure 14.6). This solution does not have the highest reliability, because the border router (as the one running BGP is called) can be a single point of failure. It's preferable to maintain two separate routes to the ISPs, with separate routers and firewalls for each path, as shown in Figure 14.7.

Even this might not be a perfect solution, however. The main problem with this configuration is that most firewalls do not share information about their connections; if one connection point fails, the information about the sessions using it cannot generally be passed on to the second

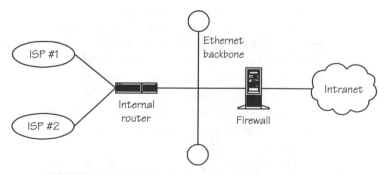

FIGURE 14.6 Multihomed connection to two ISPs.

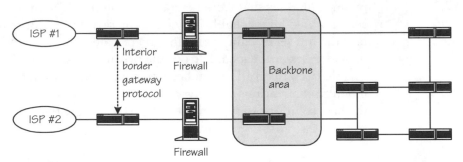

FIGURE 14.7 Multihomed connection using multiple routers and BGP.

connection point so that it can pick up where the failed connection left off. Most security gateways behave similarly, although at least one product, Bay Networks' Contivity Extranet Switch, has a failover system that provides communications between multiple servers.

If the security gateways and firewalls are either simple packet filters or can share state, you can use two routers and firewalls to connect to the Internet—provided the internal hosts have registered IP addresses that can be advertised to the Internet. If you've used privatized addresses with NAT to connect to the Internet, this won't work.

IPv6

Although we've focused on the current version of IP, IPv4, throughout most of this book, we would be remiss if we didn't write a few words about the next generation of IP, IPv6.

The current IPv4 address size for a node is only 32 bits, providing for 4,294,967,296 addresses. Although that may have seemed like enough when the protocol was first created in 1978, we're starting to see saturation of the available address space. That's partly due to the class-related method for allocating blocks of addresses—assigning contiguous blocks of addresses for Class A, B, and C networks is easy to implement but does not efficiently distribute addresses, especially for small- and medium-sized organizations. Some steps, such as *Classless Inter-Domain Routing* (CIDR), have been used to make address allocation more efficient, but these are stop-gap measures that don't address the crucial issue of the size of the address space itself.

But, IPv6 promises to solve that problem. The first notable difference between IPv6 and IPv4 is the length of its address field—it's 128 bits, or four times as long as that found in IPv4. In addition, IPv6 includes built-in support for such options as multicast support, IPSec, and flow control for quality of service, which have all been tested in IPv4 but had to be tacked on in a less-than-optimal fashion. Also, although the IPv6 header is larger than IPv4's, it has fewer fields, which should make routing more efficient as routers will have to do less processing per header (see Figure 14.8).

IPv4's 32-bit addresses are subdivided into four 8-bit groupings called octets, which are then expressed in what's known as the dot notation (i.e., 252.123.345.004). The designers of IPv6 have chosen a similar format composed of eight 16-bit integers separated by colons. Each integer is represented by four hexadecimal digits, as in FEDC:BA98:7654:3210:FEDE:BA98:7655:2130. Some IPv6 addresses can be obtained by prepending 96 zero bits to an IPv4 address. These IPv4-compatible addresses, as they're called, are important if you're planning

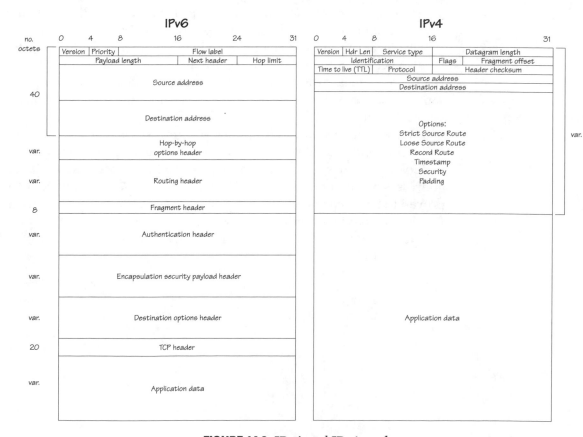

FIGURE 14.8 IPv4 and IPv6 packets.

to tunnel IPv6 packets through an IPv4 network, because the prepended zeros can be easily added to, or removed from, the IPv4 address.

The larger IPv6 addresses affect just about every part of your network; not only will you have to upgrade IP stacks for client and host computers, but you'll also have to upgrade your DNS servers and routers. DNS servers simply have to be refitted with software that can handle the larger IP addresses, which is a straightforward extension of DNS. But, switching to IPv6 will enable you to create a global addressing scheme for all your VPN sites without resorting to NAT and, therefore, reduce the need for extra reconfiguration of firewalls and DNS servers.

Summary

IP address allocation to networked devices within a company can be a painstaking, time-consuming, and error-prone task if handled manually. One solution to this problem is to utilize dynamic IP address allocation via DHCP. Because address-to-name mapping is an integral of any IP network, it's also necessary to link DNS to DHCP; this is now accomplished via DDNS, or Dynamic DNS. Special DNS configurations using multiple servers are needed if a firewall is used to separate the private corporate network from the rest of the Internet.

Allocation procedures for public IP addresses, along with the limited number of addresses defined in IPv4, have made it necessary to adopt a variety of solutions to simplify routing on the Internet and to use IP addresses on corporate networks. *Network Address Translation* (NAT) has proven to be a popular solution for enterprises wanting to keep a private IP address space for their intranet while still maintaining some connectivity with the public Internet. Unfortunately, NAT also can make it difficult to easily build VPNs.

15

Performance Management

It's an unwritten law of networking that, like nature and a vacuum, users abhor unused bandwidth and fill it quickly. The resulting network congestion can wreak corporate havoc, preventing high-priority traffic from getting through, frustrating users, and overwhelming network devices.

Furthermore, by combining many different types of traffic, today's multiservice networks, which may handle messaging, transactions, video, telephony, and more, are making it more difficult to allocate bandwidth and control the network.

Network performance and VPNs are inextricably interlinked. If VPN tunnels are to appear transparent to users and applications so that all sites appear as one large enterprise network, then the tunnels cannot act as performance bottlenecks. At the same time, these links may well not have the same bandwidth as that found on each site's LAN, so some care has to be exercised to ensure proper performance between VPN sites.

Since security gateways for a VPN often link two disparate bandwidth domains—that of the LAN and the usually significantly slower WAN—they are chokepoints for the flow of network traffic and can serve as ideal locations for controlling traffic based on application or user priorities. With this in mind, some vendors already have included support for traffic prioritization and bandwidth management within their VPN products; two noteworthy examples are Bay Networks' Contivity Extranet Switches and Check Point Software's Firewall-1.

This chapter covers the basics of network performance and related application requirements as well as methods for offering network services to your customers that can be differentiated on the basis of those application and/or user requirements. Then we'll talk about how policy-based network management can be used to help maintain control over network configurations and bandwidth control. Finally, the chapter discusses the role your ISP plays in supporting your VPN's performance.

Network Performance

Let's investigate the components of network performance before we move on to discuss how it can be managed.

Although bandwidth is the crucial factor when precise amounts of data must be delivered within a certain time period, latency affects the response time between clients and servers. Latency is the minimum time that elapses between requesting and receiving data and can be affected by many different factors, including bandwidth, an internetwork's infrastructure, routing techniques, and transfer protocols.

A network can contribute to latency in a number of ways:

1. *Propagation delay.* The length of time it takes information to travel the distance of the line. This type of delay is mostly determined by the speed of light and isn't affected by the networking technology in use.
2. *Transmission delay.* The length of time it takes to send the packet across a given medium. Transmission delay is determined by the speed of light and the size of the packet.
3. *Processing delay.* The time required by a router for looking up routes, changing the header, and other switching tasks.

Another factor, that of jitter, also affects real-time network traffic. Jitter is the variation in the latency. Irregular packet delays due to jitter can introduce distortion, making the multimedia signal unacceptable.

If we take a look at the best-effort delivery offered by IP, we see that IP networks treat every packet independently; a source may transmit a packet to a destination without any prior negotiation or communication.

Furthermore, the network has no information that a particular packet belongs to a suite of a packets, such as a file transfer or a video stream. The network will do its best to deliver each of these packets independently. This approach often introduces considerable latency and jitter in end-to-end paths, which aren't compatible with much of the data generated by the newer applications seen on networks that depend on known delays and little, if any, data loss. But, that's unsuitable for real-time applications, such as interactive multimedia, which often cannot tolerate retransmitted packets or indeterminate delays.

Requirements of Real-Time Applications

A wide variety of applications can run on networks. In addition to the bulk transfer applications like ftp, netnews, and e-mail, there are interactive applications ranging from a terminal emulator that requires entering commands to control responses from a remote host or using a Web browser to view pages on another site to interactive simulations between players in a multiplayer network and the even faster interactions required for transaction processing of online orders.

In the past, network managers could predict fairly well what the traffic patterns of their networks would be, because there were only a limited number of servers, legacy databases, and other network resources that most users accessed. But, that's changed considerably over the past few years as the World Wide Web and collaborative applications have changed interactions between users, both within, and among, subnets of an internetwork. At the same time, other new applications, utilizing streaming multimedia, videoconferencing, and so on, have increased the traffic on networks.

Traffic flowing across integrated enterprise networks can be grouped into three basic categories: real-time traffic, interactive traffic, and bulk transfer traffic (see Figure 15.1).

Real-time traffic, such as conversational voice, video conferencing, and real-time multimedia, requires very short latency and controlled jitter. Once minimum bandwidth requirements are met, higher available bandwidth can bring increased quality if the applications are designed to use it.

Interactive traffic, such as transaction processing, remote data entry, and some legacy protocols (e.g., SNA), requires latencies of approximately one second or less. Greater latencies cause processing delays as the users must wait for replies to their messages before they can continue their work. Interactive traffic is not sensitive to bandwidth beyond that needed to satisfy their latency requirements.

Bulk transfer traffic accepts virtually any network latency, including latencies on the order of a few seconds; it is more sensitive to the available bandwidth than to the latency. Increased bandwidth can result in sharply decreased transfer times; virtually all bulk transfer applications are designed to use all available bandwidth.

With the move to interactive multimedia, applications now require control over the QoS they receive from the networks. To support the different latency and bandwidth requirements of multimedia and other real-time applications, networks can use QoS parameters to accept an application's network traffic and prioritize it relative to other QoS requests from other applications. QoS provides network services that are differentiated by their bandwidth, latency, jitter, and error rates.

The increased use of multimedia is not the only reason to differentiate services and control traffic on your network. Some of the traffic flowing on your network is more critical to the running of your business than others; this traffic must go through, even if it means throttling back other, less essential traffic. It thus becomes important to be able to differentiate

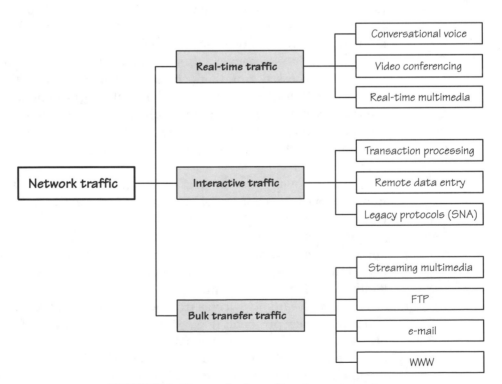

FIGURE 15.1 Networked application categories.

classes of network traffic and to have a system for dealing with these classes in different ways.

Supporting Differentiated Services

As you might expect, there's more than one approach to providing differentiating services to help deal with network congestion. The five commonly proposed techniques are as follows:

1. Over-provisioning network bandwidth.
2. Bandwidth conservation.
3. Traffic prioritization.
4. Static resource reservation.
5. Dynamic resource reservation.

Over-provisioning isn't exactly a method for differentiating services, but it can help deal with network congestion by allowing the network to handle a larger traffic volume. It's a reasonable solution for local and campus LANs. But, for WANs and VPNs, over-provisioning the bandwidth may not be a viable solution due to the high cost of the added bandwidth. Because there's often a noticeable mismatch in bandwidth (perhaps 100 to 1, or greater) at the LAN-WAN boundary (and hence the LAN-VPN tunnel boundary), some form of traffic management or control is needed.

Bandwidth-conservation techniques improve overall network performance by trying to ensure the most efficient use of the available network capacity rather than differentiating services. Some of the current conservation techniques are IP multicasting, data compression, and bandwidth-on-demand.

IP multicasting reduces the total amount of traffic on a network by eliminating the forwarding of redundant traffic. (For more details, see *IP Multicasting: The Complete Guide to Interactive Corporate Networks* by John Wiley and Sons, Inc., 1998.) The second technique, *bandwidth compression,* can be accomplished in routers to reduce bandwidth demands for a WAN link by a factor of two to four. Lastly, *bandwidth-on-demand* (BOD) can be used to provide additional bandwidth as needed by using additional analog or digital phone lines when the WAN interface becomes congested.

Each of these approaches may be usable in VPNs, but their applicability depends on the nature of your application demands. IP multicasting only works well when the same data is being transmitted to a number of receivers. If each session travelling across a VPN tunnel is between a different client and a different server, multicasting is of little help. Bandwidth compression may prove more useful, and some vendors (VPNet, for example) already have included it in their security gateways for processing IPSec traffic. But, the bandwidth savings may not be sufficient to meet your needs, and it does not address any latency problems. BOD also can prove useful by providing more bandwidth as needed, but the added links may cause configuration problems on VPNs or may not be able to inexpensively provide sufficient bandwidth (or latency) for your needs.

Traffic prioritization, or *Class of Service* (CoS), is a simple but useful tool for providing differentiated services. Routers can differentiate between service classes according to the precedence field in the header of each packet (IPv4's Type of Service, or TOS, field). This method offers a small fixed number of service classes and only guarantees that packets with higher precedence get better service than packets with lower precedence. Since there is no admission control, there is no mechanism to prevent classes from becoming overloaded.

To improve on CoS support, the major networking product vendors, like Cisco and 3Com, program admission control at edge routers, (i.e., routers that interface between a LAN, such as a branch office's LAN and a core network, such as the Internet or the main corporate network). These edge routers use preset policies, or rules, to assign traffic to classes before the traffic is forwarded to the core network (see Figure 15.2). The routers in the core network use one of a variety of algorithms to process the traffic classes, each of which has its own queue. A common algorithm for processing the queues is called *Weighted Fair Queueing* (WFQ), which prohibits large flows of packets from consuming large amounts of bandwidth, which could keep smaller flows from being transmitted. Because CoS is implemented at edge routers, those same routers can be the security gateways for your VPN, enabling you to combine VPN control and traffic control at the same point.

But, if traffic prioritization using classes is insufficient for your needs, and you choose to allocate network resources between real-time and non-real-time applications, then you have two choices. Either you can statically allocate the resources or you can allow resources to be reserved dynamically.

Static resource allocation enables you to reserve a portion of a network's capacity for a particular type of traffic, usually based on protocol, application, or user. In many enterprise networks, routers are often configured to devote a certain amount of their capacity to SNA traffic, for instance, to accommodate the requirements of legacy data transactions.

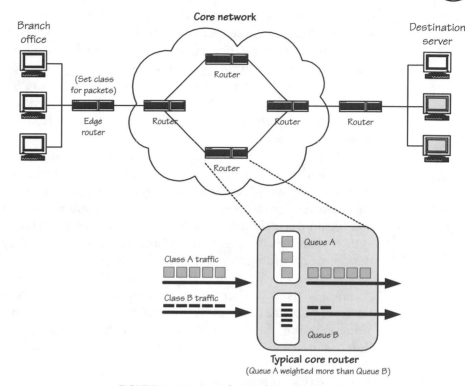

FIGURE 15.2 How class of service works.

When the capacity is reserved for a specific protocol or application, the capacity should be large enough to meet the demands of all traffic of that type. If not, the traffic exceeding the allotted capacity will most likely be subject to delays and/or discards. If the allotted capacity isn't used, it's possible for other traffic to use the remaining bandwidth.

Last, but not least, we come to *dynamic resource reservation.* The approach that's received most of the attention and efforts of Internet engineers has been that of Integrated Services and RSVP. (For more details on QoS and the many ways to provide it on IP, ATM, and frame relay networks, take a look at Paul Ferguson & Geoff Huston's, *Quality of Service: Delivering QoS on the Internet and in Corporate Networks,* John Wiley & Sons, Inc., 1998.)

Anticipating the variety of real-time applications and services that could be used on IP networks, the IETF formed the *Integrated Services* (INTSERV) Working Group, which set out to design a set of extensions to the best-effort delivery model currently used on the Internet. This framework, the Integrated Services Architecture, provides special handling for certain types of traffic flows and includes a mechanism for applications to choose between multiple levels of delivery services for their traffic. A fundamental precept of the Integrated Services Architecture is that network resources must be controlled in order to deliver QoS, which requires the inclusion of admission controls. Along with this, there must be a way to reserve resources.

As part of the architecture, the Integrated Services Working Group has defined several service classes that, if supported by routers, can provide a data flow with certain QoS commitments. This contrasts with best-effort traffic, which receives no such service commitment from a router and has to make do with whatever resources are available. The level of QoS provided by these enhanced QoS classes is programmable on a per-flow basis according to requests from the end applications. These requests can be passed to the routers by network management procedures or, more commonly, using a reservation protocol such as RSVP. The requests dictate the level of resources (e.g. bandwidth, buffer space) that must be reserved along with the transmission scheduling behavior that must be installed in the routers to provide the desired end-to-end QoS commitment for the data flow.

The first of these classes, best-effort delivery, is, of course, the default delivery mode for Internet traffic and doesn't receive any special consideration within the Integrated Services Architecture. Of the remaining classes only two of these, Guaranteed Service and Controlled-Load Service, have been formally specified within the framework of the Integrated Service Architecture for use with RSVP.

Controlled-Load Service provides approximately the same quality-of-service under heavy loads as under light loads. The important difference from the traditional Internet best-effort service is that the Controlled-Load flow does not noticeably deteriorate as the network load increases. In contrast, a best-effort flow would experience progressively worse service (greater delay and packet loss) as the network load increased. The controlled load service is intended for those classes of applications that can tolerate a certain amount of loss and delay provided it is kept to a reasonable level, such as adaptive real-time applications.

Guaranteed Service guarantees that packets will arrive within a guaranteed delivery time and will be discarded due to queue overflows, as long as the flow's traffic stays within the bounds of its specified traffic parameters. The guaranteed service does not control the minimal or average delay of traffic, nor does it control or minimize the jitter, only the maximum queueing delay. It is intended for applications with stringent real-time delivery requirements such as certain audio and video applications that have fixed playout buffers and are intolerant of any datagram arriving after their playback time. Guaranteed service is designed to address the support of legacy applications that expect a delivery model similar to traditional telecommunications circuits.

In the Integrated Services Architecture, there's a logical separation between the QoS control and the protocol designed for resource reservation, *The Resource Reservation Protocol*, (RSVP). That's because RSVP can be used with a variety of QoS services, and the QoS services that were designed as part of the Integrated Services Architecture can be used with a variety of setup schemes. If we think of RSVP as the signaling system, then the QoS control information is the signal content.

RSVP operates on top of IP; it is an Internet control protocol like IGMP or ICMP, but it is not a routing protocol. It uses underlying routing protocols to determine the destination for reservation requests. As routing paths change, RSVP adapts its reservation to new paths if reservations are in place. The RSVP protocol is used by routers to deliver QoS control requests to all nodes along the paths of the flows (see Figure 15.3) and to establish and maintain state to provide the requested service. After a reservation has been made, routers supporting RSVP determine the route and the QoS class for each incoming packet and the scheduler makes forwarding decisions for every outgoing packet.

RSVP has yet to see wide-scale deployment; many of the protocols were only admitted to the IETF standards track in the last half of 1997. Although some routers and security gateways already have shipped with RSVP support, there are still concerns about RSVP's scalability. Deployment of RSVP will depend on work that's progressing on QoS-based routing and methods for propagating network policy to the routers that take part in an RSVP path between source and destination. (A protocol called *Common Open Policy Service* (COPS) is being developed for the latter purpose.)

RSVP's biggest benefit is that it dynamically sets up and tears down sessions with the appropriate service level; thereby, making the most efficient use of bandwidth for flow-type traffic. RSVP does not create additional bandwidth, it just slices the bandwidth pie differently. RSVP does not enhance the performance of best-effort data applications; it is also not useful for short-lived Web traffic because of the overhead of establishing reservations.

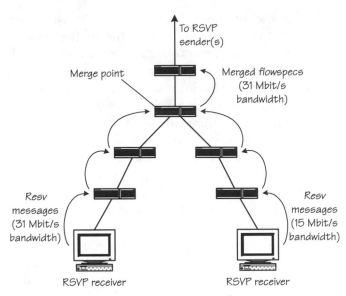

FIGURE 15.3 RSVP example.

VPN Performance

When it comes to VPNs, two major factors affect performance:

1. The speed and reliability of transmissions over the Internet.
2. The efficiency of VPN processing at hosts and security gateways.

As we've already discussed, the Internet cannot be used to provide guaranteed response times (i.e., guaranteed latencies and jitter). ISPs offering guaranteed latencies do so by circumventing the public Internet and channelling customer traffic over their own backbone network. This works for VPNs as long as all your sites can be served by the same ISP. As we pointed out back in Chapter 9, "The ISP Connection," no ISP yet offers guaranteed latencies for traffic that travels across more than one ISP's network, although it's likely that the technology and policies to do so will exist in a few years.

For all that we said earlier in this chapter on differentiated services and QoS, most ISPs are not yet prepared to offer support for these technologies. Network product vendors are pushing hard to make the requisite hardware and software available for ISPs, but few have adopted any of the technologies needed to offer customers differentiated services. The notable exceptions include MCI, UUNET, and TCG CerfNet.

Aside from the cash outlay required to purchase and install the devices, a lack of standardization for differentiated services also has contributed to ISP reluctance to adopt the techniques we've outlined. The current thinking is that RSVP will most likely not be implemented across most ISP's backbone networks and the public Internet, partly due to its scalability problems. A more likely solution for offering differentiated services is the Class of Service approach, especially since it appears that the approaches tried by different vendors, particularly Cisco and 3Com, will soon be able to interoperate.

What QoS-related services your ISP offers will have the greatest effect on your company's time-sensitive applications. If all your VPN traffic is going to be file transfers, Web browsing, and e-mail, then you won't need to be concerned with QoS. But, if transactional traffic, interactive multimedia, and IP telephony are going to a part of your VPN's traffic, then you'll need to track developments in QoS technologies and your ISP's deployment of them.

But, there's more to managing the performance of your VPN than utilizing QoS. As we mentioned at the beginning of this section, efficient VPN processing is an important factor. You do not want your security gateways to be chokepoints to network traffic due to their inability to efficiently encrypt and decrypt packets.

Depending on the computational horsepower of your VPN devices and the traffic they must process, you may have to consider installing multiple gateways at connections experiencing heavy traffic and enabling some form of load balancing between the gateways.

Since security gateways are such strategic points for creating VPN tunnels, you should plan on using them as locations for controlling the traffic

MPLS and ISPs

Another approach, *Multi-Protocol Label Switching* (MPLS), which tags IP traffic so that it can be moved efficiently over switched infrastructures such as ATM is being standardized by the IETF and is initially being offered within Ascend's products for ISPs as part of their MultiVPN product line. Because most of MPLS deployment is aimed at the ISP's backbone network, there's very little an enterprise customer would have to do to use MPLS. Only a few enterprise routers support MPLS, but expect more to become available as the protocol becomes a standard sometime in late 1998.

that enters the VPN links. For instance, if a gateway can utilize filtering rules based on time of day and application (or user), then you could set up filters to ensure that business-critical traffic is passed with a higher priority during business hours, and Web browsing might have an equal priority later in the day. Of course, setting up and managing all these rules can be a headache as you try to enforce them across numerous VPN sites; as we'll see in the next section, policy-based network management offers a potential solution.

To make the most of the bandwidth provided by your ISP, you should pay close attention to how your tunnels are created and what traffic they carry. For instance, Layer2 tunnels using L2TP can carry traffic from more than one session. But, if multiple sessions are inserted into a tunnel, it's possible that a higher priority packet can be placed in the channel first, which may disrupt any sequence-sensitive processing of packets, such as header compression. Despite the convenience multisession tunnels may offer, it's best to either restrict tunnels to single sessions or at least insert only sessions of equal priority into the same tunnel.

Aside from affecting how traffic is aggregated, the tunnels your VPN creates also can have an effect on the deployment of any QoS schemes your ISP offers. Simple approaches to tunneling like GRE (Generic Routing Encapsulation), which is used in PPTP, usually map any QoS fields of packet headers to QoS fields in the header of the tunnel packets. But, if tunnel-mode IPSec is used, the original header is encrypted; if the security gateway cannot translate QoS information from the internal host's requests in the inner header to the outer header it generates for the tunnel, then the ISP's network will not be able to provide any quality-of-service support for the tunnel's traffic.

Policy-Based Management

In past chapters, we've talked about policies in terms of security policies, covering such issues as user authentication and access rights. In the context of this chapter, however, policy-based management has a different meaning—it's using stored rules to manage bandwidth and determine what users get the quality-of-service they require. But, since in the long run all policies are focused on the user or a device, the grand vision of policy-based network management is to use a single management database (distributed or otherwise) to control all aspects of the network, including security, access rights, bandwidth requirements, and so on.

Network management has become more complicated not only as networks scale to larger sizes, but also as they become more complex, with more services coming online and application demands becoming more varied. What's needed is a better way to manage network traffic, setting priorities and bandwidth requirements in a centralized way even as the network itself becomes more distributed and decentralized.

As a form of network management, the major networking vendors, such as Cisco, Bay Networks, and 3Com, have been developing what's called policy-based network management. To help deal with the complexity of their networks, network managers can use policy-based management to implement policies that explicitly address the needs of the ever-expanding range of services.

Policy-based management has come to the fore as switches have become more important in enterprise networks. As switching becomes an integral part of enterprise networks, often displacing routers, users and managers alike are looking for ways to optimize their use of switches, especially when it comes to controlling and distributing network resources. Many networks based on a core or hierarchy of routers aren't capable of prioritizing network traffic based on either user or application priority. Similarly, ATM-based networks can offer *quality-of-service* (QoS) guarantees, but few applications have been developed to take advantage of these QoS requests at the workstation level. And RSVP, which has been developed to provide similar QoS capabilities to IP-based networks, is relatively new and hasn't yet seen wide-spread usage in networks. But, policy-based management offers the promise of working with a variety of network devices to enforce bandwidth management and admission policies for application traffic along the entire path between the source and the destination.

A fundamental tenet of policy-based management is that policies for governing network behavior are set at a high level by network managers, and intelligent network devices use these policies to adapt to network conditions (see Figure 15.4).

It's important that policies for handling priority requests are set in a centralized fashion, usually at a network-wide policy server. Thus, a network manager would set policies to determine which users and applications get the top priority when congestion slows network performance. When set, these policies can be automatically invoked by the workstations, switches, and other network devices as conditions change in the network.

As an example, see Figure 15.5; here, a network manager established priorities for applications on a user-by-user basis. These priorities, which are stored in a central policy server, are relayed to each appropriate user when the user's workstation starts up and connects to the network. Then, when a particular user launches a particular network application on his workstation, the data packets sent to the network are tagged with the

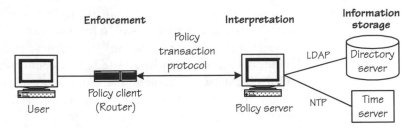

FIGURE 15.4 Basic model of policy-based network management.

appropriate priority and relayed by the switches according to their priority.

This two-dimensional matrix of priorities, sorted by user and by application, enables different users of the network to have different priorities for the same application. This way, it's possible to assign a high priority for the CEO using a SAP application while someone in technical support would have a lower priority for the same SAP application. Similarly, all uses of PointCast or similar push applications can be assigned a lower priority than the use of SAP applications. After the database on the policy server is established, network switches and routers can automatically handle high-priority traffic at the expense of lower priority traffic in the event of network congestion.

Although companies like 3Com, Bay Networks, and Cisco already have developed the first generation of proprietary policy management

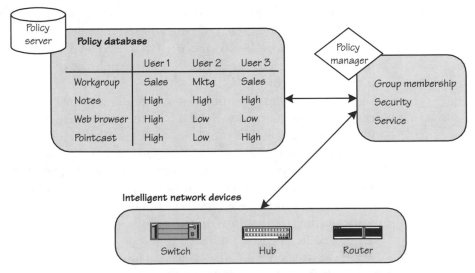

FIGURE 15.5 Example of policy-based network management.

tools, it's likely that the interoperability and capabilities will be improved over the next few years thanks to an industry effort called the *DEN Initiative* (Directory-Enable Networking). This work, originally started by Cisco and Microsoft, now has more than 20 participating vendors and is defining ways to use directories to store both user profiles and device configuration information. Although much of the initial work is focusing on using Microsoft's Active Directory, which is a part of NT Server 5.0, directories and devices will be able to query each other and exchange information using LDAP. Policy management software then can be used to set rules and store them in a DEN directory; network devices can then automatically make decisions about bandwidth and resource allocation based on the rules propagated from the policy software and user profiles stored in a DEN directory. The first products to support DEN are slated to ship in early 1999.

Because the trend in policy-based network management and DEN is to collect all network- and user-related information into one system for centralized management, both the configuration of VPN devices and traffic control of the LAN-WAN links will eventually be integrated into such systems. As we've mentioned earlier in this chapter, some VPN products are already shipping with LDAP capabilities, which will make their integration in policy-based management systems easier. But, since both policy-based management systems and DEN are relatively recent efforts, it'll still be a few years before widespread deployment is possible.

Monitoring ISP Performance and SLAs

We covered many of the details of ISP capabilities and Service Level Agreements in Chapter 9, "The ISP Connection." Remember that SLAs should be used to agree on what are reasonable expectations of service. Three basic items should be covered in every SLA: availability, effective throughput, and delay.

Monitoring your ISP's performance should be done not only to ensure that the conditions of your SLA are being met, but to determine how your VPN is behaving. For instance, if VPN traffic isn't getting through or is being delayed because of congestion at a security gateway—not because of ISP performance—then you might have to consider installing a more powerful gateway or balancing the load between multiple gateways. Alternatively, if some links aren't being heavily used, you may want to renegotiate a slower speed for those links.

Although SLAs may be based on the three items we mentioned earlier—availability, throughput, and delay—your users are going to be most concerned with the performance of their applications over the network. Always keep in mind that your performance measurements should in some way be related to actual user actions, such as the time to download a file or send a message.

Recall from Chapter 9 that where you take your measurements can have an impact on the results you get. Measurements can either be taken end-to-end or just within the ISP's network cloud (see Figure 15.6). The local loop can have a profound impact on network performance, but it is ignored in a switch-to-switch implementation. Performance measurements and troubleshooting must be performed end-to-end.

A second issue is utilizing a measurement system that is independent of the network you are measuring. Use an objective system that is not biased toward either switch or router architectures.

Many monitoring tools collect and report on data from SNMP agents. SNMP agents perform the function of accumulating real-time data, and this approach works well for bandwidth-related measurements. Most routers and other network devices are available with SNMP agents that provide most of the information needed for monitoring availability and utilization.

Other monitoring systems poll devices using specific application protocols such as FTP and HTTP or network-level polling with *Internet Control Message Protocol* (ICMP). But, polling systems can include factors that are beyond the scope (and therefore, control) of your service provider. (An overloaded Web server at a corporate site isn't the responsibility of your ISP, for instance.) A good approach would be to employ ICMP polling and to place the polling device as close as possible to the service being measured (i.e., the LAN-WAN interface in this case).

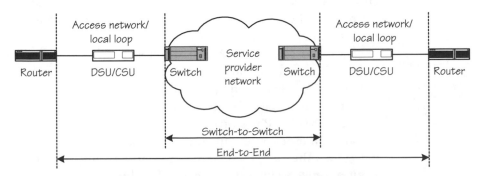

FIGURE 15.6 Measurement areas for SLAs.

Agreeing on definitions of measured parameters and how they're measured is an important task, but one that's not easy to accomplish, particularly because there's no standardization of these metrics among ISPs. Although it'll be some time before standardized metrics for IP network performance and availability are agreed upon, check out the work of the IETF's working group on *Internet Provider Performance Metrics* (IPPM) to see the latest efforts.

Many of the service providers offering guaranteed service will often locate measurement devices at your CPE. For comparison's sake, you should try to locate your own measuring devices in parallel with those installed by your ISP. You also may find that, before long, ISPs offer direct connections between their management and monitoring environment and customer-management environments, enabling customers direct access to the data that relates to their VPN.

Summary

A variety of network applications have different requirements for bandwidth, latency, and jitter, complicating the planning of bandwidth provisioning and traffic control. Many of the newer applications, such as interactive multimedia and videoconferencing, place tighter constraints on network latency and jitter than most legacy applications.

Networks can support this range of applications if they're configured for differentiated services. The five approaches to offering differentiated services are over-provisioning bandwidth, bandwidth conservation, traffic prioritization (or Class of Service), static resource reservation, and dynamic resource reservation.

Because the important components of a VPN are located at the LAN-WAN interface, they not only can become chokepoints for network traffic, but also offer the opportunity for controlling traffic and differentiated services. But, whenever ISPs offer their own support for differentiated services, special attention must be paid to mixing traffic of different priorities in the same tunnel or encrypting packet headers, which defeats most prioritization schemes.

Policy-based network management is a rapidly-developing area that promises to make device configuration and automatic control of traffic easier. Eventually, VPN configuration and user control will be included in policy-based network management systems.

Looking Ahead

VPNs are useful now and have a great deal of potential to be even more useful in the future. Standardization is just now happening, which will improve interoperability and management. Network performance over VPNs will also improve, enabling VPN links to be used for new applications, such as videoconferencing and IP telephony.

To track product interoperability, you should look at the International Computer Security Assn. (ICSA) for their tests of compliance with IPSec standards and at the Automotive Network Exchange (ANX) for valuable information on how the products work together in the real world.

16

Extending VPNs
to Extranets

The Internet and other TCP/IP networks have been around for more than 20 years. But, it's only been in the last few years that the Internet has become a household word and more businesses are paying attention to using TCP/IP and the Web for all types of communications; this includes not only communications within the enterprise, but with customers, suppliers, and business partners. The appeal of using the same protocols and in many cases the same application (a Web browser, for instance) to perform many different tasks and links to many different companies is very real and hard to pass up.

Within the business world, the biggest trend in IP networks (and perhaps the most profitable one thus far) has been to redesign corporate communications around the World Wide Web and intranets. Electronic commerce, particularly using the Internet to buy and sell goods and services, has a lot of potential, and efforts for consumer e-commerce versus business-to-business e-commerce have been following somewhat different paths of development. One of the promising efforts in business-to-business e-commerce has been dubbed an extranet, which involves opening up portions of your corporate network to access by your business partners (see Figure 16.1).

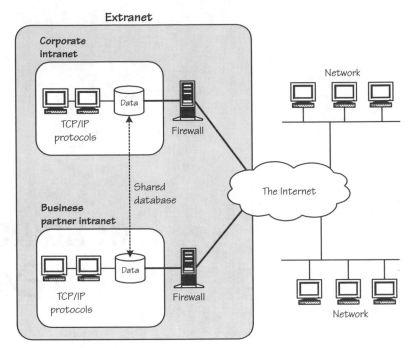

FIGURE 16.1 Intranets, extranets, and VPNs.

As we'll see in this chapter, extranets can require a great deal of coordination between businesses, perhaps more than has ever been attempted previously. And, because you're trying to control outside access to your resources and probably want to secure traffic between you and your partners, you probably already see how important security is to the proper operation of an extranet—that's where the parallel to VPNs come in. If you need the secure transmissions in addition to control of access rights for outsiders, then VPNs can be a good foundation for your extranet.

One difference between extranets and VPNs has been the focus in their evolution. Extranets are motivated more by the need for a particular business application—faster processing of purchase orders or better inventory control, for instance—and VPNs have grown out of the need to provide secure communications over the public Internet, regardless of the application. Because of this capability of VPNs, the applications you plan for your extranet can mesh nicely with the architecture of a VPN; extranet applications can be layered atop the VPN plumbing, as in Figure 16.2.

You don't have to use a VPN to create an extranet; that decision depends on the security requirements of your extranet applications. You could use SSL/TSL to secure communications between a partner's Web

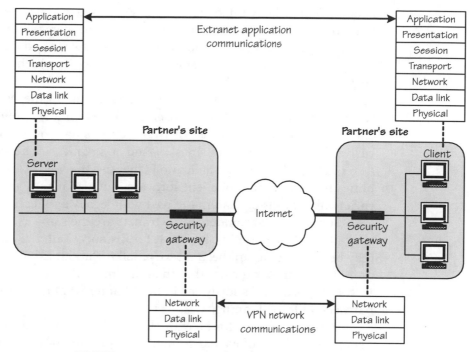

FIGURE 16.2 Extranet applications and VPN networks.

browser and a Web server maintained just for your extranet, for instance. Or, trading EDI forms via secure e-mail (using S/MIME, for instance) may be enough for your needs. But, the focus of this chapter will be how you can extend your VPN to become an extranet.

Reasons for an Extranet

Before we discuss some of the details that go into creating an extranet from a VPN, let's spend a few pages delving into extranets.

For many managers, extranets offer many advantages for communications between business partners. First, extranets are usually built using TCP/IP protocols, which means that the difficulty of linking the networks of two (or more) companies is reduced. Furthermore, since the public Internet also uses TCP/IP, partner networks can be linked to each other using the Internet instead of installing expensive leased lines or other links.

Second, using the Internet to link networks gives you more flexibility in forming and dissolving short-term partnerships as needed, which has become increasingly important in today's fast-paced business world. Sometimes you can't wait a month or more for the installation of a leased line, for instance. Or, a collaborative project between you and another company may involve only a small group of people, which would make the cost of a leased line prohibitive.

Third, many extranets revolve around the use of the World Wide Web, which helps provide a common user interface to many applications across company boundaries. The use of Web browsers has gotten to be pretty pervasive throughout many businesses, and companies are expending a great deal of effort developing applications that use the Web. This not only simplifies the distribution of client software, but also makes access to a wide variety of data easier than in the past with legacy applications.

Some of the arguments for extranets are the same as for VPNs; look back at the discussion in Chapter 1, for instance. But, the business case may be a little different because we're talking about external business communications in extranets rather than the internal communications that VPNs support. We'll shortly see in this chapter what a focus on external partners adds to planning.

Business reasons for an extranet vary, but communications with partners is at the heart of each extranet. It's a question of what kind of data you want to obtain or share: it could be inventory levels, the status of purchase orders and shipments, market data, product information, or just about any kind of business data imaginable.

One of the most popular current uses for extranets is managing the supply chain (see Figure 16.3). The idea is to tie together all the companies involved in your business: suppliers of parts, servicers of equipment, the manufacturer, and distributors, among others. Automating many of the steps in this supply chain across company boundaries can lead to faster order processing, improved inventory tracking and management, more accurate order fulfillment, support for just-in-time manufacturing, and improved customer support.

Other extranets may not be as complex; you might just want to obtain daily point-of-sale data from your distributors, for instance, or provide product information and corporate news updates to them via a Web server.

Large companies like Ace Hardware have used an extranet to provide their network of independently owned retailers access to information that previously had been stored on legacy mainframes and was difficult to access from the outside. In Ace's case, the newly accessible information on the extranet included inventory levels at the warehouse closest to the retailer, inventory-management applications to help plan reorders, and margin management and pricing tools that help store owners maintain profitability.

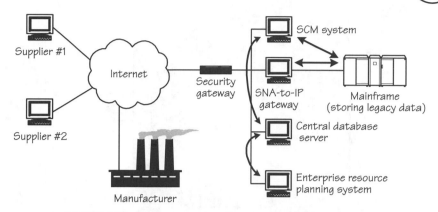

FIGURE 16.3 Components of a supply chain system.

Another area that's received a lot of attention is the purchasing process. Two different approaches to the process are worth noting: the use of on-line catalogs and the use of *Electronic Data Interchange* (EDI).

On-line catalogs have become a standard part of electronic commerce. Within the context of business-to-business e-commerce, suppliers have started to offer customized on-line catalogs for their customers; these catalogs can be based on a customer's past purchasing history or just the business type. Being electronic, they're easier to update and customize. If the catalogs are offered over an extranet, access to the proper catalogs can be easier to control.

EDI has been around since the 1960s, but it's been used mostly by large corporations and their satellite suppliers working together over a private network called a *Value Added Network* (VAN). These VANs offered reliability and security that has been difficult to duplicate on the Internet thus far. EDI data is presented in forms that are defined for a particular type of business, relayed between business parties using e-mail, and then translated into formats that the company's databases can use.

Businesses can use EDI to automate the transfer of information between corporate departments, as well as between companies. For instance, EDI-based data can be transferred between purchasing, finance, and receiving departments (see Figure 16.4) to automate the purchase-and-payment process.

Because the cost of operations on the Internet is lower than on a VAN, interest in using the Internet to transmit EDI data has increased. Some EDI vendors now offer Web-based servers that accept business data in HTML forms and translate the data to EDI formats for transmission either over a VAN or the Internet. Meanwhile, the IETF has been working

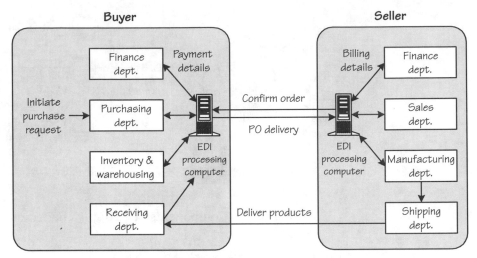

FIGURE 16.4 EDI information flow between a buyer and a seller.

on a standard for enclosing EDI form data within S/MIME messages. In addition to using EDI over the Internet, another, newer effort by the *World Wide Web Consortium* (W3C) to supplant EDI forms with the *eXtended Markup Language* (XML) will make it easier for companies to relay structured data like purchase orders within IP-based e-mail. Both EDI and XML in IP-based e-mail and on the Web will make it easier for extranet partners to exchange the information they need to tie their businesses together electronically.

Probably the largest combination of VPNs and extranets is the *Automotive Network Exchange* (ANX), which soon will be an extranet linking 8,000 suppliers and 20,000 dealers (see Figure 16.5). Organized and managed by the *Automotive Industry Action Group* (AIAG), this extranet includes certification of IP service providers as well specifications for the capabilities of each ANX member that must be met before it can become part of the extranet. The extranet relies on IPSec for communications over the network and uses EDI for automating commercial transactions between the members.

Turning a VPN into an Extranet

For the remainder of this discussion, we're going to assume that you have deployed a VPN and that you want to use the security features that it offers to create an extranet.

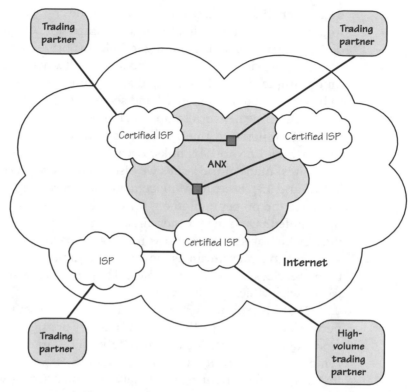

FIGURE 16.5 The Automotive Network Exchange.

The main difference between establishing your VPN and establishing an extranet is obtaining the cooperation of your business partners. Even if the extranet is your company's idea, and the applications developed for the extranet will benefit your partners, you'll still need their buy-in to make the extranet a success. For some companies, this may be the same situation they faced when getting a buy-in for a VPN from branch offices. Ah, politics . . .

We're not going to get into the details of planning your extranet applications or the development environments you can use for those applications. That could easily be the subject of another book. Because we're mainly concerned about how the extranet can use your VPN's features, we'll assume that the reasons for your extranet and the type of applications you plan to use are already settled.

Most of the concerns you'll face in linking partners to your extranet revolve around compatibility. The five main areas of compatibility are network setup, security policies, authentication servers, VPN protocols, and digital certificates. These compatibility issues may not all be of equal importance, and they will also differ in importance if you're setting up a dial-up extranet versus planning to link corporate LANs together. For instance, providing IP services and client software to your partners is much simpler if they'll be using dial-up connections than if IP LANs need to be installed or reconfigured and security gateways installed.

Regarding network setup, you'll need to know if they have the appropriate IP routers and Internet links to join your extranet, at least if you're establishing LAN-to-LAN links. Because you'll be extending VPN tunnels to their sites, many of the issues we discussed in Chapters 8, "Designing Your VPN," and 13, "Security Management," are pertinent. Does the partner's site have the proper equipment for a security gateway, or does one need to be installed? Or, if the partner already has his own VPN, can that VPN's devices be linked to yours? If you and your partners are all using private IP addresses on your intranets, how will you handle address translation and name services between companies? These are just some of the major issues with which you'll have to deal.

Dial-up extranets are perhaps a bit easier to set up when it comes to network compatibility. Even if your partner doesn't use IP as its main networking protocol, setting up a few desktop or laptop computers with remote access software, modems, and an ISP account is simpler than installing and configuring an IP network and a security gateway. It's also less expensive.

We've said a lot about security policies throughout this book. (See Chapter 13 in particular.) If you're extending your VPN to extranet partners, some agreement on security policies between you and your partners will be necessary. Whatever you do, try not to compromise your VPN's security or your internal site security to meet the wishes of your partners. If any compromise has to be made, it should favor stronger security. This may take some training on your part, because smaller companies may not have a security policy or they may not understand the value of protecting your resources. In particular, if you're going to issue passwords, security tokens, or digital certificates, be sure to impress on your partners the need to protect them against loss or theft. The question of who's legally liable for loss of data due to a lost password or security token is no doubt an important issue here, but we'll leave the coverage of legal issues to someone else.

The different partners in your extranet also may have different authentication schemes for their employees. Assuming that there's a two-way exchange of data between members of the extranet, the authentication systems will have to be able to handle some outside users (i.e., some of the employees of your partners, for instance). If different partners use different authentication servers, every system that accesses the extranet will require client software, perhaps more than one. Getting your partners to agree on one common method for authentication would simplify the configuration and use of the extranet, as well as reduce support costs in the long-run (especially for your help desk). Using RADIUS, perhaps with proxy servers, is one way to go, because many VPN systems work with RADIUS, and many companies are already adopting it for controlling remote access. Extensions to RADIUS also enable it to work with other authentication systems, such as SecurID tokens, which help make RADIUS an integrator of authentication systems.

It's also possible that you'd use digital certificates to authenticate extranets users as well as sites, much the way we described their use for VPNs in Chapter 13, "Security Management." If you do use digital certificates, check for compatibility of the certificates—not all certificates use the X.509v3 standard. The popular encryption program for e-mail, PGP, has its own certificate format that's not compatible with X.509v3, for instance. You'll also need to determine who will issue the certificates. It's possible to use either an in-house certificate server or a commercial certificate authority for your extranet, just as for your VPN. But, if the certificates are being issued by each participating business, then you'll need a way to cross-certify the *certificate authorities* (CAs) (see Figure 16.6). That's relatively easy if everyone's using commercial CAs, because they're usually already cross-certified. If you're maintaining your own certificate server, then you'll have to register your certificate server with an outside CA or your partners' certificate server.

If you're creating an extranet by combining the VPNs of business partners, there will always be the issue of interoperability between the VPNs. IPSec is a big step toward solving these interoperability issues, but don't expect all of today's IPSec-compliant products to work together automatically. The standards for key management are so new that all vendors haven't implemented them, and all the kinks haven't been worked out yet. Each partner's procedures for managing their VPN may not be the same, either, so you'll have to determine what work-arounds, if any, are needed to get each VPN to work with the other VPNs.

Two extranet-related issues don't deal with your VPN infrastructure but deserve mention. Both relate to the fact that your extranet involves sharing resources between partners.

First, some extranets are created for joint project teams, and the data that they work with and generate has to be stored somewhere. When you're designing an inventory control system for an extranet, it may be

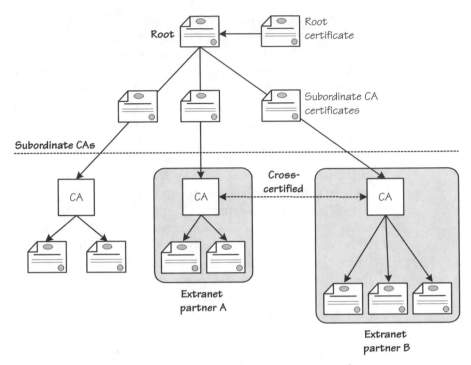

FIGURE 16.6 Linking company CAs together.

obvious where the server should reside; with joint project teams, that's less obvious. Some member of the extranet will have to decide to take ownership of the server(s) for the joint project and maintain its security.

Second is the issue of problem resolution. Even though each device on an extranet is managed by someone, the end-to-end connection crosses company boundaries. When something fails, it may be difficult to discover which device is at fault. To counter this, you'll need to institute some kind of problem-reporting procedures and methods to link together each company's help desk so that they can collaborate on solving any problems that crop up on the extranet. The last thing you want is finger-pointing.

Whether you have an in-house VPN or an outsourced VPN, you can choose to have an ISP maintain your extranet. Service providers offering extranet services usually maintain authentication servers as well as any Web and application servers that you may need for your extranet. Like an outsourced VPN, you should maintain control of user authentication and access rights for the outsourced extranet. Outsourcing the extranet may mean using a very limited portion of your VPN (your authentication servers, for example), but it's a good alternative if you feel better with separate systems for securing your internal communications and for dealing with external partners.

Just as with your VPN, you should plan to roll out your extranet in stages, starting with a pilot project. Pick a few trusted and knowledgeable customers who understand what you're trying to do with your extranet. Be sure that they're willing to deal with glitches in the system in order to make it work. If your extranet applications involve a number of different users (as in supply chain management, for instance), be sure that representatives of each class of user are included in the testing. In any case, make sure that everything that your company is responsible for works on your own network before you bring in any partners for testing.

Summary

Extranets are usually formed between business partners because of a particular business application. Because VPNs form the plumbing for secure networks and can secure any kind of network traffic, regardless of the application, you can build an extranet on top of a VPN. The main step in extending a VPN to an extranet is granting your extranet partners the access rights to specific internal resources and adding them to your authentication systems.

Many different compatibility issues will arise as you attempt to deploy an extranet because you cannot guarantee that each business runs the same types of network. Some of the compatibility issues that you'll need to resolve, revolve around security policies, existing VPNs, types of authentication deployed by the partners, and how keys and digital certificates will be distributed.

17

Future Directions

Virtual Private Networks using the Internet are an ever-increasing opportunity for businesses, vendors, and ISPs alike. It's been projected by Infonetics Research that the market for VPN products will reach $12 billion in 2001. Many of the business forces motivating the deployment of VPNs, such as cost reductions and changes in telecommunications and networking, will remain in effect for quite a few years. If anything, these forces are likely to get even stronger over time.

Let's take a look at what's likely to happen with various developments affecting VPNs over the next few years. First, we'll look at how businesses will deploy VPNs and the effects ISPs may have on future VPNs. Then we'll say a few words about the state of standards, security, and digital certificates before moving on to managing your VPN. Finally, we'll cover some of the trends in VPN product lines.

VPN Deployment

One of the major uses for VPNs currently is the replacement of existing remote access systems using modems and remote access servers with dial-in

VPNs. Not only can a dial-in VPN be less costly, but it provides more flexibility to the mobile user, whether he's a salesperson on the road or a telecommuter.

Dial-in VPNs will continue to be an important use of VPNs for some time. In fact, for some vendors and managers, it's the only VPN they know. The newly formed roaming services, which have added value to remote connections by consolidating access from different ISPs, will continue to make dial-in VPNs useful, especially for multinational businesses. As standardization of VPN protocols continue, expect roaming services to provide client support for the crucial protocols, such as L2TP and IPSec.

Even as companies move out of the pilot project stage with their VPNs, managers are looking for more uses for their VPNs. As voice over IP (or IP telephony) starts to look more attractive, the idea of combining voice and data networking over IP will become a more concrete possibility. Some care in provisioning proper latencies for voice may be required, but many ISPs' offerings are, or will be, suitable for this application. Secure videoconferencing is another application of interest, but this application may require even more constraints on bandwidth and quality-of-service.

Another trend that could drive further VPN usage is the development of the universal mailbox, in which e-mail, faxes, and phone calls can all be received and processed in a single application. The first generation of these systems is already available from Lucent/Octel and Nortel and deployed in some companies, and the standards that make it easier to transmit faxes and phone messages using e-mail are nearing completion, which will make it easier for these systems to interoperate. Transmitting these various forms of information over data networks makes it easier to secure them with a VPN.

Some companies have also talked about *internal VPNs*, which are local private networks organized around a department or project, designed to restrict access and keep communications secure against internal snooping. Many security experts have pointed out that more security breaches are due to internal attacks than any other single cause. For such applications, installing VPN software on a departmental router or firewall may suffice. Alternatively, as host-based encryption and authentication becomes more widespread, personal tunnels can be set up between team members for secure communications within the enterprise.

ISPs and the Internet

ISPs will continue to play a crucial role in the evolution of VPNs. They have very little to gain if they act only as a transmission service, and they're faced with a bigger business opportunity if they can offer value-added services. In some cases, this might be as simple as offering connections with reduced latency. But, expect ISPs to go beyond this and offer true differentiated services, probably utilizing either Class of Service technology (Cisco and 3Com already offer products for this) or *Multi-Protocol Label Switching* (MPLS), which is being offered by Ascend to ISPs and enterprise networks and also should be provided by other vendors as the protocol becomes an IETF standard.

One continued hitch in these developments is the restriction of differentiated services to a single ISP. Although it is (or soon will be) technically possible to provide such services across ISP domains, most ISPs are reluctant to consider offering such services for fear they'll loose business. Don't expect to see cross-ISP performance guarantees until the providers come up with a method for billing for different classes of traffic as it crosses from one ISP to another, which may take years. ISPs still want to show that their backbone is the best and want your traffic to travel only on their backbone if you want special treatment. (That, of course, is part of the definition of value-added services.)

Not all ISPs will be able to deploy the technologies required for differentiated services; some of them simply won't be able to afford it. Expect to see a continued dichotomy of ISPs, with the multinational and larger national and regional ISPs offering better support for VPNs and differentiated services, and smaller ISPs will continue to offer basic services and some VPN services (such as dial-in VPNs).

Although IPSec is more of a site-to-site tunneling protocol that doesn't require any ISP intervention, both PPTP and L2TP provide ISPs with an opportunity to provide value-added services for a VPN. Looking back at Chapters 6 and 7, you may recall that ISPs can use special remote access concentrators to initiate tunnels on behalf of remote callers, which allows for better control of where tunnels are terminated and avoids the need for special client software. With the high demand for dial-in VPNs, expect many ISPs will offer this type of tunneling service.

Hosting and managing outsourced VPNs is another service offered by some ISPs and one that will continue to grow. It's only been within the last year that ISPs have begun offering managed VPNs, and the market is very new. But, considering the complexity that VPNs can entail, competent ISPs, many of whom already offer managed security services for instance, will offer to manage your VPN for you.

Some of these outsourced VPN services also include hosting Web servers or other servers that can either be used internally or form the basis for an extranet. Depending on your ISP, outsourcing a VPN or extranet can include just about anything, including the network equipment, security management, serving as a certificate authority, and hosting any servers that you may need.

VPN Standards

All of the VPN protocols we covered in this book—PPTP, L2TP, and IPSec—will continue to be used over the next few years. PPTP will continue to be used due to the free availability of a Windows client and the relatively low cost of Microsoft's NT Server with RRAS. Small businesses in particular probably will use this solution for some time.

Since L2TP is just now becoming a standard, its deployment probably will take a little longer. Once again, Microsoft may have a hand in increasing its acceptance when L2TP clients get rolled out with Windows 98 and NT 5.0 includes server support. Other companies also are shipping, or will soon ship, products for L2TP, but the added complexity of L2TP and its use of IPSec for encryption may slow down its deployment, at least initially.

For anyone expecting to create a LAN-to-LAN VPN, IPSec will be the protocol of choice. The main components of IPSec, including key management via IKE, are close to standards approval by the IETF as this book goes to press. These standards will be an important step in improving the interoperability of IPSec-based products, which should help further deployment of IPSec VPNs.

IPSec currently may have some shortcomings when dealing with remote users and dial-in VPNs, but extensions to IPSec to simplify user authentication (including links to security tokens and smart cards) and to configure IPSec clients already have been proposed. With the strong interest in remote access to VPNs, it shouldn't be long before the current IPSec standards are extended to improve remote access.

IPSec client configuration will also take on a larger role when host-to-host tunnels are employed. The main emphasis in the IPSec community thus far has been on LAN-to-LAN tunneling, but some developers are already looking to tunnel creation at individual hosts for added security within the enterprise. For host-based tunneling to be feasible on the scale of large enterprise networks, the infrastructure for key management will need to be improved to handle the large number of keys, so it'll be a while before this type of tunneling becomes widespread. Furthermore, not all corporate networks will need this type of security; security gateways for LAN-to-LAN VPNs will prove to be adequate solutions for many corporations for some time to come.

Although IPSec started out as part of the development of IPv6, it has pretty much taken on a life of its own lately. For instance, this book has discussed the capabilities of IPSec in an IPv4 world, rather than limiting it to IPv6. Deployment of IPv6 will make IPSec a standard feature on any host, but it may be 5–10 years before we see appreciable deployment of IPv6. One of the principal needs for IPv6, insufficient numbers of addresses, has been somewhat alleviated by other, somewhat short-term solutions like CIDR and NAT. Current demand for IPv6 seems low, and vendor response seems correspondingly low. As far as support for IPSec is concerned, only the most basic IPSec functions have been included in commercially available IPv6 protocol stacks, so vendor support will need to be ramped up before deployment of IPv6 increases.

Security and Digital Certificates

Even as companies work to incorporate past cryptographic algorithms into their products, scientists have been developing new algorithms that are both computationally faster and more difficult to break. One of the newest algorithms that's being tested and becoming available in some commercial products (though not for VPNs yet) is *elliptic curve cryptography* (ECC). If ECC becomes more widespread and if cryptanalysts are satisfied with its robustness against attack, it's likely that the IETF will include the algorithm in its list of optional algorithms for use with IPSec.

The U.S. government also has been looking for a replacement for DES as its recommended encryption algorithm, with plans to select a new algorithm early in the next millennium. This choice will no doubt affect which algorithms are routinely selected for encryption on VPNs, as well as current governmental restrictions on exporting encryption products.

One of the most active areas of development in the security market these days is that surrounding the use of digital certificates. More products are being developed to use digital certificates for authenticating users, and these products should be readily integrated into VPN systems. One factor that's due to make the integration of use for digital certificates easier is the use of LDAP-compatible directories. X.500 and LDAP directories can be used to store certificates, and LDAP is being increasingly used as the method for accessing those certificates and related user information.

As we mentioned in Chapter 13, "Security Management," some companies are also working on the use of smart cards for carrying digital certificates. Although other card-based security tokens are available in the marketplace, the increasing number of uses for digital certificates and the deployment of LDAP-based directory infrastructures probably will drive the use of card-based certificates past that of other portable security tokens.

But, widespread use of digital certificates is still somewhat hampered by the current *Public Key Infrastructures* (PKIs). The current processes for distributing and checking Certificate Revocation Lists is both awkward and slow and poorly suited to the more dynamic uses like VPNs and secure e-mail, for example. One likely solution to this problem will be the deployment of *On-line Certificate Status Protocol* (OCSP) after it's approved as a standard.

VPN Management

For the next few years, managing VPNs will be one of the biggest concerns as standards and systems evolve. LAN-to-LAN VPNs are easier to manage because most of the VPN processes are transparent to end-users, and key management is largely based on sites rather than individuals. Of course, adding large numbers of remote users requires improved scalability of both your authentication and key-management systems.

Because IKE is only now being approved as the key-management standard for use with IPSec, expect companies to take another year to work out the kinks between their products to improve interoperability across all sizes of networks.

As we've mentioned previously, management of digital certificates is another area that needs improvement. Better handling of revoked certificates and distribution of the certificates themselves will develop over the next few years as more businesses seek to deploy PKIs both for internal uses as well as on extranets.

A relatively new line of products aimed at policy-based network management should eventually ease the management of VPNs, as well as of ordinary networks. But, policy-based network management is a very young market, and major vendors have only started to ship products in the last half of 1998. It'll still be a few more years before all installed network devices on an enterprise network will be able to take part in policy-based management.

Many policy-based management systems will come to depend on the *Directory Enabled Networks* (DEN) Initiative, which means that LDAP will become the common glue between devices and directories. Because user profiles, device configuration, and bandwidth provisioning can be lumped into DEN's framework, you can anticipate the deployment of DEN on your own networks by looking for VPN devices that include LDAP support. You will have time to plan for this, though, because the first directory and management products for DEN aren't scheduled to ship until early 1999, when Windows NT 5.0 ships.

The DEN Initiative, which started out as a collaborative effort between Cisco and Microsoft and eventually added the support of 20 other companies by early 1998, is now being managed by the *Desktop Management Task Force* (DMTF) to encourage a more open standards environment. Before DEN can be applied to VPN management, the DMTF will have to address links with IPSec as well as the security surrounding the transmission of device configurations from directories. DEN may eventually make network management easier, but it could lead to compromises in your security policies if all the exchanges of information required to keep DEN working aren't secured properly.

Product Trends

With all the hype surrounding VPNs, new developments in VPN products seem to occur on a weekly basis. Although we haven't emphasized the fact in this book, most of the current slate of products are point solutions rather than being highly integrated, which adds to the difficulty of installing, configuring, and maintaining all the pieces of your VPN. The easiest way to get an integrated solution right now is to outsource the VPN to a qualified ISP that also installs and maintain the equipment for your VPN. But, integrated solutions also will become available from vendors as well, now that the efforts on IPSec, key management, LDAP, and network management are converging on standards.

One approach to integration has been the *integrated box* product, in which a security gateway, firewall, and other network services are all bundled into one device (see Chapter 11, "VPN Hardware"). Expect to see more of these products over the next few years, with improved management applications as well. Be aware that many of these first devices included poorly designed management applications that did little to integrate the services they were meant to configure and manage.

Many of these integrated devices are combining a wide variety of network services, including Web and e-mail services as well as the security services you'd expect for a VPN. As we mentioned in Chapter 11, you'll need to decide how many of your network services you want installed in a single box. The more services in a single device, the more reliable and secure it has to be. Our own view is that distribution of services among a number of devices is preferable, as long as the services can be managed from a single workstation.

Integrated VPN devices, particularly those that are turnkey systems, require little configuration and can be particularly appealing to small businesses setting up a VPN. It's obvious that some of the products we listed in Chapter 11 are aimed at the small-business market, with more on the way. If you're in the market for this class of products, be sure to review them with future scalability in mind. Buying a product with no expansion possibilities or compatibility with accepted standards can lead to an expensive redesign of your VPN down the road as your business grows.

Although it may not be wise to add e-mail and Web servers to your integrated VPN device, letting the VPN device act as a control point for bandwidth provisioning and quality-of-service deserves consideration, as we pointed out in Chapter 15, "Performance Management." The market for QoS will mature over the next few years, so we expect that more products combining security and QoS will become available (and, of course, will be managed via DEN and/or policy-based management systems).

TABLE 17.1 Important IETF Working Groups

Group Name	Acronym	URL
Authenticated Firewall Traversal	AFT	www.ietf.org/html.charters/aft-charter.html
Common Authentication Technology	CAT	www.ietf.org/html.charters/cat-charter.html
Differentiated Services		www.ietf.org/html.charters/diff-serv-charter.html
Domain Name System Security	DNSSE	www.ietf.org/html.charters/dnssec-charter.html
Dynamic Host Configuration	DHC	www.ietf.org/html.charters/dhc-charter.html
Electronic Data Interchange-Internet Integration	EDIINT	www.ietf.org/html.charters/ediint-charter.html
Integrated Services	INTSERV	www.ietf.org/html.charters/intserv-charter.html
IPNG (IPv6)	IPNGWG	www.ietf.org/html.charters/ipngwg-charter.html
IP Security Protocol	IPSEC	www.ietf.org/html.charters/ipsec-charter.html
LDAP Service Deployment	LSD	www.ietf.org/html.charters/lsd-charter.html
Multiprotocol Label Switching	MPLS	www.ietf.org/html.charters/mpls-charter.html
Network Address Translators	NAT	www.ietf.org/html.charters/nat-charter.html
One Time Password Authentication	OTP	www.ietf.org/html.charters/otp-charter.html
Point-to-Point Protocol Extensions	PPPEXT	www.ietf.org/html.charters/pppext-charter.html
Procedures for Internet/Enterprise Renumbering	PIER	www.ietf.org/html.charters/pier-charter.html
Public Key Infrastructure (X.509)	PKIX	www.ietf.org/html.charters/pkix-charter.html
Remote Authentication Dial-In User Service	RADIUS	www.ietf.org/html.charters/radius-charter.html
Resource Reservation Setup Protocol	RSVP	www.ietf.org/html.charters/rsvp-charter.html

Keeping Up

VPNs are a dynamic market. Standards are still being developed, not only for VPN security but for digital certificates and network management as well, all of which impact your ability to design and deploy a proper VPN.

If you want to track what's going on with some of these standards efforts, check the Web sites listed in Table 17.1. Also check out the vendors themselves and other related resources that we've listed in Appendix B.

A P P E N D I X

Resources

Books

Bernstein, Terry, Anish B. Bhimani, Eugene Schultz, and Carol A. Siegel. *Internet Security for Business*. New York: John Wiley & Sons, Inc., 1996.

Comer, Douglas E. *Internetworking with TCP/IP, Vol. I, Principles, Protocols and Architecture*, Third Edition. Englewood Cliffs, NJ: Prentice-Hall, 1995.

Schneier, Bruce. *Applied Cryptography,* Second Edition. New York: John Wiley and Sons, Inc., 1996.

IETF Documents—RFCS

2315 PKCS #7: *Cryptographic Message Syntax Version 1.5*. B. Kaliski. March, 1998. (Status: INFORMATIONAL)

2314 PKCS #10: *Certification Request Syntax Version 1.5*. B. Kaliski. March, 1998. (Status: INFORMATIONAL)

2313 PKCS #1: *RSA Encryption Version 1.5.* B. Kaliski. March, 1998. (Status: INFORMATIONAL)

2307 *An Approach for Using LDAP as a Network Information Service.* L. Howard. March, 1998. (Status: EXPERIMENTAL)

2289 *A One-Time Password System.* N. Haller, C. Metz, P. Nesser, and M. Straw. February, 1998. (Obsoletes RFC1938) (Status: DRAFT STANDARD)

2284 *PPP Extensible Authentication Protocol (EAP).* L. Blunk and J. Vollbrecht. March, 1998. (Status: PROPOSED STANDARD)

2268 *A Description of the RC2(r) Encryption Algorithm.* R. Rivest. January, 1998. (Status: INFORMATIONAL)

2260 *Scalable Support for Multi-Homed Multi-Provider Connectivity.* T. Bates and Y. Rekhter. January, 1998. (Status: INFORMATIONAL)

2256 *A Summary of the X.500(96) User Schema for Use with LDAPv3.* M. Wahl. December, 1997. (Status: PROPOSED STANDARD)

2251 *Lightweight Directory Access Protocol (v3).* M. Wahl, T. Howes, and S. Kille. December, 1997. (Status: PROPOSED STANDARD)

2230 *Key Exchange Delegation Record for the DNS.* R. Atkinson. October, 1997. (Status: INFORMATIONAL)

2219 *Use of DNS Aliases for Network Services.* M. Hamilton and R. Wright. October, 1997. (Status: BEST CURRENT PRACTICE)

2215 *General Characterization Parameters for Integrated Service Network Elements.* S. Shenker and J. Wroclawski. September, 1997. (Status: PROPOSED STANDARD)

2212 *Specification of Guaranteed Quality of Service.* S. Shenker, C. Partridge, and R. Guerin. September, 1997. (Status: PROPOSED STANDARD)

2211 *Specification of the Controlled-Load Network Element Service.* J. Wroclawski. September, 1997. (Status: PROPOSED STANDARD)

2210 *The Use of RSVP with IETF Integrated Services.* J. Wroclawski. September, 1997. (Status: PROPOSED STANDARD)

2209 *Resource ReSerVation Protocol (RSVP)—Version 1 Message Processing Rules.* R. Braden and L. Zhang. September, 1997. (Status: INFORMATIONAL)

2208 *Resource ReSerVation Protocol (RSVP)—Version 1 Applicability Statement Some Guidelines on Deployment.* A. Mankin, Ed., F. Baker, B. Braden, S. Bradner, M. O'Dell, A. Romanow, A. Weinrib, and L. Zhang. September, 1997. (Status: INFORMATIONAL)

2207 *RSVP Extensions for IPSEC Data Flows.* L. Berger and T. O'Malley. September, 1997. (Status: PROPOSED STANDARD)

2205 *Resource ReSerVation Protocol (RSVP)—Version 1 Functional Specification*. R. Braden, Ed., L. Zhang, S. Berson, S. Herzog, and S. Jamin. September, 1997. (Status: PROPOSED STANDARD)

2196 *Site Security Handbook*. B. Fraser. September, 1997. (Status: INFORMATIONAL)

2182 *Selection and Operation of Secondary DNS Servers*. R. Elz, R. Bush, S. Bradner, and M. Patton. July, 1997. (Status: BEST CURRENT PRACTICE)

2181 *Clarifications to the DNS Specification*. R. Elz and R. Bush. July, 1997. (Status: PROPOSED STANDARD)

2153 *PPP Vendor Extensions*. W. Simpson. May, 1997. (Status: INFORMATIONAL)

2144 *The CAST-128 Encryption Algorithm*. C. Adams. May, 1997. (Status: INFORMATIONAL)

2139 *RADIUS Accounting*. C. Rigney. April, 1997. (Status: INFORMATIONAL)

2138 *Remote Authentication Dial-In User Service (RADIUS)*. C. Rigney, A. Rubens, W. Simpson, and S. Willens. April, 1997. (Status: PROPOSED STANDARD)

2137 *Secure Domain Name System Dynamic Update*. D. Eastlake. April, 1997. (Status: PROPOSED STANDARD)

2136 *Dynamic Updates in the Domain Name System (DNS UPDATE)*. P. Vixie, Ed., S. Thomson, Y. Rekhter, and J. Bound. April, 1997. (Status: PROPOSED STANDARD)

2132 *DHCP Options and BOOTP Vendor Extensions*. S. Alexander and R. Droms. March, 1997. (Status: DRAFT STANDARD)

2131 *Dynamic Host Configuration Protocol*. R. Droms. March, 1997. (Status: DRAFT STANDARD)

2125 *The PPP Bandwidth Allocation Protocol (BAP) / The PPP Bandwidth Allocation Control Protocol (BACP)*. C. Richards and K. Smith. March, 1997. (Status: PROPOSED STANDARD)

2118 *Microsoft Point-To-Point Compression (MPPC) Protocol*. G. Pall. March, 1997. (Status: INFORMATIONAL)

2104 *HMAC: Keyed-Hashing for Message Authentication*. H. Krawczyk, M. Bellare, and R. Canetti. February, 1997. (Status: INFORMATIONAL)

2085 *HMAC-MD5 IP Authentication with Replay Prevention*. M. Oehler and R. Glenn. February, 1997. (Status: PROPOSED STANDARD)

2078 *Generic Security Service Application Program Interface*, Version 2. J. Linn. January, 1997. (Status: PROPOSED STANDARD)

2065 *Domain Name System Security Extensions*. D. Eastlake, 3rd, and C. Kaufman. January, 1997. (Status: PROPOSED STANDARD)

2040 *The RC5, RC5-CBC, RC5-CBC-Pad, and RC5-CTS Algorithms.* R. Baldwin and R. Rivest. October, 1996. (Status: INFORMATIONAL)

2025 *The Simple Public-Key GSS-API Mechanism (SPKM).* C. Adams. October, 1996. (Status: PROPOSED STANDARD)

2008 *Implications of Various Address Allocation Policies for Internet Routing.* Y. Rekhter and T. Li. October, 1996. (Status: BEST CURRENT PRACTICE)

1995 *Incremental Zone Transfer in DNS.* M. Ohta. August, 1996. (Status: PROPOSED STANDARD)

1994 *PPP Challenge Handshake Authentication Protocol (CHAP).* W. Simpson. August, 1996. (Status: DRAFT STANDARD)

1993 *PPP Gandalf FZA Compression Protocol.* A. Barbir, D. Carr, and W. Simpson. August, 1996. (Status: INFORMATIONAL)

1969 *The PPP DES Encryption Protocol (DESE).* K. Sklower and G. Meyer. June, 1996. (Status: INFORMATIONAL)

1968 *The PPP Encryption Control Protocol (ECP).* G. Meyer. June, 1996. (Status: PROPOSED STANDARD)

1967 *PPP LZS-DCP Compression Protocol (LZS-DCP).* K. Schneider and R. Friend. August, 1996. (Status: INFORMATIONAL)

1962 *The PPP Compression Control Protocol (CCP).* D. Rand. June, 1996. (Status: PROPOSED STANDARD)

1961 *GSS-API Authentication Method for SOCKS Version 5.* P. McMahon. June, 1996. (Status: PROPOSED STANDARD)

1935 *What is the Internet, Anyway?* J. Quarterman and S. Carl-Mitchell. April, 1996. (Status: INFORMATIONAL)

1933 *Transition Mechanisms for IPv6 Hosts and Routers.* R. Gilligan and E. Nordmark. April, 1996. (Status: PROPOSED STANDARD)

1929 *Username/Password Authentication for SOCKS V5.* M. Leech. April, 1996. (Status: PROPOSED STANDARD)

1928 *SOCKS Protocol Version 5.* M. Leech, M. Ganis, Y. Lee, R. Kuris, D. Koblas, and L. Jones. April, 1996. (Status: PROPOSED STANDARD)

1918 *Address Allocation for Private Internets.* Y. Rekhter, B. Moskowitz, D. Karrenberg, G. J. de Groot, and E. Lear. February, 1996. (Status: BEST CURRENT PRACTICE)

1912 *Common DNS Operational and Configuration Errors.* D. Barr. February, 1996. (Status: INFORMATIONAL)

1900 *Renumbering Needs Work.* B. Carpenter and Y. Rekhter. February, 1996. (Status: INFORMATIONAL)

1884 *IP Version 6 Addressing Architecture.* R. Hinden and S. Deering, Editors. December, 1995. (Status: PROPOSED STANDARD)

1883 *Internet Protocol, Version 6 (IPv6) Specification.* S. Deering and R. Hinden. December, 1995. (Status: PROPOSED STANDARD)

1881 *IPv6 Address Allocation Management.* IAB and IESG. December, 1995. (Status: INFORMATIONAL)

1865 *EDI Meets the Internet Frequently Asked Questions about Electronic Data Interchange (EDI) on the Internet.* W. Houser, J. Griffin, and C. Hage. January, 1996. (Status: INFORMATIONAL)

1852 *IP Authentication Using Keyed SHA.* P. Metzger and W. Simpson. September, 1995. (Status: EXPERIMENTAL)

1851 *The ESP Triple DES Transform.* P. Karn, P. Metzger, and W. Simpson. September, 1995. (Status: EXPERIMENTAL)

1829 *The ESP DES-CBC Transform.* P. Karn, P. Metzger, and W. Simpson. August, 1995. (Status: PROPOSED STANDARD)

1828 *IP Authentication Using Keyed MD5.* P. Metzger and W. Simpson. August, 1995. (Status: PROPOSED STANDARD)

1827 *IP Encapsulating Security Payload (ESP).* R. Atkinson. August, 1995. (Status: PROPOSED STANDARD)

1826 *IP Authentication Header.* R. Atkinson. August, 1995. (Status: PROPOSED STANDARD)

1825 *Security Architecture for the Internet Protocol.* R. Atkinson. August, 1995. (Status: PROPOSED STANDARD)

1817 *CIDR and Classful Routing.* Y. Rekhter. August, 1995. (Status: INFORMATIONAL)

1794 *DNS Support for Load Balancing.* T. Brisco. April, 1995. (Status: INFORMATIONAL)

1760 *The S/KEY One-Time Password System.* N. Haller. February, 1995. (Status: INFORMATIONAL)

1702 *Generic Routing Encapsulation over IPv4 Networks.* S. Hanks, T. Li, D. Farinacci, and P. Traina. October, 1994. (Status: INFORMATIONAL)

1701 *Generic Routing Encapsulation (GRE).* S. Hanks, T. Li, D. Farinacci, and P. Traina. October, 1994. (Status: INFORMATIONAL)

1661 *The Point-to-Point Protocol (PPP).* W. Simpson, Editor. July, 1994. (Status: STANDARD)

1631 *The IP Network Address Translator (NAT).* K. Egevang and P. Francis. May, 1994. (Status: INFORMATIONAL)

1591 *Domain Name System Structure and Delegation.* J. Postel. March, 1994. (Status: INFORMATIONAL)

1531 *Dynamic Host Configuration Protocol.* R. Droms. October, 1993. (Status: PROPOSED STANDARD)

1321 *The MD5 Message-Digest Algorithm.* R. Rivest. April, 1992. (Status: INFORMATIONAL)

1320 *The MD4 Message-Digest Algorithm.* R. Rivest. April, 1992. (Status: INFORMATIONAL)

1319 *The MD2 Message-Digest Algorithm.* B. Kaliski. April, 1992. (Status: INFORMATIONAL)

1035 *Domain Names—Implementation and Specification.* P. V. Mockapetris. November 1, 1987. (Status: STANDARD)

1034 *Domain Names—Concepts and Facilities.* P. V. Mockapetris. November 1, 1987. (Status: STANDARD)

IETF Documents—Internet Drafts

IETF Internet-Drafts usually are circulated and stored for six months after publication. At the end of that period, they are either replaced with a new version, replaced with an entirely new Internet-draft, converted to an RFC, or removed. The names and dates of the drafts listed were accurate as of May, 1998.

The documents have been listed according to the working group responsible for their development. The last group, labelled individual submissions, includes any Internet-Draft that may be appropriate to the subject of this book but has not been officially generated by a specific working group.

Access, Searching, and Indexing of Directories

Genovese, Tony, M. Wahl, and Y. Yaacovi. "Lightweight Directory Access Protocol (v3): Extensions for Dynamic Directory Services," 12/23/1997, <draft-ietf-asid-ldapv3-dynamic-07.txt>

Stokes, E., R. Weiser, and Bob Huston. "LDAP Replication Requirements," 11/26/1997, <draft-ietf-asid-replica-req-01.txt>

Authenticated Firewall Traversal

Kayashima, Makoto, Tsukasa Ogino, Masato Terada, and Yoichi Fujiyama. "SOCKS V5 Protocol Extension for Multiple Firewalls Traversal," 11/26/1997, <draft-ietf-aft-socks-multiple-traversal-00.txt>

Michener, J., and Dan Fritch. "Multi-Authentication Framework Method for SOCKS V5," 03/13/1998, <draft-ietf-aft-socks-maf-00.txt>

VanHeyningen, Marc. "Challenge-Handshake Authentication Protocol for SOCKS V5," 01/07/1998, <draft-ietf-aft-socks-chap-01.txt>

VanHeyningen, Marc. "SOCKS Protocol Version 5," 03/05/1998,
  <draft-ietf-aft-socks-pro-v5-02.txt>
Zorn, Glen, Pat Calhoun, and Jeff Haag. "EAP Authentication for SOCKS
  Version 5," 03/06/1998, <draft-ietf-aft-socks-eap-00.txt>

Differentiated Services

Brim, Scott, Frank Kastenholz, Fred Baker, John Renwick, Tony Li, and
  Shantigram Jagannath. "IP Precedence in Differentiated Services
  Using the Assured Service," 04/10/1998,
  <draft-ietf-diffserv-precedence-00.txt>
Nichols, Kathleen, and S. Blake. "Definition of the Differentiated Services
  Field (DS Byte) in the IPv4 and IPv6 Headers," 05/07/1998,
  <draft-ietf-diffserv-header-00.txt>
Nichols, Kathleen, and S. Blake. "Differentiated Services Operational
  Model and Definitions," 02/11/1998, <draft-nichols-dsopdef-00.txt>

Domain Name System Security

Eastlake, Don. "DNS Operational Security Considerations," 03/12/1998,
  <draft-ietf-dnssec-secops-01.txt>
Eastlake, Don. "Domain Name System Security Extensions," 05/05/1998,
  <draft-ietf-dnssec-secext2-05.txt>
Eastlake, Don. "DSA KEYs and SIGs in the Domain Name System,"
  01/27/1998, <draft-ietf-dnssec-dss-02.txt>
Eastlake, Don. "RSA/MD5 KEYs and SIGs in the Domain Name System
  (DNS)," 01/27/1998, <draft-ietf-dnssec-rsa-00.txt>
Eastlake, Don. "Secret Key Establishment for DNS (TKEY RR),"
  02/23/1998, <draft-ietf-dnssec-tkey-00.txt>
Eastlake, Don. "Storage of Diffie-Hellman Keys in the Domain Name
  System (DNS)," 03/12/1998, <draft-ietf-dnssec-dhk-02.txt>
Gudmundsson, O., and D. Eastlake. "Storing Certificates in the Domain
  Name System (DNS)," 03/06/1998, <draft-ietf-dnssec-certs-02.txt>
Watson, Robert. "DNSsec Authentication Referral Record (AR),"
  11/26/1997, <draft-ietf-dnssec-ar-00.txt>

Dynamic Host Configuration

Droms, Ralph, and O. Gudmundsson. "Security Requirements for the
  DHCP Protocol," 03/13/1998, <draft-ietf-dhc-security-requirements-
  00.txt>

Rekhter, Y. "Interaction between DHCP and DNS," 03/05/1998, <draft-ietf-dhc-dhcp-dns-08.txt>

Electronic Data Interchange-Internet Integration

Drummond, Rik, M. Jansson, and C. Shih. "MIME-Based Secure EDI," 12/04/1997, <draft-ietf-ediint-as1-05.txt>

Drummond, Rik, M. Jansson, and C. Shih. "Requirements for InterOperable Internet EDI," 04/27/1998, <draft-ietf-ediint-req-05.txt>

IP Performance Metrics

Anon. "Connectivity," 11/24/1997, <draft-ietf-ippm-connectivity-01.txt>

Demichelis, Carlo. "Instantaneous Packet Delay Variation Metric for IPPM," 03/11/1998, <draft-ietf-ippm-ipdv-00.txt>

IP Security Protocol

Adams, R., and R. Pereira. "The ESP CBC-Mode Cipher Algorithms," 03/10/1998, <draft-ietf-ipsec-ciph-cbc-02.txt>

Bhattacharya, P., and R. Pereira. "IPSec Policy Data Model," 02/25/1998, <draft-ietf-ipsec-policy-model-00.txt>

Carrel, D., and D. Harkins. "The Internet Key Exchange (IKE)," 03/13/1998, <draft-ietf-ipsec-isakmp-oakley-07.txt>

Doraswamy, Naganand. "Implementation of Virtual Private Network (VPNs) with IP Security," 03/14/1997, <draft-ietf-ipsec-vpn-00.txt>

Doraswamy, Naganand, and C. Madson. "The ESP DES-CBC Cipher Algorithm with Explicit IV," 02/13/1998, <draft-ietf-ipsec-ciph-des-expiv-02.txt>

Kent, Stephen, and Ran Atkinson. "IP Authentication Header," 05/12/1998, <draft-ietf-ipsec-auth-header-06.txt>

Kent, Stephen, and Ran Atkinson. "IP Encapsulating Security Payload (ESP)," 05/12/1998, <draft-ietf-ipsec-esp-v2-05.txt>

Kent, Stephen, and Ran Atkinson. "Security Architecture for the Internet Protocol," 05/12/1998, <draft-ietf-ipsec-arch-sec-05.txt>

Kent, Stephen, and R. Glenn. "The NULL Encryption Algorithm and Its Use with IPsec," 03/13/1998, <draft-ietf-ipsec-ciph-null-00.txt>

Madson, C., and R. Glenn. "The Use of HMAC-MD5-96 within ESP and AH," 02/18/1998, <draft-ietf-ipsec-auth-hmac-md5-96-03.txt>

Madson, C., and R. Glenn. "The Use of HMAC-SHA-1-96 within ESP and AH," 02/18/1998, <draft-ietf-ipsec-auth-hmac-sha196-03.txt>

Maughan, D., M. Schertler, M. Schneider, and J. Turner. "Internet Security Association and Key Management Protocol (ISAKMP)," 03/11/1998, <draft-ietf-ipsec-isakmp-09.txt.ps>

Orman, H. "The OAKLEY Key Determination Protocol," 07/25/1997, <draft-ietf-ipsec-oakley-02.txt>

Patel, B. "Dynamic Remote Host Configuration over IPSEC Using DHCP," 12/04/1997, <draft-ietf-ipsec-dhcp-00.txt>

Patel, B., and Michael Jeronimo. "Revised SA Negotiation Mode for ISAKMP/Oakley," 12/04/1997, <draft-ietf-ipsec-isakmp-SA-revised-00.txt>

Patel, B., R. Pereira, and S. Anand. "The ISAKMP Configuration Method," 04/23/1998, <draft-ietf-ipsec-isakmp-mode-cfg-03.txt>

Pereira, R. "Extended Authentication within ISAKMP/Oakley," 02/24/1998, <draft-ietf-ipsec-isakmp-xauth-01.txt>

Piper, D. "A GSS-API Authentication Mode for ISAKMP/Oakley," 12/23/1997, <draft-ietf-ipsec-isakmp-gss-auth-01.txt>

Piper, D. "The Internet IP Security Domain of Interpretation for ISAKMP," 05/13/1998, <draft-ietf-ipsec-ipsec-doi-09.txt>

Piper, D., and D. Harkins. "The Pre-Shared Key for the Internet Protocol," 04/06/1998, <draft-ietf-ipsec-internet-key-00.txt>

Provos, Niels. "The Use of HMAC-RIPEMD-160-96 within ESP and AH," 02/16/1998, <draft-ietf-ipsec-auth-hmac-ripemd-160-96-01.txt>

Simpson, W., Naganand Doraswamy, Perry Metzger. "The ESP Triple DES Transform," 07/03/1997, <draft-ietf-ipsec-ciph-des3-00.txt>

Thayer, Rodney, Naganand Doraswamy, and R. Glenn. "IP Security Document Roadmap," 12/04/1997, <draft-ietf-ipsec-doc-roadmap-02.txt>

Multiprotocol Label Switching

Callon, Ross, George Swallow, N. Feldman, A. Viswanathan, P. Doolan, and A. Fredette. "A Framework for Multiprotocol Label Switching," 11/26/1997, <draft-ietf-mpls-framework-02.txt>

Callon, Ross, A. Viswanathan, and E. Rosen. "Multiprotocol Label Switching Architecture," 04/07/1998, <draft-ietf-mpls-arch-01.txt>

Davie, Bruce, Y Rekhter, A. Viswanathan, S. Blake, Vijay Srinivasan, and E. Rosen. "Use of Label Switching with RSVP," 03/12/1998, <draft-ietf-mpls-rsvp-00.txt>

Next Generation (IPv6) Transition

Anon. "Transition Mechanisms for IPv6 Hosts and Routers," 11/21/1997, <draft-ietf-ngtrans-mech-00.txt>

Durand, A., and Bertrand Buclin. "IPv6 Routing Issues," 04/24/1998, <draft-ietf-ngtrans-6bone-routing-issues-02.txt>

Srisuresh, Pyda, and George Tsirtsis. "Network Address Translation—Protocol Translation (NAT-PT)," 03/06/1998, <draft-ietf-ngtrans-natpt-01.txt>

Point-to-Point Protocol Extensions

Aboba, B., and B. Patel. "Securing L2TP Using IPSEC," 03/11/1998, <draft-ietf-pppext-12tp-security-01.txt>

Calhoun, Pat, W. Mark Townsley, Sumit Vakil, and Donald Grosser. "Layer Two Tunneling Protocol 'L2TP' Security Extensions for Non-IP Networks," 03/18/1998, <draft-ietf-pppext-12tp-sec-03.txt>

Carter, G., "PPP EAP ISAKMP Authentication Protocol," 09/20/1997, <draft-ietf-pppext-eapiskamp-00.txt>

Casner, Stephen, C. Bormann, and M. Engan. "IP Header Compression over PPP," 12/23/1997, <draft-engan-ip-compress-02.txt>

Peirce, Ken, and Pat Calhoun. "Layer Two Tunneling Protocol 'L2TP' IP Differential Services Extension," 03/09/1998, <draft-ietf-pppext-12tp-ds-01.txt>

Peirce, Ken, and Pat Calhoun. "Layer Two Tunneling Protocol 'L2TP' Multi-Protocol Label Switching Extension," 03/09/1998, <draft-ietf-pppext-12tp-mpls-00.txt>

Rubens, Allan, William Palter, T. Kolar, G. Pall, M. Littlewood, A. Valencia, K. Hamzeh, W. Verthein, J. Taarud, and W. Mark Townsley. "Layer Two Tunneling Protocol 'L2TP,' " 04/06/1998, <draft-ietf-pppext-12tp-10.txt>

Valencia, A. "L2TP Header Compression ("L2TPHC")," 12/22/1997, <draft-ietf-pppext-12tphc-01.txt>

Zmuda, James, and W. Nace. "PPP Certificate Exchange Protocol," 12/03/1997, <draft-ietf-pppext-crtxchg-01.txt>

Zmuda, James, and W. Nace. "PPP EAP DSS Public Key Authentication Protocol," 12/03/1997, <draft-ietf-pppext-eapdss-01.txt>

Zorn, Glen, and S. Cobb. "Microsoft PPP CHAP Extensions," 03/11/1998, <draft-ietf-pppext-mschap-00.txt>

Zorn, Glen, and G. Pall. "Microsoft Point-To-Point Encryption (MPPE) Protocol," 04/06/1998, <draft-ietf-pppext-mppe-01.txt>

Public Key Infrastructure (X.509)

Adams, C., and S. Farrell. "Internet X.509 Public Key Infrastructure Certificate Management Protocols," 02/26/1998, <draft-ietf-pkix-ipki3cmp-07.txt>

Adams, C., and M. Myers. "Internet X.509 Public Key Infrastructure Certificate Management Message Formats," 03/12/1998, <draft-ietf-pkix-cmmf-00.txt>

Adams, C., M. Myers, Ambarish Malpani, Rich Ankney, and Slava Galperin. "X.509 Internet Public Key Infrastructure Online Certificate Status Protocol—OCSP," 04/07/1998, <draft-ietf-pkix-ocsp-03.txt>

Branchard, Marc. "Internet Public Key Infrastructure Caching the Online Certificate Status Protocol," 04/17/1998, <draft-ietf-pkix-ocsp-caching-00.txt>

Ford, Warwick, and S. Chokhani. "Internet X.509 Public Key Infrastructure Certificate Policy and Certification Practices Framework," 04/28/1998, <draft-ietf-pkix-ipki-part4-03.txt>

Ford, Warwick, and P. Hallam-Baker. "Internet X.509 Public Key Infrastructure OPEN CRL DISTRIBUTION PROCESS (OpenCDP)," 04/22/1998, <draft-ietf-pkix-ocdp-00.txt>

Fox, Barbara, Xiaoyi Liu, M. Myers, and Jeff Weinstein. "Certificate Management Messages over CMS," 03/12/1998, <draft-ietf-pkix-cmc-00.txt>

Housley, Russ. "Internet X.509 Public Key Infrastructure Operational Protocols: FTP and HTTP," 04/16/1998, <draft-ietf-pkix-opp-ftp-http-03.txt>

Howes, Tim, S. Boeyen, and P. Richard. "Internet X.509 Public Key Infrastructure LDAPv2 Schema," 03/16/1998, <draft-ietf-pkix-ldapv2-schema-00.txt>

Howes, Tim, S. Boeyen, and P. Richard. "Internet X.509 Public Key Infrastructure Operational Protocols—LDAPv2," 03/16/1998, <draft-ietf-pkix-ipki2opp-07.txt>

Solo, D., C. Adams, D. Kemp, and M. Myers. "Certificate Request Message Format," 02/25/1998, <draft-ietf-pkix-crmf-00.txt>

Solo, D., Russ Housley, Warwick Ford, and T. Polk. "Internet Public Key Infrastructure X.509 Certificate and CRL Profile," 04/06/1998, <draft-ietf-pkix-ipki-part1-07.txt>

Remote Authentication Dial-In User Service

Calhoun, Pat, and Sumit Vakil. "RADIUS IP Security Extensions," 11/10/1997, <draft-ietf-radius-ipsec-00.txt>

Rubens, Allan, B. Aboba, and Pat Calhoun. "Extensible Authentication Protocol Support in RADIUS," 05/13/1998, <draft-ietf-radius-eap-05.txt>

Shriver, J., D. Leifer, Allan Rubens, and Glen Zorn, "RADIUS Attributes for Tunnel Protocol Support," 04/08/1998, <draft-ietf-radius-tunnel-auth-05.txt>

Zorn, Glen. "RADIUS Attributes for MS-CHAP Support," 11/06/1997, <draft-rfced-info-zorn-01.txt>

Zorn, Glen. "RADIUS Attributes for MS-CHAP Support," 11/18/1997, <draft-ietf-radius-mschap-attr-01.txt>

Zorn, Glen, and David Mitton. "RADIUS Accounting Modifications for Tunnel Protocol Support," 12/03/1997, <draft-ietf-radius-tunnel-acct-00.txt>

RSVP Admission Policy

Anon. "RSVP Extensions for Policy Control," 03/13/1998, <draft-ietf-rap-rsvp-ext-00.txt>

Herzog, Shai, A. Sastry, R. Rajan, Ron Cohen, J. Boyle, and David Durham. "The COPS (Common Open Policy Service) Protocol," 03/16/1998, <draft-ietf-rap-cops-01.txt>

Yavatkar, R., R. Guerin, and D. Pendarakis. "A Framework for Policy-Based Admission Control," 11/26/1997, <draft-ietf-rap-framework-00.txt>

Individual Submissions

Aboba, B. "Lightweight Directory Access Protocol (v3): Dynamic Attributes for the Remote Access Dial-in User Service (RADIUS)," 11/21/1997, <draft-aboba-dynradius-01.txt>

Aboba, B. "Lightweight Directory Access Protocol (v3): Extension for PPP Authentication," 11/21/1997, <draft-aboba-ppp-01.txt>

Aboba, B. "Lightweight Directory Access Protocol (v3): Schema for the Remote Access Dial-in User Service (RADIUS)," 02/05/1998, <draft-aboba-radius-02.txt>

Bartz, Larry. "LDAP Schema for Role-Based Access Control," 10/14/1997, <draft-bartz-hyperdrive-ldap-rbac-schema-00.txt>

Berkowitz, H. "To Be Multihomed: Requirements & Definitions,"
    03/11/1998, <draft-berkowitz-multirqmt-01.txt>

Carrel, D., and L. Grant. "The TACACS+ Protocol Version 1.78,"
    01/06/1998, <draft-grant-tacacs-02.txt>

Demizu, Noritoshi, and H. Izumiyama. "Dynamic Tunnel Configuration
    Protocol," 12/04/1997, <draft-demizu-udlr-dtcp-00.txt>

Ellesson, Ed, Dinesh Verma, R. Rajan, and S. Kamat. "Schema for Service
    Level Administration of Differentiated Services and Integrated
    Services in Networks," 02/25/1998, <draft-ellesson-sla-schema-00.txt>

Ferguson, P. "Simple Differential Services: IP TOS and Precedence, Delay
    Indication, and Drop Preference," 03/12/1998,
    <draft-ferguson-delay-drop-02.txt>

Heinanen, Juha, and E. Rosen. "VPN support for MPLS," 03/09/1998,
    <draft-heinanen-mpls-vpn-01.txt>

Jamieson, Dwight, Scott Pegrum, and Matthew Yuen. "VPN Multipoint to
    Multipoint Tunnel Protocol (VMMT)," 03/16/1998,
    <draft-pegrum-vmmt-00.txt>

Karn, P., and W. Simpson. "Photuris: Extended Schemes and Attributes,"
    03/06/1998, <draft-simpson-photuris-schemes-05.txt>

Karn, P., and W. Simpson. "Photuris: Session Key Management Protocol,"
    02/27/1998, <draft-simpson-photuris-18.txt>

Li, Tony, and Y Rekhter, "Provider Architecture for Differentiated Services
    and Traffic Engineering," 01/14/1998, <draft-li-paste-00.txt>

McDonald, D., B. Phan, and C. Metz. "PF_KEY Key Management API,
    Version 2," 02/27/1998, <draft-mcdonald-pf-key-v2-05.txt>

Moskowitz, Robert. "Network Address Translation Issues with IPsec,"
    02/12/1998, <draft-moskowitz-net66-vpn-00.txt>

O'Hara, John. "Configuration of Tunnel Mode IPSec Endpoint
    Parameters," 11/26/1997, <draft-ohara-ipsecparam-00.txt>

Ravikanth, Ravadurgam, and Pasi Vaananen. "Framework for Traffic
    Management in MPLS Networks," 03/19/1998,
    <draft-vaananen-mpls-tm-framework-00.txt>

Simpson, W. "Photuris: Secret Exchange," 05/06/1998,
    <draft-simpson-photuris-secret-00.txt>

Simpson, W., and Perry Metzger. "IP Authentication Using Keyed SHA1
    with Data Padding," 05/01/1996, <draft-simpson-ah-sha-kdp-00.txt>

Srisuresh, Pyda, and Kjeld Egevang. "The IP Network Address Translator
    (NAT)," 03/05/1998, <draft-rfced-info-srisuresh-05.txt>

Suzuki, M. "Architecture of the Resource Reservation Service for the
    Commercial Internet," 02/09/1998, <draft-rfced-info-suzuki-00.txt>

Web Sites

Internet and ISP Information

CIX (Commercial Internet Exchange)   www.cix.org

IETF   www.ietf.org/

Internet Infrastructure, Service Provider Links, Topology Maps
   www.clark.net/pub/rbenn/isp.html

Mapnet   www.caida.org/Tools/Mapnet/Backbones/

Russ Haynal's ISP Page   navigators.com/isp.html

Security

Bruce Schneir   www.counterpane.com

Cryptographic Protocols and Standards
   www.cs.hut.fi/ssh/crypto/protocols.html

International Computer Security Association   www.icsa.net/

Koops' Crypto Law Survey   cwis.kub.nl/~frw/people/koops/
   bertjaap.htm

NIST Computer Security Resource Clearinghouse   csrc.nist.gov/
   publications/welcome.html

VPN-Related Information

IPSec Papers, RFCs   www.ietf.cnri.reston.va.us/ids.by.wg/ipsec.html

L2F vs PPTP   www.nortel.com/rapport/product/faqpptp.html

L2TP   www.totalb.com/~12tp/

Point-to-Point Tunneling Protocol   www.microsoft.com/
   communications/PPTP.htm

Automotive Network eXchange   www.aiag.org/anx/

ANX Ottawa Test Results   www.aiag.org/anx/ottawa.html

Dynamic Virtual Private Networks
   esp.tradewave.com/papers/securevpn.html

NewOak ROI Calculator
   m80.environs.com/newoak/roi/advanced.asp

VPN ROI Calculator   www.baynetworks.com/products/switches/
    roi_calculator/index.html

Security Working Group News
    www.cs.arizona.edu/xkernel/www/ipsec/ipsec.html

S/WAN   www.rsa.com/rsa/SWAN/home.html

SKIP IP-level Encryption   skip.incog.com/

VPN Information Center   www.checkpoint.com/vpn/index.html

VPN Source Page   techweb.cmp.com/internetwk/VPN/default.html

B

VPN Vendors and Products

For more information on new product and industry updates, please visit the book's companion Web site at www.wiley.com/compbooks/kosiur

3Com Corporation, 5400 Bayfront Plaza, Santa Clara, CA 95052, (408) 764-5000, www.3com.com
NETBuilder routers
Dual Processing Engine (DPE) for NETBuilder II routers
Dial Access Outsourcing (VPN bundle)
Virtual Leased Lines (VPN bundle)

Ascend Communications, Inc., 1701 Harbor Bay Parkway, Alameda, CA 94502, (510) 769-6001 or (800) 621-9578, info@ascend.com, www.ascend.com/
MultiVPN Architecture (IP Navigator, Customer Network Management Platform)
Pipeline 220 router
SecureConnect (family of VPN software products)

Assured Digital, Inc., P.O. Box 248, 9–11 Goldsmith Street, Littleton, MA 01460, (978) 486-0555, www.assured-digital.com/
ADI VPN-100 (remote dial-up software)

ADI VPN-500 (PC-based encryptor)
ADI VPN-1000 (VPN hardware, 10-Mbps Ethernet)
ADI VPN-2000 (VPN hardware, 10-Mbps Ethernet)
ADI VPN-4500 (VPN hardware, 100-Mbps Ethernet)
ADI Management System

Aventail Corporation, 117 South Main Street, Fourth Floor, Seattle, WA 98104, (206) 215-1111 or (888) 762-5785, sales@aventail.com, www .aventail.com/
Mobile VPN (server and client software)

Axent Technologies, Inc., 2400 Research Blvd., Rockville, MD 20850, (301) 258-5043, (800) 298-2620 ext. 801, fax: (301) 330-5756, info@axent.com, www.axent.com
PowerVPN software

Bay Networks, Inc., 4401 Great America Pkwy., Santa Clara, CA 95054, (800)-8-BAYNET, www.baynetworks.com/
Contivity (formerly Extranet Switch) –1000, –4000
VPN Secure Manager
VPN Secure Client software
VPN 500n, 550n (integrated VPN hardware)
BayStream Dial VPN Service (BayDVS)

CheckPoint Software Technologies Ltd., Three Lagoon Drive, Suite 400, Redwood City, CA 94065, (650) 628-2000, info@checkpoint.com, www.checkpoint.com/
Firewall-1
Firewall-1 SecuRemote (dial-in client software)
Floodgate-1 (bandwidth-management software)

Cisco Systems, Inc., 170 West Tasman Drive, San Jose, CA 95134, (408) 526-4000 or (800) 553-6387, www.cisco.com/
PIX Firewall
IOS 11.2 (operating software for routers, switches, etc.)

Compatible Systems, 4730 Walnut Street, Suite 102, Boulder, CO 80301, (303) 444-9532 or (800) 356-0283, info@compatible.com, www.compatible.com/
IntraPort (self-contained VPN hardware)

Cylink Corporation, 910 Hermosa Court, Sunnyvale, CA 94086,
(408) 735-5800 or (800) 533-3958, info@cylink.com, www.cylink.com/
SecureDomain (self-contained VPN hardware)

Data Fellows Inc., 675 N. First Street, 8th Floor, San Jose, CA 95112,
(408) 938-6700, info@DataFellows.com, www.datafellows.com/
F-Secure VPN (VPN software for Intel PCs)

Digital Equipment Corp., Littleton, MA (978) 493-5111,
fax: (978) 506-2017, altavista.software.digital.com/
AltaVista Tunnel (VPN software)

Entrust Technologies, 2323 North Central Expressway, Suite 360,
Richardson, TX 95080, (972) 994-8000, entrust@entrust.com,
www.entrust.com/
Entrust/Directory (LDAP-compatible certificate server)
Entrust/Manager

Extended Systems, Inc., 5777 N. Meeker Avenue, Boise, ID 83713, (208)
322-7800 or (800) 235-7576, info@extendsys.com, www.extendsys.com/
ExtendNet VPN (remote access VPN server)

Fortress Technologies, Inc., 2701 N. Rocky Point Drive, Suite 650,
Tampa, FL 33607, (813) 288-7388, info@fortresstech.com,
www.fortresstech.com/
NetFortress VPN-1, VPN-3 (VPN hardware)

FreeGate Corporation, 1208 East Arques Avenue, Sunnyvale, CA 94086,
(408) 617-1000, sales@freegate.com, www.freegate.com/
Multiservices Internet Gateway

Frontier Technologies, 10201 N. Port Washington Rd., Mequon, WI
53092, (414) 241-4555, (800) 929-3054, fax: 414-241-7084,
Info@FrontierTech.Com
E-Lock Desktop (PKI and VPN client software)
E-Lock Director (PKI and VPN server software)

Indus River Networks, Inc., 31 Nagog Park, Acton, MA 01720, (978)
266-8100, fax: (978) 266-8111, www.indusriver.com/
Riverworks Enterprise VPN (hardware for dial-in VPNs)
RTS-5000 Tunnel Server

InfoExpress, Inc., 1270 Payne Dr., Los Altos, CA 94024, (650) 969-9609, fax: (650) 969-6924, info@infoexpress.com, sales@infoexpress.com for sales, www.infoexpress.com
    VTPC/Secure

Information Resource Engineering, Inc. (IRE), 8029 Corporate Drive, Baltimore, MD 21236, (410) 931-7500, www.ire.com/
    SafeNet/LAN (encrypting firewall for VPN)
    SafeNet/Soft, SafeNet/Soft-PK (client software)
    SafeNet/Smart (smart card-based VPN software)
    SafeNet/Security Center (management workstation)
    SafeNet/Dial (encrypting modem with smart card and software)
    SafeNet/Firewall (proxy firewall)
    SafeNet/Trusted Service (managed VPN service)

Intel Corp., Santa Clara, CA, www.intel.com/network/doc/1460/INDEX.COM
    IntelExpress Router

IBM, www.software.ibm.com/enetwork/technology/vpn/
    2210 Nways Multiprotocol Routers
    Nways Multiprotocol Access Services
    AIX Firewall

Internet Devices Inc., 1287 Anvilwood Avenue, Sunnyvale, CA 94089, (408) 541-1400 or (888) 237-2244, sales@InternetDevices.com, www.InternetDevices.com/
    Fort Knox (integrated VPN hardware)

Internet Dynamics, Lombard, IL, (630) 953-7700, fax: (630) 953-7701, sales@interdyn.com, www.interdyn.com/
    Conclave (integrated VPN software)

Microsoft Corp., Redmond, WA, (425) 882-8080, fax: (425) 936-7329, www.microsoft.com/
    NT Server with Routing and Remote Access Services (software)
    Proxy Server

Milkyway Networks Corp., 2650 Queensview Dr., Suite 150, Ottawa, ON, CANADA, K2B 8H6, (613) 596-5549, fax: (613) 596-5615,

www.milkyway.com/
>SecurIT Firewall (encrypting firewall)
>SecurIT Access (remote access software)

NEC Systems Laboratory, Inc., 110 Rio Robles Drive, San Jose, CA 95134, prod-info@socks5.nec.com, www.socks5.nec.com
>SOCKS5 E2 Client
>SOCKS5 Internet Access Management Framework

NetScreen Technologies Inc., 4699 Old Ironsides Drive, Suite 300, Santa Clara, CA 95054, (408) 970-8889 or (877) NETSCREEN, info@netscreen.com, www.netscreen.com/
>NS-10, NS-100 (integrated VPN hardware)

Novell Inc., Provo, UT (801) 861-5588 or (800) 638-9273, fax: (801) 861-5155, www.novell.com/bordermanager/
>Bordermanager (integrated software including VPN functions)

RADGUARD, 24 Raoul Wallenberg Street, Tel Aviv 69719 ISRAEL, +972 3 645 5444; fax: +972 3 648 0859, www.radguard.com/
>cIPro-VPN (VPN hardware)
>NetCryptor (hardware encryptor)
>CryptoCA (certificate server)
>CryptoManage

Raptor Systems, Inc., 266 Second Avenue, Waltham MA, 02154, (800) 9-EAGLE-6, (781) 530-2200, fax: 781-487-6755, info@raptor.com, www.raptor.com
>Eagle (firewall)

RedCreek Communications, Inc., 3900 Newpark Mall Rd., Newark, CA 94560, (510) 745-3900, fax: (510) 745-3999, www.redcreek.com/
>Ravlin-4, −10, −100 (VPN hardware)

Secure Computing Corporation, One Almaden Blvd., Suite 400, San Jose, CA 95113, (408) 918-6100 or (800) 379-4944, www.securecomputing.com/
>BorderWare (firewall)
>SideWinder Security Server
>SecureZone (firewall)

Security Dynamics Technologies, Inc., 20 Crosby Drive, Bedford, MA 01730, (800) SECURID, www.securid.com/index.html
    SecurID (token-based authentication system)

Shiva Corporation, 28 Crosby Drive, Bedford, MA 01730-1437, (781) 687-1000, fax: (781) 687-1001, sales@shiva.com, www.shiva.com/
    LANRover VPN Gateway
    VPN client software
    Certificate Authority software

Storage Technology Corporation, 2270 South 88th Street, Louisville, CO 80028, (800) STORTEK or (800) 786-7835, www.network.com/
    NetSentry BorderGuard (VPN software)
    Sun Microsystems, Inc., Palo Alto, CA, www.sun.com/
    Sunscreen EFS (firewall)

TimeStep Corporation, 362 Terry Fox Drive, Kanata, Ontario, Canada K2K-2P5, (613) 599-3610 ext. 4532, info@timestep.com, www.timestep.com
    PERMIT/Connect (VPN hardware and Entrust certificate server system)
    PERMIT/Gateway 4520 (VPN hardware)
    PERMIT/Client (remote access software)
    PERMIT/Config
    PERMIT/2505, 4505 (hardware-based firewalls)

Trusted Information Systems, 1-888-TISFIRST or 1-888-FIREWALL, sales@tis.com, www.tis.com/
    Gauntlet (firewall)

UAC, 200 Lincoln Street, Suite 201, Boston, MA 02111, (617) 695-0137 ext. 19, www.uac.com/uacpn7.htm
    PN7 (firewall)

V-ONE Corporation, 20250 Century Blvd., Suite 300, Germantown, MD 20874, (301) 515-5200, sales@v-one.com, www.v-one.com/
    SmartGate Enterprise (VPN server)
    SmartPass (token-based remote access)
    SmartAdmin (management software)
    SmartWall (firewall)

VPNet Technologies, Inc., 1530 Meridian Avenue, San Jose, CA 95125, (408) 445-6600 or (888) VPNET-88, sales@vpnet.com, www.vpnet.com/
    VSU-10, –1010 (integrated VPN hardware)
    VPNmanager (management software)

VPNywhere (VPN hardware with roaming services)

Watchguard Technologies, Inc., 316 Occidental Avenue S., Suite 200, Seattle, WA 98104, (206) 521-8340, fax: (206) 521-8342, www.watchguard.com/
> Firebox II
> Global Security Manager
> Watchguard Security System (Firebox II, management and authentication tools)

Commercial VPN Providers

ANS, www.ans.net/

AT&T WorldNet VPN Services, (800) 831-5259, www.att.com/worldnet/wmis/virtual.html

Compuserve Network Services, Columbus Center, 6550 Metro Place South, Suite 560, Dublin, OH 43017, (614) 792-1901, networkinfo@csi.compuserve.com

Concentric Network, www.concentric.net/business/vpns/

GRIC Communications (roaming service), 1421 McCarthy Blvd., Milpitas, CA 95035, (408) 955-1920, gricinfo@gric.com, www.gric.com/

GTE Internetworking, 150 Cambridge Park Dr., Cambridge, MA 02140, (617) 873-2000, fax: (617) 873-5011, www.bbn.com, www.gte.net

iPass Inc. (roaming service), 650 Castro Street, Suite 500, Mountain View, CA 94041, (650) 237-7300, fax: (650) 237-7321, www.ipass.com

Netcom, www.netcom.com/

networkMCI, www.networkmci.com/Contactus/index.html

TCG CERFnet, P.O. Box 919014, San Diego, CA 92191-9014, (800) 876-CERF (2373), (619) 812-5000, fax: (619) 812-3990, www.cerfnet.net

UUNET (Extralink), Fairfax, VA, www.uunet.net/

C

What's on the Web Site?

The companion Web site to "Building and Managing Virtual Private Networks" is located at www.wiley.com/compbooks/kosiur. The site aims to be your central source of information on VPNs and includes the following sections:

- Information about new VPN products
- Pointers to published reviews of VPN products and services
- Pointers to information on VPN protocols (IETF RFCs and Internet-drafts)
- Information on the latest VPN-related tests and reports from ANX and ICSA
- Pointers to Web sites on security, network management, and VPNs
- Feature checklists of available VPN products
- A directory of VPN vendors
- Corrections and addenda to the book

Glossary

aggressive mode   In Oakley, the name of a mechanism used in the first phase of establishing a security association. In aggressive mode, the sender and receiver negotiate the basic algorithms and hashes for remaining SA exchanges. Unlike main-mode exchanges, aggressive mode accomplishes the exchange in three packets rather than six.

application gateway (or application proxy)   A type of firewall that controls external access to applications within a network.

ARPANET   The predecessor of the Internet, ARPANET was the first wide-area data communications network. It was originally funded by the Department of Defense's *Advanced Research Project Agency* (ARPA) to provide nationwide connectivity among military, educational, and research sites.

authentication   In cryptography, the process of ensuring that the data is coming from the source it claims to come from.

Authentication Header (AH)   In IPSec, the IP header used to verify that the contents of a packet haven't been altered.

automatic rekeying   The process of changing a key used for encryption periodically without any manual intervention. If rekeying intervals are kept short, automatic rekeying can help defeat attacks because the amount of data subject to the attack is relatively small, and the attacker has less time in which to crack the key.

biometrics   Using a unique physical trait to identify the user. Biometric technologies measure human characteristics such as fingerprints, voice recordings, iris and retinal scans, heat patterns, facial images, and even keystroke patterns.

block cipher   A crypto algorithm that encrypts data in blocks of a fixed size.

blowfish   A 64-bit block cipher with a variable-length key designed by Bruce Schneier for implementation on large microprocessors. It's optimized for applications in which the key does not change often.

brute force attack   The process of trying to recover a cryptographic key by trying all reasonable possibilities.

Certificate Authority (CA)   A trusted company or organization that will accept your public key, along with some proof of your identity, and serve as a repository of digital certificates. Others then can request verification of your public key from the certificate authority.

Certificate Revocation List (CRL)   Certificate authorities must maintain a list of digital certificates that are no longer valid (not including those expired).

Challenge Handshake Authentication Protocol (CHAP)   A protocol for authenticating remote users. CHAP incorporates three steps to produce a verified link after the link is first initiated. Instead of a simple two-step password/approval process, CHAP uses a one-way hashing function.

challenge-response   An authentication mechanism in which the authentication process sends a challenge to a process that requests authentication; the latter is authenticated only if it sends the correct response to the authentication process.

Channel Service Unit/Data Service Unit (CSU/DSU)   An interface between a digital line and a communication device used to provide the interface for circuit data services, which includes the physical framing, clocking, and channelization of the circuit.

Cipher Block Chaining (CBC)   A block cipher mode that combines the previous block of cipher text with the current block of plain text before encrypting it.

circuit gateway (circuit proxy)   A type of firewall that forms circuit-level connections between an external computer and a computer inside the network.

compulsory tunnel   Tunnels created without the user's consent, which may be transparent to the end user. The client-side endpoint of a compulsory tunnel typically resides on a *remote access server* (RAS). All traffic originating from the end user's computer is forwarded over the PPTP tunnel by the RAS. Access to other services outside the intranet would be controlled by the network administrators.

confidentiality   Preventing anyone from reading or copying your data as it travels across the Internet.

Data Encryption Standard (DES)   A block-cipher algorithm created by IBM and endorsed by the U.S. government in 1977; uses a 56-bit key and operates on blocks of 64 bits; relatively fast and used to encrypt large amounts of data at one time.

Demilitarized Zone (DMZ)   A portion of a network in which the traffic is not yet screened or regulated; commonly delineated by two firewalls: one forming the boundary between the public network and the DMZ and the other forming the boundary between the DMZ and the internal network.

Diffie-Hellman   A system designed to allow two individuals to agree on a shared key, even though they only exchange messages in public. This oldest public-key cryptosystem is still in use but does not support either encryption or digital signatures.

Digital Certificate   An electronic document, issued by a certificate authority, that's used to establish a company's identity by verifying its public key. (See Public Key Certificate.)

Digital Data Service (DDS)   DDS was the first digital service for private line applications, offering 56-Kbps connections to corporate customers. (Also called Dataphone Digital Service.)

Digital Signature Algorithm (DSA)   Developed by NSA and based on what's called the El Gamal algorithm, the signature scheme uses the same sort of keys as Diffie-Hellman and can create signatures faster than RSA. DSA is being pushed by NIST as DSS, the Digital Signature Standard.

Domain Name Service (DNS)   The network service responsible for converting numeric IP addresses into text-based names.

Domain of Interpretation (DOI)   In IPSec, the specification of which protocols and parameters are required for negotiation of security association.

Encapsulating Security Payload (ESP)   In IPSec, an IP header that contains the encrypted contents of an IP packet.

encapsulation   Placing the contents of one network's packet into that of another network's packet. (The protocols for the two networks can be identical.)

encryption   Conversion of human-readable cleartext (or plaintext) to ciphertext, using cryptographic algorithms.

firewall   A device acting as a network filter to restrict access to a private network from the outside, implementing access controls based on the contents of the packets of data that are transmitted between two parties or devices on the network.

frame relay   A high-speed, connection-oriented, public data packet switching technology that provides a very reliable and efficient packet delivery over *virtual circuits* (VCs). It supports access speeds up to 1.544 Mbps (T1) or 2.048 Mbps (E1) in Europe. The basic transport unit, which is called frame, can be up to 4,096 bytes and carries both routing and user information.

HMAC-MD5   A message authentication algorithm coupled with the MD5 hash function; operates on 64-byte blocks of data and produces a 128-bit authentication value.

HMAC-SHA-1   A message authentication algorithm coupled with the SHA-1 hash function; operates on 64-byte blocks of data and produces a 160-bit authentication value.

International Data Encryption Algorithm (IDEA)   A cryptographic algorithm using a 128-bit key for strong encryption and designed to be efficient to compute in software.

Internet Architecture Board (IAB)   The primary decision-making body regarding the Internet. The IAB sets research and engineering directions and oversees the IETF.

Internet Assigned Number Authority (IANA)   The organization responsible for assigning Internet address blocks, protocol identifiers, and TCP/UDP port numbers.

Internet Engineering Task Force (IETF)   A worldwide organization that develops new technology and standards for the Internet.

Internet Key Exchange (IKE)   The key-management protocol used in conjunction with IPSec.

Internet Service Provider (ISP)   A company that provides Internet access services to individual users and businesses.

IPSec   The network cryptographic protocols for protecting IP packets.

ISAKMP   A key-management protocol accepted for use with IPSec; now combined with Oakley to form the Internet Key Exchange (IKE) protocol.

jitter   The variation in latency. In traditional terms, it is the variation between voice samples generating distortion in the delivered voice signal. The distortion of a signal as it is propagated through a network, in which the signal varies from its original reference timing. In packet-switched networks, jitter is the distortion of the interpacket arrival times as compared to the interpacket times of the original transmission.

key   A string of digits, which when used with a cryptographic algorithm, produces cipher text.

LAN-to-LAN tunnel   A VPN tunnel created between two security gateways, each of which serves as the interface between the LAN it's protecting and the public network.

latency   Network delay; the minimum time that elapses between requesting and receiving data.

Layer2 Forwarding (L2F)   A tunneling protocol originally developed by Cisco.

Layer2 Tunneling Protocol (L2TP)   A tunneling protocol that combines many of the features of L2F and PPTP; also uses IPSec for encryption; supports encapsulation of packets other than IP.

leased line   A dedicated, private line provided by a carrier or local telephone company for the exclusive use of the customer.

Lightweight Directory Access Protocol (LDAP)   An IP-based protocol that governs how information within X.500-format directories can be obtained.

main mode   In Oakley, the name of the mechanism used in the first phase of establishing a security association. In main mode, the sender and receiver negotiate the basic algorithms and hashes for remaining SA exchanges.

Network Access Point (NAP)   On-ramp to the high-speed Internet backbone maintained by Sprint, Ameritech, Worldcom, and others.

Network Address Translation (NAT)   A procedure for translating private IP addresses used on an internal network to a special reserved block of IP addresses for communications on the public Internet.

nonce   A random value sent in a communications protocol exchange; often used to detect replay attacks.

Oakley   A key exchange protocol used in IPSec as part of the Internet Key Exchange protocol.

one-way hash function   A formula used to convert a message of any length into a string of digits called a message digest. The length of the function determines the length of the digest, and no key is required.

packet filter   Hardware or software that discards packets based on the contents of the packet; used in firewalls.

Password Authentication Protocol (PAP)   A simple authentication protocol that uses passwords using a two-way handshake; passwords are sent in the clear and, therefore, are not secure.

Permanent Virtual Circuit (PVC)   A *virtual connection* (VC) established by the network management between a source and a destination, which can be left up permanently (used in X.25 and frame relay protocols).

Point-of-Presence (POP)   Local access point to a national or international communications network. Users dial into their networks by calling a local phone number, rather than a toll-free number or a long-distance call to a centralized location.

Point-to-Point Protocol (PPP)   An Internet data-link protocol used to frame data packets on point-to-point links, such as modem links.

Point to Point Tunneling Protocol (PPTP)   A tunneling protocol originally developed by Ascend and Microsoft that operates at the Link layer of a network. It depends on PPP for its basic functionality and uses *Generic Routing Encapsulation* (GRE) for encapsulating packets; supports encapsulation of packets other than IP.

proxy agent   A proxy server software module that's programmed to handle one specific type of data transfer (e.g., FTP or TCP).

proxy server   A type of firewall that employs a store-and-forward approach to protecting crucial data and applications. The proxy server terminates the incoming connection from the source and initiates a second connection to the destination, ensuring that the incoming user has appropriate access rights to use data requested from the destination before passing that data on to the user.

Public Key Certificate   Specially-formatted data blocks that tell us the value of a public key, the name of the key's owner, and a digital signature of the issuing organization. These certificates are used to identify the owner of a particular public key.

public-key cryptography   An encryption method that uses a pair of keys: one public and one private. Messages encoded with either key can be decoded by the other. Also called *asymmetric encryption*.

Public Key Infrastructure (PKI)   The organization of certificate issuers and certificate management processes.

Public Switched Telephone Network (PSTN)   A generic name for the worldwide public telephone network.

Quality of Service (QoS)   A term used to describe a set of performance parameters that characterize the transmission quality over a given connection.

quick mode   In Oakley, the name of the mechanism used after a security association has been established to negotiate changes in security services, such as new keys.

RC2   Designed by Ron Rivest. A variable key-size cipher for very fast bulk encryption. RC2 is a block cipher and can be used in place of DES.

RC4   Another variable key-size cipher designed by Ron Rivest for very fast bulk encryption. RC4 is a stream cipher and is as much as 10 times faster than DES.

Remote Authentication Dial-In User Service (RADIUS)   A protocol that uses a client/server model to securely authenticate and administer remote network connection users and sessions. It can support other types of user authentication, including PAP and CHAP.

Resource reSerVation Protocol (RSVP)   A control protocol developed for supporting different QoS classes for IP applications (such as video-conference and multimedia) and to reserve resources in an IP-based network. RSVP uses a soft state mechanism to maintain path and reservation state in each node along the reservation path and can be changed dynamically by the requesting host.

roaming service   A service for remote users that enables them to use a local ISP instead of their corporate-selected ISP. A broker service manages the roaming service, handling settlement charges between ISPs and distribution of client software.

RSA   Named after Rivest, Shamir, and Adelman, its designers. Public-key algorithm supports a variable key length as well as variable blocksize of the text to be encrypted. The plaintext block must be smaller than the key length. Common key length is 512 bits.

Secure Sockets Layer (SSL)   A protocol that provides authentication for servers and browsers as well as confidentiality and data integrity for communications between a Web server and a browser. SSL can be used for transactions other than those on the Web, but it's not designed to handle security decisions based on authentication at the application or document level.

Security Association (SA)   In IPSec, an agreement between two communicating parties on which authentication and encryption algorithms will be used, along with related data, such as key lifetimes.

security gateway   Security gateways sit between public and private networks, preventing unauthorized intrusions into the private network. They also may provide tunneling capabilities and encrypt private data before it's transmitted on the public network.

Security Parameter Index (SPI)   In IPSec, specifies to the device receiving the packet what group of security protocols the sender is using for communications.

Service Level Agreement (SLA)   A contract between a service provider and a customer that specifies the parameters defining acceptable network performance to be provided and the type of remuneration for failing to meet the guaranteed performance.

session key   A cryptographic key intended to encrypt data for a limited period of time, typically only for a single communications session between a pair of correspondents. When the session is over, the key is discarded and a new one established when a new session takes place.

Skipjack   The NSA-developed encryption algorithm designed for the Clipper, Capstone, and Fortezza systems. The algorithm is an iterative 64-bit block cipher with an 80-bit key.

smart card   A credit card-sized plastic card with a special type of integrated circuit embedded in it. The integrated circuit holds information in electronic form and controls who uses this information and how.

SOCKS   An application proxy protocol that passes only traffic processed from specific (i.e., SOCKS) clients.

Stateful Multi-Layer Inspection (SMLI)   A type of firewall mechanism that uses smart packet filters that compare each packet with bit patterns of similar friendly packets.

Symmetric Encryption   An encryption method in which both the sender and the receiver possess the same cryptographic key, which means that both parties can encrypt and decrypt data with that key.

T1   A WAN transmission circuit that carries DS1-formatted data at a rate of 1.544 Mbps over two twisted pair wiring.

T3   A WAN transmission circuit that carries DS3-formatted data at a rate of 44.736 Mbps.

Terminal Access Controller Access Control System (TACACS)   A protocol that uses a client/server model to securely authenticate and administer remote network connection users and sessions. It can support other types of user authentication, including PAP and CHAP.

token-based authentication   A system using a hardware device that generates a one-time password to authenticate its owner; occasionally used to describe software programs that generate one-time passwords.

Transport-Mode IPSec   An IPSec mode, used either in AH or ESP, that leaves the original IP addresses in plaintext.

Triple DES   Based on DES, this cryptographic algorithm encrypts a block of data three times with two (or three) different keys.

Tunnel-Mode IPSec   An IPSec mode, used either in AH or ESP, that encrypts the original IP addresses of the source and destination and uses the IP addresses of the security gateways to route the packet through an IPSec tunnel.

tunnel or tunneling   The process of encapsulating one type of packet in another packet type so that the data can be transferred across paths that otherwise would not transmit the data. To avoid any confusion with the media-dependent virtual circuits, the paths that the encapsulated packets follow in Internet VPNs are called tunnels, not virtual circuits.

Virtual Private Network (VPN)   A private network built atop a public network (in this book, the Internet), in which secure connections are set up dynamically between a sender and a receiver.

voluntary tunnel   Voluntary tunnels are set up at the request of the end-user. When using a voluntary tunnel, it is possible for the end-user to simultaneously open a secure tunnel through the Internet and access other Internet hosts via basic TCP/IP protocols without tunneling. The client-side endpoint of a voluntary tunnel resides on the user's computer.

Wide Area Network (WAN)   A network environment in which the elements of the network are located at significant distances from each other, and the communications facilities typically use carrier facilities rather than private wiring. Typically, a routing protocol is required to support communications between two distant host systems on a WAN.

X.509   A specification for public-key certificates, originally developed as part of the CCITT's X.500 directory specification.

I N D E X

Page references in italic type indicate illustrations. Numbers are treated as if spelled out. Thus "T1 lines" would be found as if spelled "Tone lines," and "L2F" and "L2TP" as if spelled LtwoF and LtwoTP respectively.

A

access concentrators, *see* network access
    servers
access control, 42, 286–288
    design issues, 178–179
Ace Hardware, 326
address allocation, 292–295
address management, *see* IP address
    management
ADI, 250 *table*
aggressive mode, ISAKMP/Oakley, 106,
    108–109
AltaVista Tunnel 98, 259, 265 *table*
analog phone lines, 18
ANS VPDN Services, 208, 367
Appletalk, PPP handling, 148
application proxies, 219–220, *221*
applications, 170–171
ARPANET, 7–8

Ascend Communications, Inc., 121–122,
    361
ASICs, 253
Assured Digital, Inc., 361–362
asymmetric encryption, 74
asynchronous transfer mode (ATM), 20,
    315
AT&T WorldNet VPN Services, 209–210,
    367
authentication, 42
    extranets, 330–331
    and firewalls, 227
    IPSEC, 92–94, 96–98, 101, 113
    ISPs, 199–200
    L2TP, 146, 152–153, 281
    PPTP, 133
    types, 62
    VPN hardware, 242, 246
authentication header (IPSec), 92–94,
    96–98, 101, 113

authentication services, 63–72, 280–282

automatic rekeying, 180, 199, 229

Automotive Industry Action Group, 214, 328

Automotive Network Exchange (ANX), IPSec-compliance certification, 115–116, 328, *329*

Aventail Corporation, 362

Axent Technologies, Inc., 362

B

bandwidth, 34, 194
  design considerations, 169, 171
  different applications, *170*
  performance issues, 304
  scalability, 32

bandwidth conservation, 307

bandwidth-on-demand, 307

bandwidth over-provisioning, 307

Bay Networks, Inc., 362

BioAPI Consortium, 72

Biometric API, 71

biometric systems, 71–72

Blowfish, 81

Boardwatch Web site, 205

book resources, 345

border gateway protocol, 299

Borderguard, 259, 260, 265 *table*

bottlenecks, 35

brownouts, 10

business, changing environment, 4–6

C

CallID, L2TP, 149

CERT Coordination Center, 223

certificate authorities, 54, 82–83, 85–89
  extranets, 331
  in-house, 181–182, 282–286
  ISPs as, 200

certificate revocation lists (CRLs), 88, 277, 283, 286, 340

certificates, *see* digital certificates

certificate servers, 284–286

challenge, token devices, 70

challenge handshake authentication protocol (CHAP), *see* CHAP

CHAP, 66–67
  with L2TP, 146
  with PPTP, 122, 124–125, 133

CheckPoint Software Technologies Ltd., 362

Chicago AADS NAP, 49

cipher, 72

cipher text, 72

ciPro-VPN, 250 *table*, 253

circuit proxies, 219, *220*

Cisco Systems, Inc., 122, 362

CIX NAP, 49

classes, of network addresses, 53, 292, 300

classless inter-domain routing (CIDR), 291, 300

class of service (CoS), 308
  IPv6 headers, 119

client-to-LAN tunneling, 41

closed user groups, 20

collision attacks, 97

.com domain names, 8

committed information rate, 22

common open policy service (COPS), 311

communication, 3

Compatible Systems, 362

compression control protocol (CCP), 133–134

compulsory tunnels
  L2TP, 150–151, 154
  PPTP, 128

CompuServe Authentication Service, 211
CompuServe IP Link, 210–211
CompuServe Network Services, 367
Concentric Network, 213, 367
Conclave, 259, 265 *table*
conditioned lines, 18
confidentiality, 42
Contivity Extranet Switch, 241, 252 *table*, 253, 300, 304
controlled-load service, 310
corporate networks, *see* private corporate networks; virtual private networks
CoS, *see* class of service (CoS)
cost comparisons, 26–31
cost savings, 25–26
Crypto API, 69
CryptoCard, 235
cryptographic chips/cards, 174, 240, 241
cryptography, 72. *See also* encryption; public-key cryptography
CSU/DSU devices, 50
    costs, 26–30
    ISP requirements, 198
    location, *216*
customer premises equipment, 33
CyberTrust, 87, 245
Cylink Corporation, 363

D

Data Fellows, Inc., 363
data integrity, 42
demilitarized zone (DMZ), 179
DEN (Directory Enabled Networks) Initiative, 317, 340–341
deployment
    future directions, 335–336
    IPSec, 116–118
    L2TP, 162–164
    planning, 184–185
    PPTP, 139–142
DES (data encryption standard), 81
    IPSec, 93
design
    deployment planning, 184–185
    ISP issues, 182–184
    network issues, 174–178
    requirements determination, 168–174
    security issues, 178–182
Desktop Management Task Force, 341
dial-in VPNs
    design considerations, 171, 175
    firewalls, 225–227
    future directions, 335–336
    IPSec client software, 111, 114–115
    management protocols, 47
    PPTP deployment, *140*
    tunnels, 41
    VPN hardware, 240–241
dial-up extranets, 330
Dial-Up Network Pack (Windows95), 124
dictionaries, 382
differentiated services, 307–312
Diffie-Hellman public-key cryptography, 77–79, 81
    IPSec implementation, 93, 96–108
digital certificates, 54, 82–83, 282–283
    classes, 87–88
    deployment issues, 185
    design issues, 180–182
    distribution, 84–85
    and firewalls, 227
    future directions, 339–340
    IPSec, 93
    ISPs, 200
    VPN hardware, 245–246, 247–248
    VPN software, 262
digital data service (DDS), 19, 192
Digital Equipment Corporation, 363

Directory Enabled Networks (DEN)
    Initiative, 317, 340–341
domain name service (DNS), 36, 293–295
    design issues, 177–178
    internal *vs.* external, 295–297
domain of interpretation (DOI), IPSec, 94
DSA (digital signature algorithm), 81
DSO streams, 20
dynamic address allocation, 292–295
dynamic DNS, 290
dynamic host control protocol (DHCP),
    290, 292–293
dynamic key management, 278
dynamic tunnels, 40, 128, 129
    with RADIUS, 131–133

E

ECI Telematics, 122
electronic commerce, 4, 323
electronic data interchange (EDI),
    327–328
electronic eavesdropping, 61–62
elliptic curve cryptography (ECC), 339
E-Lock, 265 *table*
e-mail security, 58
encapsulating security payload (ESP),
    92–94, 98–101, 113
    header, *99*
    modes, 101–103
encrypting routers, 234
encryption, 72–74. *See also* key manage-
    ment; public-key cryptography
    future directions, 339–340
    government restrictions, 119
    Internet security, 11
    IPSec, 92–94, 98–103, 113
    L2TP, 153–156, 274
    method selection, 79–82, 274–280

Network-layer vs. Link-layer, *59*
PPTP, 124, 133–134
system comparison, 80 *table*
VPN hardware, 242, 243, 253
encryption algorithms
    commonly used, 81
    computational requirements, 35, 174,
        175
    and firewalls, 228–229
    ISPs, 199
    remote users, 176
    VPN software, 262–263
Encryption Service Adapter (ESA), 236
end-to-end security, 43–44
Enterprise-Quality VPN, 213
Enterprise VPN, 213
Entrust Technologies, 181, 363
equipment requirement reduction, with
    VPNs, 33
Ethernet, 239
    sniffing, 61
Ethernet VPN gateways, 243
ExpressRouter, 235, 236
extended markup language (XML), 328
Extended Systems, Inc., 363
ExtendNet, 252 *table*
extensible authentication protocol (EAP),
    125, 152
external DNS, 295–297
ExtraLink, 212–213
extranets, 12–13, 323–325
    design considerations, 173–174
    motivations, 325–328
    VPN conversion, 328–333

F

face-to-face key exchanges, 104
failover features, 253

Firewall-1, 225, 231, 304
firewalls, 51–52, 216–217
  access control and, 287–288
  design issues, 174
  gateways as, 242
  location, *216*
  port numbers, 223
  product overview, 230–231, 232–233
    table
  product requirements, 227–230
  remote access, 225–227
  security policies and, 217, 225
  stateful multi-layer inspection,
    222–223
  types, 217–221
  VPN application, 224–225
flattening, of business organizations, 5
flexibility, 4–5
  design issues, 183
  ISPs and, 200
  VPN benefits, 31
Fort Knox Policy Router 5000, 250 *table*
Fortress Technologies, Inc., 363
frame relay networks, 20–23
  costs, 25, 31
FreeGate Corporation, 363
Frontier Technologies, 363
F-Secure VPN, 265 *table*
FWZ, 212

G

gateways, *see* remote VPN gateways;
    security gateways; VPN gateways
Gauntlet, 231
generic routing encapsulation (GRE) pro-
    tocol, 122, 126, 127
geographic scalability, 32
Gigabit Ethernet, 170, 194

global business, 5–6
GRIC Communications, 195, 367
GTE Internetworking, 211, 367
guaranteed service, 310–311

H

hardware, *see* VPN hardware
hardware-based encryption, 278
hash functions
  IPSec, 93, 96–98
  MS-CHAP, 133, 134
  one-time password systems, 64
  public-key cryptography, 76
header cut-and-paste attacks, 113
HMAC hash function, 93, 96–98
host-to-host VPNs, 260–261
hub-and-spoke network topology, 21
Human Authentication API, 71–72

I

IBM, 364
IBM routers, 236
IDEA (international data encryption
    algorithm), 81
IETF Documents
  Internet Drafts, 350–357
  RFCs, 345–350
IETF Working Groups, 342 *table*
IKE, 103–111, 158, 242. *See also*
    ISAKMP/Oakley
  unproven nature of, 119
incident logging
  VPN hardware, 249
  VPN software, 263
Indus River Networks, Inc., 363

Infocrypt Enterprise, 250 *table*
InfoExpress, Inc., 364
information, 14
Information Resource Engineering, Inc., 364
information technology departments, 6
inner header, IPSec, 103
Integrated Services Architecture, 310–311
Integrated Services (INTSERV) Working Group, 309–310
integrated solutions, 37, 239–242
integrated VPN devices, 52–53, 341–342
Intel Corporation, 364
InterLock, 208
InterManage, 208
internal DNS, 295–297
internal VPNs, 336
International Computer Security Association (ICSA)
    firewall certification, 223
    IPSec-compliance certification, 116
Internet, 3–4
    business opportunities, 11–14
    capabilities-benefits mapping, 14
    components, 48–51
    connectivity options, 9
    future directions, 336–338
    governance, 6–7
    growth, 7–8
    infrastructure, 8, *9*
    map of U.S., *10*
    multimedia capability, 11
    multiple links to, 182–183, 299–300
    offerings, 9–11
    reliability, 10
    Web sites with information on, 358
Internet Architecture Board (IAB), 7
Internet Assigned Numbers Authority (IANA), 7

Internet control message protocol (ICMP), 318
Internet Devices, Inc., 364
Internet Drafts, 350–357
Internet Dynamics, 364
Internet Engineering Task Force (IETF), 6
    documents, 345–357
    working groups, 342 *table*
Internet key exchange (IKE), *see* IKE
InternetMCI VPN, 211–212
Internet network access points (NAPs), 8, 48–51, 191–192
Internet protocols, 7, 9–11. *See also* specific protocols
Internet Provider Performance Metrics (IPPM) working group, 204, 319
Internet Research Task Force (IRTF), 7
Internet security association and key management protocol (ISAKMP), *see* ISAKMP/Oakley
Internet service providers (ISPs), 8, 48, 189–190. *See also* Service Level Agreements
    connectivity options, 198
    cost, 25
    design issues, 182–184
    expectations of, 195–196
    for extranet maintenance, 332
    firewall management, 223
    future trends, 213–214, 336–338
    infrastructures, 196–197
    network performance and management, 197–198
    network service providers contrasted, 50
    outsourcing to, 205–207
    performance guarantees, 11, 34
    performance monitoring, 203–205, 317–319

point-of-presence (POP), 23, 32, 50–51, 192–193
   security, 198–201
   types, 48, 190–195
   Web sites with information on, 358
Internet Society (ISOC), 6
Internet VPNs, *see* virtual private networks
interoperability, 35–36
   VPN hardware, 242
intranets, 12–13, 323–324. *See also* extranets
Intraport VPN Access Server, 252 *table*
IP addresses, 43, 53
IP address management, 36, 289–290
   address allocation, 290–297
   IPv6, 289, 300–302
   network address translation, 177–178, 297–299
iPass Inc., 195, 367
IP authentication header (IPSec), 92–94, 96–98, 101, 113
IP Link, 210
IP multicasting, 307–308
   IPv6 built-in support, 301
   tunnels, 40
IP packets
   IPSec handling, 92, *93*
   L2TP handling, 148
   PPTP handling, 124
IPSec, 45, 47
   access control, 54
   advantages, 91–92
   architecture, 92–94
   authentication header, 92–94, 96–98, 101, 113
   components, 95–103
   deployment, 116–118
   encapsulating security payload, 92–94, 98–103, 113

encryption, 274–275
   extranet application, 331
   features, 46 *table*
   firewalls, 225, 226, 228–230
   future directions, 337–339
   hardware compliance, 242
   interoperability, 35
   IPv6 built-in support, 301
   ISAKMP/Oakley, 106–111
   key management, 103–106
   with PPTP, 153–155, 160
   PPTP architecture contrasted, *136*
   problems with, 118–119
   products, 115 *table*
   relative emphasis, 242
   router support, 234–236
   security associations, 94–96, 110–111, 113
   SKIP key exchange, 104–106
   using, 111–118
   VPN hardware, 242, 249
IPSec client software, 111, 114–115
IPSec security gateways, 111–112
IP Security Working Group, 92, 115
IP switches, 50
IP telephony, 169, 171
IPv4
   address space inadequacy, 43, 177, 289, 292, 300
   authentication header, 98
   IPSec, 114
   packet headers, 92, *93*
IPv6
   authentication header, 98
   IP address management, 289, 300–302
   IPSec, 114
   packet headers, 92, *93*
IPX, 36
   L2TP handling, 146, 148
   PPTP handling, 122, 124

ISAKMP/Oakley, 45, 47. *See also* IKE
   aggressive mode, 106, 108–109
   IPSec application, 106–111
   main mode, 106, 107–108
   quick mode, 106, 109–110
ISAKMP SA, 106
ISDN lines, 32

J

jitter, 194, 304

K

key lengths, 275–276
key management, 273
   design issues, 180–182
   gateways, 276–279
   IPSec, 103–106
   L2TP, 157–159
   PPTP, 134
   session key handling, 278–279
   users, 279–280
   VPN hardware, 242, 245–246, 248–249,
     253
key recovery system, 182
keys, 72–74

L

LADP, 86, 228, 248, 285–286, 339–340
LanRover VPN, 250 *table*, 253
LAN-to-LAN tunneling, 41
   L2TP, 156–157
   PPTP, 134–135

LAN-to-LAN VPNs
   design considerations, 169–171, 175
   future directions, 338
   IPSec security gateways, 111–112
   management, 340
   management protocols, 47
   PPTP deployment, *141*
   VPN hardware, 240–241
laptop theft, 280
latency, 194, 304
   different applications, 170
Layer2 forwarding protocol (L2F), *see*
   L2F
Layer2 protocols, 44–45. *See also* L2F;
   L2TP; PPTP
Layer3 protocols, 45. *See also* IPSec
Layer2 tunneling protocol (L2TP), *see*
   L2TP
leased Internet lines, 25
leased phone lines, 4, 17–23
   star topology, 21
legacy integration, 33, 34
lightweight directory access protocol
   (LADP), 86, 228, 248, 285–286,
   339–340
link control protocols (LCPs), 124
The List (of ISPs), 205
local exchange carriers, 25
long distance charge elimination, 25–26
L2F, 44–45, 121–122, 145
   features, 46 *table*
L2TP, 45, 47, 145
   applicability, 164–165
   architecture, 146–147
   authentication, 146, 152–153, 281
   deployment, 162–164
   encryption, 153–156, 274
   features, 46 *table*
   firewalls, 230
   future directions, 337–339
   hardware focus, 242

key management, 157–159
LAN-to-LAN tunneling, 156–157
multiprotocol support, 36–37
non-IP networks, 155, 157, 164
PPP, 146–149
products, 163 *table*
relative emphasis, 242
tunnels, 150–152
using, 164–165
L2TP access concentrators, 149, 152, 161–162
L2TP network servers, 149, 160–161

M

Macintosh, PPTP clients, 138
MAE East NAP, 49
MAE West NAP, 49
main mode, ISAKMP/
Oakley, 106, 107–108
manageability, 33–34
managed access, 207
management protocols, 47–48
man-in-the-middle attack, 62–63
manual keying, 103, 105
MCI Internet backbone, 8
MD5 hash function, IPSec, 93, 97
MD4 hash function, MS-CHAP, 133, 134
message digest, 76
Microsoft Corporation, 364
L2TP support, 147
PPTP support, 122–124
Microsoft Point-to-Point encryption
(MPPE), 123, 133–134
Milkyway Networks Corporation, 364
mobile IP, 40
mobile users, *See also* dial-in VPNs;
remote users
address allocation, 290
client-to-LAN tunnels, 41

design considerations, 169
security, 35
modem banks, 4, 50, 131
modems, 18, 32
modular construction, 34
MS-CHAP, 133–134, 135, 138
multimedia, 11, 194
design considerations, 169, 171
performance requirements, 305–307
multiplatform issues, 176
multiprotocol label switching (MPLS), 313, 337
multiprotocol support, 36–37
Multiservices Internet Gateway, 250 *table*

N

NETBEUI
L2TP handling, 146, 148
PPTP handling, 122, 124
Netcom, 213, 367
NETCOMplete for Business service, 213
NetFortress VPN, 250 *table*
NetScreen, 250 *table*, 365
NetWare, 119, 247
network access points (NAPs), 8, 48–51, 191–192
network access servers, 175–176
L2TP, 160–161
PPTP, 130, 136, 138–139
network address translation, 177–178, 297–299
network control protocols (NCPs), 124
network file system (NFS) protocol, 218
network interface card, 61
networkMCI, 367
network operating systems (NOS), VPN
support, 216, 259–260
network operations center, 198

networks
   design issues, 174–178
   performance, 304–307
   performance management (ISPs),
      197–198
   security threats, 59–63
network service providers (NSPs), 50
Network Solutions, Inc., 6–7
Network Wizards survey, 8
new group mode, ISAKMP/Oakley, 106
node-to-node security, 43–44
nonrepudiation, 74
Nortel, 87
Novell, Inc., 365

O

Oakley protocol, 105
   modes, 106–110
Omniguard/Power VPN, 265 *table*
one-armed VPN gateway configuration,
      245
one-time password systems, 63–65
one-way hash functions, 76
online catalogs, 327
online certificate status protocol (OCSP),
      278, 284, 340
outer header, IPSec, 103
outsourcing, 26, 32, 205–207
over-provisioning, of bandwidth, 307

P

PAC Bell NAP, 49
packet filters, 217–218
PAP, 65
   with L2TP, 146
   with PPTP, 122, 124–125, 133

password authentication protocol (PAP),
      see PAP
passwords, 63–65
   remote users, 178
PC cards, 69–70
peering points, 192
perfect forward secrecy, 79
performance, 33, 34, 36
   design issues, 183–184
   factors influencing, 312–314
   firewall effects, 231
   ISP monitoring, 203–205
performance guarantees, 11, 34. *See also*
      service level agreements
performance management, 303–304
   differentiated services, 307–312
   ISP performance monitoring, 314–317
   networks, 305–307
   policy-based management, 314–317
permanent tunnels, 40
permanent virtual connections, 22
PERMIT security gateway, 225, 251 *table*
PGP (Pretty Good Privacy), 58, 331
Pilot Network Services, 213
pipes, tunnels, 40
PIX, 224–225
PN7, 251 *table*
point-of-presence (POP), 23, 32, 50–51,
      192–193
point-to-point protocol (PPP), *see* PPP
point-to-point tunneling protocol (PPTP),
      see PPTP
policy-based management, 228, 314–317
   VPN hardware for, 248, 254–255
port numbers, 223
Postal Service, 88
PPP
   with L2TP, 146–149
   with PPTP, 122–127
PPPEXT Working Group, 164

PPTP, 45. *See also* RADIUS
  access control, 54
  applicability, 142–143
  architecture, 122–124
  authentication, 133, 281
  deployment, 139–142
  encryption, 124, 133–134, 274
  features, 46 *table*
  firewalls, 230
  future directions, 337–339
  hardware focus, 242
  IPSec architecture contrasted, *136*
  LAN-to-LAN tunneling, 134–135
  multiprotocol support, 36–37
  network access servers, 130, 136,
    138–139
  popularity, 121–122
  PPP, 122–127
  products, 140 *table*
  RADIUS with, 124, 130–133
  relative emphasis, 242
  tunnels, 127–130, 134–135
  using, 135–142
  Windows-friendly nature, 123
PPTP client software, 136, 137–138
PPTP filtering, 137
PPTP Forum, 122
PPTP servers, 136–137
Pretty Good Privacy (PGP), 58, 331
private addresses, 297
private corporate networks, 12–13, 17.
    See also extranets; intranets; virtual
    private networks
  evolution, 18–23
  Internet application, 23–24
private key, 74–76
PrivateWire, 265 *table*
promiscuous mode network operation, 61
proxy agents, 219
proxy servers, 131, *132*, 219

PSInet network, 8
public-key certificates, *see* digital certificates
public-key cryptography, 74–76. *See also*
  key management
  Diffie-Hellman technique, 77–79, 81,
    93, 106–108
  IPSec, 93, 106–108
  method selection, 79–82
  RSA technique, 79, 81
public key infrastructures (PKIs), 82–89
public keys, 74–76
  distribution, 84–85
  generation, 84
public switched telephone networks, 18

Q

quality of service (QoS), 184, 310
  ATM networks, 315
  IPv6 built-in support, 301
  ISPs, 197, 213–214
  market for, 342
  multimedia, 194, 306
  routers, 236
  VPN integration, 255
quick mode, ISAKMP/Oakley, 106, 109–110

R

RADGUARD, 365
RADIUS, 47–48, 246
  authentication, 281–283
  compulsory tunnels, 130
  defined, 68–69
  extranet application, 331

RADIUS authentication servers, 50
    with L2TP, 151–152
    with PPTP, 124, 130–133
Raptor Systems, Inc., 365
Ravlin, 251 *table*
RC2, 81
RC4, 81
realm, 129
realm-based tunneling, 130
real-time applications, 36
    design considerations, 169, 171
    performance requirements, 305–307
RedCreek Communications, Inc., 365
reliability, 33, 34, 36
    design issues, 183
    multiple Internet links, 299–300
remote access servers, *see* network access
        servers
remote authentication dial-in user service
        (RADIUS), *see* RADIUS
remote users, *See also* dial-in VPNs;
        mobile users
    design issues, 175–176
    firewalls, 225–227
    IPSec, 111, 113–116
    multinational, 182–183
    password policies, 178
remote VPN gateways, 241, 246
    product overview, 249, 250–252 *table*,
        253–255
replay attacks, 229
requirements determination, 168–174
resource reservation protocol (RSVP),
        213–214, 311
RFCs, 345–350
Riverworks, 252 *table*
roaming service, 130, 183, 195
root certificate, 285
root public keys, 85
routers, 50, 51, 234
    costs, 26–30

design issues, 174
IP addresses and, 53
ISP requirements, 198
location, *216*
product overview, 235 *table*, 236–237
product requirements, 234–235
traffic prioritization, 308
Routing and Remote Access Server
        (RRAS), 133–135, 137, 139, 259
    features, 265 *table*
    packet filtering with, 230
RSA chips, 253–254
RSA public-key cryptography, 79, 81

S

SafeNet/LAN, 251 *table*
scalability, 31–32, 33–34
secret-key encryption, 73, *74*
Secure Computing Corporation, 363
secure HTTP (SHTTP), 58
secure MIME (S/MIME), 58
Secure Road Warrior service, 213
secure sockets layer (SSL), 58, 181
SecureVision, 251 *table*
SecurID, 227, 235
security, 35, 57–58. *See also* authentica-
        tion; certificate authorities; digital
        certificates; encryption; key manage-
        ment
    authentication services, 63–72,
        280–282
    deployment, 184–188
    design issues, 178–182
    encryption method selection, 79–82,
        274–280
    future directions, 339–340
    in-house certificate authorities,
        181–182, 282–286

integrated solutions, 241–247
Internet, 11
ISPs, 198–201
secure system components, 272
Web sites, 358
security associations
L2TP, 157–159
negotiating, 110–111
PPTP, 94–96
wild card, 112–113
security audit, 184
Security Dynamics Technologies, Inc.,
    365
security gateways, 40–41, 51–54
centralized configuration, 185
IPSec, 111–112
key management, 276–279
VPN hardware, 240, 247
security parameters index (SPI), 96, 99,
    155, 279
security policies, 272–273
consistency across sites, 246
extranets, 330–331
firewalls and, 217, 225
security protocols, 44–47, 46 *table. See
    also* IPSec
non-interoperability, 35
security services, 41–44
security threats, 59–63
seed, one-time passwords, 64
servers, 50
Service Level Agreements, 34, 183,
    201–203
performance monitoring, 203–205,
    314–318
session hijacking, 60–61
session key handling, 278–279
SHA-1 hash function, 93, 97–98
Shiva Corporation, 365
simple key management for IP (SKIP),
    104–106

Site Patrol, 211
Site Security Handbook, 178
S/Key, 64–65
Skipjack, 81
SKIP key exchange, 104–106
smart cards, 69–70, 339–340
SmartGate, 265 *table*
sniffers, 61
sniffing, 61–62
SNMP agents, 318
SOCKS proxy, 221
SOCKS v5, 47
features, 46 *table*
software, *see* VPN software
Speaker Verification API, 72
spoofing, 59–60
Sprint, 8
Sprint NAP, 49
standards, 33
future directions, 338–339
star network topology, 21
stateful multi-layer inspection (SMLI),
    firewalls, 222–223
static address allocation, 292–295
static resource allocation, 308–309
static tunnels, 40, 128–130
Stentor Alliance, 130
Storage Technology Corporation, 366
strong authentication, 62, 63
supply chain management, 326, *327*
SureRemote, 208
S/WAN Initiative, 105, 114
symmetric encryption, 73, *74*

T

TACACS, 67–68
TACACS+, 68
authentication, 281
TCG CERFnet, 213, 367

TCP/IP, 7
  extranets, 323, 325
  intranets, 12–13
  security and, 58
teams, 5
tech support reduction, 32
temporary tunnels, 40
terminal access controller access-control
      system (TACACS), 67–68, 281
theft, 280
3Com Corporation, 122, 361
Tier One Internet providers, 48–49,
      190–192
Tier Two Internet providers, 49, 192
TimeStep Corporation, 366
token-based authentication, 70–71, 282
  deployment issues, 185
T1 lines, 19–20, 31
  bandwidth scalability and, 32
  costs, 25, 26–30
traffic prioritization, 308
transfer control protocol/Internet proto-
      col, *see* TCP/IP
transparent key distribution, 85
transport mode ESP, 101–103
triple DES, 81
Trusted Information Systems, 366
trusted third-parties, 181, 282
T3 lines, 31
  bandwidth scalability and, 32
  costs, 25
TunnelBuilder, 251 *table*
tunneling protocols, 44–47. *See also* L2F;
      L2TP; PPTP
  feature comparison, 46 *table*
  non-interoperability, 35
tunneling software, 258–259
tunnel mode ESP, 101–103
tunnels, 24, 40–41. *See also* IP address
      management
  L2TP, 150–152

PPTP, 127–130, 134–135
  remote users and, 176
  VPN hardware, 242–245, 253, 254
tunnel switches, 137, *138*
turnkey solutions, 240, 241

U

UAC, 366
unified name space, 177
universal mailbox, 336
US Robotics, 122
UUNET Extralink, 8, 212, 367

V

value added network (VAN), 327
VeriSign, 87, 181, 245
videoconferencing, 169, 171
virtual circuits, 18, 24
Virtual Private Data Network (VPDN) ser-
      vices, 208–209
virtual private networks (VPNs), *See also*
      authentication; dial-in VPNs;
      encryption; Internet; key manage-
      ment; LAN-to-LAN VPNs; tunnels
  architecture, 39–44
  benefits, 24–33
  commercial providers, 24–33, 208–213
  components, 48–51
  concerns, 33–37
  cost comparisons, 26–31
  cost savings, 25–26
  defined, 17–18, 19
  design, *see* design
  future directions, 335–342
  Internet application, 23–24

outsourcing, 26, 32, 205–207
product trends, 341–342
resources, 345–359
vendors and products, 361–366
voluntary tunnels
    L2TP, 150–151, 154
    PPTP, 128
V-ONE Corporation, 366
VPNet Technologies, Inc., 118, 366
VPN gateways, 240–241
    access control and, 287–288
    configurations, 242–247
VPN hardware, 52–53, 215–216
    configurations, 242–247
    integrated solutions, 239–242
    product overview, 249, 250–252 *table,*
      253–255
    product requirements, 247–249
    types, 240–241
VPN software, 53–54, 215–216
    product overview, 263–266, 265 *table*
    product requirements, 261–263
    types, 258–261
VSU-1000/1010, 251 *table*
VTPC/Secure, 265 *table*

VPN hardware, 240, 242–243
Watchguard Technologies, Inc., 366
weak authentication, 62
Web, *see* World Wide Web
weighted fair queueing (WFQ), 308
wide area networks (WANs), *see* WANs
wild card security associations, 112–
    113
Windows environments
    L2TP for, 123–124
    PPTP for, 147
Windows NT servers, cost effectiveness,
    30
Worldcom, 8
WorldNet VPN Services, 209–210, 367
World Wide Web, 4. *See also* Internet
    and extranets, 323, 326
    offerings, 10
    security, 58
    site hosting, 49
    VPN-related information sites,
      358–359
    Web-based EDI, 327–328
World Wide Web Consortium (W3C), 6,
    328

W

WAN-capable VPN gateways, 242–243
WANs, 19
    equipment reduction from VPNs, 33

X

X.500 directories, 228, 248, 285, 339
X.25 networks, 20
X.509 standard, 83, 331, 355